Praise for *Haydn and the Valve Trumpet: Literary Essays*

'Eliot was no scholar, but he was a great poet. Raine is a considerable poet and a great reader ... This is a big and stimulating collection.'

Anthony Burgess in the *Observer*

'This is a gloriously enjoyable collection of writings ... Raine is the liveliest, most readable of explainers, as well as the sharpest.'

Paul Driver in the *Financial Times*

'These essays are intelligent (as opposed to just clever), deeply learned, hungry for rectitude. They live in literature, breathe it ...'

James Wood in the *Sunday Correspondent*

'Written with wisdom and humour and pleasure; they seem made of power and light and make one beam. They will certainly be read by the discerning for a hundred years.'

Peter Levi in the *Spectator*

'Exhilarating and engrossing ...'

Peter Kemp in *The Times Educational Supplement*

'Shrewd and sensitive ... He admires Dickens for what he calls his "almost abnormal sensitivity to language" because that is a quality he, too, shares.'

A. Alvarez in the *Sunday Times*

'The periodical and occasional criticism collected here is of an exceptionally high standard.'

Frank Kermode in the *Independent on Sunday*

'Carnivorously enjoyable ...'
Sean French in the *New Statesman*

'Rip-roaringly enjoyable ... devilishly fleet and precise ... a whiplash wit ...'

Rupert Christiansen in the *Spectator*

'Raine on Canetti leaves blood on the page . . .'

Martin Cropper in the *Daily Telegraph*

'I highly recommend Craig Raine's distinguished, wilful collection of essays.'

Ian McEwan in the *Independent on Sunday* Books of the Year

'Funny, serious and vigorous-minded – a tonic for flabby thinkers.'

Candia McWilliam in *Independent on Sunday* Books of the Year

'Neither donnish nor journalistic, positively danced with wit, energy and scholarship . . .'

Roger Lewis in the *Financial Times* Books of the Year

*Other books by Craig Raine*

The Onion, Memory

A Martian Sends a Postcard Home

Rich

The Electrification of the
Soviet Union

'1953'

History: The Home Movie

Clay. Whereabouts Unknown

Haydn and the Valve Trumpet: Literary Essays

Collected Poems 1978–1999

A la recherche du temps perdu

Craig Raine

# In Defence of
# T. S. Eliot

PICADOR

First published 2000 by Picador
an imprint of Macmillan Publishers Ltd
25 Eccleston Place, London SW1W 9NF
Basingstoke and Oxford
Associated companies throughout the world
www.macmillan.com

ISBN 0 330 37577 6

1 3 5 7 9 8 6 4 2

A CIP catalogue record for this book is available from
the British Library.

Typeset by SetSystems Ltd, Saffron Walden, Essex
Printed and bound in Great Britain by
Mackays of Chatham plc, Chatham, Kent

TO
ANNALENA McAFEE
AND
IAN McEWAN

# Contents

# CONTENTS

# A Criticism of Life

In my naive, untheoretical, writerly way, I believe in language.

Edmund White's autofiction, *The Farewell Symphony*, tells us that 'the tragedy of sex is that one can never know what this most intimate and moving form of communication has actually said to the other person and whether the message, if received, was welcome'. I have annotated this sentence with one tart word: *talk*?

Steven Pinker is a professor in the Department of Brain and Cognitive Sciences at MIT. He specializes in the psychology of language. In 1994, he wrote a brilliant book, *The Language Instinct*. His initial proposition is that human beings can shape events in each other's brains with exquisite precision. 'I am not referring to telepathy or mind control or the other obsessions of fringe science,' he writes. 'These are blunt instruments compared to an ability that is uncontroversially present in every one of us. That ability is language. Simply by making noises with our mouths, we can reliably cause precise new combinations of ideas to arise in each other's minds.' We are, says Pinker, liable to forget what a miracle this is.

Indeed we are. Deconstruction maintains the opposite. Far from being an instrument of exquisite precision, language is a self-referential system with no necessary purchase on reality – a system in which meaning is endlessly deferred and often contradictory.

But consider Steven Pinker's example of language at work. When octopuses mate, the male octopus's normally grey body suddenly becomes striped. He caresses the female with seven of his arms, slipping the eighth into her breathing tube. A series of sperm packets moves slowly through a groove in his eighth arm, finding rest in the mantle cavity of the female.

The tragedy of sex here is that the male can't ask the female if his intentions are desired. The triumph of language is that, should you now see an octopus turn stripy, you will know *exactly* what is going on. Simple, isn't it?

Over thirty years ago, Ted Hughes published *Poetry in the Making*. Part anthology, part instruction manual, it is a pedagogical guide to writing poetry – culled from radio programmes made for the BBC Schools Broadcasting Department. It is an unsurpassed masterpiece of suggestion and provocation, sparky, inspiring, spontaneous still, engaging and impossible not to engage with. Its afterword, for example, is curiously unconvinced by language's ability to cope with the sheer immediacy, the *thinginess* of the world: 'there are no words to capture the infinite depth of crowiness in the crow's flight'.

Oddly for a writer, Hughes here adopts the position of the literary theoretician for whom the inadequacy of language is axiomatic – for whom the signifier is merely the thin, arbitrary representative of this or that aspect of reality, the signified. A few years later, in 1970, Hughes was at Persepolis, with the theatre director Peter Brook, inventing a universal language, Orghast, whose words would have a more inevitable relationship to reality. After a few false starts, Orghast emerged directly from the Hughes diaphragm, not from ingenuity or adaptation, but from pure intuition and naked inspiration.

At the time, Tom Stoppard wrote a puzzled but fascinated account of this linguistic experiment in *The Times Literary Supplement*. He was admiring, amused, bemused and undecided. Who can blame him? Orghast for 'darkness opens its womb', the staple of any phrase book, is BULLORGA OMBOLOM FROR. As a language, it seems especially suited to the mega-concept, its natural fount the upper case, and less useful for more fiddly, mundane, lower-case items. Where tin-openers and electric hairdryers are concerned, Orghast seems less well provided for, even a touch skimped. In the event, Hughes felt he had created something musical, choral, rather than something capable of semantic intricacy.

The strange thing is that Hughes's practice effortlessly contradicts his theoretical stance. As he bewails the inadequacy of language – 'all we can do is use a word as an indicator, or a whole bunch of words as a general directive' – he also demonstrates the power of words not only to equal reality, but to surpass it. 'But the ominous thing in the crow's flight, the barefaced bandit thing, the tattered beggarly gypsy thing, the caressing and shaping yet slightly clumsy gesture of the downstroke, as if the wings were both too heavy and too powerful, and the headlong sort of merriment, the macabre pantomime ghoulishness, and the undertaker sleekness – you could go on for a very long time with phrases of that sort and still have completely missed your instant, glimpsed knowledge of the world of the crow's wingbeat.' Even as he employs it so brilliantly, Hughes obviously underrates the power of language. But the root misapprehension is the assumption, natural enough, that reality is real. It isn't. Most of the time, reality, as most people perceive it, is experientially impoverished. When we see a crow, for instance, we don't in fact see it. Or we don't see it with an iota of the vividness conveyed by Hughes's phrases. Just as the word 'crow' merely denotes a particular bird, so the bird signified is merely registered in the normal course of things. We do not apprehend it. Language can do that for us, which is why we value art.

Good writing is a criticism of life: it describes, selects, contemplates defining features, beauties, flaws; it puts reality on pause; it searches the freeze-frame; it is an act of measured consideration, of accurate re-presentation. When Marianne Moore compares the top of a fir tree to 'an emerald turkeyfoot', we see the fir tree more stereoscopically than before. The metaphor involves two bits of knowledge, common to most of us, but kept separate – the top of a fir and the shape of a turkey's foot. Moore brings them together in an act of shared recognition. But re-cognition is how we should understand this process. We are being asked to re-think, to *think again*, because our first thoughts are barely thoughts at all. They are reflexes. As the crow flies. Think how little that means. Consider, then, how much Hughes and language have contributed to reality: focus, sharpness, magnification, intensification and, yes, reality. To 'reality' art lends *reality* – italics, emphasis.

# The Catcher in the Rye

Boy, what a phoney. According to the jacket copy – not much of *that* on any of fastidious old Salinger's works – 'this new edition reproduces, for the first time in Penguin Books, the original American text'. Very big deal. In practice this means American orthography and a few extra fidgety italics to emphasize the dynamic of American speech. Thanks for *tell*ing me, but it isn't that *diff*erent. It means that Holden gets the ax from Pencey Prep and an attack of diarrhea in the museum. When they see that '– you' was actually all along the unguessable 'Fuck you', some readers may have about two hemorrhages apiece. Or not. The first sentence now wittily concludes its aria of reticence with this ironic extra clause: 'if you want to know the truth'. And the novel is dedicated to the author's mother. As I almost said, what a phoney.

*The Catcher in the Rye* is catching, a masterpiece of intense orality – a great soliloquy of American vernacular which is the heir of Mark Twain ('You don't know about me, without you have read a book by the name of *The Adventures of Tom Sawyer*, but that ain't no matter') and the benefactor of Saul Bellow ('Some people thought he was cracked and for a time he himself had doubted that he was all there'). From Huck to Holden to Herzog the line of language stretches itself – unbroken, supple, sassy, streetwise. As well as Holden's hypnotic idiolect, Salinger captures perfect specimens of other speech: taxi-driver's twang ('What're ya tryna do, bud?'); pimp's

*The Catcher in the Rye* by J. D. Salinger, Penguin Books.

parlando ('Innarested in a little tail t'night?'); highball high style ('So you and Pencey are no longer one'); prostitute politesse ('Well, ordinary, I'd say grand. I mean I'd love to have you drop up for a cocktail . . .'); sophisticated sophomore ('*Must* we pursue this horrible trend of thought?'). And so, flawlessly, on. Salinger has pitch so perfect it's a surprise he hasn't had a *succès fou* at baseball as well.

But there is more to *The Catcher in the Rye* than ventriloquism and the virtual reality of an American adolescent mind rendered down to the last mental detail. All *that*, of course, is there in the novel, dazzling and three-dimensional, just waiting for some trite, dazed and tone-deaf academic to dismiss it as 'merely verbal'. Nevertheless some of Salinger's shapeliness has become more visible as the surface pyrotechnics blaze a mite less fiercely, though the obvious brilliance will never seem other than just that – obvious and brilliant.

Mark Twain was shifty about lit. crit. and his author's note to *Huckleberry Finn* is resolutely facetious: 'Persons attempting to find a motive in this narrative will be prosecuted.' Salinger's dedication to *Raise High the Roof Beam, Carpenters* is emulative in its determination to hightail it the hell away from hermeneutics: 'If there is an amateur reader still left in the world – or anybody who just reads and runs – I ask him or her, with untellable affection and gratitude, to split the dedication of this book four ways with my wife and children.' The trouble with this is that Salinger (and Twain, for that matter) is a real pro. *The Catcher in the Rye*, as one rereads it, is a surprisingly literary book, a searchingly sad book, a novel of real artistic cunning – and not just the hilariously sustained solo of popular memory.

In includes, for example, its own oblique artistic credo. One of its most sly jokes is that Holden, of *all* people, flunks Oral Expression. He explains to his old teacher, Mr Antolini, that 'the boys that got the best marks in Oral Expression were the ones that stuck to the point all the time'. Holden, however, *likes* it when somebody digresses. The novel itself is mercurial with digressions, a great gorgeous spatter – but they issue from

Holden, whose spirit has been broken. And locating the leak is the point of the novel, the point from which he flinches as often as he looks.

One key to his character is Holden's grey hair: 'I was sixteen then, and I'm seventeen now, and sometimes I act like I'm about thirteen. It's really ironical, because I'm six foot two and a half and I have gray hair. I really do. The one side of my head – the right side – is full of millions of gray hairs.' This premature greyness is set against persistent infantility because Holden's problem is his fear of entering the adult world. As Carl Luce says, 'Same old Caulfield. When are you going to grow up?' In fact, old Luce says it again ('When in *hell* are you going to grow up?'), and he puts his finger near the problem when he recalls his advice that Holden should see a psychoanalyst. Their drink in the Wicker Bar of the Seton Hotel may look like a digression, a *happening*, but actually it is purely functional. Luce comes and goes but doesn't conform to Holden's gloomy and twice-repeated statement that 'people never give your message to anybody'. Old Luce delivers. He tells us that Holden is in denial, that he doesn't want to grow up.

The greyness is commensurate with Holden's premature encounter with the adult world – in which his adored younger brother, Allie, has died of leukemia, leaving Holden with an injured fist and an unhealed wound at the heart. The former results from breaking all the goddam garage windows with his fist the night his brother dies. The broken heart is referred to with brilliant comic indirection: throughout the novel, Holden has a fantasy that he is concealing a wound. 'When I was *really* drunk, I started that stupid business with the bullet in my guts again. I was the only guy at the bar with a bullet in their guts. I kept putting my hand under my jacket, on my stomach and all, to keep blood from dripping all over the place. I didn't want anybody to know I was even wounded.' The bravura digression here is the point: he *is* 'a wounded sonuvabitch'. Like Hamlet, his pretended madness conceals a profound psychological disturbance.

So it is hardly accidental that Hamlet should be alluded to –

specifically, when Holden criticizes Olivier's Hamlet because 'he was too much like a goddam general, instead of a sad, screwed-up type guy', and more generally whenever Holden swears to God he's crazy, or apologizes 'like a madman', or swears to God he's a madman, or notices that hangers in a closet 'rattle like madmen'. Nor is it surprising that Holden should be suicidal. Not just 'damn depressed and lonesome', 'blue as hell', but fully prepared 'to sit right the hell on top of' the atomic bomb. The larkiness in the teeth of tragedy is explained by the discussion of *Romeo and Juliet* – and in particular Holden's favourite character, Mercutio, who dies with a jest on his lips. Not a naive work, then, but rather literary. Rather well read despite its air of illiteracy.

In the first chapter, Holden confides: 'After I got across the road, I felt like I was sort of disappearing.' Though there are bags of ontological insecurity on view throughout *The Catcher*, it isn't until near the end that this particular evocation recurs. The morning after Mr Antolini has made his pass at Holden, 'something very spooky started happening' – Holden prays to his dead brother, Allie, to stop him disappearing before he gets to the other side of the street. Holden doesn't stop 'till I was way up in the Sixties'. This refers, of course, to the Manhattan grid, but also to Holden's fear of ageing into the adult world. As he walks uptown, he also 'ages' away from his youthful self.

Holden can remember the precise date of his brother's death (18 July 1946). His mother's grief is poignantly and laconically evoked: 'Half the time she's up all night smoking cigarettes.' *The Catcher in the Rye*, like Tennyson's *In Memoriam*, is a great anatomy of prolonged grieving. The title's (inaccurate) allusion to Burns's 'Coming through the Rye' is an allegory of vulnerability and the desperate need to protect. Holden wants to be the catcher, who stops the kids plunging over the brink of the chasm. It is a myth to place against death. Mummification is another, twice alluded to in the novel, each time in a comic context, though the drift is perfectly, deadly serious. Holden's failed history paper for Mr Spencer refers to the preservation of the *face* by a secret chemical. Later, the idea is repeated, again in a comic context (the kids says 'toons' when they mean 'tombs'), but the reader is quite clear that individuality, the *face*, is what Holden believes is preserved.

Holden refuses to go to Allie's grave. Why? Because *twice* it rained: 'all the visitors could get in their cars and turn on their radios and all and then go some nice place for dinner – everybody except Allie. I couldn't stand it.' Eventually, Holden *does* stand it, but only by an act of total solidarity with the dead. At the very end of the novel, it starts to rain heavily. Everyone except Holden takes shelter under the carousel. He remains out on a bench, getting soaked to the skin – out in the elements with his dead brother. The incident is bizarre, pure with quiddity, utterly convincing but inexplicable without reference to the shape of anguish which is the template organizing the novel. Holden never stops mourning Allie. Which is why he identifies not with Christ's disciples but 'that lunatic and all, that lived in the tombs'. He lives in the tomb of grief. Grief explains, too, why, when Holden is describing how his sister Phoebe used to amuse Allie, he inserts a sore, uncharacteristic correction of his headlong vernacular: 'She killed Allie, too. I mean he liked her, too.' His death is too real to be mistaken for a figure of speech. Grief and growing up – they account for Holden's jaundiced meditation on marriage and adulthood in Chapter 17, which follows Holden's failure to join two kids playing on a see-saw at the end of the previous chapter. So much that seems random and chaotic in this great novel is ultimately accounted for by the devastating debit in Holden's life – Allie. 'God, he was a nice kid, though.'

# Bad Language: Poetry, Swearing and Translation

Translation, like politics, is the art of the possible – with all the inevitable compromise implicit in that parallel with politics. The main reason for this can be summed up in a quotation from *Tender is the Night*. At the moment when the tendresse between Nicole Diver and the martial Tommy Barban is about to harden into something more sexually definite, the pair flirt between languages:

> 'Talk English to me, Tommy.'
> '*Parlez français avec moi, Nicole.*'
> 'But the meanings are different. In French you can be heroic and gallant with dignity, and you know it. But in English you can't be heroic and gallant without being a little absurd, and you know that, too. That gives me an advantage.'
> 'But after all – ' He chuckled suddenly. 'Even in English I'm brave, heroic, and all that.'

Barban is right, or translation would not be possible at all. But Nicole is right, too. French comes, as in this passage, with italics. The spirit of each language is different. Cognac, as it were, somehow becomes whisky. And occasionally cognac becomes a ginger beer shandy or a lager and lime – a phenomenon noted by Bruce Chatwin in his profile of André Malraux, where he remarks that Malraux's rhetoric is magnificent in French and fatuous in English. So what *is* possible?

Famously, pithily, undeniably, Robert Frost long ago found

that poetry is what is lost in translation. And it was many years before D. J. Enright made his pragmatic rejoinder that even more is lost if you do not translate. Translation, then, is better than nothing.

As an answer, this is better than nothing. Nevertheless, Frost has the better of the argument. And if Henry James anticipates Frost, at least by implication, it is because Frost's truism happens to be true. In *The Portrait of a Lady*, Edmund Ludlow, a New York lawyer, has the following exchange with his wife Lilian about her sister, Isabel Archer. Lilian mildly grumbles: 'I don't see what you've got against her except that she's so original.' Ludlow replies: 'Well, I don't like originals; I like translations.' We can tell from this that the translation is staider, thicker-waisted, less pliant, less athletic, slower on its feet than the *original* stuff. More of a home-body, in fact.

Swearing is another example of untranslatability, though a recent one because latterly swear words were expunged before they needed to be translated. Before swear words, however, there was the exclamation – often untranslatable in an identical way. When Santiago has lost his harpoon in the first shark and then sees the first *pair* of sharks, Hemingway's *The Old Man and the Sea* gives us this disquisition on translation. ' "Ay," he said aloud. There is no translation for this word and perhaps it is just a noise such as a man might make, involuntarily, feeling the nail go through his hands and into the wood.' In *Little Dorrit*, Dickens observes the same phenomenon: ' "ALTRO!" returned John Baptist, closing his eyes and giving his hand a most vehement toss. The word being, according to its Genoese emphasis, a confirmation, a contradiction, an assertion, a denial, a taunt, a compliment, a joke, and fifty other things, became in the present instance, beyond all power of written expression, our familiar English, "I believe you".'

Swearing is a more extreme instance of untranslatability. Let me give you four examples. Fuck to bloody shithouse. Shite and onions. I besmirch the milk of thy duty. What are you doing now, you lazy drunken obscene unsayable son of an unnameable gipsy obscenity?

I hope no one has taken any of these last four tetchy remarks personally. I offer them generally, in a forensic spirit, as part of an investigation into the nature of language and the limitations of translation. And I venture to say that only one brief expletive runs the risk of personal offensiveness to an English-speaking audience. All four are quotations, but only one is *echt*, or *pukka* or authentic. It is 'shite and onions', a personal coinage of Simon Dedalus in *Ulysses*. Because Dedalus is an English speaker, he has what used to be known as a generative grammar: he can work a plausible variation on the vernacular, a variation which is readable to the rest of us, if we, too, are native English speakers. All swearing possesses its proper penumbra of impropriety, and 'shite and onions' is reasonably versatile. Yet the tragic note is well beyond its range, and it is impossible to imagine it replacing Lear's brute howl as he bears the dead Cordelia in his arms. No, as English speakers we know from our bat-like linguistic radar that the tonal range of 'shite and onions' is restricted to the expression of rueful exasperation at the contingencies and incongruities of fate. 'Shite and onions' is never tragic, most often wryly comic, and very occasionally expressive of the note of incredulous sternness. *Shite and onions.* This last variant I can *say*, but I cannot write.

My first quotation, 'Fuck to bloody shithouse', is oddly opaque by comparison. It shares grammatical ambiguity with the now long-vanished legend over varnished train lavatory seats which Jonathan Miller analysed three decades ago in *Beyond the Fringe*. Was the unpunctuated phrase, 'Gentlemen lift the seat', a definition, an imperative or a loyal toast? 'Fuck to bloody shithouse' might conceivably be an imperative, though the context to justify this interpretation might require a Joe Orton to script something sufficiently plausible. In fact, the phrase was the favourite expletive of a boy called Charlie Wong at my boarding school. He arrived there at the age of seventeen from either Hong Kong or Singapore and never quite managed, therefore, the art of swearing in fluent English. He could conduct a normal conversation. He could make himself understood. But his deep generative grammar was faulty and his favourite expletive, 'fuck to bloody shithouse', was fatally tone deaf. The finer points of the English language – swearing and poetry – were equally beyond him.

The second pair of quotations is from Hemingway's *For Whom the Bell Tolls*. 'I besmirch the milk of thy duty' is what Agustin says to his fellow-partisan Fernando. 'What are you doing now, you lazy drunken obscene unsayable son of an unnameable unmarried gipsy obscenity?' is the rhetorical question of Pilar to the morally crumbling Pablo, her consort. The two quotations are different. One is a translation, of sorts, and the other is an edited obscenity not unlike Conrad's *Typhoon*, where the spaces left by censorship figure as euphemisms and propriety reaches for colouristic synonym: 'he didn't mind, he said, the trouble of punching their blanked heads down there, blank his soul'; 'to shove the unmentionable instrument down his gory throat. Who cared for his crimson barometer...' Compare Mr Polly's interior monologue in which adjectives like 'sanguinary' replace 'bloody' over a number of lines:

> 'Arf a mo',' said the figure, as if in response to his start, and speaking in a hoarse whisper. 'Arf a mo', mister. You the noo bloke at the Potwell Inn?'
>
> Mr Polly felt evasive. 'S'pose I am,' he replied hoarsely, and quickened his pace.
>
> 'Arf a mo',' said Uncle Jim, taking his arm. 'We ain't doing a (sanguinary) Marathon. It ain't a (decorated) cinder track. I want a word with you, mister. See?'
>
> Mr Polly wriggled his arm free and stopped. 'Whad is it?' he asked, and faced the terror.
>
> 'I jest wanted a (decorated) word wiv you. See? – just a friendly word or two. Just to clear up any blooming errors. That's all I want. No need to be so (richly decorated) proud, if you *are* the noo bloke at the Potwell Inn. Not a bit of it. See?'

'You lazy drunken obscene unsayable son of an unnameable' is, of course, the bowdlerized version and yet it is more effective on the page than the more nearly accurate but also edited 'I besmirch the milk of thy duty', where, I take it, 'besmirch' stands for 'shit in' or 'shit on'. The point about the blanks offered by Hemingway – 'obscene', 'unsayable' – is that we can fill them convincingly and quickly from the word-hoard of the English language. We are given the opportunity to substitute, whereas the other phrase, 'I shit on the milk of your duty', is a translation in which the force has been lost, in which the poetry has gone missing. Here is another brief extract from Hemingway's novel: ' "Then go and befoul thyself," Pilar said to him without heat. "Thy mother," Agustin replied.'

*Tu madre* is a serious swear word, like *madonna putana* in Italy, but the literal translations, 'your mother' and 'madonna whore', are without force, without patina, without the weight of tradition, without the context of Catholicism. One of Hemingway's linguistic projects is to write in Spanish using English. I myself once began a translation of Marina Tsvetayeva's 'An Attempt at Jealousy' in which I aimed to write a kind of Russian-English, without articles and reproducing the Russian word-order. In the event, Tsvetayeva's subject matter, jealousy, interested me more than the linguistic project and I ended up writing a traditional ballad, though in another poem, 'Purge', I did my best to re-create the linguistic surprises of the Siamese-English spoken by a lodger at my mother-in-law's house, the tricks and tropes of which I had noted down a decade previously. Hemingway, clearly, can sense some such linguistic spin-off when he has Robert Jordan discuss the psychological requirements of the saboteur as follows: 'In this you have to have very much head and be very much cold in the head.' It isn't English, but we know what he means and that he is really speaking in Spanish. Of course, we also know that Jordan, though fluent, is not bilingual. Were he bilingual, the texture of foreignness would disappear. The feel of the language would feel like English to an Englishman, but where would that leave Hemingway's vaunting expertise? It would leave it unadvertised. And is this actually what we want? Instead of the flavour of foreignness, would we prefer it if Agustin said, for example,

'You can take your sense of duty and stick it up your arse, sunshine'? When Tom Stoppard reviewed Hemingway's posthumous *The Garden of Eden* in the *Observer* (8 February 1987), he noted the 'flourishing of small expertise' and referred to E. B. White's famous parody in which the Hemingway figure takes a girl to Schrafft's, 'where my old friend Botticelli is captain of girls and where they have the mayonnaise in fiascos'. Stoppard then quoted Hemingway's description of gazpacho: 'it came in a large bowl with ice floating with the slices of crisp cucumber, tomato, garlic bread, green and red peppers, and the coarsely peppered liquid that tasted lightly of oil and vinegar. "It's salad soup," Catherine said. "It's delicious." "*Es gazpacho*," the waiter said.' Hungry? Or perhaps you'd rather have the paella from *For Whom the Bell Tolls*:

> we ate in pavilions on the sand. Pastries made of cooked and shredded fish and red and green peppers and small nuts like grains of rice. Pastries delicate and flaky and the fish of a richness that was incredible. Prawns fresh from the sea sprinkled with lime juice. They were pink and sweet and there were four bites to a prawn. Of those we ate many. Then we ate *paella* with fresh sea food, clams in their shells, mussels, crayfish, and small eels. Then we ate even smaller eels alone cooked in oil and as tiny as bean sprouts and curled in all directions and so tender they disappeared in the mouth without chewing. All the time drinking a white wine, cold, light, and good at thirty centimos the bottle. And for an end: melon. That is the home of the melon.

Gazpacho, paella, both brilliantly described, both expertly evoked. I side with Stoppard, who wrote: 'Well, it isn't Hemingway's fault that you can now get the stuff in cans at Safeway's.' And I would want to add a codicil to Stoppard's defence. It is this. Open the can from Safeway's, cook the paella-in-the-packet and neither will have the authenticity of Hemingway's account: art transcends life in a way which would have brought a Q.E.D.

to Oscar Wilde's full lips. It is said that some gourmets read recipe books as if they were pornography. Hemingway's descriptions of food are a kind of paunchography with strong sexual undertones. Take that melon, for example. Fernando disagrees with Pilar. ' "The melon of Castile is better," Fernando said. "*Qué va*," said the woman of Pablo. "The melon of Castile is for self-abuse. The melon of Valencia for eating." '

Which returns the argument to the role of swearing in translation theory. In Alfred Jarry's *Ubu Roi*, Ubu refers now and again to various obscene instruments in his possession: *le croc à merdre* and *le cisaux à merdre*. If we can, so to speak, leave the strangely singular *cisaux à merdre* at the back of the bathroom cabinet, we can concentrate on *le croc à merdre*. How exactly do we translate this obscenity? It is, literally, the 'crook' for 'shit' or the 'shit crook'. Were I a translator of the Nabokov persuasion, I should leave the matter there, accurately rendered but scarcely Englished. The 'crook for shit' doesn't even convey a kind of Frenchness as Agustin's 'I shit in the milk of your duty' conveys an unmistakable Spanishness as it strikes the English ear. I have given *le croc à merdre* considerable thought, convinced that the novelty of Jarry's French must require a similar novelty in English, however free the translation. Turd tongs, shit pliers, shit shifters, a bowel probe are some of my suggestions. My final choice, however, is that Ubu should reach for his *No. 2 iron*.

Behind Jarry's *le croc à merdre* are lined up a host of untranslatable things, objects and concepts, which have no currency outside their country of origin. Of course *le croc à merdre* has no currency *in* its country of origin, but it serves as a symbolic hook to join poetry and swearing to those other untranslatable things, *things*.

Recently, I have been translated into Dutch, Polish and American. I leave the American translation till last. My Dutch translator is a poet who has translated John Donne's songs, sonnets, elegies and holy sonnets, as well as work by contemporary English poets for every Poetry International at Rotterdam. His name is Jan Eijkelboom and the consensus is that he is the best Dutch translator of poetry. He had two problems. My poem 'Gauguin' is a linguistic experiment, not unlike Hemingway's desire to reproduce in English certain Spanish qualities. I wished to invent a kind of pidgin, inspired by certain brilliant and possibly apocryphal pidgin periphrases like the pidgin for 'helicopter', 'mixmaster blong Jesus Christ', or the pidgin for playing the piano, 'man in bockis, you fight him, he cry'. My poem's subject was sex:

> He stickyout number2tongue
> because he magnetized to she.
>
> Which she hide in shesecrets,
> Because she magnetized to he.

And so on. In Rotterdam, Eijkelboom told me that the poem was impossible to translate *because* the Dutch language has a dialect of pidgin – which would be seen as racist. The problem of connotation is like that associated with swearing – but in reverse. The neutral and harmless, when translated, becomes lethal and poisonous. (Later, though, when translating my *Selected Poems*, the resourceful, gifted Eijkelboom obviously found a solution because, in that volume, the poem *is* translated.) The other Dutch problem was disclosed by a member of the public who wrote to me after he had seen Jan Eijkelboom's translation of my poem 'In Modern Dress', in which I describe a small child trailing a comforter across a muddy garden so that the child looks like Sir Walter Ralegh laying down his cloak for Queen Elizabeth. My correspondent told me that in Dutch my child was now sucking a dummy, a different kind of comforter.

In Polish, the problem for my brilliant translator, Jerzy Jarniewicz, was a stanza largely consisting of the names of English sheep breeds – Devon Longwool, Derbyshire Gritstone, Beulah Speckle-Faced, to name three from a list of twelve or more. Obviously these local sheep don't exist in Poland, and my translator at first decided to leave the bulk of the stanza in

English. Then he discovered that although Poland had no Hill Radnor or North Country Cheviots, it did have its own comparably varied sheep strains, which he was able to use instead.

My experience of being translated into American came as more of a surprise, even if, years ago, I had a similar experience in *Poetry Chicago*, to whom I had given a poem called 'The Explorers' that included the line 'tights as tight as a Durex' to describe some ballet dancers. At the suggestion of the editor, I altered this to the more alliterative 'tights as tight as a Trojan'. (You will recall that Bette Midler once said of her all-women backing group that the only thing they knew about classical literature was Trojans.) In 1991, I wrote a profile of Seamus Heaney for *Vanity Fair* and had an educational encounter with Wayne Lawson, the magazine's executive literary editor. For instance, the acronym D-I-Y means nothing to an American audience and has to be expanded to Do-It-Yourself. The allusion to 'a line of Keith Douglas' has to tote extra, necessary information, so little known is Douglas to American readers: thus, 'Heaney evoked a line of Keith Douglas's poem "The Marvel" in one lapidary phrase'. The concept of the 'review front' had to be explained to Americans as (the slightly inaccurate) 'Lowell's poetry could command a review on the front page of the arts section in a national Sunday newspaper' – whereas what I intended was a reference to the publication of several of Lowell's *Imitations* on the front page of the *Observer*'s review section, rather than a review as such. Similarly, what one of my informants described as 'a kind of desolate secondary school' became 'a kind of desolate secondary intermediate school'. Other things simply had to be dropped. For instance, praising Heaney's fine ear and his ability to capture sounds like a tape-recorder, I quoted one of the Glanmore sonnets, which refers to 'the sibilant penumbra of close-down'. American radios are different. The thing doesn't exist: no sibilance, no penumbra, and close-down is called something else. I referred also to a Derek Mahon poem which describes a pub singer with one hand to his ear and the other earthing himself through his girlfriend's hand. The American verb is 'grounding', not 'earthing'. More recently, I have discovered from the copy-editor of Doubleday that 'caliper' means 'dividers' in America – and if you have polio there, your leg will end up in a *brace*, not a calliper.

It is, however, a translation, whereas 'the sibilant penumbra of close-down' cannot be translated from English into American-English because the thing itself doesn't exist. In the same way, English potato peelings differ from American 'potato peels' (see Mary Karr's essay 'Against Decoration' in a 1991 *Parnassus*), which derive rather from the English orange peel – all of which differ from the untranslatable *dacha*, a word which is defined in Marcus Wheeler's Oxford Russian–English dictionary as '*dacha* (holiday cottage in the country in environs of city or large town)'. A *dachnik* is defined as '(holiday) visitor (in the country)'. 'Chalet' is the only English word to come within megaphone distance of *dacha* – and it is fatally associated with the sea, whereas *dacha* is firmly associated with the countryside. In Ronald Hingley's translation of Chekhov's 'Lady with a Dog', Gurov, on his return to Moscow after his seduction of Anna Sergeyevna, lapses into a gross unspirituality: he can eat a whole plateful of 'Moscow hot-pot'. Constance Garnett's version of this coarse materialism is a whole plateful of 'salt fish and cabbage'. S. S. Koteliansky prefers to stay with the original Russian: 'he could eat a whole plateful of hot *sielianka*'. What Chekhov actually wrote was *selyanka*, for which Wheeler's Oxford Russian–English dictionary gives: '(culinary) hot-pot; (*fig*) hotch-potch, hodge-podge'. In other words, Hingley's translation is more accurate than Garnett's 'salt fish and cabbage' or Koteliansky's muffed transliteration. However, perverse as it may seem, I think 'hot-pot', even with the prefix 'Moscow', has connotations too restricted to Lancashire. *Selyanka*, like *dacha*, is in reality untranslatable. What these examples show is that general rules are very difficult to establish, but that accuracy is less important than effect: 'hot-pot' is correct, but makes the effect of coarse Englishing, as if 'sausage roll' were used to translate *piroshki*. *Piroshki* are best described using French vocabulary: they are like a brioche with a savoury meat filling, a million wursts away from sausage rolls.

On the whole, I think it best to transliterate the original where there is no equivalent entity in the host language. In Chapter 2 of *The Gift*, Nabokov sensibly writes: 'the greasy, clayey *zemskaya* (rural district) road'. On the same principle, it might be better to translate *sirnik* not as 'curd fritter', the suggestion of Marcus Wheeler's dictionary, but as *sirnik*, a cheese fritter. 'Curd' in English has stronger sweet connotations than sour ones: we think of lemon curd before we think of curd cheese. In this limited sense, it can sometimes be better for a translator to know his *own* language better than the foreign original.

Even a great writer like Nabokov makes mistakes in the move from his 'infinitely docile' Russian to the less flexuous English language. In *The Gift*, we read: 'the paired pack-loads of equal weight are seized twice with lariats so that nothing can shift'. Elsewhere, a young man 'in his hard, sinewy way' is 'remindful of a gundog'. Nabokov doesn't give us the *development* of a friendship, but, pursuing the photographic idea, 'the exposure of their friendship'. I wonder, too, exactly what distinction he is making when he writes that Godunov-Cherdynstev's father 'could not stand procrastination, hesitation'. The translator must be good at the language he is translating from but perfect in the language he is translating into. With this saving thought in mind, I want now to quote from a letter written to Ian McEwan by one of his many translators. I deliberately refrain from disclosing the language into which the translation is being made:

Dear Ian,
I've just (three minutes ago) finished to translate your *The Comfort of Strangers*. It's been a real hard job, not because of the language, your english is translator's delight, but because of the story. I've told the publisher I'm not sure I'm going to translate your next works, because there's too much gap between us, and I believe it's real better when you feel what you translate. I've already had it bad with *The Cement Garden*, and since it seems that every new novel or story of yours is a lil' bit

crueller and more full of corpses than the one before,
what next then? Anyway, you're real great writer.

There is something as disturbing here as Koteliansky's translation of Gurov's name in 'The Lady with the Dog' as Gomov.
It is difficult to feel any confidence when your translator writes
that 'your english is translator's delight'. Nevertheless, I cling,
charitably, to the idea that one's real expertise should be in
one's own language. To return to swearing, I recall Thom Gunn
asking me in San Francisco if I had really published a poem
entitled 'Arsehole'. I had. It was a version of the Rimbaud–
Verlaine sonnet called 'Sonnet d'un trou de cul'. Gunn's comment was a poet's comment on two languages. 'Gee, "arsehole"
is so much dirtier than "asshole".' Where most translations fail
is by choosing what is possible in English, rather than what is
right in English. 'Asshole' is a possible translation of 'arsehole'
but it isn't the right translation – not only for the reason given
by Thom Gunn. To call someone an 'arsehole' is quite different
from saying someone is an 'asshole'. The former is malignant
where the latter is harmless. To be on a desert island with an
asshole would be irritating perhaps. To be on the same desert
island with an arsehole might even be dangerous.

On 16 June 1991, the *Observer* published an interview with
the French prime minister Edith Cresson – a reject from Naim
Atallah's book of interviews with women which suddenly
became newsworthy when Madame Cresson was elevated by
President Mitterrand. Nowhere did the piece say that the interview was conducted in French and translated into English, but
there was a moment when the internal evidence made this clear.
Naim Atallah's question was: 'Appearance is also very important to men; you rarely see a rich, successful man with a woman
who isn't pretty.' The answer began: 'That isn't my opinion.'
This is possible in English, but we are more likely to say 'I
disagree', or 'That isn't what I think', or 'Not in my opinion'.
Another question ('Do you think that, today, there are advantages in being a woman?') received this answer: 'If you know
how to draw them out, I believe there are many advantages in

being a woman.' I suspect that Madame Cresson meant something closer to 'If you know how to make the most of them . . .'

In Chapter 14, Part 5, of Milan Kundera's *Immortality*, the translation from Peter Kussi gives us this: 'She is at the dentist's, sitting in a crowded waiting room; a new patient enters, walks to the couch where she is seated and sits down on her lap; he didn't do it intentionally, he simply saw an empty seat on the couch; she protests and tries to push him away, shouting . . .' So far, so good. It is what she shouts which is strange – possible, but wrong. ' "Sir, can't you see? This seat is taken! I am sitting here!" ' Trying her exclamations on one's tongue, we can see that the mistake is one of punctuation. That 'Can't you see?' is a possible but unlikely question. Any of the following are more plausible: 'Are you blind?'; 'Look what you're doing'; 'Look out.' But best of all is the Kussi with its punctuation altered. Instead of the stiffly lapidary 'Can't you see? This seat is taken!' one might substitute the more fluent 'Can't you see this seat is taken?'

Translation is the art of compromise. It should be theoretically impure and practically impure. Rigid rules are its enemy. Ask your mouth to tell you not if what is written is *allowable* in English but if what is written is *right* in English. And then beware of clichés – which always sound right.

I now want to discuss the translation of Brecht's 'To Those Born Later' in *Poems 1913–1956*, edited by John Willett and Ralph Manheim with the co-operation of Erich Fried. Many of the poems have the initials of a translator appended, but this particular poem has not. The *apparatus* explains: 'Those translations which bear no translator's initials involve a degree of collaboration on the Editors' part which makes final responsibility difficult to establish.' This is the beginning (of 'An die Nachgeborenen') in the Willett–Manheim–Anonymous version:

Truly, I live in dark times!
The guileless word is folly. A smooth forehead
Suggests insensitivity. The man who laughs
Has simply not yet had
The terrible news

What kind of times are they, when
A talk about trees is almost a crime
Because it implies silence about so many horrors?
That man there calmly crossing the street
Is already perhaps beyond the reach of his friends
Who are in need?

It is true I still earn my keep
But, believe me, that is only an accident. Nothing
I do gives me the right to eat my fill.
By chance I've been spared. (If my luck breaks, I am lost.)

Derek Mahon's translation of this poem (in *The Hunt by Night*)
is at first closely related to the Brecht. His inspired rendition of
the Willett–Manheim–Anonymous's 'A smooth forehead/ Suggests insensitivity' shows what can be done by a good poet-
translator: 'A clear brow argues/ A thick skin.' Soon, though,
Mahon's impatience shows, and translation shades into version
and version ends up as imitation – a Mahon poem nourished by
Brecht. My own partial attempt follows. I have no German to
speak of or speak with, but I have attempted my own 'translation' of this Brecht poem, using the Willett–Manheim–Anonymous translation as if it were a rough literal version. It isn't
really a translation so much as a critique of the Manheim–
Willett–Anonymous version.

It's true, we live in dark times.
The unconsidered word is naive. A placid brow
Indicates callousness. The man who is laughing
Just hasn't heard the dreadful news yet.

What sort of a world is it, when
Talking about trees is almost criminal
Because it implies silence about so much horror?
When that man there calmly crossing the street
May already be beyond the reach of his friends
Who need his help?

> OK, I still earn enough,
> but, believe me, that's only luck. Nothing
> I do gives me the right to eat till I'm full.
> I've been spared by accident. (If my luck runs out, I've
> > had it.)

Impudently, for a non-Germanist, I've tried to eliminate the clichés in the Willett–Manheim–Anonymous version ('earn my keep', 'eat my fill') and to eradicate all those heavy touches of translationese: you can say 'If my luck breaks, I am lost', but it is better to say 'If my luck runs out, I've had it'; 'Truly, I live in dark times!' has a more pronounced German accent than 'It's true, we live in dark times'; 'A talk about trees' suggests a lecture or an address, whereas 'talking about trees' is idiomatic; 'The guileless word is folly' might have been written by Schiller and translated by Coleridge, so I prefer the less antique 'The unconsidered word is naive'. Later in the Willett–Manheim version, we encounter 'But those in power/ Sat safer without me'. I'm hardly sure what this means, so odd is the English. It may be an oblique reference to show trials, but it's a phrase of English which is hardly even as allowable as the other phrases were that I've been quibbling over. If I knew German better, I dare say I'd be much less worried by the English. Is there a case for translation in tandem with one translator who knows both languages well and one translator who is only a gifted monoglot?

Sometime in 1987, I was commissioned by Jonathan Miller to translate Racine's *Andromaque* for his opening season at the Old Vic in 1988. Miller wanted a clean, modern translation – without, for example, any of the 'thees' and 'thous' which Richard Wilbur uses in his version, following the usage of his country neighbours in Connecticut. I began with an octosyllabic line and rhyming couplets. And I quickly realized that Miller's simple request was impossible. One of Racine's most famous lines, about Hector's son, Astyanax, occurs in Pyrrhus's first speech adumbrating the war just past:

> Un fleuve teint de sang, des campagnes désertes,
> Un enfant dans les fers . . .

The problem here is that there can be no room in a 'clean, modern translation' for *un enfant dans les fers*: 'a child in chains' is the obvious route and that chosen by Robert Henderson, but those 'chains' take us out of the twentieth century if not to the seventeenth century. This pressure is constant, though perhaps less obviously pronounced. The result is an idiom which is neither contemporary nor anything approaching Racine's poetic diction, either in its genuine reach or in its artificiality. It is easy to write a kind of formal civil service speech, reaching – in anger or fear or jealous passion – for rather dated colloquialisms and the clichés of sentiment. This language is occasionally heightened but never attempts the sublime. In no time at all, 'under' has become 'beneath' and 'on' has become 'upon'. The solution, it seemed to me, was to update the entire piece in order to use contemporary English fearlessly. Miller disagreed with me and replaced my version with Eric Korn's more literal translation, which wasn't without its resourcefulnesses. However, the night I saw the production, the audience laughed every time Eric Korn used a contemporary idiom. In the inevitable overall artificiality of the faithful Racine translation – the result of the original's restricted vocabulary and marzipan diction for the emotions – anything remotely natural is liable to strike an audience as laughable. By setting my free version in a fictitious 1953, I could be confident of what was for me the most important thing – a clean, modern language. I could use my own voice.

Admirers of Racine will already be appalled. I wish to add, all the same, that Racine's greatness, for me, lies less in the language than in the plot. Of course, the plot of *Andromaque* is full of improbabilities – like, for instance, Andromaque's pious hope that Pyrrhus will care for Astyanax, despite her suicide, because she has gone through the marriage ceremony. George Steiner told me, when I jeered at this particular improbability, that I did not understand the code of Pyrrhus's *parole d'honneur*. I'm afraid that I responded by pointing out that Pyrrhus has already given his *parole d'honneur* to Hermione – and broken it. By plot I really mean the system of frontal conflicts, however contrived their inception may be.

Anyone who has heard my French accent will know that my inwardness with the French language isn't adequate to a full appreciation of Racine's poetry. I am sure this is true. In his 'Anniversaries', Donne has this wonderful line: 'Thinke thee laid on thy death-bed, loose and slacke.' Metrically, it would be difficult to find a looser, slacker or deader pentameter. And the tautology there, 'loose and slacke', is acceptable to a native English speaker in the way that Nabokov's 'procrastination, hesitation' was not. This is an anthology of padding from *Macbeth*, all of it acceptable: 'thou sure and firm-set earth'; 'stop up the access and passage to remorse'; 'the vile blows and buffets of the world'; 'to trade and traffic with Macbeth'; 'a wild and violent sea'; 'a good and virtuous nature'. None of these examples, perhaps, would be acceptable outside dramatic poetry, where repetition is permissible and, arguably, necessary for audience comprehension. A foreigner, though, would be unable to gauge the linguistic allowance to be made. What is padding, what is repetition of a telling kind, and what is pure tautology? Translating Racine, I found myself, as a foreigner, unable to tolerate the tautology (as I perceived it) of the French and its total absence of economy. Act 5, Scene 1, will illustrate. Hermione is speaking after having sent Orestes to murder Pyrrhus, the man she really loves, in the temple before he can marry her rival Andromaque:

> Où suis-je? Qu'ai-je fait? Que dois-je faire encore?
> Quel transport me saisit? Quel chagrin me dévore?
> Errante, et sans dessein, je cours dans ce palais.
> Ah! ne puis-je savoir si j'aime ou si je hais?
> Le cruel! . . .

Yet, while I found this insufferably stylized and repetitive, I noticed comparable repetition in my own version, which alter-

26

nated between ametrical lines and rigid octosyllabic lines with a full rhyme – the idea being to drop in and out of metre. This is my Andromaque pleading with Hermione for her son Astyanax:

> I don't want to antagonize
> your royal highness. That would serve
> no purpose at all. Please don't misconstrue
> straightforwardness as brazen nerve.
> You have everything. You want for nothing.
> I have nothing but the task
> of saving my son. I'm desperate. Forgive me.
> I ask because I have to ask.
> I have no husband. I have only a son.
> You'll marry soon and have a child.
> Then you'll feel what I feel, what all mothers feel.
> We're not quite civilized. We're wild,
> instinct with instincts . . .

That last repetition is an attempt to make over Racine's linguistic turn and return, but those immediately before strike me as acceptable because dramatically necessary. The point is that a foreigner would be unable to gauge the weighting of each decision – and the result would be boredom. Repetition is the area of poetry where translation is the most likely to fail, where a calculated risk, full of tension, can appear in another language as 'loose and slacke'.

Let me conclude this deliberately inconclusive essay with one consolatory certainty. It is a certainty which returns us to our starting point. Isn't it wonderful that FUCK and STOP, the words for licence and prohibition, are so universally understood that they need no translation?

# James Joyce's *Ulysses*

Alan Bennett, à propos Kafka, once defined 'classic' as an author no one has read – hence their unassailable classic status. At any dinner party, someone has read 'Metamorphosis', a select few *The Trial*, but no one has read *Amerika*. Unless George Steiner is a guest. Or Milan Kundera.

Another kind of classic is the text which starts with stardom and subsequently achieves permanent status. Nabokov's *Lolita* was a *succès de scandale* first, then a *succès d'estime*.

*Ulysses* is both kinds. If the novel had stardom, its stardom was modelled on Greta Garbo – the glamour of the unknown. Initially, *Ulysses* was not famous, but banned and infamous – a dirty book in which the hero sat on the lavatory and his wife fantasized about fellatio and the sexual possibilities of the banana. For many English readers, the book was available only via Stuart Gilbert's 'study'-cum-digest, published in 1930, eight years after its first appearance in Paris. Original copies had to be smuggled, since the book was banned. Unread because forbidden – what better guarantee of popular readership? Just as well. Rivals greeted the book with less than unanimous acclaim – Virginia Woolf thought it 'underbred' and reading it like watching the boot boy at Claridge's pick his pimples. D. H. Lawrence abhorred its 'deliberate dirty-mindedness'. In other words, it shocked them by the extraordinary candour with which it records the ordinary, unedited life of an average man. Outside and in.

*Ulysses* is a modernist work of realism. Like the greatest literature, it sees the object as it really is and re-presents it to us.

Great writing corrects our automatic perceptions of reality. Leopold Bloom may say 'miaow' to his cat, but the cat says 'mkgnao'. We think we say 'tut-tut', but Joyce knows we say 'Dth! Dth!' Realism in literature means the correction of literary conventions by reference to 'reality'. Sometimes it is also unfairly taken to mean a novel which aspires to encompass the whole of reality – an impossible task and, by definition, not worth undertaking. 'University modernism', academic modernism, therefore opposes realism and modernism, pits me against the other. *Ulysses* is effortlessly both.

And it is this that has given the novel its staying power, its classic status. Visibly experimental and virtuoso, the book has every trick in the book. It parodies the whole of English prose; Molly Bloom's soliloquy is unpunctuated stream of consciousness; the prose of another section aspires to the condition of music.

On the other hand, the twenty-four hours in Dublin it describes are virtually free of plot – of contrived excitements – and simultaneously charged with reality, the very textures of life. Davy Byrne, the publican, has 'tuckstitched shirtsleeves'. Bloom's copy of *The Poetical Works of Denis Florence M'Carthy* has a 'copper beechleaf bookmark at p. 5'. Bloom's chest measurement is 28″ – and 29½″ expanded.

This brings me to Joyce's simple, central achievement – though he begins with the statutory contempt of the highbrow, he forges a great democratic imagination. Even George Orwell, as he sometimes knew, is contaminated with class contempt – 'we may find in the long run that tinned food is a deadlier weapon than the machine gun'. In Joyce, the ordinary man – undernourished, under-educated, physically feeble – takes the limelight from the intellectual Stephen Dedalus. And takes it without the sentimentality of Chaplin's or H. G. Wells's celebrations of the little man. For a long time, Joyce's epic parallels – between Homer's *Odyssey* and the narrative of a (surprisingly uncircumcised) Jewish advertisement canvasser in Dublin – were wrongly thought to ironize contemporary modern life. Courageous on occasion, a trimmer on others, fastidious and farting ('Pprrpffrrppffff'), Bloom is a hero, but one recognizably human.

# *Ulysses*

In the 'Ithaca' section of *Ulysses*, the penultimate episode of question and answer, Leopold Bloom, ever the diplomat, dissents 'tacitly' from Stephen Dedalus's views 'on the eternal affirmation of the spirit of man in literature'. For his part, Stephen dissents 'openly' from Bloom's views on 'the importance of dietary and civic selfhelp'.

In this, the driest section of the novel, favoured by Joyce above the rest as the 'ugly duckling' of his masterpiece, the text is functional, a virtuoso pastiche of scientific technical prose. The author is writing up the experimental data garnered in the course of his narrative – and adding to it. It is, therefore, Euclidean, skeletal, summary – and teeming with extra observation. 'Ithaca' may tempt the reader to equate its method with Zola's idea of the 'experimental' novel – 'simply the report of the experiment that the novelist conducts before the eyes of the public' – but Joyce's prose is at once more forbiddingly forensic and, in its way, joyously prodigal. It demonstrates the fundamental artistic principle which animates the whole – 'the art of surfeit', a phrase Stephen applies to Shakespeare in the 'Scylla and Charybdis' section. It isn't difficult to connect Stephen's pell-mell exempla, 'hot herringpies, green mugs of sack, honeysauces, sugar of roses, marchpane, gooseberried pigeons, ringocandies', with the lists in the later chapter: 'hydraulic millwheels, turbines, dynamos, electric power stations, bleachworks, tanneries, scutchmills'. But there is more to Joyce's surfeit than mere enumeration. He was photographed many times with a magnifying glass, thanks to the weakness of his eyesight, and the optical aid is a truer emblem of his art than 'factification' – since his art of surfeit is the art of magnification.

Nothing is too small to escape his attention. Not even a clothes line in Bloom's kitchen: 'under a row of five coiled spring housebells a curvilinear rope, stretched between two holdfasts athwart across the recess beside the chimney pier, from which hung four smallsized square handkerchiefs folded unattached consecutively in adjacent rectangles and one pair of ladies' grey hose with lisle suspender tops and feet in their habitual position clamped by three erect wooden pegs two at their outer extremities and the third at their point of junction'. Dry, objective, swimming in descriptive lust, there is the sagging line – held in granular close-up by Joyce's telephoto lens like the last numinous example of a threatened species. And how satisfying to know that those nameless fixtures, like miniature straight handlebars, are called 'holdfasts'.

'Ithaca' is the section new readers of *Ulysses* tend to dislike, understandably but unjustly, because it imposes its exhaustiveness on attention already exhausted by 700-odd pages of taxing narrative. Yet it is full of idiosyncratic beauty ('the plump mellow yellow smellow melons of her rump'), frank poetry ('the heaventree of stars hung with humid nightblue fruit') and sly comedy. When Bloom bumps his head, Joyce's hilariously unsmiling pedantic account anticipates Kingsley Amis at his most comically periphrastic: 'the right temporal lobe of the hollow sphere of his cranium came into contact with a solid timber angle where, an infinitesimal but sensible fraction of a second later, a painful sensation was located in consequence of antecedent sensations transmitted and registered'. Richmal Crompton frequently adopts a related Latinate gravitas for the more egregious exploits of William Brown. Likewise P. G. Wodehouse's Jeeves.

A different kind of comedy, more human, less verbal, animates the tacit and open disagreements between Bloom and Stephen. The confident (and intoxicated) artist can object to Bloom's dietary and civic theories 'openly', without giving offence – or without noticing he has given offence. But the proposition from which Bloom dissents is of a different order of magnitude. Saying 'no' to 'the eternal affirmation of the spirit of man in literature' is like withholding applause and merely clearing your throat after a private performance of a full symphony when the conductor turns, drenched in sweat like an exhausted duellist. Tacit dissent is all that is possible. The applause is not prolonged.

As a human transaction, the exchange shows Stephen's praiseworthy candour and his possible brusqueness. It shows us, too, Bloom's tact and equanimity, his common sense opposed to Stephen's tendency to magniloquence. And yet it is equally possible that it is Stephen who *denies* 'the eternal affirmation of the spirit of man in literature'. The relevant sentence will allow this reading. Bloom then becomes the one who wishes to affirm the proposition. 'Bloom dissented tacitly from Stephen's views on the eternal affirmation of the spirit of man in literature.' What those views are is not specified. We know, of course, that Bloom is a down-to-earth type from the 'Hades' section at Paddy Dignam's funeral in Glasnevin cemetery:

> Mr Kernan said with solemnity:
> – *I am the resurrection and the life.* That touches a man's inmost heart.
> – It does, Mr Bloom said.
> Your heart perhaps but what price the fellow in the six feet by two with his toes to the daisies? No touching that. Seat of the affections. Broken heart. A pump after all, pumping thousands of gallons of blood every day. One fine day it gets bunged up and there you are. Lots of them lying around here: lungs, hearts, livers. Old rusty pumps: damn the thing else. The resurrection and the life. Once you are dead you are dead. That last day idea. Knocking them all up out of their graves. Come forth, Lazarus! And he came fifth and lost the job.

The interior monologue shows us Bloom's toughness, an unsentimental outlook almost verging on the callous. If the Order of the Service for the Burial of the Dead proves so resistible to him, it seems unlikely that he would maintain that literature eternally affirmed the spirit of man. Stephen, on the other hand, has shown himself capable of fatuous pretence ('Proudly walking. Whom were you trying to walk like?') and overweening intellectual vanity: 'Books you were going to write with letters for titles. Have you read his F? O yes, but I prefer Q. Yes, but W is wonderful. O yes, W. Remember your epiphanies on green oval leaves, deeply deep, copies to be sent to all the great libraries of the world, including Alexandria?' This is manifestly the Dedalus of whom Mulligan says he 'proves by algebra that Hamlet's grandson is Shakespeare's grandfather and that he himself is the ghost of his father'. There is no shortage of hostile witness against Stephen. We should remember, however, that the most hostile witness is Stephen himself. It is he who records damningly: 'You bowed to yourself in the mirror, stepping forward to applause earnestly, striking face. Hurray for the Goddamned idiot!' And even as Stephen elaborates his Shakespeare theories, less absurd than Mulligan's travesty, he mentally disowns their extravagance: 'I think you're getting on very nicely. Just mix up a mixture of theologicophilolological. *Mingo, minxi, mictum, mingere.*' This tart self-satirist might easily attack the idea that literature embodies 'the eternal affirmation of the spirit of man'. Just as plausibly, the mostly robust and commonsensical Bloom is nevertheless capable of aesthetic lapses. It may be unfair to tax him with the sentimental vision of his dead son Rudy, in the phantasmagoric 'Circe' episode: '*A white lambkin peeps out of his waistcoat pocket.*' However, Joyce clearly sets ironical limits to Bloom's literary judgement in 'Calypso', the fourth chapter. There, in the outside lavatory, Bloom is made to wipe himself with half of the *Titbits* story he has just read and admired for its narrative smartness and morality. And only seconds before, ruminating on Ponchielli's 'Dance of the Hours', Bloom is shown to be a sucker for kitsch: 'Evening hours, girls in grey gauze. Night hours then black with daggers and eyemasks. Poetical idea pink then golden, then grey, then black. Still true to life also.' Throughout *Ulysses*, poetry betrays Bloom's limitations, exposing his banal preconceptions to unforgiving daylight:

> *The hungry famished gull*
> *Flaps o'er the waters dull.*

That is how poets write, the similar sounds. But then Shakespeare has no rhymes: blank verse. The flow of the language it is. The thoughts. Solemn.

Seen thus, Bloom is clearly capable of finding in literature a venue for the eternal affirmation of the spirit of man.

In fact, when the passage occurs in 'Ithaca', there is no way of establishing with complete certainty whether Bloom or Stephen is to be held responsible. Yet this isn't a fault in the novel. In *The Making of 'Ulysses'*, Frank Budgen, a painter and confidant of Joyce, records this early conversation: 'You seem to have read a lot, Mr Budgen. Do you know of any complete all-round character presented by any writer?' Because Bloom is this fictional rarity, the complete all-round character, he is just as capable as Stephen of sentimentalizing literature as he is of assessing its limitations more realistically. In the bath, Bloom bestows on his penis the epithet 'limp father of thousands'. Of his own character, he could say further, with Whitman: 'Do I contradict myself? / Very well then I contradict myself, / (I am large, I contain multitudes.)' No wonder Joyce ends the 'Ithaca' chapter with the alphabetically disordered, alliterative roll-call: 'Sinbad the Sailor and Tinbad the Tailor and Jinbad the Jailer and Whinbad the Whaler and Ninbad the Nailer . . .' Of course, Sinbad in *A Thousand and One Nights* is a version of Odysseus and shares several of his adventures, including that with Polyphemus. But the more obvious reason for the roll-call is that Bloom is a kind of everyman who contains multitudes – even the sleepy 'Xinbad the Phthailer', who is merely Sinbad drowsily pronounced from the threshold of sleep. It is more important to grasp this fundamental than it is to know, say, the dream of Er in Book 10 of Plato's *The Republic* – which tells us, not irrelevantly, that a soldier watches the souls choose their fates before drinking from the river of Oblivion, prior to entering on their human existences. Agamemnon chooses to be an eagle, but Odysseus chooses to be the most modest, the most unknown of men.

The length of *Ulysses* is a crucial part of Joyce's achievement, the creation of this unknown man, who is not a flat character, nor even a rounded character, but a real person. By the adjective 'real' I do not mean that I am unable to distinguish between fiction and reality. I mean only that Joyce gives his readers more information about Bloom than any other character in the history of literature. We know him better than we know most of our friends. Even 'Ithaca', the factual skeleton of *Ulysses*, is, as we have seen, alive with detail, fleshed out with circumstance, and articulated by context and event. As a result of Joyce's huge effort of consciousness, we are able to scrutinize the changing litmus of Bloom's character – to watch, for instance, prudence shading into expediency shading into cowardice, and vice versa. For one of literature's great modernists, this may seem an oddly traditional achievement. It is. But *Ulysses*, for all its vaunted difficulty, for all that Joyce appears to abjure standard ideas of plot, offers its readers many of the ordinary pleasures which the novel generally supplies – particularly character, of course, but also suspense. Molly's adultery may be given, fated, but the reader must wait until the last pages for the physical detail and, more important, Molly's attitude to her marriage and to Bloom now that Boylan has made his conquest. And though *Ulysses* observes the temporal and spatial unities, it actually contains the whole of Bloom's life, or the greater part of it, recorded with more lavishness than the average Victorian three-decker. *Ulysses* is *nouvelle cuisine*, exquisitely crafted in every detail, with all the satisfactions of an old-fashioned feast. One might almost risk praising it for being a work of literature in which the spirit of one man is eternally confirmed in all its complexity: equable, slow to anger, modest, charitable, tender, filial, lecherous, fatuous, kind, satirical, gentle, callous, contradictory . . . There is no particular reason why the list should stop.

Complexity and mass are the keys to Joyce's fiction, a fiction that questions clichés of every kind – and which, characteristically, allows its great dump of clichés in 'Eumaeus' to self-destruct under its own weight because Joyce manages the extraordinary feat of writing seventy-odd pages of prose without once deploying an expression that isn't identifiably clichéd. The comic effect is not unlike the failure of Tom Stoppard's Rosencrantz and Guildenstern to toss a coin so that it comes down tails. The ultra-usual, the entirely familiar, the old straight and narrow is made to seem loopy and weird by the simple ploy of sustained accumulation. In the 'Hades' section, we might reasonably expect grief – and we get some, among a great many other things demanded by Joyce's realism. There is, for instance, laughter at this funeral: John O'Connell, the caretaker, greets his acquaintances with 'Did you hear that one about Mulcahy from the Coombe?' and tells the joke discreetly 'to their vacant smiles'. Bloom, remembering a phrase of Simon Dedalus describing one Father Coffey, has to repress a chuckle: 'Burst sideways like a sheep in clover Dedalus says he will. With a belly on him like a poisoned pup. Most amusing expressions that man finds. Hhhn: burst sideways.' Like Mr Chick in Dickens's *Dombey and Son*, Bloom has a tendency to lapse into absent-minded singing under his breath: 'The ree the ra the ree the ra the roo. Lord, I mustn't lilt here.' And the grief when it occurs is observed minutely by Joyce: 'Mourners came out through the gates: woman and a girl. Leanjawed harpy, hard woman at a bargain, her bonnet awry. Girl's face stained with dirt and tears, holding the woman's arm *looking up at her for a sign to cry*.' (My italics.) This is very acute. Joyce has captured an enigma. The behaviour here is caught between the insincerity of crying on cue and the sincere mutuality of grief – what Wilfred Owen called 'the eternal reciprocity of tears'. Here, too, Joyce identifies the element of self-pity and display which sometimes infiltrates grief – from David Copperfield watching his tears in the mirror, to Stephen Dedalus imagining his own death ('And Wells would be sorry then for what he had done. And the bell would toll slowly'), to this unnamed girl anxious to cry in unison. There is something equally self-centred in Mr Dedalus's sudden show of grief as he catches sight of his wife's grave: ' – Her grave is over there, Jack, Mr Dedalus said. I'll soon be stretched beside her. Let Him take me whenever He likes. Breaking down, he began to weep to himself quietly, stumbling a little in his walk.' Merely maudlin and swiftly erased.

Joyce's task, here as elsewhere in *Ulysses*, is to reproduce, as far as possible, the restless stream of consciousness. Mental attention is not monolithic, even at moments of great seriousness. This isn't Joyce's exclusive discovery any more than the stream of consciousness technique, which Joyce admitted taking from the French novelist Dujardin, but which can be found in Miss Bates's torrential monologues in *Emma* or in the idiolect of Dickens's Flora Finching. Joyce, however, applied with more thoroughness than any previous writer the principle enunciated by John Donne in a sermon of December 1626, on the subject of prayer: 'a memory of yesterdays pleasures, a feare of tomorrows dangers, a straw under my knee, a noise in mine eare, a light in mine eye, an any thing, a nothing, a fancy, a Chimera in my braine, troubles me in my prayer'. The chimera in Bloom's brain turns out to be the idea of remembering the dead: 'Besides how could you remember everybody? Eyes, walk, voice. Well, the voice, yes: gramophone. Have a gramophone in every grave or keep it in the house. After dinner on a Sunday. Put on poor old greatgrandfather Kraahraark! Hellohellohello amawfullyglad kraark awfullygladaseeragain hellohello . . .' The noise in Bloom's ear is 'Rtststr!' – the noise of a rat which 'crushed itself in under the plinth, wriggled itself in under it'. And the straw under Bloom's knee? 'My kneecap is hurting me. Ow. That's better.' The fancy is Bloom's sudden thought: 'If we were all suddenly somebody else.'

In 'Wandering Rocks', everyone *is* somebody else, in a sense. At Dignam's funeral, Bloom's odd hypothesis, which flits into his mind as he stands at the graveside, is provoked by two things. He has just noticed that Ned Lambert's dark suit is, in fact, dyed, and not what it seems. This is the immediate cause. Then Joyce wishes the reader to realize again that the characters in his novel, or some of them, are ghosted by parallel figures in Homer's epic *The Odyssey* – as are several events also. 'Wandering Rocks' further complicates this complication. Its theme is the idea of confusion. The wandering rocks are a navigational hazard of classical times because they are lethally unfixed. The chapter therefore follows the criss-crossing progress of several Dubliners, while Joyce multiplies the ambiguities with his usual immense, calm thoroughness. Throughout the nineteen sections, there are interruptions as Joyce interpolates actions simultaneous in time. Thus, while Katey and Boody Dedalus are cooking soup and boiling clothes in their kitchen – in themselves a possible source of confusion – there are three intrusions from other areas of Dublin: Father Conmee walking on Clongowes field; the leaflet thrown away by Bloom into the river Liffey; and the lacquey shaking his handbell outside Dillon's auction rooms. When, in due course, we reach the lacquey's section, the bell is echoed by the bell for the last lap of a half-mile race. Not only that, the lacquey himself is doubled in the mirror of a cabinet which is for sale. Doubling and repetition is a feature constantly inconstant in 'Wandering Rocks': we see Parnell playing chess, but it is Parnell's brother, the 'ghostbright' John Howard Parnell; as the viceregal procession passes, Joyce gives us, beautifully, aptly, 'outriders leaping, leaping in their, in their saddles'; Tom Kernan preens himself before his double in the mirror of Peter Kennedy, hairdresser; we see 'the stalwart back of Long John Fanning ascending towards Long John Fanning in the mirror'. As Joyce multiplies his spells, things are left progressively uncertain. As Father Conmee boards a tram, the Revd Nicholas Dudley steps off another. All greetings and salutes supply a pseudo-mirroring: 'Father Conmee began to walk along the North Strand road and was saluted by Mr William Gallagher who stood in the doorway of his shop. Father Conmee saluted Mr William Gallagher . . .' Father Conmee is the focus of some delicate syntactical comedy. Sentence after sentence, like those just quoted, begins 'Father Conmee'. To avoid confusion, the pronoun 'he' is sparely used at the beginning of a sentence. But since this violates the reader's expectation, the stylistic tic creates the very ambiguity it is apparently designed to banish. There appears to be a new Father Conmee created for every paragraph. Other characters have misleading appearances: Mrs M'Guinness is 'like Mary, Queen of Scots' but is actually a pawnbroker; Denis J. Maginni is dandified enough to be a toff, but isn't; Maginni is a dancing master, just as Mr Eugene Stratton isn't a Negro, but a blackface comedian; when Blazes Boylan orders fruit, it is for Molly, and not for the 'invalid' he indicates. Father Conmee reads 'Nones' out of sequence and sees himself in his mind's eye conducting the holy sacrament into an old man's trembling mouth when he is actually on a tram.

Set out like this, Joyce's industry perhaps looks a mite tedious and over-applied. But apart from the interpolations, the formal requirement of the episode is as tactful as it is relentless, paradoxical as that may sound. It is the least obscure, the most accessible episode of *Ulysses*. The section dealing with Dignam's young son shows how this comes about. He has been sent out for a pound and a half of porksteaks from Mangan's, the butchers. Which was formerly, possibly confusingly, Fehren- bach's. As he dawdles home, he stops to look in the window of a milliner's shop, where there is a poster advertising a boxing match. Two boxers oppose each other, putting up their 'props' like mirror images. Meanwhile, Master Dignam is reflected in the sidemirrors: 'two mourning Masters Dignam gaped silently'. Disappointed to find that the contest is over, Master Dignam reflects on boxing in general: 'the best pucker for science was Jem Corbet before Fitzsimmons knocked the stuffings out of him, *dodging and all*'. (My fixative italics.)

At this point, Master Dignam recalls his dead father in a passage of hard brilliance equal to anything in *Ulysses* or the rest of literature:

His face got all grey instead of being red like it was and there was a fly walking over it up to his eye. The scrunch that was when they were screwing the screws into the coffin: and the bumps when they were bringing it downstairs. Pa was inside it and ma crying in the parlour and uncle Barney telling the men how to get it round the bend. A big coffin it was, and high and heavylooking. How was that? The last night pa was boosed he was standing on the landing there bawling out for his boots to go out to Tunney's for to boose more and he looked butty and short in his shirt. Never see him again. Death, that is. Pa is dead. My father is dead. He told me to be a good son to ma. I couldn't hear the other things he said but I saw his tongue and his teeth trying to say it better. Poor pa. That was Mr Dignam, my father. I hope he is in purgatory now because he went to confession to Father Conroy on Saturday night.

What a wonderfully sustained and flawless interior monologue. And, though we notice the doubling in the phrase 'screwing the screws', the two-facedness of grey death and raddled life, the double image of Paddy Dignam alive and Paddy Dignam dead, the passage is valuable for its human truth – Joyce's unflinching, open-eyed analysis of the way in which piety almost immediately begins to tidy up our emotions and tidy away unpleasant details. The passage ends on the note of religious overlay, but not before Joyce has shown us that tongue struggling to make itself under-stood to a son who, on the day of his father's funeral, is already responding to life's distractions – the straw under his knee, the new mourning collar that keeps springing up, the thought of his name in the evening paper.

All this would tell even to a reader uninterested in pursuing the Homeric parallels in their several ramifications. This is true of *Ulysses* as a whole. Ezra Pound in *The Dial* (May 1922) wrote: 'These correspondences are part of Joyce's mediaevalism and are chiefly his own affair, a scaffold, a means of construc-tion, justified by the result, and justifiable by it only.' If you consider 'Sirens', you can see what Pound means. There, Joyce has to find an equivalent for Ulysses binding himself to the mast so that he doesn't succumb to the Sirens. He has Bloom take an elastic band: 'Bloom wound a skein round four forkfingers, stretched it, relaxed, and wound it round his troubled double, fourfold, in octave, gyved them fast.' Most of us have done this. All of us have seen it done. Joyce is the first writer to include it in a novel, driven by the requirements of his Homeric scheme.

Rudyard Kipling in his introduction to the Outward Bound edition of his work, wrote: 'it is not needed to show strangers our charts, for these be of man's making and each must prick out his own for himself'. Joyce, on the other hand, did allow his own charts a limited currency – charts showing that each episode not only had an Homeric parallel, but also an organ, an art, a colour, a symbol and a technic. The scheme comes in three slightly different versions, given to Carlo Linati, Stuart Gilbert and Herbert Gorman, three early employees in the Joyce explication industry. In fact, complex though the scheme purports to be, Joyce used the Homeric myth as and when it suited him, and certainly not with the intention of using Homer to belittle the contemporary world and Bloom in particular. It was a resource. Characteristically, 'Wandering Rocks' is based on a phenomenon referred to in Homer but never actually encountered by Ulysses. It is clear, too, that in the first three chapters, the 'Telemachia', the Homeric parallels fit only loosely. Joyce was more exercised by the real events of his autobiography. Mulligan is a usurper without being a suitor. Stephen is more concerned with his mother's death than with her wooing by unwanted suitors. Of course, there are nice touches, like the pseudo-Ulysses at the men's bathing place: 'An elderly man shot up near the spur of rock a blowing red face. He scrambled up by the stones, water glistening on his pate and on its garland of grey hair, water rilling over his chest and paunch and spilling jets out of his black sagging loincloth.' The exactness of this description needs no help from Homer. It justifies itself, as does the rat at Dignam's funeral, which, unforgettably, 'crushed itself' under the plinth. The baldness conveyed by the 'garland' of hair, the jets of water spilling from the 'black sagging loincloth', are confident, vivacious and assured touches which compel us to see. We cannot look away. Yet 'garland' and 'loincloth' are two words which require us to look beyond the present. As well as visual immediacy, there is semantic association, as well as phanopoeia, logopoeia – recalling the archaic world of myth.

On the whole, though, the opening chapters are driven by the engine of Joyce's autobiography. Not only had he scores to settle with Oliver St John Gogarty, the model for Malachi Mulligan, but *Ulysses* clearly begins as a continuation of *A Portrait of the Artist as a Young Man*: Stephen refers, for example, without a word of explanation, to Cranly, a character from the earlier novel. It wasn't until later, when Bloom began to replace Stephen as the prime focus of interest, that Joyce was released from the bondage of autobiographical truth and left free to let the Homeric possibilities realize their potential. They could suggest Bloom's biography, whereas before they could only conform, reluctantly, intermittently, with the given events of Joyce's own life. In the 'Telemachia', a fundamentally inno-cent narrative is made to confess, as it were, to possession of Greek substance. It is incriminated in the mythic rather than founded on it. The evidence is circumstantial – Mulligan's name is 'two dactyls' and he wants to 'Hellenize' the island. The real substance of the opening, though, is Stephen's hypnotized guilt about his mother's death – a death which runs counter to Homer's mythos. Nor is Mulligan a convincing usurper, except in the most general way, since he has no designs on Penelope. Nor can he have designs, since, if we are to press the parallels, Telemachus's mother is deceased at this point.

So what is the status of the parallels? When *Ulysses* was published in book form, Joyce dropped the Homeric chapter headings which had sometimes been used in the magazine publication. Yet he released the schema of the novel, as if, says Richard Ellmann in *Ulysses on the Liffey*, 'he was not comfort-able at the thought that his art might too successfully conceal his art'. In November 1921, he lent Valery Larbaud a copy of the schema because Larbaud was to lecture on the novel in December. Joyce professed to his patron, Harriet Shaw Weaver, that the aim was 'to confuse the audience a little more'. He admitted, however, that he 'ought not to have done so'. Jacques

Benoist-Méchin, who was to translate excerpts for Larbaud's lecture, also asked to see the plan. At first, Joyce fobbed him off with fragments. Finally, the whole schema was handed over and thereafter passed around surreptitiously by people sworn to secrecy – until Joyce consented to let Stuart Gilbert publish it.

In a conversation with the young Vladimir Nabokov, Joyce remarked that his use of Homer was whimsical. Nabokov countered: 'But you collaborated with Gilbert.' Joyce dismissed the collaboration as a 'terrible mistake', as an 'advertisement for the book' which he now very much regretted. This anecdote was told by Nabokov to Alfred Appel in 1974, many years after the event. We should, therefore, approach it warily. The collaboration with Gilbert was not a 'mistake', so much as a necessary evil. *Ulysses* was then a banned book in English-speaking countries, and Gilbert's summary chapters were a way of reaching readers, however unsatisfactory. Gilbert's revelations, his scholarly explications of schema and background, made it clear that the law was wrong to assume that *Ulysses* was just another dirty book. Nevertheless, this calculated response to the obscenity laws brought disadvantages in its train and Joyce's regrets were probably twofold.

Twofold, but not logically compatible, since the regrets stem from different sides of his character. The side which nourished Bloom's personality may have felt the apparatus was liable to distract attention from the primary text and its urgent human concerns. We know that Eliot came to feel this way about the notes to *The Waste Land*. The side of Joyce's character which created Stephen was decidedly more devious, calculating and egotistical: the publication of the schema would solve a whole series of problems that might have occupied academics for generations. Richard Ellmann's great biography quotes Joyce's confession to Jacques Benoist-Méchin: 'I've put in so many enigmas and puzzles that it will keep the professors busy for centuries.'

Even here, we should be careful. When I interviewed Benoist-Méchin in 1981, for a BBC radio documentary, he said exactly the same thing – of *Finnegans Wake*, to which the comment applies with more justice. *Ulysses* is a remarkably approachable modernist work. In fact, the end result of the disclosure of the schema has been to place the Homeric material fairly exactly – as important, generative, but, in the last analysis, a secondary subtext. *Ulysses* has thus escaped the fate of much academically studied literature, where the primary text is perceived as mere camouflage for what is waiting to be discovered underneath. Saul Bellow describes the process in *To Jerusalem and Back*: 'there is a clever, persistent young woman who writes to me often from Italy, who insists upon giving the most ordinary occurrences in my novels a political interpretation. A cafeteria lunch in New York actually refers to a meeting in Canada between Churchill and Roosevelt . . .' By leaking his subtext, Joyce at least stopped critics inventing a subtext – and claiming primacy for it.

The mythic framework has been widely influential. John Updike once told me that he could not have written *The Centaur* without the example of *Ulysses*. But although Updike borrows Joyce's mythology, magnifying glass and tape-recorder, the result is nothing like an exact academic pencil study of an antique cast. Updike's mythology is unrestricted and ennobling, at once casual and allusive – the luncheonette counter of Minor, where Mrs Passify (Pasiphae) works, is 'a maze' – and coexistent, eruptive and supplanting. Characters like Chiron are taken over bodily by their mythic counterparts. Despite calculated differences, Updike is still in debt to his great predecessor. An early Updike story, 'You'll Never Know, Dear, How Much I Love You', takes 'Araby', an early Joyce story, as its template. Both are stories of disillusionment – with a bazaar and with an American fairground – in which boyish protagonists are stung out of romance by vulgar reality. Updike doesn't copy. Rather he follows Joyce's narrative shape, even down to the final, rhetorical sentence of bitterness, given a paragraph to itself. Joyce ends: 'Gazing up into the darkness I saw myself as a creature driven and derided by vanity; and my eyes burned with anguish and anger.' Updike ends on the same tone of febrile declamation: 'Thus the world, like a bitter coquette, spurns our attempts to give ourselves to her wholly.' There is nothing slavish here. We identify emulation as much as imitation – as we do when we realize that the middle-aged Toyota-franchise-holder 'Rabbit' Angstrom is a fictional figure conceived by an admirer of Joyce's average sensual man, Leopold Bloom. Innocent of culture but carnally knowing, greedy, Angstrom is, if anything, even more basic a challenge to the novelist's redemptive imagination.

Joyce is present, too, in Updike's eye for detail. Joyce brings his magnifying glass to tea-making: 'the sluggish cream wound curdling spirals through her tea'. Updike, less masterfully, scrutinizes the minutiae of coffee-making: 'the brown powder, Maxwell's Instant, made a tiny terrain on the surface of steaming water, and then dissolved, dyeing the water black. My mother stirred with my spoon and a spiral of tan suds revolved in the cup.' The attention Joyce brings to excretion, Updike brings to teeth being cleaned. Without Joyce, this rapt contemplation of trivial particulars would not be admissible. Again, Joyce can reproduce exactly the voices of the non-human world – that rattle of pebbles saying 'Rtststr!', the 'sllt' of a quire-folding machine, a cat's impatient, imperious 'Mrkrgnao!' Updike's competitive admiration leads him, in *The Centaur*, to some botched approximations: the '*skrkk, scrak*' of chalk on a blackboard, the '*txz! aeiii*' of wood being sawn. He has borrowed the maestro's tape-recorder without Joyce's electric talent.

Updike isn't Joyce's only debtor. Orwell copied the 'Circe' episode in *A Clergyman's Daughter* – incompetently. Nabokov, despite his several denials, owes a good deal to *Ulysses* – particularly the passages of interior monologue in *The Gift*, a novel written in Berlin between 1935 and 1937: 'Did not have time to make out my third line in that burst of light,' muses the composing Fyodor to himself. 'Pity. All gone now, missed my cue.' Saul Bellow's *Herzog* gracefully acknowledges Joyce's enabling priority by naming his hero after the Herzog in *Ulysses*

– Moses E. Herzog. Bellow's main debt is to Joyce's fluid interchange between 'he' and 'I': 'A paper. He liked to read at stool. Hope no ape comes knocking just as I'm.' Parallels in Bellow are too plentiful to cite. In any case, Bellow's gratitude is openly expressed in a *Paris Review* interview.

The same interview strangely describes *Ulysses* as a 'masterpiece of confusion' – an eccentric opinion, but one which used to exert a powerful orthodoxy, even after T. S. Eliot published his influential, agenda-setting essay in 1923, '*Ulysses*, Order and Myth': 'Mr Joyce's parallel use of the *Odyssey* has a great importance. It has the importance of a scientific discovery . . . It is simply a way of controlling, of ordering, of giving a shape and a significance to the immense panorama of futility and anarchy which is contemporary history.' Orwell, too, thought that if art implied selection, there was 'as much selection in *Ulysses* as in *Pride and Prejudice*'. In the same letter of December 1933, Orwell says that *Ulysses* 'sums up better than any book I know the fearful despair that is almost normal in modern times.' And here he agrees with Eliot, who saw an 'immense panorama of futility and anarchy' – and with Bellow, for whom *Ulysses* shows 'humankind has reached a terminal point'. The diagnosis is superficially plausible. In Eliot's own poetry, the Golden Age is also a gold standard and it would not be difficult to see the Homeric framework ironically opposed to a sordid present – in which the faithful Penelope of legend is become the adulterous Molly Bloom, while the heroic voyager Ulysses has shrunk to the dimensions of a canvasser for ads in dubious Dublin.

It is true, too, that intellectuals at the beginning of the century shared a self-congratulatory *contemptus mundi*. Joyce was no exception – initially. In July 1904, he wrote to C. P. Curran: 'I am writing a series of epicleti – ten – for a paper. I have written one. I call the series *Dubliners* to betray the soul of that hemiplegia or paralysis which many consider a city.' To his publisher, Joyce spoke with relish of the 'special odour of corruption' which floated over the stories. Nevertheless, 'The Dead', the last story in *Dubliners*, transcends this smug, fashionable, French-influenced orthodoxy. Mined with ironies against modern life though it is – 'The men that is now is only all palaver and what they can get out of you' – the story represents a readiness to swim in Yeats's 'filthy modern tide'. It is a turning point, and *Ulysses* itself is accurate, unflinching and accepting – undismayed and undisgusted by humanity.

It is a great novel and an influential one, but not, therefore, without faults. Joyce becomes fatally impatient with his first, brilliant stylistic discovery – the friction-free traffic between exterior objective narrative and an interior subjectivity which need not make grammatical sense. 'On the doorstep he felt in his hip pocket for the latchkey. Not there. In the trousers I left off. Must get it. Potato I have.' The simple, supremely flexible stylistic device is laid aside in the latter part of *Ulysses* as Joyce wills into existence a series of newly patented inventions. The greatest of these is Molly's peerless soliloquy, rightly seen by Joyce as the *clou* of the book. The dramatic form of 'Circe' is a tour de force of stage direction and 'Sirens' invents an orchestral musical prose of great charm – but the remainder, for all its manifest variety, leans too heavily on the parodic mode: 'Nausicaa' parodies the breathless prose of the woman's magazine; 'The Oxen of the Sun' is a tedious anthology of parodied English prose styles; 'Ithaca' pastiches scientific prose with a droll factuality that was to influence Samuel Beckett; and 'Cyclops' has several passages of mock-epic parody that demand all the reader's stamina and little of his intelligence.

There must be some doubt also as to whether Joyce really delivers the advertised peristaltic prose rhythms in 'Lestrygonians', or whether the surrogate father–son relationship between Bloom–Ulysses and Stephen–Telemachus is properly established. Bloom's attitude is clarified for attentive readers of the Malory parody in 'The Oxen of the Sun'. There he remembers his dead son Rudy and the lambswool jacket knitted for him by Molly – and transfers his longing to Stephen: 'and now Sir Leopold that had of his body no manchild for an heir looked upon him his friend's son'. This superimposition is repeated in the Pater parody, where Bloom imagines his dead son as 'a lad of four or five in linseywoolsey' – frowning 'just as this young man does now'.

But nowhere in *Ulysses* does Stephen reciprocate. In the library episode, he announces in the Shakespeare discussion that 'paternity may be a legal fiction' – but this negative, unfilial disposition hardly amounts to a positive recognition that Bloom would be a truer parent. Moreover, Stephen's Shakespearean theorizing is so clearly guyed by Joyce that Stephen's notion of the consubstantiality of father and son is caught up in the comedy and discredited. Its status is more a vague rumour than a structural armature.

Bloom, of course, behaves in a quasi-fatherly way by taking Stephen to 7 Eccles Street. And perhaps this 'homing' in 'Ithaca' would be an adequate fulfilment of Homeric requirements, were it not that the slaying of the suitors is managed so perfunctorily by Joyce. The perfunctoriness is necessary because Frank Budgen's explanation of the slaughter is surely correct: 'it is in the unsmiled smile of his equanimity that the bowstring of the lord of 7 Eccles Street most loudly twangs. It slaughters the suitors of Marion as effectively as did the divinely aided Ulysses those of Penelope.' There can be no pother if Bloom's cool indifference is to be lethal. But the relevant pages listing and dismissing Molly's suitors are few. The rest of the section appears to have its own parodic momentum, unrelated to Homeric requirements – though one might argue, rather desperately, that the crucial suitor-slaying paragraphs are only the cool climax to an episode of remarkable scientific *froideur*.

When Joyce was having his portrait painted by Patrick Tuohy in 1924, he was impatient with the artist's pretensions: 'Never mind my soul. Just be sure you have my tie right.' This is a long way from the dedicatory page of Joyce's first work, a play prophetically entitled *A Brilliant Career*: 'To my own soul I dedicate the first true work of my life.' Finally, all the complex structures in the world, all those affirmations of the spirit of man, will fail unless the tie is right. *Ulysses* is a work crammed with such rightnesses at the opposite pole from righteousnesses. A game of bowls: the 'brief alert shock' of collision. A man

48

lighting a pipe: 'Mr Dedalus struck, whizzed, lit, puffed savoury puff after. Puff after stiff, a puff, strong, savoury, crackling. He puffed a pungent plumy blast.' A man yawning: 'Davy Byrne smileyawnednodded all in one: – Iiiiiichaaaaaaach!'

# *Anna Livia Plurabelle*

Almost exactly two years after the publication of *Ulysses*, Joyce was busy explaining *Anna Livia Plurabelle* to his patron Harriet Shaw Weaver: 'it is a chattering dialogue across the river by two washerwomen who as night falls become a tree and a stone. The river is named Anna Liffey.' Five years later, in 1929, he again writes to Miss Weaver about *Anna Livia Plurabelle*: 'T.S.E. [T. S. Eliot] most friendly. He wants his firm to publish S.G.'s book [Stuart Gilbert's study of *Ulysses*] and to bring out an English papercover edition at 2/- of A.L.P.' This latter, one of the first paperbacks, has now been reissued in the excellent Faber Library series of sewn hardbacks, printed on acid-free paper.

Joyce, ever the entrepreneur, was quick to supply advertising copy. This was his suggested blurb, which, to his chagrin, Faber's publicity department used only on a mimeographed press release:

> Buy a book in brown paper
> From Faber & Faber
> To see Annie Liffey trip, tumble and caper.
> Sevensinns in her singthings,
> Plurabelle on her prose,
> Seashell ebb music wayriver she flows.

The liquefaction of the old standard – she shall have music wherever she goes – is lucid, unstrained and perfect. And it

*Anna Livia Plurabelle* by James Joyce, Faber.

explains why a poet like Seamus Heaney once brilliantly encapsulated Joyce's project in *Finnegans Wake* as masturbatory,
linguistically erotic and self-pleasuring. The language, he said, is
'slippy with delight'.

This verbal onanism can sometimes seem excluding, however.
For Esther Greenwood in *The Bell Jar*, the semantic shiftiness
becomes a kind of quicksound in dialogue with her derangement: 'my eyes sank through an alphabet soup of letters to the
long word in the middle of the page . . . Words, dimly familiar,
but twisted all awry, like faces in a funhouse mirror, fled past,
leaving no impression on the glassy surface of my brain . . . I
decided to junk my thesis.' Funhouse or madhouse? Arrangement or derangement? The prose of *Finnegans Wake* can appear
to be both.

It is easy to respond to the verbal ingenuity of Joyce's
'puntomime' when the text retains a certain semantic and con-
textual stability. Here are the two old washerwomen, recognizably feeling the nip in the air: 'my hands are blawcauld between
isker and suda like that piece of pattern chayney there, lying
below'. Hands blue with cold, then, like a bit of willow-pattern
on the bottom of the stream. But not only blue with cold, also
blown on to warm them up a bit. And what about 'between
isker and suda'? Whisky and soda, plus the two rivers Iskar and
Suda, we inconclusively conclude. What does it mean? Whisky
is, of course, hot – even when it is cold. Soda water can cool a
drink, but caustic soda is capable of burning skin. Might the
explanation be this? – that certain degrees of coldness are
registered as their opposite by the nervous system. Tom Stoppard's *The Invention of Love* invokes the one surviving sentence
of Sophocles's lost play, *The Loves of Achilles*, which compares
love to ice held in the hand by children: 'the ice that burns who
clasps it'. Here, we can solve Joyce's conundrum by an appeal
to experience. We could also cite, say, Elizabeth Bishop's poem
'At the Fishhouses', which tells us that the sea is so cold, 'If you
should dip your hand in, / your wrist would ache immediately, /
your bones would begin to ache and your hand would burn' –
much as if you were one of Joyce's washerwomen, in fact. But

where Elizabeth Bishop beautifully takes her time, Joyce is all thrift and speed – a virtuoso of microwriting.

And it is this laconic method, this concentration, which explains the one obscure phrase in that Faber and Faber jingle: 'Sevensinns in her singthings'. First, Anna Livia is prone to the seven deadly sins in her transgressions, her sinkings. Second, she is a plurabelle rather than singular: there are seven senses or meanings in her singing and her sighings, which also amalgamate in 'singthings', additionally to 'sinkings'. The method here was epitomized by Joyce in another Faber jingle as 'kinks english'. Sometimes, though, the kinks cannot be straightened out in the way we have so far managed.

Harriet Shaw Weaver's coolness about *Work in Progress* was swiftly registered by Joyce. After all, she wasn't alone in her scepticism and bafflement: 'your letter gave me a nice little attack of brainache. I conclude you do not like the piece I did?' Joyce wrote. 'I am rather discouraged about this as in such a vast and difficult enterprise I need encouragement. It is possible Pound is right but I cannot go back.' Pound's verdict on the undertaking was funereal: 'I will have another go at it, but up to the present I make nothing of it whatever. Nothing so far as I can make out, nothing short of divine vision or a new cure for the clapp can possibly be worth all the circumnambient peripherization.' Miss Weaver was less brutal, only proffering the suggestion of an annotated edition, so that the ordinary reader could benefit, like her, from Joyce's glossaries and notes.

Actually, Joyce wasn't interested in the ordinary reader. For him, the ideal reader of his 'nightmaze' was specified in the text as 'suffering from an ideal insomnia' – ironically enough. Stung by the criticism, his broader response was to insist on the context, the setting of *Finnegans Wake*. Byron's Don Juan knows 'a third of Life is passed in sleep'. For Joyce, this was territory to be annexed, using appropriate tactics: 'one great part of every human existence is passed in a state which cannot be rendered sensible by the use of wideawake language, cutandry grammar and goahead plot'. In other words, when we are asleep, we are *in*sensible. It is this state which Joyce sets out to capture – where linear time, physical laws, consistency of any kind, conventional morality, are all suspended. This one condition alone makes for obscurity, and the *Wake* is full of injunctions to the reader: 'now, patience; and remember patience is a great thing, and above all else we must avoid anything like being or becoming out of patience'. Joyce was aware of his demands on the reader's attention: we 'may have our irremovable doubts as to the whole sense of the lot, the interpretation of any phrase in the whole, the meaning of every word of a phrase so far deciphered out of it'. Ironic, how lucid these disquisitions on obscurity are. Read twice, their pedantic pedestrianisms are clearly authorial send-ups of the worthy, conventional reader.

Once we know that Joyce's aim is to render the experience of sleep, just as in *Ulysses* he once rendered the inner, expanding universe within the waking world, we are in a better position to assess his method and his achievement. Milan Kundera has said that *Ulysses* is a great act of espionage – that Joyce secretes a microphone into the mind of Leopold Bloom. Nabokov, on the other hand, had reservations about Joyce's success. For him, thought processes – processes which are sometimes non-verbal – could not be accurately rendered in linguistic terms. Faced with the task of 'feeling aslip', of catching the evanescent Gestalt of sleep, we may think that Lewis Carroll's *Alice's Adventures in Wonderland* both anticipates and surpasses Joyce in rendering the peculiar conditions of sleep – for instance, the defining arbitrariness of control and lack of control, the Sisyphean thwarting of desire only matched by the miraculous gratification of desire, malleability, metamorphosis, mutability. What Carroll conveys better than Joyce is the inevitability of dream, the vivid sensation of logic without the faintest trace of its substance. Whatever is, is right – even as it feels obscurely wrong. The other authors, besides Carroll, to have captured this sensation are Stoppard in *Rosencrantz and Guildenstern are Dead* and Kafka in the definitive *Metamorphosis*.

Joyce was certainly uneasy when accused of belatedness: in May 1927, he wrote to Harriet Shaw Weaver about his critics: 'another (or rather many) says he [Joyce] is imitating Lewis

Carroll. I never read him till Mrs Nutting gave me a book, not *Alice*, a few weeks ago – though, of course, I heard bits and scraps.' In the next sentence, Joyce denies ever having read Rabelais. It is pretty unconvincing, the debtor in denial, given the intrinsic role Humpty Dumpty plays in *Finnegans Wake*. Not that this would matter if Joyce's treatment of dreamtime had the immediate conviction of Carroll's. Carroll calls up abrupt but irrefutable transitions, whereas, for Joyce, *transition* rather represents the experimental, avant-garde magazine of that name. Carroll simply does it, simply. Joyce's method is encrusted with programmatic modernism – self-consciously virtuosic, straining to be all-encompassing, to be at once Irish and local and universal and omni-linguistic. And, in the end, the medium is frequently its own subject. *Finnegans Wake* is not an account of dream conditions. It is rather an account of dream conditions applied to language alone – shifts, slips, slides, the simulacrum of sense which evaporates as we look away from the dream of language.

Now and then, particularly in *Anna Livia Plurabelle*, Joyce transcends the purely verbal and touches on the final frailty of consciousness, when the scintilla of life faints into earth's dumb, material process. Clive Hart, the doyen of Joyce scholars, finds the end of *Anna Livia Plurabelle* sentimental in its easy lyricism. He is wrong. Joyce has, by some miracle, found a way to sing without raising his voice above a whisper. It is one of literature's great experiences and worth all the minor irritations en route.

# Sex in Nineteenth-Century Literature

In 1924, Virginia Woolf perversely insisted – aping T. S. Eliot –
that 'human character changed' 'in or about December 1910'.
Eliot had famously declared in 1921 that 'the mind of England'
had changed sometime after the metaphysical poets and Tennyson and Browning to produce a dissociation of sensibility. By
1941, Virginia Woolf was more mature, less polemically emulative, and more amused by the alleged changes brought about by
the conventions of periodicity – as she records in *Orlando* and
in *Between the Acts*, where Lucy Swithin insists on the solidarity
of human experience. Speaking for her creator, she says the
Victorians were exactly like us, except that they wore different
clothes. We are the Victorians, in that case, give or take the odd
stove-pipe hat, frock coat and a set of scimitar sideburns.

But are we all the same in the buff? In bed? The Victorians
are a bit like our parents. We can imagine them having sex –
but it is sex in the abstract, deprived of specificity. Of course,
we say, they did what we do. But then we ask what we do. Only
think of Kundera's *Immortality* and think again: 'he would
therefore slide off her and resort to a method which he considered both a capitulation and a piece of technical virtuosity
worthy of a patent: he stuck his hand inside her and moved his
fingers powerfully upwards . . .' You can find the same sexual
topos frequently revisited in D. M. Thomas's *The White Hotel*.
But the *Victorians* . . . Congress, perhaps, yet little (surely) in
the way of what Humbert Humbert calls fancy embraces –
meaning fellatio in this instance.

So what better place to start than with fellation. Here are

55

two examples – one inadvertent, one intended, I believe. In Milan Kundera's *Slowness*, Vincent simulates love-making with Julie because his 'member is as small' 'as a great-grandmother's thimble', 'as a wilted wild strawberry'. Hardy uses the same image in *Tess of the d'Urbervilles*, though, not having Kundera's licence, he suppresses the tenor. The sexual relations between Tess and Alec are proleptically adumbrated by Hardy when he has Alec override her wish to eat a strawberry from her own hand, not his: ' "Nonsense!" he insisted; and in a slight distress she parted her lips and took it in.' The insinuation here is so obvious, so gross, that it seems impossible. And Hardy is careful to discount his visual symbolism and its undertow of compulsion by insisting on the strawberry's literalness: it is 'a specially fine product of the "British Queen" variety'. The conflation of horticulture and Her Royal Majesty, Queen Victoria, is at once impudent and unassailable – the perfect example of the principle of deniability.

My other example of fellatio occurs in a sacred context, stanzas 7 and 8 of Hopkins's 'The Wreck of the *Deutschland*':

> . . . How a lush-kept plush-capped sloe
> Will, mouthed to flesh-burst,
> Gush! – flush the man, the being with it, sour or sweet . . .

The linguistic trigger, I'd guess, is stanza 7's 'dense and driven Passion' – in which the theological and the sexual connotations of the word 'passion' unintentionally come together, embarrassingly for Hopkins, if only in retrospect. Had he been asked about the hidden sources of the stanza, he might have turned to literature rather than to his own tormented sexuality: 'Veiled Melancholy has her sovran shrine, / Though seen of none save him whose strenuous tongue / Can burst Joy's grape against his palate fine.' Keats, of course, but consider that 'sour or sweet' and think yet again. Undeniably unintended and undeniably there.

And then there is Clough, so famous for his theological doubts and so widely unread in academia that I recall a fellow-examiner justifying a discrepant low mark by explaining the candidate thought (hilariously) that Clough was full of sex. As of course he is. In 1852, Clough was in the States. Blanche, his fiancée, wrote him that she had come on his manuscript of *Dipsychus*. Clough's reply was prompt and a touch anxious, as well it might be: 'Please don't read Dipsychus yet. I wish particularly not. You shall see it sometime – but not now – please.' Could it be that Clough had this (later deleted) stanza in mind:

> While street on street she winds about,
> Heedful at corners, but *du reste*
> Assured, and grandly self-possessed,
> Trips up a stair at last, and lands me;
> Up with her petticoats, and hands me
> Much as one might a *pot de chambre*
> The vessel that relieves *le membre*.
> No would-be-pretty hesitation
> No farce of female expectation
> Most business-like in her vocation
> She but the brief half instant lingers
> That strikes her bargain with five fingers.
> 'Twas well enough – I do not mean
> Voluptuous, but plain and clean;
> Doctors perhaps might recommend it,
> You step and do the thing and end it.

Even in his published work, Clough was risqué, but so risqué that he effectively risked very little. Elspie in the *Bothie of Tober-na-Vuolich* relates a sexually transparent dream, whose very transparency is its protection from prudish objections. Prurience is in the eye of the beholder:

> Sometimes I find myself dreaming at nights about arches
>                                                 and bridges, –
> Sometimes I dream of a great invisible hand coming
>                                                 down, and

Dropping the great key-stone in the middle: there in my
                                                    dreaming,
There I feel the great key-stone coming in, and through it
Feel the other part – all the other stones of the archway,
Joined into mine with a strange happy sense of
                                        completeness. But, dear me,
This is confusion and nonsense. I mix all the things I can
                                                    think of.
And you won't understand, Mr Philip.

Philip Hewson chooses to interpret her dream of copulation as
divine intervention:

See the great key-stone coming down from the heaven of
                                                    heavens!
And he fell at her feet, and buried his face in her apron.

In January 1849, J. A. Froude wrote to Clough that he was
'forever falling upon lines which gave me uneasy twitchings'.
Quite so. But then Froude arrives at his example – an example
that reminds one of the Abbey Theatre riot caused by Synge's
use of the word 'shift' – 'for example, the end of the love scene'
where Hewson buries 'his face in her apron'. Froude is in a
pother: 'I dare say,' he daringly writes, 'the head would fall
there, but what an image!' Given his mind-set, Froude is blind
to the infinitely greater offence of the key-stone because it is
unthinkable. Nor does he quote this powerful, messy, accurate
evocation of what Sid Vicious a hundred years later was to
designate as having a squelch:

You are too strong, you see, Mr Philip! just like the sea
                                                    there,
Which *will* come, through the straits and all between the
                                                    mountains,
Forcing its great strong tide into every nook and inlet,
Getting far in, up the quiet stream of sweet inland water,

Sucking it up, and stopping it, turning it, driving it
backward,
Quite preventing its own quiet running: and then, soon
after,
Back it goes off, leaving weeds on the shore, and wrack
and uncleanness:
And the poor burn in the glen tries again its peaceful
running,
But it is brackish and tainted, and all its banks in
disorder.
That was what I dreamt all last night. I was the
burnie . . .

'Brackish and tainted': such sexual realism must have seemed out of the question to Froude. And it was this very incredibility that allowed Clough to engross the gross. Had he been accused, he could have responded with a look of incredulity.

Victorian literature is a fertile source of accidental sexual reference. Think of Emily Dickinson in her Freudian slip in 520, 'I started early – took my Dog', where she is pursued by the sea until her shoe is full of pearl and the sea 'withdrew'. Or think of Christina Rossetti's 'Goblin Market'. More interesting to me are the deliberate, disguised, unequivocal equivocations – the transgressions of writers desperate to address a fact of life.

During the European Enlightenment, English poetic diction was more refined and polite than ever before or since. At the same time, it was capable of a candour bordering on the coarse – as coarse as anything before or since. For example, Swift's notorious 'Celia shits' and Pope's 'And Maids turn'd Bottels, call aloud for Corks'. But let us begin at the end of the Enlightenment with two literary orgasms. They occur in novels by Laurence Sterne and, while it is quite clear what is being written about, Sterne's finger is equally clearly to be seen on the dimmer switch. The effect is comic, but the comedy is touched with prurience. *Tristram Shandy* opens with the author's conception: '*Pray, my Dear*, quoth my mother, *have you not forgot*

to *wind up the clock?* ——*Good G—!* cried my father, making
an exclamation, but taking care to moderate his voice at the
same time, —*Did ever woman, since the creation of the world,
interrupt a man with such a silly question?'* The explanation,
and our enlightenment, is postponed for the space of three short
chapters – when we learn that Mr Shandy, on the first Sunday
of every month, wound up the 'large house-clock' and, at the
same time, undertook to dispatch other 'family concernments'
so as not to be 'plagued and pestered with them the rest of the
month'. At the actual moment of orgasm and interruption,
perfectly timed, Sterne's innocent reader inquires of the interruption, 'Pray, what was your father saying?' And receives for
answer, 'Nothing'. He was *doing*, not saying, Sterne coyly would
have us infer.

Sterne's other orgasm is equally oblique, a footnote to Yor-
ick's receipt of his passport: 'But there is nothing unmix'd in
this world; and some of the gravest of our divines have carried
it so far as to affirm that enjoyment itself was attended even
with a sigh – and that the greatest they knew of terminated in a
general way, in little better than a convulsion.' Behind the sexual
innuendo, in both cases, is a larger innuendo that sex is small
beer – a shandy rather than a powerful intoxicant, like a brandy,
say. The body was already being put in its place – to be replaced,
in Coleridge's poem 'This Lime-Tree Bower My Prison', by
landscape as a source of pleasure implicitly in opposition to the
body: 'yea, gazing round / On the wide landscape, gaze till all
doth seem / Less gross than bodily.' *Less gross than bodily.*
With these words, a century of euphemism was inaugurated.

In 'The Eve of St Agnes', Keats in stanza 36 is exercised by
the requirements of propriety when Porphyro and Madeline
come to grips:

> Beyond a mortal man impassioned far
> At these voluptuous accents, he arose,
> Ethereal, flushed, and like a throbbing star
> Seen mid the sapphire heaven's deep repose;
> Into her dream he melted, as the rose

> Blendeth its odour with the violet,
> Solution sweet – meantime the frost-wind blows
> Like Love's alarum pattering the sharp sleet
> Against the window-panes; St Agnes' moon hath set.

*Into her dream he melted.* Keats's friend Woodhouse wrote to another friend that Porphyro 'acts all the acts of a bona fide husband, while she fancies she is only playing the part of a Wife in a dream . . . tho' . . . all is left to inference, and tho' profanely speaking, the Interest on the reader's imagination is greatly heightened, yet I do apprehend it will render the poem unfit for ladies'. *Into her dream he melted.* Against this stanza, Kingsley Amis is reported to have written as an undergraduate, impatiently, 'You mean he fucked her, do you?' One can sympathize with the young Amis's irritability at Keats's insistent soft-focus. Nevertheless, Keats does smuggle in an actual orgasm: 'Love's alarum pattering the sharp sleet.' Desire thinly disguised as meteorology. And, of course, deniable. As it has to be, given the climate of opinion. The rest of the century is poised perfectly between suggestibility and deniability, as in Browning's 'Meeting at Night', which precedes the illicit meeting of the lovers with the act, the sexual act, their assignation will bring about: the narrator comes by boat:

> And the startled little waves that leap
> In fiery ringlets from their sleep,
> As I gain the cove with pushing prow,
> And quench its speed i' the slushy sand.

In *A Sentimental Journey*, Sterne famously begins: ' – They order, said I, this matter better in France – ' And it is true that sexual frankness is greater in France. It is literally more literal. The hiss of Emma Bovary's corset, the slither of stays, can stand for a whole French literature of lingerie as writers wish their dirty linen on the reading public. Take Maupassant's *Bel-Ami* when the hero seduces Madame Walter, bringing her from church to boudoir for her first marital infidelity:

Again he said: 'I swear to respect you.'

A restaurant-keeper standing in his doorway eyed them with curiosity. In an access of terror, she dashed into the house.

'It's here, on the ground floor.'

And he pushed her into his flat.

As soon as he had shut the door he seized her, as though she were his prey. She struggled and fought, babbling all the while: 'Oh my God – Oh my God.'

He showered kisses on her neck and eyes and lips in a sort of frenzy, and she could not avoid his furious caresses; and, as she thrust him away, and tried to evade his mouth, she returned, despite herself, his kisses.

Suddenly she ceased to struggle; vanquished and resigned; she allowed herself to be undressed. One by one, skilfully and quickly, he took off all her garments with a lady's maid's deft fingers. She had snatched her bodice out of his hands, to hide her face in it, and she stood, a white figure, amid the clothes now scattered at her feet.

He left her boots on, and carried her towards the bed. Then, she murmured into his ear in broken tones: 'I swear . . . I swear . . . I have never had a lover before'; just as a girl might have said: 'I swear I am a virgin.'

And he thought to himself: 'Much I care whether she has or not.'

This is a brilliantly cynical piece of writing about an expertly cynical seducer, Georges Du Roy, whose expertise is there in the phrase 'with a lady's maid's deft fingers' and whose erotic cynicism is conveyed by the educated decision to leave on her boots, items both pedestrian and piquant.

When Henry James, in the autumn of 1894, came to plan *The Wings of the Dove*, his initial sense of his subject was of envy for French licence. His plot, in the original donnée, was for a young man to give his love to a young rich heiress, whose tragedy was to be that, while having everything, she had no expectation of living long enough to enjoy it. James is still feeling his way towards an ironic complication of his subject which he can elaborate. At this stage, he sketches out what will be in fact the basis of the finished novel – that the young man will have a prior attachment and commitment to another woman 'whom he has never doubted (any more than this person herself has) that he loves'. A young man, then, in love with two women in different ways. At first, James is a little querulous in his meditation on the subject's difficulty: 'If I were writing for a French public the whole thing would be simple – the elder, the "other", woman would simply be the mistress of the young man, and it would be a question of his taking on the dying girl for a time – having a temporary liaison with her. But one can do so little with English adultery – it is so much less inevitable, and so much more ugly in all its lying and hiding side.' This last observation may seem puzzling – why should French adultery be more inevitable and less ugly than English adultery? – but James explains what he means. Adultery in England, he argues, is 'so undermined by our immemorial tradition of original freedom of choice, and by our practically universal acceptance of divorce'. In other words, France has a tradition of arranged marriages (where adultery isn't seen, therefore, as a betrayal of love) and, being a Catholic country, no ease of divorce, so that adultery is often, of necessity, rendered consequenceless.

But it is precisely on difficulty that James's genius thrives. In this early entry, one can already see him rejecting the obvious as gross – and as much because it is *obvious* as because it is gross:

> It has bothered me in thinking of the little picture – this idea of the physical possession, the brief physical, passional rapture which at first appeared essential to it; bothered me on account of the ugliness, the incongruity, the nastiness, *en somme*, of the man's 'having' a sick girl: also on account of something rather pitifully obvious and vulgar in the presentation of such a remedy for her despair – and such a remedy only. 'Oh, she's dying without having had it? Give it to her and let her die' – that strikes me as sufficiently second-rate. Doesn't a greater prettiness, as

63

well as a better chance for a story, abide in her being already too ill for that, and in his being able merely to show her some delicacy of kindness, let her think that they might have loved each other *ad infinitum* if it hadn't been too late.

The absence of French latitude, the constraint of English morality, and James's appetite for subtlety come together in a kind of analytic lust to produce something more satisfying than the original, obvious plot-line.

Not that I wish to suggest that, in every case, the public constraint inevitably increases imaginative invention. Apart from anything else, it would be unjust to a writer like Maupassant, who uses his considerable literary freedom to give his readers the gross as it is in real life – however much Henry James would prefer a more artistic treatment than life, clumsy Life, as he calls her, can manage on most occasions. This is *Bel-Ami* again. This time, Bel-Ami is bent on discovering his wife, Madeleine, in flagrante with M. Laroche-Mathieu, a minister who has advanced Bel-Ami's career, but whose usefulness is now at an end and whose adultery can therefore be exposed instead of bitterly tolerated:

'If you will not open,' said Georges, 'we shall break down the door.'

He gripped the brass handle, and pushed slowly with one shoulder. As there was no response, he flung his full weight so violently against the door that the frail old apartment-house lock gave way. The screws were wrenched out of the wood, and the young man nearly fell on to Madeleine who was standing in the hall, wearing a vest and skirt, with hair dishevelled, bare legs, and carrying a candle.

'That's her,' he exclaimed. 'We've got them.'

And he dashed into the flat. The Commissaire, taking off his hat, followed him in. And the scared lady walked behind holding up the candle. They went through a dining-room where the table was still covered with the remains of dinner; some empty champagne bottles, an opened jar of foie gras, the carcase of a chicken, and half-eaten bits of bread. Two plates on the sideboard were covered with oyster shells.

The bedroom looked as though it had been the scene of a struggle. A dress was flung over the back of one chair, and a pair of trousers hung cross-legged over the arm of another. Four boots, two large and two small, lay where they had been kicked off at the foot of the bed.

It was the typical bedroom of an apartment house, vulgarly furnished and pervaded by the disagreeable stale smell that haunts such rooms, the smell of curtains, mattresses, walls and chairs, the smell of all the people who have slept or lived, for a day or for six months, in this public lodgement, and left in it something of their own odour, that human odour which, added to all the rest, concentrates into a sort of nondescript, sickly, loathsome stench, the same in all such places.

A plate of cakes, a bottle of Chartreuse, and two small glasses still half full, stood on the mantelpiece; and a large masculine hat had been clapped over the bronze figure on the clock.

The Commissaire turned briskly round, and looked steadily at Madeleine.

'You are – are you not? Mme Claire Madeleine Du Roy, legal wife of M. Prosper-Georges Du Roy, journalist, here present?' And in a strangled voice she managed to articulate:

'Yes, monsieur.'

'What are you doing here?'

She did not answer.

'What are you doing here?' repeated the magistrate. 'I find you away from your home, half undressed, in a furnished flat. For what purpose did you come here?'

He waited for a few moments. Then, as she still said nothing:

'If you will not admit the facts, Madame, I shall be compelled to establish them for myself.'

On the bed the outline of a body could be seen hidden under the sheet.

The Commissaire went up to it, and said:

'Monsieur?'

The prostrate form did not move. He seemed to have turned his back on the proceedings, his head buried underneath a pillow.

The magistrate touched what appeared to be a shoulder, and went on:

'Monsieur, pray do not force me to take action.'

But the veiled body remained as motionless as a corpse.

Du Roy, who had marched into the room, pulled down the bedclothes, snatched away the pillow, and uncovered the livid countenance of M. Laroche-Mathieu. He leaned over him, and quivering with the desire to take him by the neck and throttle him, he said, between clenched teeth:

'You might at least have the courage of your infamy.'

Again the magistrate asked: 'Who are you?'

As the distraught lover did not answer, he went on:

'I am the Commissaire of Police, and I demand your name.'

Georges, who was trembling with bestial fury, shouted:

'Answer, you blackguard, or I will give it myself!'

The figure on the bed then blurted out:

'Monsieur le Commissaire, you should not let me be insulted by this person. Am I dealing with you or with him? Which of you am I to answer?'

He seemed to have no saliva left in his mouth.

The magistrate replied: 'You will address yourself to me alone, Monsieur. I ask you who you are.'

The other was silent. He was clutching the sheet against his neck, his eyes upturned in terror. His small moustache stood out black against his colourless face.

The Commissaire went on: 'Do you refuse to reply? In

that case, I shall be forced to arrest you. In any case, get up. I will question you when you are dressed.'

The body in the bed shook and the head murmured:

'But I can't in front of you.'

'Why not?' demanded the magistrate.

'Because,' stammered the other. 'Because ... I'm ... I'm naked.'

Du Roy laughed contemptuously, and picking up a shirt from the floor, he threw it on to the bed, and exclaimed: 'Nonsense! ... Get up ... Since you undressed in front of my wife, you can quite well dress in front of me.'

Then he turned and went back to the mantelpiece.

Madeleine had recovered her composure, and seeing that all was lost, she no longer minded what she did. The audacity of bravado gleamed in her eye: and, making a spill out of a bit of paper, she lit, as though for a reception, the ten candles in the hideous candelabra on each corner of the mantelpiece. Then she stood with her back against it, and extending one of her bare feet to the dying fire, thus lifting the back of the skirt which hung precariously from her hips, she took a cigarette out of a pink packet, lit it and began to smoke.

The Commissaire had returned to her, leaving her accomplice to get up.

'Do you often do this job, Monsieur?' she asked insolently.

'As seldom as I can, Madame,' he replied gravely.

She smiled in his face. 'I congratulate you, it isn't a nice one.'

She affected not to look at, nor see her husband.

Obviously, there is an argumentative temptation to prefer Jamesian subtlety and imaginative intricacy to this dirty realism *avant la lettre*, to prefer the ingenious to the infamous. All the same, the Maupassant is very great literature too. *Bel-Ami* is not perhaps a Jamesian moral gymnasium for stretching the reader's sympathies and intellect, but neither does it suffer from the intermittent sense in James that the reader is attending, blind-fold, a high-powered seminar of disembodied voices – all of them sounding suspiciously like the Master. Maupassant is alert to the power of externals in a way that James seldom is – or *could* be, in this instance. Where James is moral and philosoph-ical, Maupassant is documentary. Contrast the use of detail here with James's account, in *The Wings of the Dove*, of Merton Densher returning to his rooms in Venice where Kate Croy has had sexual intercourse with him once, as her guarantee of good faith before Densher embarks on his *tendresse* with the invalid Milly Theale. In *Bel-Ami*, Maupassant is purely factual, true to clumsy Life: the sexual greed of the adulterers is there in the detritus of the half-eaten feast, the broached jar of foie gras, the unfinished bits of bread, details which tell us that the sexual business is also incomplete. Those screws 'wrenched *out* of the wood'. James tells us why people behave as they do, Maupassant *how* they behave: they clap a hat over the clock, their bodies shake with terror, they hide under the sheets, their terror is overtaken by desperate bravado, they take a cigarette from a pink packet and talk themselves into boldness. Best of all, Bel-Ami's wife 'affected not to look at, nor see her husband'. How true this is of guilty behaviour.

Densher, by contrast, relives his encounter with Kate every time he re-enters his rooms: 'He remained thus, in his own theatre, in his single person, perpetual orchestra to the ordered drama, the confirmed "run"; playing low and slow, moreover, in the regular way, for the situations of most importance.' It is hard not to read this metaphor as verbose and distracting, a desperate attempt by James to talk his way out of an embarrass-ing fact. Like Bel-Ami's wife, he affects not to look at or see his narrative difficulty. He protests too much and the nearest he comes to directness is 'when, with each return, he worked his heavy old key in the lock' – a piece of symbolism bluntly used by Sterne to suggest the mechanical nature of Mr Shandy's sexual urge, but here presented with studied neutrality by James, except perhaps for the verb 'worked'. The innuendo is, as it must be, in the mind of the beholder.

Could this be the same Henry James who wrote to Robert Louis Stevenson: 'Oh, yes, dear Louis, "Tess of the D'Urbervilles" is vile. The pretence of sexuality is only equalled by the absence of it.' This sounds odd coming from a writer who, in *The Turn of the Screw*, deliberately adopted as his narrative strategy the total occlusion of the evil transactions between Quint, Miss Jessell and the two children, Miles and Flora. For James, the refusal to name the evil was a way of magnifying it: each reader would supply his own horror. In practice, the novella's restraint goes for nothing. The reader rapidly supplies the only solution commensurate with the narrative's squeals of horror – sexual abuse. Moreover, one knows that James's protestations in his preface about his ingenuity are merely *faute de mieux*. He doesn't mention the central evil because it is unmentionable – not because he has discovered a better way to make the reader's flesh creep. According to Steven Marcus in *The Other Victorians*, his study of Victorian sexuality, Dickens's readers would have swiftly identified Major Bagstock in *Dombey and Son* as a child molester. I think the same readers would have suspected Quint and Miss Jessell rather more readily.

Sexuality, in Victorian literature, is a train of consequences rather than a source of pleasure. The fallen woman is a familiar figure, but the fall itself tends to take place between the end of one chapter and the beginning of the next – which is why it is impossible to say whether Tess is raped or seduced by Alec d'Urberville when he carries her off to the Chase. In *Adam Bede*, the same strictures obtain: George Eliot shows the reader a little canoodling between Hetty Sorrel and the squire, Arthur Donnithorne, but the extent of their real intimacy is touched on only when Arthur has decided to break off their relationship by letter: 'A sudden dread here fell like a shadow across his imagination – the dread lest she should do something violent in her grief; and close upon that dread came another, which deepened the shadow.' The letter itself repeats this dark hint: 'if any trouble should come that we do not now foresee, trust in me to do everything that lies in my power'. When she is pregnant, Hetty takes the only course open to fallen women in Victorian fiction. Like Lady Dedlock in *Bleak House* and little Emily in *David Copperfield*, when Steerforth has had his upper-class way with her, Hetty takes to her heels and goes walkabout. Where her seduction is skimped, the walking and its culmination in infanticide are portrayed unflinchingly. Various reports and gradual disclosures climax in the evidence of the yokel who first hears the cry of the abandoned baby: 'I thought it didn't come from any animal I knew, but I wasn't for stopping to look just then. But it went on, and seemed so strange to me in that place, I couldn't help stopping to look. I began to think I might make some money of it, if it was a new thing.' He can't find it, however. Returning later, he sees 'something odd and round and whitish lying on the ground under a nut-bush by the side of me. And I stooped down on hands and knees to pick it up. And I saw it was a little baby's hand.'

The detail here – including the incomparable lateral thinking that produces the labourer's mercenary aside, 'I began to think I might make some money of it, if it was a new thing' – this detail isn't possible in a sexual context. Other strategies have to be employed by the resourceful novelist. The sexual failure of the marriage between Dorothea and Casaubon in *Middlemarch* is conveyed to us obliquely when Dorothea breaks down on her honeymoon while looking at nude statuary. Or, more precisely, *after* looking at nude statuary, here evoked somewhat obscurely in the phrase 'long vistas of white forms whose marble eyes seemed to hold the monotonous light of an alien world'. Although George Eliot is careful to add in other forms of art and to generalize the cultural shock that Dorothea receives from Rome, the significant sentence is surely this: 'Forms both pale and glowing took possession of her young sense, and fixed themselves in her memory even when she was not thinking of them.' While not once mentioning the word 'nudity' and while being careful to paint a general contrast between Dorothea's puritanism and Rome's eclectic Catholicism, the real nature of her upset is made available to the shrewd reader. When the word 'nudity' *is* mentioned, it is prudently attached to the soul: 'many souls in their young nudity are tumbled out among incongruities and left to "find their feet" among them, while their elders go about their business'. The meta-communication is clear enough through the overt sense: a young nudity is left by an elder to fend for itself.

The enigma of Nancy's attachment to Bill Sikes in *Oliver Twist* is another example of strategic displacement. Why doesn't Nancy leave him? Why is she loyal? Dickens cannot tell his readers that Sikes has a sexual hold over her. Instead, he dramatizes her predicament and parallels it using Sikes's dog – which is also astonishingly loyal, though regularly beaten by his owner. The dog even stays with Sikes when it knows that Sikes wants to kill it, fearing its presence will give away his identity. It keeps its distance, of course, but is loyal right to the end, jumping from the tiles towards Sikes's hanged body. How else was Dickens to expatiate on the animal hold that Sikes has over Nancy, except by giving her psychology to a dog?

If seduction presents difficulties to the Victorian writer, how much more problematic are the more intricate reaches of human sexuality. Perversion, for example, is practically absent. Sexual success can be assumed, more or less, by the writer. It is in theory at any rate by and large *uniform*. Sexual failure, as we know from Masters and Johnson, can take a large variety of forms. Dysfunction isn't short of options. This is something Hardy makes clear in a letter dated 20 November 1895, written about the character of Sue Bridehead in *Jude the Obscure*: 'You are quite right; there is nothing perverted or depraved in Sue's nature.'

The abnormalism consists in disproportion, not in inversion, her sexual instinct being healthy as far as it goes, but unusually weak and fastidious. Her sensibilities remain painfully alert notwithstanding, as they do in nature with such women. *One point illustrating this I could not dwell upon;* that, though she has children, her intimacies with Jude have never been more than occasional, even when they were living together (I mention that they occupy separate rooms, except towards the end), and one of her reasons for fearing the marriage ceremony is that she fears it would be breaking faith with Jude to withhold herself at pleasure, or altogether, after it; though while uncontracted she feels at liberty to yield herself as seldom as she chooses. This has tended to keep his passion as hot at the end as at the beginning, and helps to break his heart. He has never really possessed her as freely as he desired.

Sue is a type of woman which has always had an attraction for me, but the difficulty of drawing the type has kept me from attempting it till now.

*One point illustrating this I could not dwell upon. The difficulty of drawing the type has kept me from attempting it until now.* In France, on the other hand, Zola in *Germinal* could show the hero Etienne, his rival Chaval and his beloved Catherine trapped in a mining accident behind a rock fall. They have to relieve themselves in front of each other. Chaval attempts to swap food for sexual favours. He is murdered by Etienne, who then, rather improbably, achieves sexual intercourse with the dying Catherine on a narrow ledge while the corpse of his rival bobs in the flood-water immediately below. 'Feeling her half naked body through her rags, so close to his, his virility returned and he took her.' Hardy, by contrast, is compelled to characterize his heroine so vaguely that lesbianism is a possibility that needs elimination – though only in his correspondence is this possible.

Nevertheless, *Jude the Obscure* is a novel in which Hardy attempts to delineate a particular type of sexual failure – at once subtly and crudely, using symbolism and deliberate lacunae in the narrative. His strategy isn't often read correctly and, for that reason, might be said to fail. In my view, Hardy has been failed by his readers, for reasons which are obvious enough. They jump to conclusions too quickly. For instance, in *Far from the*

*Madding Crowd,* the demonstration of swordplay by Sergeant Troy to Bathsheba is clearly sexual. We could deduce this from Hardy's end to the chapter in which it takes place, even if we did not know that the 'short-sword' was a popular euphemism for the penis. You can find it used unambiguously in this way by Kipling in his story of a rake, 'The Dream of Duncan Parrenness'. Hardy ends his account of Troy's military virtuosity in terms which are meaningful only if the virtuosity is also sexual:

> He drew near and said, 'I must be leaving you.' He drew nearer still. A minute later and she saw his scarlet form disappear amid the ferny thicket, almost in a flash, like a brand swiftly waved.
>
> That minute's interval had brought the blood beating into her face, set her stinging as if aflame to the very hollows of her feet, and enlarged emotion to a compass which quite swamped thought. It had brought upon her a stroke resulting, as did that of Moses in Horeb, in a liquid stream – here a stream of tears. She felt like one who has sinned a great sin.
>
> The circumstance had been the gentle dip of Troy's mouth downwards upon her own. He had kissed her.

Quoted thus, the hint – 'she felt like one who has sinned a great sin' – may read a little crudely. Hardy, of course, could not afford to be crude. His novel would have been banned, burned or both. Which is why this chapter begins with a deliberate, pedantic and above all literal exposition of the various thrusts: 'first, we have four right and four left cuts; four right and four left thrusts. Infantry cuts and guards are more interesting than ours, to my mind; but they are not so swashing.' And so on. And on. All in the interest of deniability. Hardy's other sexual symbol in this chapter is so bold that most people don't see it. If there is a penis in the chapter, there is also a vagina. The chapter is called 'The Hollow Amid the Ferns'. This is how Hardy describes it. Judge for yourselves.

'I heard you rustling through the fern before I saw you,' he said, coming up and giving her his hand to help her down the slope.

The pit was a saucer-shaped concave, naturally formed, with a top diameter of about thirty feet, and shallow enough to allow the sunshine to reach their heads. Standing in the centre, the sky overhead was met by a circular horizon of fern: this grew nearly to the bottom of the slope and then abruptly ceased. The middle within the belt of verdure was floored with a thick flossy carpet of moss and grass intermingled, so yielding that the foot was half-buried within it.

This passage of Hardy's has retained its secret for over a hundred years largely because it has never occurred to his readers that Hardy would dare to do such a thing. The other reason is that the reader jumps to the nearest conclusion – the equation of sword and penis – and looks no further. In fact, Hardy's symbolism is capable of conducting an argument, of diagnosing and describing a sexual dysfunction.

He does so in *Jude the Obscure*. Everyone is familiar with the incident in which Arabella, the coarse animal type, throws a pig's pizzle at the young dreamer, Jude. The bluntness of the symbolism makes obvious the nature of Arabella's appeal to Jude – and readers tend to leave the matter there. But Hardy continues the train of ideas with considerable delicacy. Arabella traps Jude into marriage by pretending to be pregnant. Yet it is she who terminates the marriage after only one quarrel – about a pig. The couple have been fattening a pig for slaughter, but when Challow the pig-man fails to turn up, the couple decide to kill it themselves – in itself a very unlikely decision, taken because there is no more food for the pig. 'He ate the last mixing o' barleymeal yesterday morning,' says Arabella. But since the pig has been starved for two days anyway, 'to save bother with the innerds', another day would make little difference. Jude then botches the slaughter out of pity for the pig. It is supposed to bleed to death slowly, so that the flesh will be white and the blood collected in a bucket for black pudding. 'He ought to be eight or ten minutes dying, at least,' Arabella instructs. However, Jude plunges in the knife 'with all his might'. ''Od damn it all!' she cried, 'that ever I should say it! You've over-stuck un!' Shortly afterwards, Jude hears two of Arabella's friends laughing over her deception – the false pregnancy – and reproaches her with it. Though there is ill-feeling, they don't quarrel and she gets on with preparing the pig fat. The next day, she picks a quarrel deliberately, pretends he has misused her and leaves for good while he is out getting drunk in his misery. Considering the trouble she has gone to to marry him, the sudden departure scarcely makes sense. In a letter, she merely states that 'she had grown tired of him', that 'he was such an old slow coach, and she did not care for the sort of life he led'. These reasons are suspiciously perfunctory – deliberately so. Hardy intends us to meditate on the juxtaposition of the pig-killing with her termination of the marriage. One interpretation might be that the animal passion, signalled by the thrown pizzle, is dead. But the pizzle itself wasn't exactly alive when she first threw it. Rather, Hardy intends to adumbrate the nature of their sexual relationship. Not only is Jude too fastidious for Arabella, he is also inept in bed. The act, like the pig-killing, is over sooner, much sooner than it should be. Jude's attraction for Arabella is nothing to do with his virtuoso work with the short-sword. It is his fine feeling, his romantic aura, a commodity that loses its power almost as quickly when she remarries him at the end of the novel. There, Hardy subtly resumes the pig imagery in a way that makes obvious the equation between marriage, sex and the pig-killing. Arabella gets Jude drunk, wanting to persuade him to consent to remarry: 'the quiet convivial gathering, suggested by her, to wind Jude up to the sticking point, took place'. Lest we fail to make the equation, Hardy's next paragraph begins with this ostensibly random information: 'Donn had only just opened his miserable little pork and sausage shop, which had as yet scarce any customers . . .' This train of imagery couldn't be clearer without leaving the novel liable to prosecution.

With D. H. Lawrence, we move from the oblique presentation

of sex to the explicit, from *The White Peacock*, which is nineteenth-century in its procedures, to *Lady Chatterley's Lover*, a novel that doesn't beat about the bush. In *The White Peacock*, George Saxton and Lettie Beardsall dance together. They are a couple who should marry. There is real sexual magnetism between them. But they marry other people, largely for reasons of class: George marries Meg of the Ram public house, Lettie the upper-class Leslie.

> Lettie helped to clear away – sat down – talked a little with effort – jumped up and said:
> 'Oh, I'm too excited to sit still – it's so near Christmas – let us play at something.'
> 'A dance?' said Emily.
> 'A dance – a dance!'
> He suddenly sat straight and got up:
> 'Come on!' he said.
> He kicked off his slippers, regardless of the holes in his stockinged feet, and put away the chairs. He held out his arm to her – she came with a laugh, and away they went, dancing over the great flagged kitchen at an incredible speed. Her light flying steps followed his leaps; you could hear the quick light tap of her toes more plainly than the thud of his stockinged feet. Emily and I joined in. Emily's movements are naturally slow, but we danced at great speed. I was hot and perspiring, and she was panting, when I put her in a chair. But they whirled on in the dance, on and on till I was giddy, till the father, laughing, cried that they should stop. But George continued the dance; her hair was shaken loose, and fell in a great coil down her back; her feet began to drag; you could hear a light slur on the floor; she was panting – I could see her lips murmur to him, begging him to stop; he was laughing with open mouth, holding her tight; at last her feet trailed; he lifted her, clasping her tightly, and danced twice round the room with her thus. Then he fell with a crash on the sofa, pulling her beside him. His eyes glowed like coals; he

76

was panting in sobs, and his hair was wet and glistening. She lay back on the sofa, with his arm still around her, not moving; she was quite overcome. Her hair was wild about her face. Emily was anxious; the father said, with a shade of inquietude:

'You've overdone it – it is very foolish.'

When at last she recovered her breath and her life, she got up, and laughing in a queer way, began to put up her hair. She went into the scullery where were the brush and combs, and Emily followed with a candle. When she returned, ordered once more, with a little pallor succeeding the flush, and with a great black stain of sweat on her leathern belt where his hand had held her, he looked up at her from his position on the sofa, with a peculiar glance of triumph, smiling.

'You great brute,' she said, but her voice was not as harsh as her words. He gave a deep sigh, sat up, and laughed quietly.

The equation of dance with sex is one which Lawrence repeats in his early short story 'The White Stocking'. The meta-textual content is even clearer there – not that it is obscured here. And this *is* an advance on the nineteenth century; though the method of symbolic displacement is the same, the principle of deniability has quietly vanished. In Lawrence, unlike the nineteenth century, though sexual intercourse cannot be described directly, it can be acknowledged obliquely. The symbolism is now transparent in its intention.

In the nineteenth-century novel, the climate of repression, occlusion and exclusion of sexual matters occasionally meant that complete transparency became a form of concealment. Because the prevailing assumption was that the physical side of love was to be hidden, it was now and then possible to hide things by leaving them so in the open that they couldn't possibly mean what they appeared to mean. Earlier, I contrasted Maupassant's feel for the concrete with Henry James's disembodied theory. There is a real and surprising exception to this proposition. It occurs in *The Golden Bowl* at the point where Maggie is the centre of consciousness. Her husband, Amerigo, returns to their house in Portland Place after an excursion on which he has committed adultery with Charlotte Stant, an old flame who has married Maggie's father, Adam Verver. Before Amerigo met his wife Maggie, he had a *tendresse* with Charlotte. But this relationship did not develop because Charlotte has 'very small means'. It wasn't a sexual relationship either: 'on his own side there had luckily been no folly to cover up'. After his marriage to Maggie, who has money and is moreover a friend of Charlotte Stant, Maggie is preoccupied with her children and her father. Charlotte, therefore, becomes a social companion for Amerigo, while their respective spouses stay at home. This leads to their adultery. Maggie and her father spend most of their time together at his house in Eaton Square. On this occasion, Amerigo returns to Portland Place and, to his surprise, for once finds Maggie in their own home. They chat about his doings with Charlotte ('all their cathedral-hunting adventure, and how it had turned out rather more of an affair than they expected') and then he goes off for a bath. Never has a bath meant more in a novel because it means only and exactly what it is – a way of getting clean.

> He had told her of his day, the happy thought of his roundabout journey with Charlotte, all their cathedral-hunting adventure, and how it had turned out rather more of an affair than they expected. The moral of it was, at any rate, that he was tired, verily, and must have a bath and dress – to which end she would kindly excuse him for the shortest time possible. She was to remember afterwards something that had passed between them on this – how he had looked, for her, during an instant, at the door, before going out, how he had met her asking him, in hesitation first, then quickly in decision, whether she couldn't help him by going up with him. He had perhaps also for a moment hesitated, but he had declined her offer, and she was to preserve, as I say, the memory of the smile with

which he had opined that at that rate they wouldn't dine till ten o'clock and that he should go straighter and faster alone. Such things, as I say, were to come back to her – they played, through her full after-sense, like lights on the whole impression . . .

In its way, this is more sordid than anything in the Maupassant passage I quoted from *Bel-Ami*. It is completely explicit and has, therefore, paradoxically, remained invisible and unnoticed for nearly a hundred years.

# Emily Dickinson – Paleface Redskin

In 1957, considering 'the immense contrast between the draw-ing-room fictions of Henry James and the open-air poems of Walt Whitman', Philip Rahv famously divided American writers into palefaces and redskins.

The upstairs room in Amherst where Emily Dickinson spent most of her reclusive adult life seems a long way from Mark Twain's worldly milieu, where a whorehouse filled with dead bodies and obscene graffiti is found floating down the Missis-sippi. Her grandfather, Samuel Fowler Dickinson, was largely responsible for founding Amherst College as a bulwark of religious orthodoxy. Her father and brother were both lawyers, important public figures and treasurers of Amherst College. In 1857 she won second prize in the Cattle Show for her rye and indian bread. The survival of this fact is an index of how uneventful her life was. Whitman's vaunted grey neck contrasts with Emily Dickinson's legendary indoor pallor. She was liter-ally a paleface.

Yet she, too, like Twain, like Whitman, is faithful to the emphases of excited speech – its interjections, its breathlessness, its cries, its syncopations, its italic mode. Thomas H. Johnson's critical biography points to the influence of Isaac Watts, who provided her with the basic model of rhyme and metres. Watts's *Christian Psalmody* and his collection *The Psalms, Hymns, and Spiritual Songs* were in her father's library, bearing his signature. To this formal template she added the American speaking voice, her own particular excitable tones. As the harmonium wheezed and pumped out its four-square melodies, she added disgraceful grace notes and set up a disreputable descant. Like Twain, she *uses* italics. 234 is a poem in which she not only interrogates complacent Christian orthodoxy but actually *interrupts* it in mid-sentence. All the heat of argument is preserved miraculously on the page:

> You're right – 'the way *is* narrow' –
> And 'difficult the Gate' –
> And 'few there be' – Correct again –
> That 'enter in – thereat' –
>
> *Tis* Costly – So are *purples*!
> Tis just the price of *Breath* –
> With but the 'Discount' of the *Grave* –
> Termed by the *Brokers* – 'Death!'
>
> And after *that* – there's Heaven –
> The *Good* Man's – '*Dividend*' –
> And *Bad* Men – 'go to Jail' –
> I guess

What sarcastic italics and how well they work in tandem with her bluntly ironic metaphor from brokerage and investment – a metaphor which finally, implicitly, leads her and us to the idea of bankruptcy. 'And *Bad* Men – "go to Jail" ': the application of the idea of bankruptcy transfers itself to the religion it is meant to explicate. Her target could be Calvinism or religion as arithmetic, calculation, commerce, rather than selfless commitment to Christian principles like renunciation of things material. And that last truncated, colloquial line – 'I guess' – allows the poem to end on an utterly inconclusive note of disbelief. A note, too, which is authentically American.

This redskin note of informality is struck again and again: 'Flowers – Well – if anybody / Can the ecstasy define' 95; 'How lonesome the Wind must feel Nights' (1418); 'It don't sound so terrible – quite – as it did – '(426).

But Dickinson's greatest discovery was the dash, a device whose power all readers feel without, perhaps, being able to analyse. From my point of view, it isn't punctuation so much as war-paint, a definitely redskin device. But how exactly does it work? Consider this poem: an elegy for a dead woman.

> To the spirit its splendid – conjectures
> To the flesh – its sweet despair,
> Its tears – o'er the thin-worn locket
> With its anguish – of deathless hair!
>
> That little shoe – in the corner
> So worn – and wrinkled – and brown,
> With its emptiness – confutes you,
> And argues your wisdom – down.

Dickinson's dash inscribes spontaneity into her poetry – and wasn't restored until Thomas H. Johnson's 1955 edition. It is reminiscent of the jazz singer's vernacular phrasing, that calculated air of spoken improvisation, of making it up as you go along – a hesitation, almost, which is utterly alien to opera.

In fact, this isn't a poem by Emily Dickinson at all. It is a poem by James Russell Lowell, 'After the Burial', to which Emily Dickinson alludes in a letter to Higginson of December 1879. I have taken the fourth and the final stanzas and mocked up an Emily Dickinson poem deploying the Dickinson dash – which is, of course, a misnomer, since what it does, primarily, is stop and hesitate. As readers, we experience what Dickinson (in 293) calls 'That Stop-sensation – on my Soul'. It is an effect related to musical phrasing, what Larkin in 'Love Songs in Age' calls 'word after sprawling hyphenated word', stretched across the notes in the score. Updike's 'Rabbit' Angstrom notes the same visceral effect in *Rabbit at Rest*, when he explores the mnemonic tug of popular music: 'Then, "Mule Train", by Frankie Laine, not one of the great Laines but great enough, and "It's Magic", by Doris Day. Those pauses back then: *It's ma-gic*. They knew how to hurt you . . .'

Dickinson introduces into poetry something new – verbal

suspense, the ache for completion, a poetic brinkmanship, a sense of danger prolonged and safety achieved. This quality of the tantalus, of the withheld and the finally conferred, arrives in our ears as a modern effect – comparable to the pauses in Pinter and Beckett, when both playwrights toy with the terror of extended stage silence. Remove the pauses from the James Russell Lowell stanzas and you restore a fatal rapidity:

> To the spirit its splendid conjectures,
> To the flesh its sweet despair,
> Its tears o'er the thin-worn locket
> With its anguish of deathless hair!
>
> The little shoe in the corner,
> So worn and wrinkled and brown,
> With its emptiness confutes you,
> And argues your wisdom down.

Dickinson uses rubato, distorting the time signature in order to bring sharpness and intention to the phrasing. The words are not merely spoken. They are given expressiveness. Thus 'splendid conjectures' has a completely different semantic penumbra from 'splendid – conjectures' because the latter creates an ironic oxymoron, by giving 'splendid' its full weight before introducing 'conjectures' with its terrible weightlessness. Essentially, Dickinson's dashes are conscious acts of direction – intent on making her readers intent. It is like watching a movie with a remote control – using the pause to isolate and concentrate.

But the other effect is a coexistent quality of improvisation. On the one hand, there is the frank mimesis of 360, her guidance of the reader:

> Death sets a Thing significant
> The Eye had hurried by
> Except a perished Creature
> Entreat us tenderly
>
> To ponder little Workmanships

> In Crayon, or in Wool, With 'This was last Her fingers
> did' –
>
> Industrious until –
>
> The Thimble weighed too heavy –
> The stitches stopped – themselves

The Dickinson dash can make us linger, confer significance, as in 'So worn – and wrinkled – and brown', saving the colour of the little shoe from being a mere makeweight rhyme word and making it instead part of the enigmatic factuality of things, making the colour's contingency seem deliberate. Dash 'sets a Thing significant / The Eye had hurried by . . .' It can mimic the faltering of the sewing fingers: 'The stitches stopped – themselves.' The effect is conscious and chosen. The dash, however, can also mimic a hesitation designed to subvert poetry's artfulness and its general air of contrivance and happy arrangement. Like the greatest actors, Dickinson, by using her dash, can persuade us that she is making it up as she goes along:

> The World – feels Dusty
> When We stop to Die –
> We want the Dew – then –
> Honours – taste dry –

This is the parched vernacular of the death-bed rather than the padre's polished, palefaced address from the pulpit.

In 1939, Jean Rhys published the last of her novels before she disappeared from the literary world for thirty years. It was called *Good Morning, Midnight* and its title was a quotation from Emily Dickinson. It is an odd conjunction – the New England spinster in her white frock, who shied away from visitors, and the murkily scarlet Rhys, who knocked around all over the world and was knocked up and knocked about for her pains. Dickinson described her eyes to her mentor, Thomas Wentworth Higginson, as 'like the Sherry in the Glass, that the

Guest leaves'. Jean Rhys was an alcoholic, the author of *Sleep It Off Lady*. How do the proper and the improper conjoin?

First, Dickinson, though punctilious, was not truly proper. Underneath the ditsy ingénue there was a profound eccentricity, a personality helplessly *sui generis*. Her erotic entanglements with married men, Samuel Bowles, the editor of the *Springfield Daily Republican*, and Judge Otis P. Lord, seem conventionally unconventional only at first. What, if anything, took place, is impossible to disentangle. She loved and loved passionately. That much is certain. But she seems to have feared the dilution of passion involved in day-to-day transactions, let alone sex and practising the sack arts. This is the subject of her great poem 'I cannot live with You – ', whose second line is 'It would be Life – '. Dickinson gave *everything* to her lovers, every iota of her erotic and emotional capital – they couldn't spend it, that's all.

She was religiously heterodox, though capable, in her poems, of ventriloquizing conventional Christian sentiments for speakers other than herself. In 1859, she writes, 'Mr S[eelye] preached in our church last Sabbath upon "pre-destination", but I do not respect "doctrines", and did not listen to him, so I can neither praise, nor blame.' To Higginson, she was even more forthrightly atheistical as she introduced her family context: 'they are religious – except me – and address an Eclipse, every morning – whom they call their "Father" '.

Her attitude is theologically relaxed rather than atheistically militant. She can be sarcastic about sectarianism yet tender towards the central Christian myth. In 527 she is touched by Christ's relinquishing of his life and scathing about 'the Brand of the Gentile Drinker / Who endorsed the Cup – ' She entertains pity for Moses excluded from the Promised Land and simultaneously denies his historical reality in 597: 'tho' in soberer moments – / No Moses there can be / I'm satisfied.' 1,317 is an acid meditation on Abraham's proffered sacrifice of Isaac: 'Flattered by Obeisance / Tyranny demurred.' By and large, though, Dickinson can leave it and take it, like the minister in Frost's 'The Black Cottage': 'For, dear me, why abandon a belief / Merely because it ceases to be true.'

Jean Rhys could have known none of this, so what attracted her to Dickinson's poem? Partly, perhaps, that its radical defeatism ('You – are not so fair – Midnight – / I chose – Day – / But – please take a little Girl – / He turned away!') is smokily cognate with the Blues. One thinks of Billie Holiday's vulnerable, cracked rendition of the Fisher–Higginbotham–Drake classic 'Good Morning, Heartache': 'Might as well get used to you / Hanging around. / Good morning, heartache, / Sit down.'

The bond between Rhys and Dickinson isn't an accident but an affinity – accurately sensed by Jean Rhys. Both writers share with Tennyson not just a pervasive melancholy but also an acute awareness that emotional states may be interior yet they descend on us like the weather – and are to be suffered in their several manifestations as they occur, apparently for ever. There is no remote control to change channels. We are helpless to alter the stasis of feelings, just as we cannot stop it raining.

Jean Rhys's 1966 novel about Antoinette Bertha Mason, the mad Creole wife of Mr Rochester in *Jane Eyre*, is called *Wide Sargasso Sea*. Though most of the action is set in Jamaica and the Windward Isles, the Sargasso Sea is not a setting. Nor is it even mentioned in the novel. It is not a geographical reality but a psychological equivalent of Antoinette's inability to alter her fate, of the way she discovers, like other Rhys heroines, that the becalmed moment of sadness can continue unbroken to become, unbelievably, a life.

If you want a translation of *Wide Sargasso Sea*, you could do worse than turn to the collection of undated fragments in the Johnson–Ward edition of Dickinson's letters. One phrase, the merest wisp, preserves the iron perfume of Dickinson: 'What Lethargies of Loneliness'. That one word, 'Lethargies', takes the reader directly into the stale, debilitated air of authentic loneliness, the very room.

Dickinson is an authority on the emotions, with a genius for classification and discrimination that makes her the Linnaeus of psychology. Half-tones, quarter tones, chords and discords, the queer but authentic atonalities that sound within us – she is the pitch-perfect poet, with an unmatched gift for transcription, a tape-recorder of the soul. 'What Lethargies of Loneliness': an Edward Hopper subject, in her slip, on the edge of a bed, smoking.

'How do most people live without any thoughts. There are many people in the world (you must have noticed them in the street). How do they live. How do they get strength to put on their clothes in the morning.' This last sentence is Emily Dickinson, but it could be Jean Rhys, spokeswoman for the becalmed who are unable to organize their *areté* – or to put on their clothes – the spiritually sluttish, with their torpid accuracy. In *Good Morning, Midnight*, Rhys makes us privy to Sasha Jensen's tipsily repetitive inventory of her life and immediate surroundings:

> *The House in the Boulevard Magenta.*
> The sage femme has very white hands and clear, slanting eyes and when she looks at you the world stops rocking about. The clouds are clouds, trees are trees, people are people, and that's that. Don't mix them up again. No, I won't.
> And there's always the tisane of orange-flower water.
> But my heart, heavy as lead, heavy as a stone.
> He has a ticket tied round his wrist because he died. Lying so cold and still with a ticket round his wrist because he died.

The last two nearly identical sentences refer to Sasha's dead baby son. The bleak affectlessness of Sasha's alcoholic anaesthesia is reproduced in the sentence's repeated unadorned notation. The preceding sentence is untrue because it is a cliché: 'But my heart, heavy as lead, heavy as a stone.' What we have here is *cinéma vérité* – hand-held camera prose. Rhys wants to create sympathy for her heroine, to give her the proper feelings about her dead child – 'my heart, heavy as lead, heavy as a stone' – but succeeds in something more difficult, by accidentally insisting on the bald factuality of the death. Instead of the immediacy of grief, she records the great distance that sometimes opens up

87

between tragic events and our emotional response. 'He has a ticket tied round his wrist because he died.' Not, you notice, 'He *had* a ticket tied round his wrist because he died.' This is the continuous present. It will never change. 'Lying so cold and still with a ticket round his wrist because he died.' Clear but seen through the wrong end of a telescope. Rhys has recorded, unforgettably, *by chance*, not a heart 'heavy as lead, heavy as a stone', but the clinical state of shock.

The lesser known, more fugitive emotions, the shy sensations, the unrecorded, unringed fauna of the mind and the heart are Dickinson's field of research, too. Like Rhys, but less haphazardly, she is an expert on shock.

> After great pain, a formal feeling comes –
> The Nerves sit ceremonious, like Tombs –
> The stiff Heart questions was it He, that bore,
> And Yesterday, or Centuries before?
>
> The Feet, mechanical, go round –
> Of Ground, or Air, or Ought –
> A Wooden way
> Regardless grown,
> A Quartz contentment, like a stone –
>
> This is the Hour of Lead –
> Remembered, if outlived,
> As Freezing persons, recollect the Snow –
> First – Chill – then Stupor – then the letting go –

Keats, another interesting anatomist of the emotions, coined the useful expression 'the feel of not to feel it'. In this numb world of emotional Novocaine, the heart is no longer the reliable, voluble witness, but an organ uneasily amnesiac – 'The stiff Heart questions was it He, that bore, / And Yesterday, or Centuries before?' 'Stiff' is wonderfully chosen, carrying its own shock when applied, of all things, to the heart. It picks up the adjective 'formal' in the first line, but it is immediately clear that the stiffness is also physical – the result of having carried a great weight, 'was it He, that bore'. And the adjective also anticipates the poem's frozen conclusion. There is something brilliantly surprising, too, in the line: 'The Nerves sit ceremonious, like Tombs'. The unexpected quiescence of the nerves is conveyed by 'ceremonious' − the ritual of mechanical behaviour − but the swollen, gigantified potential is implicit in the comparison of small to large, 'like Tombs'. The weakness of the Rhys passage conveniently provides us with a check-list for Dickinson's strengths. 'But my heart, heavy as lead, heavy as a stone' is rescued from complete feebleness − if it *is* rescued − by the sentence's verbless, grammatically truncated finality. Yet when you compare Dickinson's use of lead and stone, she can be seen alert and in charge. 'A Quartz contentment, like a stone − // This is the Hour of Lead − '. So, not a heart 'heavy as a stone', but 'a Quartz contentment, like a stone', where the stoniness is qualified by 'contentment, and the 'contentment' drastically modified by the adjective 'Quartz'. This is a state of mind poised between total lack of feeling and a mutedness almost pleasurable. 'This is the Hour of Lead' equally avoids the cliché, since the property of *heaviness* isn't specified: the reader is left at liberty to consider the grey colour and the dull pliancy of lead, as well as its insulating property.

If modernism means anything in the twentieth century, it must mean the exploration of emotions, the discovery of feelings which, while not new, have so far escaped description in poetry − an art which, more than the novel, prefers the tried and the tested conservative emotions. Hence Eliot's irritable enjoinder in 'The Metaphysical Poets': 'Racine and Donne looked into a good deal more than the heart. One must look into the cerebral cortex, the nervous system, and the digestive tracts.' This was in 1921. Dickinson was before him. For instance, we can all respond to Dickinson's assertion (281): ''Tis so appalling − it exhilarates.' However unreasonable this facet of human psychology, it is well and extensively documented: one thinks, for instance, of Paul Morel and his sister being stricken with explosive hilarity after they have administered a lethal overdose to their dying mother. Equally, 1,175's claim that 'We like a

Hairbreadth 'scape / It tingles in the mind' is at once perverse and an explanation of adrenalin as it affects the playgoer watching a tragedy or a participant at a funfair. Likewise, Dickinson's assertion (770) 'I lived on Dread – / To Those who know / The Stimulus there is / In Danger – Other impetus / Is Numb – and Vitalless . . .': this isn't great poetry, but it is immediately intelligible and uncontroversial as an account of an emotion not exactly new but seldom notated.

Dickinson was perfectly aware of the difficulty implicit in accurate expression of emotion. 314 draws a contrast between dumb nature and even more mute humanity: dumb nature cannot conceal its calamities, but man is stifled despite his intrinsic capability:

> Nature – sometimes sears a Sapling –
> Sometimes – scalps a Tree –
> Her Green People recollect it
> When they do not die –
>
> Fainter Leaves – to Further Seasons –
> Dumbly testify –
> We – who have the Souls –
> Die oftener – Not so vitally –

The emotions, of course, are volatile and subjective, and introspection, as Gilbert Ryle has said, is no guarantee of Cartesian clear and distinct perception – hence poetry's preference for the primary colours. It takes a great poet, like Dickinson, to write about depression, as she does in 430:

> When – suddenly – my Riches shrank –
> A Goblin – drank my Dew –
> My Palaces – dropped tenantless –
> Myself – was beggared – too –
>
> I clutched at sounds –
> I groped at shapes –
> I touched the tops of Films –

> I felt the Wilderness roll back
> Along my Golden lines –
>
> The Sackcloth – hangs upon the nail –
> The Frock I used to wear –
> But where my moment of Brocade –
> My – drop – of India?

There is some undeniable weakness in the writing here – the fairy-tale props and imagery of goblins, palaces and beggars – but Dickinson nevertheless conveys the sudden absoluteness with which depression falls. Another strength of her presentation is that the term 'depression' isn't once mentioned, probably because it wasn't current at the time, about 1862. According to the *OED*, 'depression of spirits' is the preferred formula before 1862. The first modern usage of 'depression' on its own in the *OED* is *Daniel Deronda* (1876): 'He found her in a state of deep depression, overmastered by those distasteful miserable memories.'

The poem begins with the enigmatic but confident pronouncement that 'It would never be Common', which expansively metamorphoses into the assertion that 'that old sort – was done'. In effect, this unnamed unspecified 'It' broods, therefore, over the poem's catalogue of recovered joys. It creates suspense in the interstices of celebration. By the poem's end, the initial prognosis has been thrown into reverse: the prediction was that 'It', still undescribed, would occur only rarely or not at all; that if 'It' did reappear, its ability to incapacitate would be weakened by all the years of bliss:

> Such bliss – had I – for all the years –
> 'Twoud give an Easier – pain –

But when it *does* arrive, this 'Easier – pain' is not merely a diversification in a life essentially joyous. On the contrary, the extended period of happiness is itself diminished and dwindles to 'my moment of Brocade – / My – drop – of India'. Here, in the concluding oxymorons, Dickinson dramatizes the swiftness and the scope of the shrinkage: a 'moment' seems more than a 'drop' just as 'brocade' seems less lavish than 'India'. By the last line, the intensity of contrast is at the maximum, eked even smaller by the almost faltering punctuation. India is wonderfully laconic hyperbole and successfully supplants the stale Cinderella myth which appears to be the poem's metaphorical starting point.

In *Middlemarch*, Harriet Bulstrode discovers her husband's moral disgrace by degrees. Lydgate turns aside her inquiry. Her friend, Mrs Hackbutt, hints at something in her manner. A subsequent visit to Selina Plymdale produces nothing definite, but an unfocused dismay is conveyed by something occult in Selina's manner. Finally her brother tells her everything. Harriet Bulstrode's reaction is to change her manner of dress to something plainer, nearer mourning. From an accumulating apprehension, then, to revelation: 'That moment was perhaps worse than any which came after,' writes George Eliot. Some similar gradualist scenario underpins 1,277's account of a deferred but inevitable tragedy:

> While we were fearing it, it came –
> But came with less of fear
> Because that fearing it so long
> Had almost made it fair –
>
> There is a Fitting – a Dismay –
> A Fitting – a Despair –
> 'Tis harder knowing it is Due
> Than knowing it is Here.
>
> The Trying on the Utmost
> The Morning it is new
> Is Terribler than wearing it
> A whole existence through.

What makes this such a powerful account of tragedy is that the word 'tragedy' is never used. The dress-making imagery gives the sense that, while things have gone wrong, the wrongness is tailor-made for the particular person. The sense that the fittings are unsatisfactory – 'a Dismay', and then 'a Despair' – doesn't quite eliminate the suspicion that a personal tragedy, not something off-the-peg and accidental, is being perfectly made. Behind everything, too, is a terrible, authentic sense of impotence – which is inseparable from tragedy and tailors, as Dickinson's source, *Great Expectations*, comically records: 'Probably every new and eagerly expected garment ever put on since clothes came in, fell a trifle short of the wearer's expectation. But after I had my new suit on, some half an hour, and had gone through an immensity of posturing with Mr Pumblechook's very limited dressing glass, in a futile endeavour to see my legs, it seemed to fit me better.'

And then there is the poem's poisoned consolation – that you will get used to the tragedy because it will last your entire life. The human capacity for accommodation, even to the most terrible circumstances, has never been more graphically evoked.

Dickinson is, in her way, an expert on the accommodation of pain and suffering. She is a deft analyst of survival modes in extreme circumstances. Take 650: 'Pain has an element of blank.' Take 599:

> There is a pain – so utter –
> It swallows substance up –
> Then covers the Abyss with Trance –
> So Memory can step
> Around – across – upon it –
> As one within a Swoon –
> Goes safely – where an open eye –
> Would drop Him – Bone by Bone

Is there a better account of trauma and its burial in the subconscious, of involuntary strategic amnesia and clinical repression? Unsystematic, of course, yet Dickinson has a great psychological talent and an unapproachably unique gift for formulation. Her behaviour myths are manifestly true *and* memorably expressed.

'So Memory can step / Around – across – upon it – / As one within a Swoon': how difficult it is to read these lines without recalling Sasha Jensen's glazed anomie and drained reminiscence: 'He has a ticket tied round his wrist because he died.' Another piece of poetic case law, less powerfully expressed, again recognizable as instinctive protective behaviour, occurs in 859:

> A doubt if it be Us
> Assists the staggering Mind
> In an extreme Anguish
> Until it footing find.

The divided self can be both strategy and affliction. In Rhys's Sasha Jensen, strategy and affliction are inseparably confused. At the end of *Good Morning, Midnight*, she shows us classic self-destructive alcoholic behaviour as Sasha drives off the man with whom she wants to spend the night: 'Who is this crying? The same one who laughed on the landing, kissed him and was happy. This is me, this is myself, who is crying. The other – how do I know who the other is? She isn't me.' In fact, everyone, not only alcoholics, knows behaviour which is designed to conclude difficult situations rather than solve them in our own interests. Human beings are drawn to extreme resolutions, as Yeats notes in *The Countess Cathleen*: when the people sell their souls to the devil, the first merchant explains that some do it 'because there is a kind of joy / In casting hope away, in losing joy'. Not *perversity*, merely normal perversity and heightened contrariness.

Melancholia is a common subject in nineteenth-century poetry, but depression makes its debut in Dickinson's poetry. Pathology proves an attractive subject to Tennyson in *Maud* and to Browning in 'Porphyria's Lover', but neurosis and nerves are discovered for literature by Dickinson. We think of Eliot's 'A Game of Chess' – 'My nerves are bad to-night. Yes, bad. Stay with me.' – as the *locus classicus* in English poetry, though neurotics are common enough in French poetry, from Baudelaire

94

to Laforgue. However, Dickinson has some claim to the role of originator: 'The Nerves sit ceremonious, like Tombs'; 'The glittering Retinue of Nerves' (786); 'I laughed a crumbling Laugh' (609). In 1861, when she was thirty, Dickinson developed a neurosis which eventually confined her to the house. This is how she describes it to Higginson (25 April 1862): 'I had a terror – since September – I could tell to none – '. Though one can't be sure, the letters show not a sudden affliction but an insidious growth of agoraphobia, a condition whose panic attacks aren't always consistent or, initially, uncontrollable. The agoraphobia began, I believe, as early as 1853. This is a letter written when the railroad, in which her father was a major investor, came to Amherst with a grand opening ceremony: 'I sat in Prof Tyler's woods and saw the train move off, and then ran home for fear somebody would see me, or ask me how I did.' On 15 January 1854, seven months later, she writes to Susan Gilbert, the wife-to-be of her elder brother Austin: 'I'm just from meeting, Susie, and as I sorely feared, my "life" was made a "victim".' On her way to church, she is subject to fluctuating panic until she can reach the comparative safety of her seat:

> I walked – I ran – I turned precarious corners – One moment I was not – then soared aloft like Phoenix, soon as the foe was by – and then anticipating an enemy again, my soiled and drooping plumage might have been seen emerging from behind a fence, vainly endeavouring to fly once more from hence. I reached the steps, dear Susie – I smiled to think of me, and my geometry, during the journey there – It would have puzzled Euclid, and it's doubtful result, have solemnized a Day. How big and broad the aisle seemed, full huge enough before, as I quaked slowly up – and reached my usual seat!

Although she manages to calm herself 'during the exercises' and gets out of church 'quite comfortably', once outside the situation deteriorates: 'Several roared around, and, sought to devour me, but I fell easy prey to Miss Lovina Dickinson, being much too exhausted to make any further resistance.' Six months later, in July 1854, her solution is one of avoidance and she writes to Abiah Root: 'I thank you Abiah, but I don't go from home, unless emergency leads me by the hand, and then I do it obstinately, and draw back if I can.' These early symptoms, however, need reconciling with her assertion to Higginson that she 'had a terror' *in September of 1861.*

A few years of strategic avoidance of situations likely to trigger attacks of agoraphobia probably lulled her into the belief that she was immune. Indeed, it is quite possible that she tested herself and the particular circumstances allowed her to remain stable – only to find in September 1861 that other circumstances triggered a massive attack of agoraphobia, a Terror much worse than anything she had ever experienced before. Thereafter, she was housebound. She continued to see some people, including strangers like Higginson. Higginson inquired about her 'shunning men and women' and she replied: 'they talk of Hallowed things, aloud – and embarrass my dog'. The 'talk of Hallowed things' which she wanted to avoid at all costs was probably endless discussion and analysis of her phobic condition. She herself felt free, nevertheless, to explore her neurosis in a poem (327):

Before I got my eye put out
I liked as well to see –
As other Creatures, that have eyes
And know no other way –

But were it told to me – Today –
That I might have the sky
For mine – I tell you that my Heart
Would split, for size of me –

The Meadows – mine –
The Mountains – mine –
All Forests – Stintless Stars –

As much of Noon as I could take
Between my finite eyes –

The Motions of the Dipping Birds –
The Morning's Amber Road –
For mine – to look at when I liked –
The News would strike me dead –

So safer – guess – with just my soul
Upon the Window pane –
Where other Creatures put their eyes –
Incautious – of the Sun –

Though often read as a love poem spoken by someone tragically hurt by her experience with 'the sun', someone for whom a successful love affair would be equivalent to ownership of the world, I think the blinding is also a metaphor for her crippling phobia.

The absoluteness of 'Before I got my eye put out', the sense that the disablement is permanent, applies equally well to miscarried love and to her confining phobia. And once more the element of finality and the unexplained in 'Before I got my eye put out' reminds one of Jean Rhys: 'You are walking along a road peacefully. You trip. You fall into blackness. That's the past – or perhaps the future. And you know that there is no past, no future, there is only this blackness, changing faintly, slowly, but always the same.'

Another poem addresses the subject of her phobia as it affected her meetings even with her loved ones. It is 398:

I had not minded – Walls –
Were Universe – one Rock –
And far I heard his silver Call
The other side the Block –

I'd tunnel – till my Groove
Pushed sudden thro' to his –

97

> Then my face take her Recompense –
> The looking in his Eyes –
>
> But 'tis a single Hair –
> A filament – a law –
> A Cobweb – wove in Adamant –
> A Battlement of – Straw –
>
> A limit like the Veil
> Unto the Lady's face –
> But every Mesh – a Citadel –
> And Dragons – in the Crease –

What is the obstacle preventing her from looking at her loved one? What is the 'limit like the Veil'? The most plausible reading is that the poem attempts to encapsulate the inexplicable but immovable prohibitions of neurosis. We know that, on occasion, Dickinson was unable to see Bowles. At least once, Bowles was successfully impatient of an interview conducted from the top of the stairs. As a subject, phobia disappears from view, though not from real life, until it reappears in Virginia Woolf's *The Waves*, where Rhoda is given her creator's own irrational behavioural tic. In *A Writer's Diary* for 30 September 1926, Virginia Woolf recalls: 'as a child – couldn't step across a puddle once, I remember, for thinking how strange – what am I? etc. But by writing I don't reach anything. All I mean to make is a note of a curious state of mind.' Like Dickinson, Woolf is engaged in the task of cataloguing curious states of mind. Thus Rhoda in *The Waves*: 'Also, in the middle, cadaverous, awful, lay the grey puddle in the courtyard, when, holding an envelope in my hand, I carried a message. I came to the puddle. I could not cross it. Identity failed me. We are nothing, I said, and fell.'

These interior, fluttered, abysmal sensations plague everyone. We learn, if we are lucky, to stave off their tyrannies. Elizabeth Bishop's poem 'Man-Moth' is another example of this terrorized but nervously intrepid inner self. 'But what the Man-Moth fears most he must do.' Bishop is one writer who not only read Dickinson but was also influenced by her. 'The Weed' takes as its donnée Dickinson's insight that 'After great pain, a formal feeling comes – / The Nerves sit ceremonious, like Tombs – / The stiff Heart questions . . .' Bishop's 'The Weed' begins with the same funereal numbness and the same stiff heart:

> I dreamed that dead, and meditating,
> I lay upon a grave, or bed,
> (at least, some cold and close-built bower).
> In the cold heart, its final thought
> stood frozen, drawn immense and clear,
> stiff and idle as I was there . . .

These parallels demonstrate Dickinson's anomalous placing among the Victorians. Eliot, Woolf, Bishop and Rhys are truer contemporaries. Like them, Dickinson was fully aware of the magnitude of her task and its particular difficulties. She was not, *pace* Larkin, a Grandma Moses figure. She was self-conscious. To set up as a poetic electroencephalograph registering the delicate voltage of brain waves was something she, like other writers, knew to be fraught with difficulty. Writing to Higginson about the worth of her poetry, for instance, she adumbrates Ryle's idea of introspection: 'Are you too deeply occupied to say if my Verse is alive? // The Mind is so near itself – it cannot see, distinctly . . .' In spite of this intrinsic difficulty, Dickinson is a great, gifted and precise cartographer of the human soul.

When in January 1856 the family moved house, she left this account of the difficulty and triumph of self-consciousness: 'I took at the time a memorandum of my several senses, and also of my hat and coat, and my best shoes – but it was lost in the *mêlée*, and I am out with the lanterns, looking for myself.' Thus far her account of everything gone to scatteration, to use Twain's coinage. She continues: 'Such wits as I reserved, are so badly shattered that repair is useless – and still I can't help laughing at my own catastrophe. I supposed we were going to make a "transit", as heavenly bodies did – but we came budget by budget, as our fellows do, till we fulfilled the pantomime contained in the word "moved".' At this juncture, Dickinson identifies the fugitive feeling which had gone missing: 'It is a kind of *gone-to-Kansas* feeling, and if I sat in a long wagon, with my family tied behind, I should suppose without doubt I was a party of emigrants!'

Modern, then; ahead of her time. In another sense, however, she is of her time. Any writer of importance and originality is bound to be, as it were, a borderline case – with progenitors and an originality manifesting itself as literary influence in the future. All writing of any significance is influenced and influential. Yet, here again, Dickinson is exceptional. Her influence is belated by the problematic publication history of her work. Rather than influence, we tend to find coincidence of temperament. In Jean Rhys, we encounter sadness overwhelming everything: 'And it can be sad, the sun in the afternoon, can't it? Yes, it can be sad, the afternoon sun, sad and frightening.' In Dickinson, too, afternoons can be sad and frightening:

> There's a certain Slant of light,
> Winter Afternoons –
> That oppresses, like the Heft
> Of Cathedral Tunes –
>
> Heavenly Hurt, it gives us –
> We can find no scar,
> But internal difference,
> Where the Meanings, are –

It is the interior, the darkest interior, which counts. The outside reality counts, too, of course, but the interior counts more. 411 contrasts the external grave with the internal grave.

> The Color of the Grave is Green –
> The Outer Grave – I mean –
> You would not know it from the Field –
> Except it own a Stone –
>
> To help the fond – to find it –
> Too infinite asleep

To stop and tell them where it is –
But just a Daisy – deep –

The Color of the Grave is white –
The outer Grave – I mean –
You would not know it from the Drifts –
In Winter – till the Sun –

Has furrowed out the Aisles –
Then – higher than the Land
The little Dwelling Houses rise
Where each – has left a friend –

The Color of the Grave within –
The Duplicate – I mean –
Not all the Snows could make it white –
Not all the Summers – Green –

You've seen the Color – maybe –
Upon a Bonnet bound –
When that you met with it before –
The Ferret – cannot find –

The tone of this poem has something of the quality of a first
reader – a determined simplicity reinforced by the repeated
pedantry of 'The outer Grave – I mean'. Two terrible touches
transport us beyond the flat clarities on offer: 'just a Daisy –
deep' isn't deep and wishes an invasive intimacy on us; the other
touch is 'The Ferret', an animal acutely contrasted with the
childlike diction of the verse. The 'Grave within' is at first
ambiguous: we think initially that Dickinson means the grave
under the soil which doesn't modify with the seasons, as we
have been shown the 'Outer Grave' does. In fact, she means 'the
Duplicate', the mental burial place. It is the black of mourning
crêpe. It is grief – a grief which is eternally fresh, eternally newly
encountered, never familiar.

This is deceptive in its simplicities of tone. As are 87's laconic
four lines on death and mourning:

A darting fear – a pomp – a tear –
A waking on a morn
To find that what one waked for,
Inhales the different dawn.

It is a terse, swift masterpiece – at once controlled and head-long. In form, a near-perfect rhyming quatrain and, initially, almost callous in its *notation* of grief's strange blanknesses. The first line evokes the onset of illness ('a darting fear'), the funeral ('pomp') and mourning ('a tear') in near-recipe form. It is per-functory but this proves to be the shocking perfunctoriness of death. Without antibiotics, death could be implacably brusque. Even in 1931 Arnold Bennett died of typhoid after drinking the water in a Paris hotel to prove it was safe. Here, the real subject is the profound after-shock of a grief which makes life meaningless. In the last three lines, sorrow comes into focus finally. The indefinite articles of the first line continue half automatically into the second, so that everything seems dis-tanced and innocuous enough. It is, apparently, any morning. And the third line disguises its import, its poison, by substitut-ing 'what' for 'whom'. 'What one waked for' could be almost anything from breakfast cereal to a longed-for letter in the post. With the last line the damage is done, massively inflicted. The verb 'inhales' means that 'what one waked for' can only be a person. And the first definite article is so definite as to be irrevocable – 'the different dawn'. We turn towards our loved one out of sleep – and find her gone. Like Mr Ramsay in *To the Lighthouse*: 'Mrs Ramsay having died rather suddenly the night before, he stretched his arms out. They remained empty.'

There is a story by Kipling, 'The Gardener', in which the heroine conceals almost from herself the truth – which is that her nephew is in fact her illegitimate son. She brings him up with their true relationship unacknowledged. When he is killed at Ypres, her grief, the imperious inner force, has to be con-trolled. Dickinson knew the stresses of such deception, or at least could imagine them, as she records in 734:

If He were living – dare I ask –
And how if He be dead –
And so around the Words I went –
Of meeting them – afraid –

I hinted Changes – Lapse of Time –
The Surfaces of Years –
I touched with Caution – lest they crack –
And show me to my fears –

Reverted to adjoining Lives –
Adroitly turning out
Wherever I suspected Graves –
'Twas prudenter – I thought –

And He – I pushed – with sudden force –
In face of the Suspense –
'Was buried' – 'Buried'! 'He!'
My Life just holds the Trench –

The situation here is Hardyesque in the ironic discrepancy between the internal devastation and the necessary exterior control. It is impossible to trace this situation back to any specific autobiographical event. But it is clear that Dickinson was drawn to the psychology of deception – the need for caution, underpinned by reluctance to hear the worst, only to yield to impulse at the last. 'I pushed – with sudden force – / In face of the Suspense.' Another poem (272) begins in the same kind of territory. 'I breathed enough to take the trick', it starts. Catastrophe at the card table.

*Good Morning, Midnight* provides a strangely apt parallel. Sasha Jensen has met a fat man in a bar. He says: 'Life is too awful. Do you know that story about the man who loved a woman who was married to somebody else, and she fell ill? And he didn't dare go and ask about her because the husband suspected her and hated him. So he just hung about the house and watched. And all the time he couldn't make up his mind whether he'd be a coward if he went and asked to see her or whether he'd be a coward if he didn't. And then one day he went and asked, and she was dead. Doesn't that make you laugh?' It is possible that Jean Rhys got the idea from Dickinson's poem, which was published in 1929 in *Further Poems of Emily Dickinson* edited by Martha Dickinson Bianchi, the same volume in which 'Good Morning, Midnight' first appeared. There is a kind of acknowledgement in the fat man's conclusion: 'That's an old story, but doesn't it make you laugh? It might be true, that story, mightn't it?'

Emily Dickinson's *Letters* tell us clearly enough whom among her contemporaries Emily Dickinson admired – George Eliot, the Brownings, Dickens, Tennyson and the Brontë sisters. Shakespeare, Milton and the Bible are also frequently mentioned or alluded to in the letters.

Two things explain the traffic between the Brontës and Dickinson. She was subject to powerful emotion and drawn to it as subject matter. She could encompass what Sir Walter Scott called the 'Big Bow-wow', an aptitude for passion he felt was beyond the range of Jane Austen. Charlotte Brontë agreed. Reading *Pride and Prejudice*, she acidly adjudicated: 'an accurate daguerreotyped portrait of a commonplace face'. The Brontës were Dickinson's beloved 'Yorkshire girls', role models and literary idols, reread into intimacy. *Jane Eyre* and *Wuthering Heights* are romantic pattern books for her – of imagery, incident and attitude. The fierce exclusiveness, the almost cruel elementalism of love which we find in Cathy's cry to Nelly Dean – 'my love for Heathcliff resembles the eternal rocks beneath: a source of little visible delight, but necessary' – is reproduced faithfully in Dickinson: 'Alter! When the Hills do – / Falter! When the Sun / Question if His Glory / Be the Perfect One – '. Time and again, Dickinson hits the top note of rich romanticism, purified of any dark, ironic colours: 'Where Thou art – that – is Home— / Cashmere – or Calvary – the same – '.

Were that note predominant, it would eventually prove wearisome – in principle, at least. In practice, the linguistic gifts carry their own conviction: consider the perfect, laconic alliteration of 'Cashmere – or Calvary – '. Still, with so much displayed sentiment, it is refreshing to note her frequent unsentimentalities. She once said that she 'sang from Charnel steps'. There are heartbreaking poems, piercing elegies in the canon. There is also this cool, true observation of how quickly the dead leave no trace. They are gone. And that is that. Dickinson could be very tough:

> As Sleigh Bells seem in summer
> Or Bees, at Christmas show –
> So fairy – so fictitious
> The individuals do
> Repealed from observation – [i.e., dead]
> A Party that we knew –
> More distant in an instant
> Than Dawn in Timbuctoo.

The linguistic genius here is in the 'ugliest' line: 'more distant in an instant', with its syncopated sound of *an, in, an, in, an* – a prestidigitation that transforms 'distant' into 'instant' almost before you can blink. Just as the dead are swallowed swiftly away.

The emotional assumptions Dickinson shares with the Brontës centre on the imperious, anarchic centrality of romantic love, accompanied by a frequent contempt for the traffic of ordinary existence. This temperament is fundamentally at one with the reckless exultation of Marina Tsvetayeva, who, in a poem about Joan of Arc (and herself), wrote: 'The transcript of the trial is theirs. / The pyre is mine'. It was Tsvetayeva, too, who wailed, a martyr to the disproportion between her feelings and the world, 'What shall I do . . . with all this immensity in a measured world?'

'All overgrown by cunning moss' is a poem about the grave of Currer Bell, Charlotte Brontë. And *Jane Eyre* is the source for at least two of Emily Dickinson's poems, 'The Soul has Bandaged moments' (512) and 'A still – Volcano – Life' (601).

> The Soul has Bandaged moments –
> When too appalled to stir –
> She feels some ghastly Fright come up
> And stop to look at her –
>
> Salute her – with long fingers –
> Caress her freezing hair –
> Sip, Goblin, from the very lips
> The Lover – hovered – o'er

Charlotte Brontë cannot match the opening line, 'The Soul has Bandaged moments', but the next seven lines owe everything – perhaps too much – to this passage from *Jane Eyre*: 'A dream had scarcely approached my ear, when it fled affrighted, scared by a marrow-freezing incident, enough. This was a demoniac laugh – low, suppressed, deep-uttered, as it seemed, at the very key-hole of my chamber door. The head of my bed was near the door, and I thought at first the goblin-laughter stood at my bedside – or rather, crouched by my pillow . . .'

601 completely re-imagines and transfigures the essentially stock image of the volcano as we find it in *Jane Eyre*: 'To live for me, Jane,' says Rochester, 'is to stand on a crater-crust which may crack and spew out fire any day.' A little earlier in the novel, Jane herself feels as if she 'had been wandering amongst volcanic-looking hills, and had suddenly felt the ground quiver, and seen it gape'. In 601, Dickinson is less concerned with hyperbole than with invisible, repressed passion. And the volcanic activity she so vividly imagines is quietly lethal rather than showily pyrotechnic:

> A still – Volcano – Life –
> That flickered in the night –
> When it was dark enough to do
> Without erasing sight –
>
> A quiet – Earthquake Style –
> Too subtle to suspect

By natures this side Naples –
The North cannot detect

The Solemn – Torrid – Symbol –
The lips that never lie –
Whose hissing Corals part – and shut –
And Cities – ooze away –

Charlotte Brontë's volcano is a cliché. Dickinson's is vividly placed before us – the more so because she dispenses with its fretful and bellicose eructations, giving us instead a pair of lips and three deliberately sober verbs, 'part', 'shut' and 'ooze', of which the last is granted an almost transitive force by the context.

In 640, the famous 'I cannot live with You – ', a poem which argues that the greatest passion cannot permit itself the wear-and-tear of ordinary intercourse, Dickinson borrows from *Wuthering Heights* the idea of a human passion so great that it usurps even the love of God:

> Nor could I rise – with You –
> Because Your Face
> Would put out Jesus' –
> That New Grace
>
> Glow plain – and foreign
> On my homesick Eye –

If you can detect the faint noise of something clearing its throat as a way of attracting attention, it is this passage from *Wuthering Heights*: 'I was only going to say,' says Cathy, 'that heaven did not seem to be my home; and I broke my heart with weeping to come back to earth; and the angels were so angry that they flung me out into the middle of the heath on the top of Wuthering Heights; where I woke sobbing for joy.'

Robert and Elizabeth Barrett Browning leave their trace elements and Tennyson's lyric 'Go not, happy day', from *Maud,*

surely lies behind 72's 'Glowing is her Bonnet, / Glowing is her
Cheek, / Glowing is her Kirtle, / Yet she cannot speak.' Think
of the euphoric narrator in Tennyson babbling away: 'Rosy is
the West, / Rosy is the South, / Roses are her cheeks, / And a
rose her mouth . . .' Neither Tennyson nor the Brownings is a
particular surprise, but Edgar Allan Poe is – if only because, in
her letters, Dickinson refers only once to Poe, confessing her
ignorance: 'Of Poe, I know too little to think.' All the same,
414, ''Twas like a Maelstrom, with a notch', clearly owes its
central image of threat and last-minute reprieve to Poe's 'A
Descent into the Maelstrom' – though that extraordinary telling
'notch' is Dickinson's own incomparable addition to her source.
Equally clearly, 'William Wilson', Poe's story of self-haunting, is
the template behind 670, 'One need not be a Chamber – to be
Haunted'. In Poe's tale, the profligate hero is dogged through
life by a person with the same name, but who otherwise
resembles him not at all. This other William Wilson speaks
always in a whisper – and the whisper is an exact replica of the
hero's voice. The whisper is, of course, the voice of Wilson's
conscience, but Poe's ploy is to externalize this better self – so
that, for example, the better self exposes Wilson when he is
cheating at cards at Oxford. Finally, Wilson challenges the
whisperer to a duel and runs him through in an antechamber to
a ballroom in Rome. At first, Wilson thinks his bloody antag-
onist is his own reflection in a previously unseen mirror, but the
other Wilson, by now completely identical, is dying on the floor,
with these final words: 'How utterly thou hast murdered thyself.'
Poe's story is one of his better tales and is also the source for
Kipling's story 'The Dream of Duncan Parrenness'. But 'William
Wilson' *is* Gothic and Dickinson's poem is explicitly contemptuous of the Gothic and its props – the assassin hidden in the
apartment, the gallop through an abbey at night. What frightens
Dickinson isn't conscience either:

> Ourself behind ourself, concealed –
> Should startle most –

And the denouement of 670 is the contrast between the reaction to a physical threat, which is to take up a weapon ('The Body – borrows a Revolver – '), and the impossibility of knowing how to behave when confronted by a self 'behind ourself':

> He bolts the door –
> O'erlooking a superior specter –

One thinks perhaps of R. D. Laing's *The Divided Self*, of schizophrenia *avant la lettre*, of identity and its frail illusion of stability, of the terrible possible selves in all of us. The well-read paleface has adapted Poe's essentially polite horror to something more queasily disturbing, redskin and primitive.

Nothing is lifted without being set down again in a slightly better light. If she pilfers, she polishes. Take, for example, the concluding paragraph of Chapter 11 of *Dombey and Son*: 'He sat, with folded hands, upon his pedestal, silently listening. But he might have answered "weary, weary! very lonely, very sad!" And there, with an aching void in his young heart, and all outside so cold, and bare, and strange, Paul sat as if he had taken life unfurnished, and the upholsterer were never coming.' That 'aching void' is a little vacuous and there is a coarse reminiscence of Tennyson's 'Mariana' in that slightly null anthology of adjectives, 'weary, weary! very lonely, very sad!' And we can see Dickens dickering about and going to some lengths to arrange his image satisfactorily – *posing* the metaphor. To get from inner misery to its objective correlative, unfurnished rooms, Dickens constructs a little causeway of adjectives designed to apply to either – 'cold', 'bare', 'strange'. Then there is the actual awkward moment of introduction – 'as if he had taken life unfurnished' – where the discrepancy between tenor and vehicle, notwithstanding that causeway, is all too evident. 'Life' is too grandly abstract for the offered concrete equivalent of unfurnished rooms. Dr Johnson's objection to the metaphysical conceit applies here – things too dissimilar have been yoked by violence together. Only Dickens's final flourish brings it off – the absent upholsterer carries the reader unresistingly away from the moment of comparison into the particularity of the image.

Dickinson's version of the Dickens occurs in 393 – condensed to four words which are all the more powerful for being utterly unexpected and unprepared for. 393 is a poem in which she compares the exalted emotional moment with the synthetic high produced by narcotics:

> Did Our Best Moment last –
> 'Twould supersede the Heaven –
> A few – and they by Risk – procure –
> So this Sort – are not given –
>
> Except as stimulants – in
> Cases of Despair –
> Or Stupor – The Reserve –
> These Heavenly Moments are –
>
> A Grant of the Divine –
> That Certain as it comes –
> Withdraws – and leaves the dazzled Soul
> In her unfurnished Rooms.

Four words of bleak finality, awesome in their obliteration of joy.

'Immature poets imitate; mature poets steal,' wrote Eliot in his essay on Massinger. 'The good poet welds his theft into a whole of feeling which is unique, utterly different from that from which it was torn.' Misery is Dickens's subject as it is Dickinson's, but her poem is a different 'whole of feeling' because it is about the suddenness of sadness and because it has shed Dickens's undertow of humour.

These literary sources complicate our view of Dickinson. We should be guarded in our assumptions about her biography since there is little known with complete certainty. More, there are several poems which are clearly voiced for speakers other than herself. 631 has one married girl addressing another dead girl married on the same day ('Ourselves were wed one summer – dear – '); 588 is spoken by a dead child; 538 is spoken by another corpse, possibly a child, too, since the content is naive pleas for the forgiveness of those who 'shut me in the Cold'; 518 is voiced for a man whose bride has died soon after marriage and has a thoughtfully real sense of the woman's physical solidity in the first line: 'Her sweet Weight on my Heart a Night / Had scarcely deigned to lie – '; 493 is spoken by a newly married woman: 'The World – stands – solemner – to me – / Since I was wed – to Him – '. 467 is spoken by dead children and is remarkable for the unbearably painful, naive callousness of the children, who dislike their gloomy adult visitors and so keep their distance; 461 equates death and loss of virginity: 'A Wife – at Daybreak I shall be – '; 445 begins ''Twas just this time, last year, I died' and catalogues a child's memories: 'I wondered which would miss me, least'; 389 is young male again and innocently hard in the use of 'it':

> Somebody flings a Mattress out –
> The Children hurry by –
> They wonder if it died – on that –
> I used to – when a Boy –

158 is the wail of someone dying quite young: 'Dying! Dying in the Night!':

> Somebody run to the great gate
> And see if Dollie's coming! Wait!
> I hear her feet upon the stair!
> Death won't hurt – now Dollie's here!

215 has a boy wondering about life after death: 'Do they wear "new shoes" – in "Eden" – '.

In his essay on Dickinson, Tom Paulin misreads her great poem 'I never lost as much but twice' as addressed to a lover and as protesting 'against the dominant masculine values of

nineteenth-century American culture'. In fact, it is addressed to
God and voiced for a bereaved mother:

> I never lost as much but twice,
> And that was in the sod.
> Twice have I stood a beggar
> Before the door of God!
>
> Angels – twice descending
> Reimbursed my store –
> Burglar! Banker – Father!
> I am poor once more!

The Lord giveth (Banker) and the Lord taketh away (Burglar).
Even this anthology of dramatis personae shows Dickinson's
addiction to the bizarre end of the psychological spectrum, her
determination to record unflinchingly the blunt and the callous.
'They wonder if it died – on that – ' She was drawn to the
unpredictable and the thought which is unsayable. Though
famous for telling things slant, Dickinson should be equally
renowned for telling things straight. 561: 'I measure every Grief
I meet'; 887: 'We outgrow love, like other things'; 856: 'There
is a finished feeling / Experienced at Graves'; 241: 'I like a look
of Agony'.

At her best, even Dickinson's treatment of emotions in the
higher register effortlessly escapes the Brontës' mechanical duali-
ties – foliage versus the eternal rocks beneath; horse-trough versus
sea; oak tree and flower pot. Poem 754 is a classic of originality,
what Larkin called 'romantic love in a nutshell', and begins:

> My Life had stood – a Loaded Gun –
> In Corners – till a Day
> The Owner passed – identified –
> And carried Me away –

The difficulty for the romantic poet is to find an effective means
of expression. Charlotte Brontë, for instance, fails continually,

as does Emily Brontë, often in the same way. This is Jane Eyre on learning that Rochester has a living wife by a previous marriage: 'My nerves vibrated to those low-spoken words as they had never vibrated to thunder – my blood felt their subtle violence as it had never felt frost or fire.' This is Cathy drawing a distinction between Heathcliff and Edgar Linton: 'Whatever our souls are made of, his and mine are the same; and Linton's is as different as a moonbeam from lightning, or frost from fire.' Clearly, both sisters have drawn the standard allowance of frost and fire from stores.

Though Dickinson could be terse, her preferred mode was one of extended invention, a swift and lucid multiplication, of sustained fantasy. Her gift for fantasy looks back to Dickens and ahead to Disney, comparable geniuses both. While it is possible to pinpoint a couple of poems influenced by Words-worth (804, 742) and several which seem co-authored by the Brownings in their intimate, exalted mode (for instance, 275's 'Doubt me! My Dim Companion', 268's 'Me, change! Me, alter!' or 704's give-away sense of the body warmth of an interlocutor which is so Browningesque: 'No matter – now – Sweet'), it is true to say that Dickens is a more pervasive and important presence in her poetry. We've already noted the debt to *Dombey and Son*. The letters show more than a scattering of direct references. They show the tribute of imitation – direct copying. David Copperfield's distracted musings in church about Dora are made over, twice, to Susan Gilbert. Dickens's techniques of vigorous cartoon animation are also mastered in a more general way. It is surely the Inimitable who is being imitated in this sally of 7 May 1850: 'Twin loaves of bread have just been born into the world under my auspices – fine children – the image of their *mother*. . .' She can reproduce Dickens's compulsion to energize the inanimate in a way that anticipates Disney's version of 'The Sorcerer's Apprentice' in *Fantasia*: alone in the house in March 1859, she writes, whim-sically paradoxical, that she has no cause to complain: 'Of course one can't expect one's furniture to sit still all night, and if the Chairs do prance – and the Lounge polka a little, and the shovel give it's arm to the tongs, one don't mind such things!'

As a poet of last things, her greatness lies in her almost indecorous accuracy. She was early suspicious of poetry consisting entirely of sonorous organ chords in a minor key. There had to be room for lucidity, wit, melody, invention and charm. Here she is in 1854, writing to her brother about his poetry: 'I have had some things from you, to which I perceived no meaning. They were either very vast, or they didn't mean anything. I don't know certainly which.' The poet of last things, then, was a severe critic of opacity, an advocate of embroidery as well as of contemplation of the needle's eye. In 391, these two impulses come wonderfully together. In the letter about the prancing furniture already quoted, Dickinson also says: 'I am somewhat afraid at night, but the Ghosts have been very attentive, and I have no cause to complain.' A humorously intended oxymoron, yet one which is a useful introduction to 391, a poem about a visitation, a dreaming of the dead:

> A Visitor in Marl –
> Who influences Flowers –
> Till they are orderly as Busts –
> And Elegant – as Glass –
>
> Who visits in the Night –
> And just before the Sun –
> Concludes his glistening interview –
> Caresses – and is gone –
>
> But whom his fingers touched –
> And where his feet have run –
> And whatsoever Mouth he kissed –
> Is as it had not been –

The poignancy here is all in the suggestion: does the adjective 'glistening' refer to the bodiless presence, or to the tears in its eyes? And that 'it' in the last line, taken with the rhythmic breakdown, does it refer to the kissing and touching? Or the numb sense of loss in the fingers and the mouth? Or does it mean that it is as if the ghost had *never* been? There is something thrillingly unexpected in the toying with flowers, the arrangement symbolizing care.

And then we realize that 391 is a poem about frost.

Or, rather, *also* a poem about frost, because the return of the dead cannot be fully explained away.

391 shows that the serious and the playful emerge from the same matrix. Unusually among poets, Dickinson shows both sides in her work. Virtually all poets show happiness in their lives, but many are like Lowell, who confessed in his Afterword to *Notebook*, 'In truth I seem to have felt mostly the joys of living; in remembering, in recording, thanks to the gift of the Muse, it is the pain.' In Dickinson, happiness and horror share a family resemblance. In 1883, she wrote to Maria Whitney: 'To have been made alive is so chief a thing, all else inevitably adds. Were it not riddled by partings, it were too divine . . .' This gusto is evident in the sustained anthropomorphized tours de force like 1,405: 'Bees are Black, with Gilt Surcingles – / Buccaneers of Buzz.' Now and then this homocentricity of the imagination can be predictably cute – for instance, 634's Robin, whose complete wardrobe is out of Beatrix Potter. Now and then, too, one can be unpersuaded by the automatic, irreversible direction of the metaphorical arrow, which always humanizes the non-human and sometimes diminishes nature. Nevertheless, these trim, witty transformational cartoons have enduring charm – and if they remind us of Disney, they are no worse for that. Mary de Rachelwiltz remembers in *Indiscretions* being taken to Disney films in Venice by her father, Ezra Pound – who, returning home from the cinema, across the deserted Venetian squares, would imitate Donald Duck and Goofy. Even without this endorsement from the high priest of modernism, it is impossible to resist, say: 'The Day undressed – Herself – / Her Garter – was of Gold' (716) or 737's moon which starts as 'but a Chin of Gold' and ends with the stars as 'Trinkets at Her Belt – / Her Dimities – of Blue'. Can this transformation of early autumn be bettered? 'Summer laid her simple Hat / On its

boundless Shelf – / Unobserved – a Ribbon slipt, / Snatch it for yourself.'

One playfully inclined poem (318) illustrates that Dickinson's fantasy can embody pleasure and pain, modulating from sunrise to sunset:

> I'll tell you how the Sun rose –
> A Ribbon at a time –
> The Steeples swam in Amethyst –
> The news, like Squirrels, ran –
> The Hills untied their Bonnets . . .

The fantasy is confident and one line is touched with genius: 'The Steeples *swam* in Amethyst.' The territory is comic, domestic, delightful. Then the sun sets:

> But how he set – I know not –
> There seemed a purple stile
> That little Yellow boys and girls
> Were climbing all the while –
> Till when they reached the other side,
> A Dominie in Gray –
> Put gently up the evening Bars –
> And led the flock away –

This was the first poem sent by Dickinson to Thomas Higginson for his verdict. It isn't difficult to see why it was chosen. It is playful, inventive, even extravagant, yet controlled and finally serious and touchingly sad. It has everything. No wonder he undervalued it and found it too odd. I am moved by the way the poem suggests, by complete omission, the almost biblical swiftness of life's passing. There is nothing between sunrise and sunset. Hardly time to grow up in – hence the boys and girls being led into school after their brief playtime. Poetically, I am impressed by the modulation from the celebratory to the sombre and even more impressed by the radical nature of the metaphorical transformations, which, though radical, have a completely unforced effect. They *assume* what a metaphysical poet would strenuously argue – the equation of dusk to a dominie, the rays of the sun to children, and so forth.

Dickinson's genius is for emblems, extended fantasies and objective correlatives. On the whole, with some stunning exceptions – 'The clouds – like listless Elephants – ', 'The quiet nonchalance of death – ' – her gifts are not for description in the conventional sense. Evocation is her forte from 1,628's 'Jamaicas of Remembrance stir – ' to the sunset's 'harrowing Iodine' of 673, from 697's 'Odors from St Domingo' to 409's 'They perished in the Seamless Grass – '. A letter of consolation to Perez Cowan, dated October 1869, ends: 'Dying is a wild night and a new road.' In 722, the mountains turn on the poet 'Their far – slow – Violet Gaze – ', a brilliant phrase halfway between evocation and description. Consider, though, the straight description of a cat in 507.

> She sights a Bird – she chuckles –
> She flattens – then she crawls –
> She runs without the look of feet –
> Her eyes increase to Balls –

This poem and other examples of telling it straight explain why Dickinson preferred to tell it slant (1,129) – a poetic mode which deepens metaphor by withholding half of the equation. Weak descriptive powers acquire an extra riddling ingredient. Thus 500 and 1,463 famously portray the humming bird as 'A Route of Evanescence': but they do not describe; they evoke. Likewise 1,034's 'His Bill is an Auger' evokes the woodpecker. The poem is not a description, so much as a recipe composed of clues.

824 is Dickinson's famous poem about the wind. The information isn't slanted, so the poem opens with a bungled, inept simile ('The Wind begun to knead the Grass – / As Women do a Dough') before it scores its sole, direct hit:

> the Dust did scoop itself like Hands –
> And throw away the Road –

It is odd that Dickinson's unslanted, straight *statements* – 'I can wade Grief'; ''Twas the old – road – through pain – ' – should be so much stronger than her straight *description*. But a comparison of 824's direct method with 1,397's indirect method of describing a rain storm, shows the indubitable superiority, for Dickinson, of the indirect way:

> It sounded as if the Streets were running
> And then – the Streets stood still –
> Eclipse – was all we could see at the Window
> And Awe – was all we could feel.
>
> By and by – the boldest stole out of his Covert
> To see if Time was there –
> Nature was in an Opal Apron,
> Mixing fresher Air.

Dickinson's deliberate, consciously indirect aesthetic is embodied in 719:

> A South Wind – has a pathos –
> Of individual Voice –
> As One detect on Landings
> An Emigrant's address.
>
> A Hint of Ports and Peoples –
> And much not understood –
> The fairer – for the farness –
> And for the foreignhood.

*The fairer for the foreignhood.* Here, in essence, is Viktor Skhlovsky's *ostranie*.

Telling things slant piqued her wit and made everything instantly more interesting. It was her *métier*. In early March 1866, she writes of her young nephew: 'Ned tells that the Clock purrs and Kitten ticks. He inherits his Uncle Emily's ardor for the lie.' Nor is it difficult to see the rewards of the technique when one considers a letter of August 1861 to Mrs Samuel Bowles: 'Vinnie would send her love,' the letter concludes, 'but she put on a white frock, and went to meet tomorrow – a few minutes ago. Mother would send her love – but she is in the 'Eave Spout', sweeping up a leaf, that blew in, last November.' How dull this would be if Dickinson said simply that her mother and her nightgowned sister were asleep – and that her mother was snoring.

In 1882, after her mother's death, Dickinson wrote to James D. Clark: 'Her dying feels to me like many kinds of Cold – at times electric, at times benumbing . . .' There is a connoisseurship at work here – the chef tasting his dish to see if the seasoning is right. When in early August 1884, she herself has a funny turn, she reports her symptoms meticulously and in a way that reminds one of Orwell's introductory comments on his wounding in *Homage to Catalonia*: 'The whole experience of being hit by a bullet is very interesting and I think it is worth describing in detail.' Among many poems about dying – the panic, the calm, the nonchalance, the exhaustion, 'Till pleading, round her quiet eyes / The purple Crayons stand' (144) – there are three poems, 465, 462 and 524, which address the subject of death-bed aloneness, as the dying person is suddenly bereft of certainty. Her subject is the falter on the threshold of eternity. Dickinson wishes to capture the blur before death with the maximum clarity. 462 is about the death of a child who repeats to itself the consolations proffered by adults, only to find that fear of hell ('the Instead') is far more powerful, so powerful that the poem goes into first person:

> But – the Instead – the Pinching fear
> That Something – it did do – or dare –
> Offend the Vision – and it flee –
> And They no more remember me –
> Nor ever turn to tell me why –
> Oh, Master, This is Misery –

524 leaves the soul similarly stranded between its two options:

> Departed – to the Judgment –
> A Mighty Afternoon –
> Great Clouds – like Ushers – leaning –
> Creation – looking on –
>
> The Flesh – Surrendered – Cancelled –
> The Bodiless – begun –
> Two Worlds – like Audiences – disperse –
> And leave the Soul – alone –

The idea of limbo is less intended than the idea of abandonment. Abandonment and complete aloneness. No wonder Dickinson said that she 'sang off Charnel steps'.

The celebrated 'I heard a Fly buzz' is a poem about disrupted certainties, about the quietly confident Christian death invaded by the tinnitus of dying as it actually is. The fly is both exterior and interior, a mild distraction and what Dickinson in a later letter called 'a great darkness coming'. What is moving is the attempt of consciousness to control the crisis by charting each abrupt stage. More piercing still is the brave, vain instinctive attempt to locate the disaster outside the self. The mind has a strong instinct for normality. During a total eclipse of the sun, the fall in temperature is large, but the brain registers it as considerably less. Dickinson knows the instinct if not the scientific fact. 'I could not see to see' represents the last bulletin of a consciousness still at its post. This death is told straight and credibly as a sort of surprise.

Another death, told slant, is 712, 'Because I could not stop for Death – '. It is another poem about death as a surprise – this time because it is a slow death, or an illness so long that the sufferer is taken aback when she realizes her illness is going to be fatal:

> We slowly drove – He knew no haste
> And I had put away

> My labor and my leisure too,
> For His Civility –

When the realization finally dawns that 'the Horses' Heads' are 'toward Eternity', time seems for a moment to stop. With shock. But the shock isn't the shock of Wyatt's courtier suddenly, sybaritically confronted with Death – and 'Dazed with dreadful face'. Nor is it the last-second stumble of 'I heard a Fly buzz – '. It is rather the surprise tinged with a sense of foolishness at one's mental slowness on the uptake. Of *course*. One learns from Dickinson to respect the most minute differences. Every death is different.

Some deaths aren't even deaths. 'It was not Death, for I stood up, / And all the Dead, lie down – ' What follows in 510 is an attempt to write up the state of emotional anaesthesia, a state of depression so hopeless that despair seems an improvement, a state of psychological insulation for which there is no precise term – though Dickinson can show us the patient and the patient's feelings. Or lack of them. You could call it heart-death. Graham Greene would call it a burnt-out case. The self-dramatizing Greene has a map of the heart with only two places marked on it, despair and suffering, the capital and the major port. Emily Dickinson has an ordnance survey map which can lead you to villages that exist even if they have no name.

# Fitzgerald's First Hit

*This Side of Paradise*, Scott Fitzgerald's first novel, was, and still is, a surprising bestseller – given the strobe effect of its intermittent narrative, its interpretative difficulties and its uneasy, insecure range of cultural reference. Almost immediately, its popular success created a more considered critical failure. It became a qualified success. There were reservations. Qualifications shaded into disqualifications. 'A Romance and a Reading List', 'derivative', fabricated, full of 'faked references', 'formless' – and these are only the authorial qualifications, Fitzgerald's confident concessions to friends who might otherwise have resented the ostentatious chorus of uncultivated acclaim. Not to mention the bravura display of literary promise. *This Side of Paradise* remains a seriously underrated novel.

The envious Edmund Wilson was the first of Fitzgerald's friends to join the chorus of friendly disparagement. For him, the novel had verve, but it was not '*about*' anything', was 'illiterate' and was derivative from 'an inferior model', Compton Mackenzie's *Sinister Street*. None of these three remarks should be accepted without reservation. As qualifications, they need qualification. *This Side of Paradise* is indebted to *Sinister Street* – Fitzgerald mentions it by name and alludes to it – but so is Joyce's *A Portrait of the Artist as a Young Man*, a novel to which Fitzgerald is more profoundly indebted – indeed, more richly indebted.

*Sinister Street* appeared in two volumes, in 1913 and 1914, at over a thousand pages in total. Its sexual frankness (now virtually invisible) made it a sensation of the publishing season.

But its real merits lay in Mackenzie's meticulously detailed rendition of childhood – teaching timetables reproduced *in extenso*; the SALVE on the doormat; a globe with a snow-storm and 'a weather-worn tin figure with a green face, blue legs and an unpainted coat'; mittens to prevent thumb-sucking. It is this spirit of unabashed accumulation which encouraged Joyce to revise *Stephen Hero*. On the one hand, Joyce felt the need for greater formal unity and omitted telling episodes (like Isabel's death from gynaecological complications) in order to focus his theme of *non serviam*. On the other hand, Joyce recognized and radicalized Mackenzie's inventory of childhood: in his more thorough account, motherese and bed-wetting find their place. Mackenzie, too, is the source for Stephen's protest to Rector Conmee after his unjust pandying by Father Dolan – an incident of which there is no autobiographical trace in Joyce's life; in fact, Stanislaus Joyce's *My Brother's Keeper* tells us that Joyce was a happy and successful schoolboy, good at games rather than otherwise. However, if we compare the protest of Michael Saxby Fane with that of the indebted Stephen Dedalus, Joyce's infinite superiority is clear. The thinness of Mackenzie's imagination is apparent in the simple heroism of Fane, whereas Dedalus is crucially urged by snobbery as well as indignation at injustice ('Dolan: it was like the name of a woman who washed clothes'). Joyce can show the timid Stephen 'swallowing down the thing in his throat' and even record the way he bumps his elbow in his hurry to regain the playground. No one now accuses Joyce of using an inferior model. Nor did they then, because he manifestly transcends his source.

The same could nearly be said for Fitzgerald. In any case, there is influence and plagiarism. And it should be said that Mackenzie's undoubted originality itself derives from Kipling's portrait of an unhappy childhood in 'Baa Baa Black Sheep', where another young boy is persecuted by a nurse who favours the sister in a perverse act of discrimination – Mackenzie's Stella and Kipling's Judy are sisters under the skin. But how much does *This Side of Paradise* owe to *Sinister Street*?

There are two or three verbal and observational parallels.

When Amory decides to get over Rosalind, he gathers together his accumulated mementoes and alludes directly to *Sinister Street*: 'As he transferred them carefully to the box his mind wandered to some place in a book where the hero, after preserving for a year a cake of his lost love's soap, finally washed his hands with it.' This refers to Chapter 13 of *Sinister Street* and the following chapter: 'The soap was called Trèfle Incarnat, and somewhat cynically Michael relished the savour of it, and even made up his mind to buy a full fat cake when this one should be finished.' Fitzgerald's talent is there in the transposition of Mackenzie's fictional incident. It remains a fictional incident – something in a book – because Fitzgerald knows, as minor writers do not, that romantic tragedy cannot obliterate the sufferer's previous mental existence. Mackenzie's episode is a dramatization of a cliché – the hero washing his hands of the (non-)affair. In Fitzgerald, there is no cliché, nothing so final, nothing so gratifyingly pat – only the sense of fine psychological realism. And something less conclusive: 'The string broke twice, and then he managed to secure it . . .' The shift is subtle but indicative.

Other echoes include Amory's penchant for supporting the losing side (Bonnie Prince Charlie, Hannibal, the Confederates), which is a trait for which Mackenzie's Michael Fane is teased by his governess. A further and minor borrowing is Beatrice Amory's observation that American women in Europe 'pick up old, moth-eaten London accents that are down on their luck and have to be used by someone. They talk as an English butler might after several years in a Chicago grand-opera company.' This is borrowed (and improved in every way) from Mackenzie's acute but pedestrianly annotated observation: 'soon Michael and Stella found themselves going out to dinner and playing bridge and listening to much admiration of England in a Franco-cockney accent that was the result of a foreign language mostly acquired from grooms'. Consider Fitzgerald's instinctive verbal play ('pick up' nodding to 'down on their luck') and you realize at once the injustice of Wilson's suggestion that Fitzgerald is somehow tainted by the inferiority of his source when he so conclusively surpasses it, sentence for sentence.

It may be that Amory's cynical short story on his father's funeral owes something to Michael Fane's affectless response to the suicide of Prescott ('Michael's first emotion was a feeling of self-interest in being linked so closely with an event deemed sufficiently important to occupy the posters of an evening paper'), but the two novels are very different. So different, in fact, that one begins to suspect Edmund Wilson of only a nodding acquaintance with *Sinister Street*. I don't myself see how Michael Fane can be described as a 'shadowy figure' when, apart from his hidden paternity, we know so much about him, from his first in History to his resolve to redeem a prostitute by marrying her. *Sinister Street* is a sprawling *Bildungsroman*. *This Side of Paradise* is a laconic exercise in narrative discontinuity, episodic, experimental in its use of dramatic form and stream of consciousness.

Of course Fitzgerald owes something to Mackenzie's concentrated exposition of undergraduate life and japes. In fact, Mackenzie's pranks are less nasty and more plausible than those of Fitzgerald's undergraduates. We dislike the persecution of the 'Jewish youth' who warrants no further characterization from Fitzgerald and we do not believe in the stripped-down and reassembled motor car which Burne Holiday impossibly insinuates into the Dean's study. In *Sinister Street*, however, Lonsdale's comic deployment of 'Sammy', his father's set of samurai armour, is funny and credible. So is the manufacture of 'a miniature chest protector' for Wedderburn's replica Venus de Milo. It may be, too, that Mackenzie's play with the paternity of his hero (he is the illegitimate son of an English milord) is the stimulus for Monsignor Darcy's toying with the notion of a part in Amory's procreation. Nevertheless, *Sinister Street* is a traditional novel, owing something to Kipling, but indebted primarily to *David Copperfield*. Fitzgerald's accomplished prose cadences, his brevity (ten pages is all it takes for Amory and Rosalind to fall tragically in and out of love), his brisk narrative discontinuities, his hospitality to bad poetry and the extended exposition of undergraduate ideas derive from something much less traditional – Joyce's *A Portrait of the Artist*.

This is Fitzgerald's far from inferior source – its radical diaristic denouement and its lisping baby-talk at the outset provide Fitzgerald with the necessary exemplary experimentation. Joyce's novel famously concludes with Stephen Dedalus's resolve 'to forge in the smithy of my soul the uncreated conscience of my race' – and Fitzgerald, mesmerized by Joyce's literary status, echoes Stephen's ejaculation three times in *This Side of Paradise* and once in a letter to Margaret Case Harriman (August 1935). Tom D'Invilliers's literary criticism is said to 'represent the critical consciousness of the race'; the romantically defeated Amory sees himself as thwarted but preserved 'to help in building up the living consciousness of the race'; and Amory defines the intellectual as one who has 'an active knowledge of the race's experience'. Another reasonably exact verbal echo of Joyce occurs when D'Invilliers recites his free-verse denunciation of contemporary American poetry. 'You win the iron pansy,' Amory applauds. In *A Portrait of the Artist*, Lynch, listening to Stephen's exposition of his aesthetic theory, suddenly interposes, 'Tell me now what is *claritas* and you win the cigar.'

The history of the English novel is the history of retreat from mere event and the decline of exaggeration. With Henry James's preface to *The Portrait of a Lady*, the direction of the novel is clear – it must play towards its strength, the exposition of character and the celebration of interiority. Isabel Archer's nightlong vigil before a dying fire is, James asserts, as ' "interesting" as the surprise of a caravan or the identification of a pirate'. With Joyce, this interiority comes into its own – in the *style indirect libre* extensively deployed in *Dubliners* and *A Portrait* as well as the pulsing stream of consciousness in *Ulysses* as it alternates with conventional impersonal narrative. Related to this movement to supplant mere event with mental event is the movement to cherish the evanescent and the trivial as they occur in the external world. Cranly picks his teeth, a stout student farts, the young Stephen blocks and unblocks his ears at refectory. Fitzgerald profits immensely by this new economy. Those reading lists that later gave him 'the pip' are a tribute to interiority, and Fitzgerald is an extraordinarily gifted observer of the purely social scene. He has a gift for showing social gifts, for swiftly sketching in that most impalpable quality – charm. 'The things Isabelle could do socially with one idea were remarkable. First, she repeated it rapturously in an enthusiastic contralto with a soupçon of Southern accent; then she held it off at a distance and smiled at it – her wonderful smile; then she delivered it in variations and played a sort of mental catch with it, all this in the nominal form of dialogue.' Evelyn Waugh admired Hemingway for his exact reproduction of drunken conversation in *Fiesta*. Fitzgerald, I think, has a rival expertise in the field of conversational flirtation – or what he so precisely designates the 'fabrication of gaiety'. Examining the instinctive good breeding of Humbird, Fitzgerald hits off exactly the aristocratic absence of strain: 'everything he said sounded intangibly appropriate'. And Fitzgerald, lest he be labelled a snob, is just as acute about servants: 'a sparkling wine was poured by an unintelligible waiter'.

There is glamour and irony in that waiter, as there is in so much of Fitzgerald. Like Clara in *This Side of Paradise*, Fitzgerald can 'make fascinating and almost brilliant conversation out of the thinnest air that ever floated through a drawing-room'. And this is the writer that Edmund Wilson stigmatized as brilliant but illiterate – a writer capable of microscopic distinctions, little miracles of precision, as here when he stipulates '*almost* brilliant', or elsewhere when he distinguishes between cardinals, queens and 'more subtle celebrities'. While it is true that Fitzgerald twice wrote 'juvenalia' for 'juvenilia' and appears to think 'chronic' means 'terrible', it is criminal of Wilson not to recognize that, beyond all this fiddle and pedantry, Fitzgerald's prose has extraordinary reach and range, moving his readers with understated husky notes as well as with notes of piercing purity. 'A small crowd of seconds swept by.' 'He apparently had none of the nervous tension that was gripping Amory and forcing his mind back and forth like a shrieking saw.' The fact is that Fitzgerald was *aware* of words. He can hear them whispering within the given semantic field of the sentence: look at the play on *constitution* in this early outing:

'But Beatrice grew more and more prone to like only new acquaintances, as there were certain stories, such as the history of her constitution and its many amendments, memories of her years abroad, that it was necessary for her to repeat at regular intervals.' And no one who could write that Monsignor Darcy was 'a trifle too stout for symmetry' can be described as 'illiterate'.

Actually, the prose is so often so good and the narrative the obverse of smoothly hypnotic that one wonders how *This Side of Paradise* ever achieved the notorious degree of popularity so unpalatable to Edmund Wilson. The answer is sex, of course, though the novel seems in that respect less sensational now than *Sinister Street*, where the murderous Meats is aroused in a monastery by Michael Fane's girlish eyes and where there is a quasi-lesbian relationship between Lily and Sylvia. Here there is more kissing than parents would have approved of, undertaken in a spirit of considered cynicism. Contemporary readers would have been intrigued by the insider view of a famous Ivy League university. The President of Princeton was cross enough at Fitzgerald's portrayal to write him a letter of reproach. Fitzgerald's novel must have seemed both inside-track and wickedly up to date: it contained women who were 'speeds' and men who were 'slickers'. In a letter to D'Invilliers after the war, Amory uses an expression which sums up the novel's appeal: 'modern, that's me all over, Mabel'. Fitzgerald, of course, isn't taken in. There is always a saving detachment: when Amory is heart-broken, he is also self-indulgent and Fitzgerald's intelligence does not spare him: 'After another glass he gave way loosely to the luxury of tears. Purposely he called up into his mind little incidents of the vanished spring, phrased to himself emotions that would make him react even more strongly to sorrow.' Likewise, though undergraduates are granted a certain intellectual glamour, Fitzgerald records some wonderful dips into absurdity:

'What on earth is the use of suddenly running down Goethe,' he declared to Alec and Tom. 'Why write books to prove he started the war – or that that stupid, overestimated Schiller is a demon in disguise?'

'Have you ever read anything of theirs?' asked Tom shrewdly.

'No,' Amory admitted.

'Neither have I,' he said laughing.

When Hemingway, another treacherous friend, betrayed Fitzgerald publicly in 'The Snows of Kilimanjaro', describing him as 'poor Scott Fitzgerald' and attributing to him a sycophantic interest in the rich, Fitzgerald wrote a restrained letter of complaint. In the postscript, Fitzgerald disclaimed any interest in the rich unless they had exceptional charm or distinction. This was too defensive. The rich relate to Fitzgerald's central perception, a perception that links him with Conrad and Conrad's fascination with the flaw of romantic temperament. It is hardly a matter for wonder that Fitzgerald and Ring Lardner should have decided to perform a dance of (intoxicated) homage for Conrad when he visited the Doubleday estate at Oyster Bay in 1923. (They were expelled for trespassing.) The eyes of Dr Eckleburg in *The Great Gatsby*, Fitzgerald's most obviously Conradian novel, tell us everything we need to know about Fitzgerald's attitude towards the rich, the glamorous, indeed to life itself. They are put there by an oculist. They signify perfect vision. And they preside over an ashy waste land. Fitzgerald knew that glamour was bound to fail, that there is an ineradicable human instinct for it which is utterly mistaken.

Edmund Wilson's third criticism of *This Side of Paradise* was that the novel seemed not to be '*about* anything'. This also happens to be untrue but it is the most intelligible of his criticisms. Here the stupidity is venial. As well as Joyce and Conrad, Wilde is an acknowledged influence on Fitzgerald – not just on the epigrammatic turn the prose frequently takes ('memory, a thermometer that records only fevers') but also on the central thematic substance of the novel. *The Picture of Dorian Gray* is alluded to when Kerry Holiday acts Lord Henry to Amory's Dorian. Wilde's novel is of course an account of artificially sustained social glamour concealing profound moral corruption. There is a Dorian Gray-like moment when the automobile death of Dick Humbird occurs and, like Dorian at the suicide of Sybil Vane, Amory experiences 'a sudden hardness' – and raises one of the dead man's hands only to let it fall back inertly. Like Dorian, too, Amory turns away to social pursuits: 'with a determined effort he piled present excitement upon the memory of it and shut it coldly away from his mind'.

Throughout *This Side of Paradise* there is an intricate struggle between good and evil – in the soul of Amory Blaine and almost everywhere else. It is simply untrue to say that the book is without theme or without form. It has both – even to excess. In Ian McEwan's *Black Dogs*, the theme is the intimate coexistence of good and evil and of how one will subtly metamorphose into its opposite – so that the destruction of the Berlin wall brings almost immediately in its train acts of skinhead brutality; so that the hero's defence of a small boy being bullied by his father at once slips into unconsciously relished sadism; so that a Polish concentration camp isn't outside the town but at its very heart. *This Side of Paradise* functions along similar lines in a way that knits together the apparently fragmented narrative. The centrality of Amory's great lost love Rosalind requires no justification. But the cameo appearance of Clara, the beautiful widow, or the more extended role of eccentric Eleanor, might seem to demand some explanation.

Clara is there because, although she is a figure of unimpeachable virtue and social charm, although her goodness is interesting, indeed, an 'asset', she is suddenly capable of asking Amory for a cigarette – and the wicked note is lightly struck. ' "Oh Clara!" Amory said; *"what a devil* you could have been if the Lord had just bent your soul a little the other way!" ' (My italics.) Eleanor is more problematic because she is more improbable. Fitzgerald said later in the margin of his own copy, 'This is so funny I can't even bear to read it'. And it is true that Eleanor is somewhat pressed into the service of Fitzgerald's polarized theme. 'Eleanor was, say, the last time that evil crept close to Amory under the mask of beauty' – the reader is summarily informed almost before the character is introduced. There is statement but little demonstration: 'they could see the devil in each other'. She recites Verlaine and he recites Poe. Neither of which enthusiasms seems a sufficient qualification for diabolism. Nevertheless, Amory is quickly muttering, '*Who the devil* [my italics] is there in Ramilly County . . . who would deliver Verlaine in an extemporaneous tune to a soaking haystack?' Soon her capacity for extrasensory perception (she can anticipate his unexpressed thoughts) is provoking some playful innuendo: 'She was a witch, of perhaps nineteen . . .' (No need for italics.) Shortly thereafter Eleanor is boasting about her materialism and, by reaction, Amory is asserting his belief in the soul: 'And like most intellectuals who don't find faith convenient . . . like Napoleon and Oscar Wilde and the rest of your type, you'll yell loudly for a priest on your death-bed.'

This fluctuation between the pagan and the Christian is first embodied in the somewhat over-convenient and over-explanatory figure of Monsignor Darcy, who has begun as a pagan only to find himself within the pale of the Catholic Church. And it is this dichotomy which explains and engrosses, which *comprehends* the two most puzzling and enigmatic episodes in a novel of 'quick, unrelated scenes' – Amory's vision of the commonplace devil in the hundreds of Manhattan and the act of self-sacrifice performed by Amory in the Atlantic City hotel for the benefit of Alec Connage.

Let us take the devil's appearance first. As elsewhere in the novel (and in a way that reminds one of the early supernatural *double entendre* in Updike's *The Witches of Eastwick*) the diabolic is initially introduced in an almost ludic fashion: the young people burst into the café 'like Dionysian revellers' and, if they don't worship a golden calf, their dancing is 'going to shake a wicked calf'. The devil, when he finally materializes, doesn't have cloven hooves, but there is definitely *something* disturbing about his moccasins. Finally, as in the classic ghost story, Amory's terrified perception is confirmed back at Princeton when Tom D'Invilliers sees something evil at their window. The omnipresence of evil lurking just under the everyday surface is the vision which animates, perhaps over-animates, *This Side of Paradise*. It is made, in the early pages of the book, to cover even petting parties: 'I'm just full of the devil', a symbolically loaded girl is made to remark guilelessly.

Literary genius is also co-opted by Fitzgerald – crudely co-opted, one might say, were it not that the theme seems to have eluded generations of professional readers. At Princeton in his freshman year, Amory tries to decide between social and literary success – both represent evil because neither is disinterested:

> 'Well,' said Kerry, as the excitement subsided, 'you're a literary genius. It's up to you.'
> 'I wonder' – Amory paused – 'if I could be. I honestly think so sometimes. *That sounds like the devil* [my italics], and I wouldn't say it to anybody except you.'

Social success is more obviously a desire tinged with the diabolic – hence the recruitment of Dick Humbird to the role of devil. Humbird's death in an automobile accident is heralded by a woman at the roadside: 'Afterward he remembered the harpy effect that her old kimono gave her, and the cracked hollowness of her voice . . .'

Granted this infernal state of affairs, it is as well that Amory has 'rather a Puritan conscience' in the earliest pages of the novel, and, at the mid-point, what Thayer Darcy conveniently informs us is 'that half-miraculous sixth sense by which you detect evil' – which is 'the half-realized fear of God in your heart'. Towards the end of the novel, this handy faculty has waned: 'Once he had been miraculously able to scent evil as a horse detects a broken bridge at night, but the man with the queer feet in Phoebe's room had diminished to the aura over Jill.' Jill is Alec Connage's sexual partner for whom Amory takes the blame in Atlantic City. In the hotel room, at the moment of crisis, Amory intuits an aura hovering over the girl and another 'presence' by the window, 'something else, featureless and indistinguishable, yet strangely familiar'. These are the rival poles of good and evil: 'two great cases presented themselves side by side to Amory'. The good, featureless yet familiar, is the ghost of Monsignor Darcy who (we later learn) has just died. The evil is the girl – so it is no surprise to read several pages on, during Blaine's stream of consciousness, 'Wonder where Jill was – Jill Bayne, Fayne, Sayne – what the devil . . .' (My aposiopesis.) Nor is it a surprise when, his money and spirits at equally low ebb, Amory should feel 'an overwhelming desire to let himself go to the devil' – or reflect that 'Misfortune is liable to make me a damn bad man.' Or even a *damned* bad man.

When you consider that Rosalind is twice called 'a vampire', once by her sister Cecilia and once by a suitor, Howard Gillespie, you wonder how Edmund Wilson could seriously conclude that *This Side of Paradise* was not really *'about* anything'. In the interests of clarity, I have laboured this exposition but any sarcasm should be sent on to Wilson and not laid at the door of Fitzgerald – the italics, after all, are mine, not his, and only necessary for the myopic sage of Wellfleet, who couldn't see the theme or hear the prose.

'The moon rose and poured a great burden of glory over the garden.' What a beautiful and beautifully characteristic sentence of Fitzgerald's – rich in sensuous appreciation, freighted with wary intelligence, poised perfectly between enjoyment and apprehension. The great burden of glory. Already, in his earliest work, this characteristic movement of mind is present – and correct. *This Side of Paradise* hasn't the greatness of *The Great Gatsby*, nor of *Tender is the Night*, nor of *The Last Tycoon*. It is flawed, massively, by the exclusion of the war and by the profusion of virtually uncharacterized names which are thrown at the reader to shore up the gaping hole in the narrative. All the same, it is an extraordinary debut – and, like all good books, improves on rereading.

# Constance Garnett – Translator

*Matrioshki* are those wooden, hollow, biologically improbable Russian dolls, sarcophagus-shaped and too rudimentary for much in the way of features or waists. In terms of beauty, they have all the allure of a thermos flask in national dress. What they lack in looks, however, they make up for in fecundity. Each holds several increasingly small replicas, one inside another. In their way, they are the perfect emblem for translation – for perfect translation, that is, where some diminishment is inevitable, but the model and the copy are otherwise identical. This depends, of course, on the given simplicity of the original. Anything too complicated – poetry, for instance – and, until quite recently, you might have found yourself looking for an entirely different image.

However, in the streets of Moscow, you can now buy a new-style *matrioshka* which is not for sale in the shops. The outside doll is Gorbachev. Inside him is Brezhnev. Inside Brezhnev, Krushchev and, finally, inside Krushchev lurks Stalin. (Ignore for the moment the political joke: don't be fooled by appearances; these guys are all the same.) In the context of translation, the new-style *matrioshka* provides a neatly cynical emblem of theoretical continuity and actual, observable divergence. The blood on Stalin's hands winds up – in the way of translation – relocated on Gorbachev's bald spot. Not so different actually from Lyubimov's wish to know, while he was directing Pasternak's translation of *Hamlet*, if an English translation of the text

*Constance Garnett: A Heroic Life* by Richard Garnett, Sinclair-Stevenson.

was available. The answer is that there is and there isn't. Shakespeare's text won't disclose what Pasternak did to it in the course of translation.

Versatile, even promiscuous, the capacious new-style *matrioshka* can also stand for what is sometimes gained in translation. For instance, the French open up Edgar Allan Poe and out pops Baudelaire. Here, what has been lost in translation – Poe's energetic vapidity – represents an enormous gain. Equally, the new-style doll will cover plagiarism, the original sin. For example, Baudelaire's essay 'Edgar Allan Poe, sa vie et ses ouvrages' is plagiarized from two articles in the *Southern Literary Messenger* by John R. Thompson and John M. Daniel. Daniel's article is plagiarized in its turn from Griswold's obituary of Poe – a fraud within a fraud within a fraud.

*Traduttore : traditore.* If, as the Italians say, to translate is to traduce, isn't plagiarism a peculiarly faithful form of betrayal, a criminalized subspecies of translation? Not if you compare, as translations, Constance Garnett's translation of Chekhov's 'Sleepy' with Katherine Mansfield's alleged plagiarism, 'The Child-Who-Was-Tired'. The Mansfield is boldly, imprudently divergent from the original. The Garnett version, however, is so utterly unobtrusive as to deserve the plaudit of William Weaver, our senior living translator, who prefaces his translation of Calvino's *If on a winter's night a traveller* with this note: 'In Chapter Eight the passage from *Crime and Punishment* is quoted in the beloved translation of Constance Garnett.' In 1921, Katherine Mansfield herself was moved, on finishing Garnett's translation of *War and Peace*, to write of this and her other translations: 'The books have changed our lives, no less.' On the other hand, Ronald Hingley, translator of the nine-volume Oxford Chekhov, strikes a note of peevish judiciousness: 'Though Garnett is far from the least competent of Chekhov translators, her English is marred by an element of quaintness.' A comparison of Garnett's 'Sleepy' with Hingley's less quaint 'Sleepy' is impossible, alas, because Volume 4 of the Oxford Chekhov, covering the years 1888 to 1889, begins, mystifyingly, in March 1888 – omitting 'Sleepy', therefore, which appeared in

January of that year. Doubtless there are excellent reasons for
this, but one can't help feeling that, with less unstinted apparatus, preface or introduction, room could have been found for a
six-page story Hingley thinks a 'minor masterpiece'.

'Sleepy' is the story of Varka, a thirteen-year-old nursemaid.
Deprived of sleep by the screaming of her small charge and then
made to work all next day by the demanding parents, she finally
strangles the baby. The story's form is the form of a *matrioshka*:
as the poor girl drifts off to sleep, reality is superseded by the
imperious reality of first one dream, then another. A broad high-
road is covered with liquid mud through which people trudge
with wallets on their backs. After a brief moment of wakeful-
ness, Varka dreams the death of her father, rolling on the floor
because 'his guts had burst' – and the way she felt for 'the
broken pot with the matches' to light the candle when the
doctor called. Instantly, Chekhov imposes the scenarios on his
reader. Like literary super-glue, they fasten on us, supplanting
the previous reality much more effectively, it has to be said, than
Calvino's much lengthier, only half-tantalizing truncated novel-
las in *If on a winter's night a traveller*. In the Calvino, the
deliberate air of pastiche alerts his reader's wariness and, since
his subject is the reading experience itself, Calvino tells his
reader he is being sucked in even as the reader begins to succumb
to the fiction – as a method, this is like someone waking you up
to say you are falling asleep. But Chekhov is simply economical
in the way that Kostya envies Trigorin in *The Seagull*: 'Trigorin's
worked out his methods, it's easy enough for him. He gives you
the neck of a broken bottle glittering against a weir and the
black shadow of a mill-wheel – and there's your moonlit night
all cut and dried.' Chekhov establishes the milieu of 'Sleepy' in
one brief authoritative paragraph – the icon lamp, 'a string
stretched from one end of the room to the other, on which baby-
clothes and a pair of big black trousers are hanging', and a
stuffy smell that is a mixture of cabbage soup and 'the inside of
a boot-shop'. It is this unassailable reality which is banished by
the irresistible competing realities of Varka's dreams.

Chekhov's denouement, flirting with melodrama as it does,

depends on the reader's habit of implicit belief in each succeeding 'reality'. The murder is predicated on the indisputability of each inner scene: when, instead of a scene, Chekhov substitutes an idea – the idea of murdering the child for peace in which to sleep – the reader accepts his sleight of hand.

Despite Chekhov's strategy, there is a slight narrative wobble as he transcribes Varka's interior monologue. Before, the dreams seemed to engross us directly, apparently unmediated by Varka's consciousness, whereas the idea of murder clearly emanates from her: 'Kill the baby and then sleep, sleep, sleep . . .' It is impossible here not to identify the two conflated voices of author and character with a third voice – that of the over-insistent hypnotist. However, as failure threatens, Chekhov's imagination, characteristically combining the commonplace with the heightened, saves the story. Already amused by the 'brilliance' of her solution to the problem, Varka advances on the cradle, 'laughing and winking and shaking her fingers' in one of those grimacing paroxysms of synthetic merriment that adults visit on surprisingly unsceptical infants.

Katherine Mansfield's 'plagiarism' of this story (a transgression for which, according to Claire Tomalin, she was blackmailed by her former lover, Florian Sobienowski) differs dramatically and instructively from the Garnett version. Whereas Garnett is everything a good translator should be, the ideal blend of saint and valet, Mansfield obtrudes everywhere. As an author in her own right, Mansfield is unable to repress her egotism, and 'The Child-Who-Was-Tired', though it derives clearly enough from Chekhov, isn't an example of plagiarism at all. It retains the central situation and the risky denouement – and changes everything else. These changes remake the narrative, not to mask the source, but the better to serve Mansfield's own gifts. The scene is now Germany and the altered emphasis is on the child's screaming: Chekhov's donnée is fleshed out, literally, as the baby 'doubled his fists, stiffened his body and began violently screaming'. The dreams are now one dream – of a little white road leading nowhere – but Mansfield's attention is given over to the horror of domestic chores, to a world of broken bootlaces, to bickering children who spit on each other's shaven heads, to a skirt full of potatoes and beetroot, to the task of pegging out twisted and wind-bulged washing, to moistening the rubber teat in your mouth before giving the baby his bottle. None of these details occur in the Chekhov.

'The Child-Who-Was-Tired', therefore, is really a palimpsest, not unlike the Picasso *Head of a Young Man* (1906) in the recent Berggruen exhibition at the National Gallery, where the gouache is laid thickly over a Japanese wood-block print, but not so thickly that one cannot see lines of the original like folds in the paper – creating a visual effect analogous to papier mâché, at a time when Picasso's pictures were seeking to annex sculptural values and effects of several different kinds.

Likewise, Katherine Mansfield has learned general lessons from Chekhov – his weaknesses as well as his strengths. Suffocation, rather than strangulation, is a more plausible form of infanticide, since the inflicted violence is unseen. Despite this improvement, Mansfield manages to introduce her own wobble: her nursemaid is characterized, unlike Chekhov's, as a simpleton, for reasons of greater plausibility. However, we learn that she is retarded because her unmarried mother attempted to kill her by 'trying to squeeze her head in the wash-stand jug'. Fearful symmetry. This unsuccessful infanticide and the successful one with which the story closes is one infanticide too many. The most useful lesson Mansfield has absorbed from Chekhov is that the short story should include purely gratuitous details, lest the narrative appear not merely short but anorexic. Mansfield gives us, therefore, a vignette of the coal cellar: 'Such a funny, cold place the coal cellar! With potatoes banked on one corner, beetroot in an old candle box, two tubs of sauerkraut, and a twisted mass of dahlia roots – that looked as though they were fighting one another.' Another brilliantly irrelevant detail occurs at lunchtime: 'dinner was eaten, the Man took the Frau's share of the pudding as well as his own'.

In Chekhov's 'The Lady with the Dog' there is a glorious supernumerary detail which perfectly illustrates the dual economy of the greatest short stories – an overall parsimony suddenly leavened by luxury. Fresh from their first adultery, the new lovers sit in the dawn's outdoor emptiness and are approached by a man who looks at them, then walks away. For the reader and the lovers, it is as if the strangeness conferred on them by the affair has been corroborated. In Garnett, this figure is 'probably a keeper'. In Hingley, he is 'a watchman, no doubt'. In Koteliansky, he is, unambiguously, 'a coast-guard'. As a non-Russian speaker, I have no idea which of these professions is correct but I don't think it matters. Garnett evidently made a number of slips in this area – Augusta Tovey notes in 'The Steppe' a confusion between *cherep* (skull) and *cherepok* (potsherd). This is hardly surprising. Her dictionaries must have been considerably worse than the Oxford Russian–English dictionary compiled by Marcus Wheeler – which my wife found less than adequate when she was translating Pasternak's poetry.

More important are mistakes of tone or straightforward clumsiness, of which there are relatively few examples in Garnett. In 'A Dreary Story', even allowing for the narrator's habitual academic delivery, one baulks at this stilted sentence: 'You may be ever so much of a gentleman and a privy councillor, but if you have a daughter you cannot be *secure of immunity* [my italics] from that petty bourgeois atmosphere.' This is exceptional and no worse than Hingley's maladroit update in 'Murder': 'Mother's breast is baby's snack-bar.' Alas, 'snack-bar' is no longer current and hasn't yet acquired an appropriately antique patina. 'Mother's breast is baby's buffet' would achieve, by contrast, a timeless and relatively placeless quality.

A comparison of three versions of 'The Lady with the Dog' (Garnett), 'A Lady with a Dog' (Hingley) and 'Lady with the Toy Dog' (Koteliansky) makes it clear that Garnett is the superior translator. Hingley, on principle, gives us what Chekhov would have written had he been an English writer. 'Snack-bar' is one unfortunate instance of where this principle leads. Chekhov's own belief was that *things* do not always translate: '*The Cherry Orchard* is being translated for Berlin and Vienna. But it won't succeed there because they don't have billiards, Lopakhins or students *à la* Trofimov.' Undeterred by this,

Hingley boldly translates the untranslatable. Anna Sergeyevna is deprived of her atmospheric and irreplaceable patronymic and becomes 'Anne'. In Garnett, Anna Sergeyevna isn't sure 'whether her husband has a post in a Crown Department or under the Provincial Council'. In Hingley, Anne's choice is between 'the County Council or the Rural District'. However, in this area, there are no absolute rules, except what works on the page, and Hingley is correct to prefer 'ENTRANCE TO CIRCLE' for the more literal 'TO THE AMPHITHEATRE' chosen by Garnett and Koteliansky. On the other hand, Hingley's 'Slav Fair hotel' doesn't sound plausibly English at all. The Commercial Hotel would be a better equivalent, but better still is Garnett's 'the Slaviansky Bazaar hotel', which is aromatic with Russianness. The replacement of 'Crown Department' by 'County Council' is equivalent to the substitution, in a translation from Italian, of the Archbishop of Canterbury for Pope. You may as well translate *matrioshka* as Cindy doll.

There are small points. The main difference between Hingley and Garnett is that Hingley's literary touch is coarser. In the Garnett, Gurov encounters the lady with the dog and reflects: 'if she is here alone without a husband or friends, it wouldn't be amiss to make her acquaintance'. What is not fully disclosed even to himself is taken by Hingley out of the arena of the half-formulated. The ambiguity in Garnett, admittedly short-lived, is between two alternatives: is his sexual interest aroused by the absence of husband and friends, or does that absence simply point up the loneliness he wishes magnanimously to alleviate? Hingley resolves the problem prematurely with jarring contemporary demotic: 'If she has no husbands and friends here she might be worth picking up.' So much for a motivation poised momentarily between the predatory and the polite.

Hingley is too prone to translate Chekhov's hints and guesses into four-square certainties. After Anna's seduction, Hingley depicts her remorse thus: 'she had struck a pensive, despondent pose, like the Woman Taken in Adultery in an old-fashioned picture'. Garnett has: 'she mused in a dejected attitude like "the woman who was a sinner" in an old-fashioned picture'. Koteliansky has: 'exactly like a woman taken in sin in some old picture'. Since Russian has no articles, definitive or indefinite, 'a woman' or 'the woman' are equally possible. But the biblical allusion, with its assumption of forgiveness, works against the idea of Anna's remorse, which is more like, say, the genre of Holman Hunt's *The Awakening Conscience*.

There are three occasions when Chekhov's characters show emotion and where Garnett outdoes Hingley because he over-does the emotion. At the theatre, the lovers meet again. Gurov sees Anna and, in Hingley, his 'heart seemed to miss a beat'. In the Garnett, 'when Gurov looked at her his heart contracted'. When Anna looks up and sees him there, she is, in Garnett, 'unable to believe her eyes, and tightly gripped the fan and the lorgnette in her hands'. Hingley overstates her action by a fatal margin: 'not believing her eyes, crushing fan and lorgnette together in her hands'. Compare, too, their first kiss. Example A: 'Then he stared at her hard, embraced her suddenly and kissed her lips. The scent of flowers, their dampness, enveloped him, and he immediately glanced round fearfully: had they been observed?' Example B: 'Then he looked at her intently, and all at once put his arm round her and kissed her on the lips, and breathed in the moisture and the fragrance of the flowers; and he immediately looked round him, anxiously wondering whether anyone had seen them.' I don't believe that you need to be told that the abrupt, parodically passionate advance of Example A, faintly reminiscent of silent films, is by Ronald Hingley. In any case, the ineptitude of 'he stared at her hard' is sufficient to trigger uneasiness. Her hard *what*? The phrase belongs with another clunking Hingleyism: 'people who would have been glad to misbehave themselves, given the aptitude'. Constance Garnett avoids Hingley's ugly retread of 'given the opportunity' and translates so: 'persons who would themselves have been glad to sin if they had been able'.

Of course, the Oxford Chekhov is nevertheless a great gift, with all its flaws, and we monoglots are properly grateful. It is simply that Constance Garnett's contribution to world literature is incomparably vast – and that where we encounter Hingley as a series of snags in his translations, she is perfectly invisible, as effective and insubstantial as the Holy Ghost, a divine nobody.

This fascinating life by her grandson, Richard Garnett, is the life of a nobody, taking on at times the authentic intonations of Mr Pooter: 'In February I had greens (which neither of us care much for) for dinner fourteen times.' But if this biography in its fullness sometimes makes over to us the genuine stupor of everyday concerns, its meticulousness also rewards us with the extraordinariness of the ordinary. Out of the *matrioshka* Constance Garnett emerge the translations of Turgenev, Tolstoy, Dostoevsky, Chekhov and Goncharov. But the Russian connection isn't just literary: as a boy, her father skated across the Baltic; she knew the Russian exiles Felix Volkhovsky (deaf after six and a half years in solitary confinement), Stepniak and Kropotkin, whose beard covered his solar plexus.

Her marriage to Edward Garnett was celibate after the birth of their only child, David or Bunny. Constance suffered a prolapse of the uterus and thereafter wore some kind of internal support. After a time, Edward, with Constance's consent, found himself a sexual partner in Nellie Heath, a painter who had previously fallen for her teacher, Sickert. Constance had her own *tendresses*, though none of these became physical, and she wrote, truthfully, to Edward that their love for each other was central and permanent: 'other interests – even other love – cannot alter it'. Curiously, it seems to have been most threatened not by illicit sexual attraction, but by Edward's lack of respect for Constance's socialism and her individuality: a bitter but generalized letter suddenly resolves itself into a particular grudge, at once trivial and humiliating: 'to call me "a boiled owl" for instance before the Lucases'.

Apart from translation, sex and sickness are the great currents through her life, sometimes flowing together. What kind of internal support must she have worn? How was it kept clean? How did she manage while menstruating? Was it feasible on long Russian train journeys? Was it specially made, like Ruskin's truss? At the end of the nineteenth century and the beginning of the twentieth, one was only a short step away from the musty atmosphere of the sick-room and everyone had their small ailment. One thinks of Eliot's truss, worn from boyhood, and of Updike's father's 'pathetic sweat-stained truss' in *Self-Consciousness*. Constance's mother dies of an aggravated rupture, caused by lifting her invalid husband from bed to bathchair and back again: 'my mother, unconscious and gasping in an awful way looked quite different – sunken and grey. Grandmamma was crying on one side of the bed, my poor father, crying too (which seemed almost the most dreadful thing of all) was saying "Oh, the little monkeys, the poor little monkeys!" – his nickname for Gracie and Katie. In the next room Robert was sitting with a book open pretending to read.'

All those ailments from a different era: ulceration of the retina, internal inflammation, sick headaches, Valentine's Meat Juice as a remedy for Edward's abscess on his tooth, the typhoid that left the 'walls of his intestines as thin as paper', the way he took quinine till it left him deaf. Mental illness: the mad brother who murdered his wife and child with the coal-hammer before killing himself; the friend who stole Constance's pistol and fired it at an editor who rejected his poems. Sex and sickness: the sister whose husband contracted syphilis in Brazil; the locomotor ataxia of Constance's father which she believed, incorrectly, was caused by syphilis. As a young man, her father made a servant girl pregnant. When he somewhat high-handedly arranged for his illegitimate son to go to boarding school, the boy's maternal grandmother wrote with all the heartbreak that unpunctuated literary incompetence can convey: 'pleas to be so kind as to Let mee know how you leave him poor little fellow he will feel very strang with all Strangers ... I cannot tell you how I feel.' In sexual matters, this biography is to be commended for its candour. David Garnett, we learn, was fundamentally heterosexual, but willing to comply with the physical demands of Duncan Grant – it was the emotional burden he found insupportable. Despite their subsequent celibacy, Constance and Edward were lovers before they married. Certainly, she was no prude and, via her husband, recommended 'Malthusian sheaths' to her son.

In fact, she was in general rather tough. Of Tolstoy she

remarked: 'these prophets are dreadful people to deal with'. She never had much time for religion and dismissed the gospels because they were 'written by ignorant men in Aramaic and translated two centuries later into bad Greek'. By the end of her life, she was thoroughly disgusted by the piety of *Children's Hour*.

All in all, she is a *matrioshka* containing multitudes – Shaw 'looking like a fairly respectable plasterer, his cuffs trimmed with scissors'; H. G. Wells, vigorous but 'a bit vulgar, you know'; D. H. Lawrence, protesting, 'Mrs Garnett says I have no true nobility – with all my cleverness and charm. But that is not true. It is there, in spite of all the littlenesses and commonnesses'; Tussy Marx; the Webbs; Yeats poor enough to black his heels where they showed through the holes in his socks; Tolstoy's wife, dismissed as 'a Philistine, admirably qualified to be the wife of the Mayor of Brighton'; and, best of all, Ford Madox Ford, telling a Russian émigré that rye was England's largest crop, but that the most profitable crop was 'a very tall cabbage, the stalks of which supplied walking-out canes for soldiers in the British army'. If you didn't know that Tolstoy was 'a keen cyclist and rode for considerable distances on a solid machine with a single-plunger brake and no mudguards' – then you need this biography, which also contains the cycling secrets of Henry James.

# Moscow Diary

**Monday, 29 January**

Things have changed. We are at the Russian Embassy to see Andrei Nekrasov's execrable biopic about Pasternak. A huge video projector squats while Sergei Shilov, the ambassador's personal assistant, presents my wife with twelve red roses, *garni*, and says a few words of introduction. He will not presume, he says, to speak of the work of Boris Pasternak because, well, there are in the audience the nieces of Pasternak, who are intelligent, well, very intelligent, and also, well, very beautiful and far more able than he is to speak about Pasternak's work. Shilov's English has that mixture of hesitation and surge normally associated with high-wire artistes. At the end of every successfully negotiated sentence, he smiles like a performer being judged – radiant with nerves.

As a diplomat, he is masterly. Faced with a straight question from a BBC interviewer, he speaks fluent fog. You want to coin, in the spirit of admiration, a new verb of speech, *to soothe*. As in, the ambassador's personal assistant soothed, 'Indeed, every generation of arts carries with it the burden of past mistakes and triumphs and is affected in everyday writings. Be it writers, painters, artists and musicians, they are affected by the history of the nation. In some ways, of course, the legacies still affect them. But it is not in the relationship of an artist via the state, it is just in the inner soul of the artist where the conflict remains.' I take my quotation from a BBC transcript. These sweet nothings, impossible to paraphrase, are virtually without content. As they are in any wooing process. And, unmistakably, we are being wooed.

My wife, Lisa, my brother-in-law and I have a last-minute telegram of invitation to the Pasternak Centenary celebrations in Moscow, sent to us by the poet Andrei Voznesensky, head of the Writers' Union. It turns out that the other English guest is Jeremy Treglown, the editor of *The Times Literary Supplement*. Josephine Pasternak, the poet's only surviving sister, and Sir Isaiah Berlin were to have been the first team, we later learn. But even as substitutes, we have everything made easy. We supply three photographs and the embassy fills in the visa application for us to sign. For my wife, the occasion is full of irony. 'I can remember,' she tells the *Today* programme, 'queuing drearily here, not in this building, in 1960, when my uncle was dying and had asked my mother to visit him at his bedside. It was only with extreme difficulty that we got a visa after his death. Now things have been completely reversed, and we've been invited to come to Moscow to attend the celebrations of his centenary. I'm a guest here to read his poetry and I shall read a poem which he kept only in manuscript, in which he talks about his time without wings, uninspired time. So this is full of the ironies of change.'

Fortunately, the BBC do not use an answer she regrets having given. Asked if she feels bitter, she answers 'no' – a reply she would want to qualify, pointing out that she herself hardly suffered anything more than the 'insolence of office', whereas her uncle was abused, isolated and deprived of his livelihood. The English instinct to be agreeable – not to cause a fuss – goes very deep. Somehow I can't imagine the Russians having, as part of their mythology of courage, the phrase 'It's only a scratch.'

### Monday, 5 February

On the other hand, have things changed all that much? Secretary Shilov telephones me at work to say our visas are ready for collection. I ask him to send them to Fabers on a motorbike. Ever the diplomat, he counters this extravagant proposal neatly, by saying he doesn't have the visas himself. I must collect them from the consulate, not the embassy. The consulate is 'only down the road'. In that case, I rejoin, can he go and collect the visas personally – to avoid any delay – and I will arrive in a taxi at the embassy in one hour's time? The air tickets must be collected separately from the Aeroflot offices ('first floor, ask for Betty') opposite Reid's Hotel in Piccadilly.

An hour later, I press the buzzer at the embassy gate, drop Shilov's name and listen uncomprehendingly to the crackle of Cyrillic. For some reason, Russian always makes me think of hallmarks on silver. Finally, a delightful woman with blonde hair and pale blue eye shadow runs down the steps to the gate, grins (one dimple), holds both my hands, and tells me that Sergei Shilov is not back from the consulate with the visas. Do I know how he looks? I do. Today, apparently, he is wearing a beige raincoat. And there our intense relationship ends. With a grin, my hands are returned to me, and I climb back into the taxi and am driven slowly back down the semi-private road.

Here is Shilov, accompanied by a burly, dark-jowled figure whom I immediately assume is 'security'. We shake hands. This time, I retain his hands in both of mine. There is difficulty, however, with the visas. I can collect them tomorrow. We agree instead to entrust them to the GPO's special delivery service. I have an idea that even his influence and status have failed to affect the due process of bureaucracy – a side of democracy we don't often see in England, but which is frequently displayed in socialist countries. In Poland, once, I remember our interpreter vainly lying about our international importance at a hotel reception desk whose magnificent unreceptiveness was explained by an explanatory notice on the counter – explaining that the staff were having their thrice-daily break. This aggressive assertion of equality makes all the service industries ghastly in the Eastern and Central European socialist bloc. Waiters and waitresses are more concerned to establish their lack of servility than they are to serve. Only in the abstract is this not such a bad thing. I grin at Shilov with genuine friendliness, as if to say that I also know what it is to have one's charm rebuffed.

After some cruising down Piccadilly, Eros comes into sight and my taxi-driver and I realize simultaneously that Reid's Hotel is elusive mainly because we should have been looking for the Ritz. £13 on the clock. I ask for a receipt. His eyes meet mine in the rear-view mirror: 'Use a lot of these, then, do you mate?' And he gives me the remainder of a book. Which contains, as it happens, only two blank receipts, and I feel gratified somehow by the idea of beating bureaucracy, of asserting the right of every freeborn Englishman to fiddle his expenses.

At Aeroflot, Betty is out to lunch. It is 4.40. Finally, at 4.50, she appears. The manager has the tickets. He is out to lunch and his office is locked. Then it transpires that he has given the tickets to another secretary – but only after my ineffectual charm has been replaced by muted truculence and a demand that Secretary Shilov should be telephoned at the number I give them. When I examine the tickets, I discover that my wife's is made out to Lisa Pasternak, whereas her passport, which dates from the bad old days, discreetly gives her name as Dr Elisabeth Raine. It is too late to have the ticket changed, so I collect a series of names and direct telephone numbers for use if the check-in at Terminal 2 becomes awkward about the ticket's validity.

**Friday, 9 February**
As it turns out, my wife's birth certificate is enough to convince the English employee at the check-in. Our flight has been cancelled, however, which means that we will definitely miss the inaugural ceremony at the Bolshoi Theatre. Our timing was, in any case, touch and go. I am not heartbroken. I have attended several opening ceremonies. On the flight, my brother-in-law, Michael Slater (Michael Pasternak, according to his ticket), is unable to read because the Aeroflot jumbo doesn't have individual seat lights. He has the aisle seat – exiled to inner darkness. Speaking of darkness, what a curious sensation it is to emerge from the gloom of the transit corridor, into the designer dusk of Sheremetievo Airport and the ring-mail burnished rust of the ceiling's empty pilchard tins.

Vladimir Stabnikov is waiting for us. I have met him before, in England and in the Soviet Union. Small, thick-set, black-eyed, densely bearded, restlessly rubbing his hands, inexplicably powerful, grinning indefatigably, he wafts our party into the VIP lounge, where six or seven Africans are torpidly toying with glasses of Pepsi. After about ten minutes, all the formalities have been completed on our behalf and we leave for Moscow in two cars. No snow. A wet night. Temperature: 2 degrees. Stabnikov tells me that he is about to become the head of Soviet PEN and that they will be hosting a conference on the literature of the Second World War. Asked for suitable names, I recommend Stephen Spender (because of his experience de-Nazifying German libraries after the war) and Alan Ross. Then I mention that Ross served in the Navy, and in poems like 'Murmansk' recalls the war in the Baltic. Stabnikov seems satisfied. We pass the now famous queue outside McDonald's, where, I am told, customers wait four hours outside and then an hour and a quarter inside before they are served. On the other hand, how can only one outlet serve Moscow's nine million inhabitants? Baskin Robbins is here. Pizza Hut, I see from the hoardings, is also on its way. Christian Dior is another sign I notice.

At the Hotel Rossia, the television and the radio in our room have been switched on to welcome us. Andrei, our interpreter, produces money to cover our expenses, meals and so forth. We sign for 130 roubles each. Andrei exists on three roubles a day. We unpack, have a swig of duty-free Jameson's, and head for Red Square, which is five minutes' walk away. Most of the five minutes is spent getting out of the vast hotel. Outside, despite my *vatnik* (a wadded jacket as worn in the gulag), we are accosted by people selling military regalia and other more obvious souvenirs. On this trip, though, no one tries to change money. A large party of Americans are taking each other's photographs outside Lenin's tomb. They are noisy, high-spirited, unabashed, triumphant. Why not? I argue with myself. The windows of GUM have considerably more than faded pyramids of *snoek*. Trainers, track suits, ski wear. There is an electric guitar even uglier than anything I've seen in the West. Its futuristic shape is based, paradoxically, on the ice-hockey stick.

## Saturday, 10 February

Bus to Peredelkino, the writers' colony. We have a programme
and a list of guests. Jeremy Treglown is there, but where are
Richard Gere and Bernardo Bertolucci? Where is Kurt Von-
negut? The bus sizzles along the roads flanked by blackened
chunks of Kendal mint cake and we debus at the tiny Peredelkino church, where a service for Pasternak is to be held. The
choir has not yet arrived, and the church is packed and stuffy.
Jeremy, Michael, my wife and I, plus Andrei, decide to take a
look at Pasternak's grave before the main party arrives. The
graveyard is set on the side of a hill. Each grave is surrounded
by its own iron fence. Paths squeeze in and out between the
railings. My wife is following her instinct. When we arrive, the
main party is well in evidence. Yevtushenko is master-of-
ceremonies, highly visible in a zoot-suit jacket of black, white
and red, like interference or a Mexican blanket. Please Do Not
Adjust Your Suit. Around me, people are asking if Raisa Gorbachev has come. She hasn't, though she attended the Bolshoi
festivities the night before: our interpreter turned, saw her, said
hello spontaneously, and was immediately closed off by her
security men. I see a couple of proprietorial Russians trying to
ferry Arthur Miller to the graveside. Squeezing past, he steps
apologetically on our toes in one direction and then again in the
other direction – but gets no nearer the epicentre represented by
Yevtushenko and the television cameras.

Yevtushenko introduces each speaker fulsomely and then
ignores what they have to say because, with urgent gestures, he
is silently cajoling the next person towards the camera. By now,
it is clear that these celebrations have a dual purpose – to pay
tribute to a great poet (Yevtushenko) and to demonstrate to the
wider world the continuing vigour of *glasnost*. All the big words
that make us so unhappy are loud on the lips of every speaker.
We decide to return to the church and get warm.

Jeremy unfolds a pair of depressed clericals that collapse into
themselves like a miniature wheelchair and, finding a bench at
the back, unfolds his long frame too and settles to read in the
fug of BO and beeswax. Earlier, he had remarked that the pew

was Protestantism's great contribution to theology. I admire the three-dimensional crucifix which hangs at the centre of the church like a magnified snowflake. On one altar, parishioners leave offerings for the priest: a bag of caramels, biscuits, a bottle of soured milk. An old woman presses her face to the iconostasis: what the sutler saw. The choir arrives and performs. It is the Russian equivalent of an accordion to evoke the streets of Paris – musical black bread. After a brisk volley at the net, one word is lobbed heavenwards and hangs in the air like the Paraclete – *Go— spodi.*

Back in the graveyard, it is still impossible to get near. My wife describes the headstone to Jeremy in case he should want to write about it. Yevtushenko appears to be in the middle of another aria, so we set off for Pasternak's dacha by road. The week after Pasternak's funeral, my wife remembers, you could still see the wide path beaten by the mourners across a field of strawberries as they took the shortest route to the cemetery from the dacha. She also treats us to a short disquisition on Pasternak as a translator of Shakespeare – how he edited, used Russian idioms, took liberties, curbed Shakespeare's verbosities, toned down the lewdness of the original. The Russians are rather prudish, as Andrei will later confirm when he describes his simultaneous translation work at the cinema. American films casually use expressions like 'motherfucker', 'scumbag' and 'asshole', which, were he to translate them accurately, would scandalize his audience. His *amour propre* as a translator is piqued, however, when mischievous members of the audience complain loudly about his euphemistic substitution of 'rascal' for 'motherfucker'.

When we reach the dacha, Yevtushenko and Voznesensky are before us once again to inaugurate the dacha's new status as a Pasternak museum. Both men's eloquent but limited gestural vocabularies are unabated. A huge crowd has gathered. Alexander Blokh from PEN, an elegant figure in a pin-striped suit and brown suede shoes, nods towards the speakers and says, 'The strong, silent Russian hasn't been invented yet.' Madame Blokh asks me if I do not think the translation of Rimsky-

Korsakov's opera rather 'unfortunate'. Our programme says we are to see it on Sunday evening. It is called *The Golden Cock* – not *The Golden Rooster*, which she thinks less improper. I explain that this regular embarrassment is so regular as to be no longer embarrassing. 'I don't know,' says Jeremy, 'what about those co'tail parties we all go to?'

Pasternak's son, Evgeny, comes to the microphone to say that he remembers this dacha very well: down there, he says, is a lilac bush planted by Pasternak's second wife, Zinaida; he also remembers, seeing this large crowd, how, after the award of the Nobel Prize, no one came to the dacha for a week, until a friend arrived by train from Georgia. For all its level, almost toneless, delivery, it is a measured rebuke.

Lisa and I are pleased to see that the old enamel bath is still there in the vegetable garden. I remember the outside lavatory and wonder if it, too, still exists. It does. A kind of sentry box with a darkly soaked seat, it has an incredibly deep shaft of about four storeys, which must have taken some digging. You can't lift the seat – like a gentleman – because the board is structurally immovable. Inevitably, I pee on the seat like everyone else, just a little bit.

Relatives seize us, but, even with their Pasternak credentials, it is difficult to get into the dacha museum. The crowd pressure never stops. 'They must be selling bananas,' someone jokes. After an hour, we are literally dragged inside by a relation. Pasternak's dacha is rather better than most writers' museums because there is an excellent display of his father Leonid's pictures, something worth seeing rather than the usual raft of pencils and pens. There is also a wonderful television set – a square yard of woodwork and upholstery framing a four-inch screen that looks like a Chiclet pellet. On the desk is a manuscript of *Doctor Zhivago*, on the flyleaf of which Pasternak has written 'And there shall be no more death' (Revelation 21:4), presumably to emphasize the meaning of *zhivago* – *life* – in Russian. Lisa sees a woman return to this quotation with tears in her eyes, saying, 'Only a great poet could write such a thing. There shall be no more death. A great poet.' She shakes her head with admiration and disbelief. By the end of this weekend, three thousand people will have signed the Visitors' Book.

Back in Moscow, we invite a gaggle of relatives to lunch in the hotel restaurant. Somehow they manage to pay – an alarming soufflé of ten-rouble notes. During the meal, I consume several glasses of vodka ('einmal ist keinmal,' a cousin assures me) and hear about Pamiat (Memory), the new Russian nationalist literary movement, which, though supported by some genuinely good writers like Rasputin, has anti-Semitic hangers-on whose strength it is impossible to gauge. The anti-Semitism is 'explained' in terms of Soviet history and a reaction to the strong Jewish presence in Bolshevism. Now, it seems, the Jews are responsible for every communist failure from collectivization to the KGB. A meeting at the Writers' Union has been broken up by anti-Semites.

Some of my relatives are puzzled when I express regret that the Lithuanians and Estonians should have embarrassed Gorbachev by pressing their nationalist programmes. Perhaps, some of them say, this was their only chance: the moment had arrived. Pragmatism sometimes seems completely alien to the Russian soul. For instance, they are paying this bill they can't afford.

We go straight from lunch to the Writers' Union, where a sumptuous reception has been laid on. There, Jeremy introduces me to Adam Michnik, who, despite his faintly grubby jeans, is a minister in the Solidarity government. Why, I wonder, is communist denim so distinctively different from capitalist denim? Why is it so insistently a work material which can never make the transition to leisure status? The truth of these ruminations strikes me so forcibly that I wonder if I'm pissed from lunch. I ask Michnik how Poland is surviving its twenty-fifth or so devaluation since Mazowiecki came to power. He fobs me off like a true professional: short-term hardships will soon give way to long-term improvements. It strikes me as classic Gorbachev-speak. On the other hand, I'm speaking French, which probably means I am drunk.

Two days later, in England, I discover one answer to my question. Now that they are part of a market economy, my

Polish publishers can no longer afford to publish my poems. A few days after that, I receive a copy of *Student Life* from Prague, which contains an interview I gave. My interviewer's letter tells the same story: 'It looks as if the magazine will be folding up very shortly, now that the state has ceased to finance the IUS to the extent it previously did, but I can't say the world will significantly mourn its passing.'

### Sunday, 11 February

We have decided to skip the organized trip to the monastery at Zagorsk. Instead we'll go to the Pushkin Museum to see the last day of its Pasternak exhibition. I suppose this isn't scheduled for the other foreign guests because Russian is required for a serious visit. Dresden have sent a van der Weyden crucifixion to illustrate the exhibition's theme – the parallel drawn by Pasternak between Christ's Passion and events in Zhivago's life. There is also a lovely Cranach of Christ at Gethsemane, in which the stereotypical spaniel-eyed Christ is as automatic as the Euclidean folds in the drapery, but redeemed by the particular, workaday faces of the apostles, who, for once, are credibly asleep, not merely models with their eyes closed. There is a photograph of Pasternak with Mayakovsky on his left, which Pasternak has annotated: 'the left eye is smaller out of respect to my neighbour'. You look again, and it is. A whole glass case in the exhibition is devoted to the denunciations of Pasternak that appeared in *Pravda* after the Nobel announcement. Also there is Pasternak's letter of retraction, with its pitiful hope that he can still do the state some service – painful if you prefer heroism to be simple; almost gratifying, if, like me, you like your heroes to be human. Nothing is hidden.

In the main gallery, there is a scrummy little Vuillard: a figure relaxes on a rose-upholstered divan with loose covers. This great blush of strawberries and evaporated milk is set off against the severely plain linoleum and a white, beautifully observed door, where Vuillard has transcribed the exact weight of the handle and the awkward broken white paint on the sturdy hinges.

From the museum, we walk to Golgolevsky Boulevard, past

the steaming open-air swimming pool. We want to see Alexander Pasternak's old flat in the building he designed himself. We stayed there in 1974. In front of the block, a man carries a bucket of hot water to his car, which is filthy like every car in Moscow. We wonder what he is going to do with the water, since he couldn't possibly intend to wash the car. But he is. We celebrate by eating an ice-cream outside Kropotkinskaya underground station. Then, for 5 copecks each, we take a journey to the outskirts of Moscow. We are going to visit yet more relatives. At the metro station where we get off, there is a market. We buy a pair of *valinki* (black felt snow boots) for one of our kids, a jar of mushrooms in oil and garlic (the plastic lid is the same price as the contents), a kilo of cranberries, a jar of hot garlic and tomato paste, a plastic bag containing shredded carrot, dressed and spiced. At the end of the stalls, there is a pale blue lorry with a high tidemark of dirt almost to the roof. The back door is open. You can see a scrap of blanket, faded green with a brown stripe, and a Tartar is lounging, half in, half out, against the hay inside, which is packing for a vast quantity of melons – the colour of giant nutmegs and individually tied with dry rushes. Below, another Tartar, vinyl-eyed, is slicing open a sample with a long, broadening blade. The flesh of the melon is brilliant white lavishly brushed with red gold. They want 3 roubles a kilo. What we want is a camera.

My brother-in-law discusses the difficulty of sex in shared accommodation, the built-in constraint of your mother only an inch of plaster away – or even only the width of a curtain. As we pick our way through the mud, I see, on cue, three pale turquoise, used condoms on the ground.

Inside the cramped flat, books, pictures, old-fashioned furniture, an atmosphere of culture, the smell of cooking. We talk to my wife's aunt Anya, who is over eighty, dignified, spruce, her hands calm in her lap. She tells us how her brother was arrested several times, released, then finally sent in 1938 to a camp 'without the right of correspondence' – in other words, liquidated. After his first arrest, in 1919, the brother could be visited only by her, because she was under ten and entitled by some legal oddity. Why was he arrested? No reason. Perhaps because William was not a normal Russian surname. This is the first time any relative has ever mentioned this murdered man. When we ask what it is like to be able to say anything, the reply comes back that now there aren't any jokes. But seriously, we persist, what is it like to be able to say anything? They catch each other's eyes, then someone says: 'We're not sure we *can* say anything.' They offer a definition of *glasnost*: the lead has been lengthened; the dish has been taken away; we can bark as much as we like.

Another story from the time of collectivization: one summer, a peasant and his small son came from the Ukraine, where their whole family was starving, to beg in Moscow. The William family let them live in their attic. They collected crusts of bread and dried them on the roof. By winter, when they returned to the Ukraine (they would have frozen to death in the attic), they had sacks and sacks of dried crusts to keep them going. It was their only food and it wasn't enough. The next summer, the father returned with his wife and baby daughter, but without the boy. The little girl was eight months old. Anya William had just given birth herself to a son – now a jovial, grey-haired architect with a bold arrangement for disguising his bald patch – and she offered their sick daughter a dish of kasha. The parents explained that the baby had only ever eaten pre-chewed bread. The little girl died, and the mother and father returned to Ukraine with their sacks. The next summer, only the father came. And the summer after that, no one came. Ten years later, the mother came on her own. She had been sent to a camp and only just released. Everyone else was dead.

The William flat had eight rooms, which were requisitioned. Ten families were billeted there, the largest total of people being thirty-six at one time. A single kitchen and lavatory were used by everyone. Personnel changed over the years, but included Lenin's bodyguard, who, family anecdote has it, wrote in his memoirs: 'I was a good friend of Lenin. Many's the time he's said to me, "Get out of my sight, Friedmann, I can't bear the sight of you."' He was married to a dancer at the Bolshoi. There were also two informers – a political informer and a police informer – and an executioner. One woman wanted to beat up another woman who was universally disliked. So there would be no witnesses, everyone agreed to stay in their rooms – where they listened to the rumpus through their closed doors. When the victim had gone to lodge a complaint to the militia, everyone emerged and the victor, when asked how she felt, said: 'It was a very *appetitlich* beating.' The flat also housed an ancient peasant woman who in the *krasni ugolok* (the red corner traditionally reserved for the icon) set up a shrine to Stalin. Its centrepiece was an embroidered, misspelt motto: THISS TOWULL IS GIVUN TO HYM WHO IS KINDE AT HART.

Vodka flavoured with aniseed is served, and I propose a toast to everyone but especially to the old, who have seen so much. Not for the first time, I'm close to tears – even as I realize that my toast is a quotation from *King Lear*: 'The oldest hath borne most: we that are young / Shall never see so much, nor live so long.'

Back at the hotel, we decided to skip *The Golden Cock* and visit another set of relatives on the opposite outskirts of Moscow. I am so tired I feel like a bluebottle toiling up a window-pane only to fall, stupefied, half the height achieved. Taxi-drivers aren't keen to take us such a long distance, but finally Lisa does a deal and a driver agrees to take us for a five-pound note. In the car, she asks him what he will do with the *valuta* (hard currency). He intends to buy a leather coat. But couldn't he buy that in a Russian shop? He points: see that *magasin* over there? Do you know what *barraban* means? (It means a drum.) Well, that shop is emptier than a *barraban*. It's a vacuum, and roubles are as much use to him as a Mongolian *tugunka*. In high spirits, the taxi-driver tells us the joke about the man who goes to hell. As he walks, the road ahead divides. There is a tall bearded person, a cross between Father Christmas and Neptune, who is carrying a trident and standing at the fork. Which road do I take? asks the man. Depends where you want to be, the Neptune figure replies. This road leads to the capitalist hell. That road leads to the socialist hell. What's the difference? asks our man.

Not much, comes the answer. In the capitalist hell, they hammer a six-inch nail up your arse every day for a month. In the socialist hell, it's the same thing – only some days there are hammers and no nails, and other days there are nails and no hammers, but at the end of the month you have thirty six-inch nails up your arse to fulfil your quota.

After forty-five minutes, we reach our destination. The taxi-driver offers to take us back for the same terms. We agree that he should return at 10.30. This flat is more cluttered than the other flat. I see a set of dumb-bells. Our hosts have a dog which prances, hoovers my crutch and barks at the top of its voice. Its name is Snap, which is pronounced 'Snep'. We eat cold cuts and apples which have been preserved in salted water. I try an apple and regret it. In this flat, there are several family drawings by Leonid Pasternak. They include a profile of Alexander Paster-nak, aged about nine. His closed lips tell you about the slightly buck teeth behind them. There is a drawing of my mother-in-law as a bold, dark-eyed three-year-old with her mother – and another of her, aged ten, sitting sideways in a Biedermeier chair, with her legs over one of the chair arms. You can see the tops of her stockings. The sketch has the informality of a snapshot and yet is precisely composed. It is as if this wisp of a young girl is cradled in the arms of the chair. It is gay, yet has the form of a *pietà*. And all of these people are dead. Art and love fill our eyes.

We mention our taxi-driver, and one cousin tells us how she took a taxi to bring a load of shopping home. The driver kept glancing over his shoulder and quizzing her: what did she do, then? A marine biologist, eh? So what did she bring home in wages? What did her husband do? Another marine biologist, eh. And his wages? When she told him, he was astounded and, switching to the intimate form of address, offered to get her husband a job as a taxi-driver.

The other topic of conversation is private property. Their parents have bought a house in a village which is a night's train journey from Moscow. Only one inhabitant of the village still lives there and he hunts for a livelihood, mostly wild boar. There is a considerable amount of paperwork but such transactions are now legal. All the owners have to give their written consent. The house cost about 300 roubles. At the moment, the official exchange rate is 10 roubles to the pound. A buyer's market.

On the return journey, our taxi-driver is more subdued. Perhaps he has realized that, in his dealings with us, it is buyer's market. We ask him about a towering chromium monument. Gagarin, he replies laconically, we call it the whistle. I half expect him to offer me a wad of receipts.

## Monday, 12 February

The international Pasternak conference begins at the Writers' Union. We can attend only the opening session. Our plane leaves in the afternoon. As security for the simultaneous translation headsets, officials are taking the foreigners' visas. I decide to forgo the pleasure. At the far end of half a mile of green baize, Voznesensky opens the proceedings, which thereafter continue inaudibly, partly because the nearby simultaneous translators kick up quite a racket in their sedan-chair hutches. My brother-in-law says their translations are criminally skimpy. I am pleased they make no attempt to translate poetry. As things muddle on, I reflect on what has been said to us – particularly the prognosis that Russia is on the verge of civil war. But a Russian civil war, in which, though the sides are not yet clear, the victorious side *is* clear. It is whichever side the army takes. Being here, being anywhere, doesn't seem to make things clearer. It isn't a guarantee of authenticity. Think of those foreigners credulously attending now to the simultaneous translation. I find myself sceptical of all analysis and inclined to make the international football match an exemplum. Stay at home and see more on television. It isn't until we return to England that we hear Nelson Mandela has been released. The Prague correspondent I mentioned earlier describes the phenomenon perfectly: 'Our Polish printing house went on strike and hot on the heels of that little rebellion came our (so-called) Velvet Revolution, about which I am sure British media have probably kept you better informed than me!' This from a student, one of those whom Tim Garton-Ash judged to be the efficient cause of Havel's revolution.

According to my wife, the proceedings of the conference are dull, except the contribution of Georges Nivat, who married and divorced the daughter of Olga Ivinskaya, Pasternak's last mistress. Nivat recalls Pasternak discussing Shakespeare's use of soliloquy – the naked artifice of the device and its blunt violation of naturalism. Then Pasternak added: 'But in the thirties, when there were things I dared not say even to my wife, I would look at the Kremlin over my shoulder, soliloquizing inside my head, saying, "One day I will stand in judgement over you."' Let us hope things don't change back again.

# Chekhov

In *The Middle Years*, Henry James recalls meeting Tennyson at Aldworth, only to discover that 'Tennyson was not Tennysonian'. In the same way, Chekhov is a tougher, more pitiless and less perfect writer than the wryly compassionate connoisseur of heat, doldrums, disappointment and defeat popularly associated with the epithet 'Chekhovian'. Like Joycean or Kafkaesque, Chekhovian is so widely current that we are disinclined to think it might be counterfeit, or have a value markedly different from that generally attributed. 'A Dreary Story' is the testy narrative of an old professor left sleepless by the unsleeping, imminent death lurking in his organism. It was written in 1889, and as early as 1886 Chekhov was apologizing for the late copy with this excuse: 'I am ill. Spitting blood and weakness . . .' His mother's side of the family was tubercular. In 1889, nursed by Chekhov, his brother Nikolai died of typhoid and tuberculosis. To his friend and mentor, Suvorin, Chekhov wrote: 'there's not a copeck's worth of poetry left in life'. And it is this mood which provides the dismal drive behind the at least quasi-autobiographical 'A Dreary Story'. Chekhov isn't totally dissociated from the professor's withering denunciation of contemporary Russian fiction which, far from being intellectually candid, is set about with debilitating conscientious objections, including the need to have 'a warm attitude to man'. There is a great deal of tonic coldness in Chekhov's report on the professor's coldness as it gradually chills every human contact. The prose is possessed of the arid inanition and unblinking pedantry which we associate with Beckett: 'as regards my present manner of life, I must give a foremost place to the insomnia from which I have suffered of late. If I were asked what constituted the chief and fundamental feature of my existence now, I should answer, insomnia.'

It isn't difficult to find in 'A Dreary Story' observations which manifestly contradict the popular image of Chekhov. The tone is scientific and dispassionate. It is the story of a soul whose central heating has failed, a tale of self-pity and repressed terror: 'is it possible that this old, very stout, ungainly woman, with her dull expression of petty anxiety and alarm about daily bread, with her eyes dimmed by continual brooding over debts and money difficulties, who can talk of nothing but expenses and who smiles at nothing but things getting cheaper – is it possible that this woman is no other than the slender Varya whom I fell in love with so passionately for her fine, clear intelligence, for her pure soul, her beauty . . .?' His daughter Liza enacts with him a ritual which has been daily from her childhood. The professor kisses her fingers, pretending each one is a different ice-cream flavour: 'but the effect is utterly different. I am cold as ice and ashamed.' It gradually emerges that this menaced egotism isn't entirely the recent result of the professor's ill-health. He has always been inadequate. When his ward, the beloved Katya, is abandoned by her lover, attempts suicide and loses her baby, the professor's testimony is culpably vague: 'Later on, from certain hints, I gathered that there had been an attempt at suicide. I believe Katya tried to poison herself. I imagine that she must have been seriously ill afterwards . . .' What a damning trio of verbs: I 'gathered', I 'believe', I 'imagine'. The central heating has never been turned up very high: 'when she wrote to me of her intention of suicide, and then of the death of her baby, every time I lost my head, and all my sympathy for her sufferings found no expression except that, after prolonged reflection, I wrote long, boring letters which I might just as well not have written. And yet I took a father's place with her and loved her like a daughter!' At the story's end, when the troubled Katya follows him all the way to Harkov, she is clearly at the end of her tether, as (brilliantly) is her hat: 'she sinks on a chair and begins sobbing. She flings her head back, wrings her hands, taps with her feet; her hat falls off and hangs bobbing on its elastic . . .' And the professor's response? It is twofold. Inwardly, he feels ashamed because he is happier than she is, despite the proximity of his death and the last-minute realization that he is soulless, a man in whom 'the most skilful analyst could not find what is called a general idea, or the god of a living man'. Outwardly, his response is an invitation to lunch. Unsurprisingly, the offer is rejected.

If Chekhov has a subject, it is the nature of feeling – its failure, its forcing, its fatuity, its pretences, its fickleness. One minute, Trigorin is begging Irina to release him so that he can pursue 'a little provincial miss' who represents for him 'young love, enchanting and magical love that sweeps you off your feet into a make-believe world – can anything else on earth give one happiness?' Two years later, Konstantin reports: 'She had a baby. It died. Trigorin tired of her and returned to his former attachments, as could only be expected.' In 'An Artist's Story', the narrator muses on his declaration to Misuce in a way which suggests the subtle and complex analysis Chekhov brought to bear on the ostensibly simple subject of love: 'I was full of tenderness, peace, and satisfaction with myself – satisfaction at having been able to be carried away by my feelings and having fallen in love . . .' In 'The Duel', the susceptible Nadyezhda Fyodorovna can simultaneously luxuriate in the prospect of her continuing an illicit affair with Atchmianov and indulge in a sentimental fantasy about her regular partner, Laevsky:

> she made up her mind to go away that she might not continue this life, shameful for herself, and humiliating for Laevsky. She would beseech him with tears to let her go; and if he opposed her, she would go away secretly. She would not tell him what had happened; let him keep a pure memory of her . . . She would live in some far remote place, would work and send Laevsky, "anonymously", money, embroidered shirts, and tobacco, and would return to him only in old age or if he were dangerously ill and needed a nurse. When in his old age he learned what were

her reasons for leaving him and refusing to be his wife, he
would appreciate her sacrifice and forgive.

In fact, Laevsky is desperate to leave her and is making plans to
disappear himself – a sexual irony that looks forward to Milan
Kundera, just as his definition of kitsch fits Nadyezhda Fyodorovna's hormonally induced hypothesizing. In *The Art of the
Novel*, Kundera formulates what Chekhov shows us in action:
'Kitsch is the translation of the stupidity of received ideas into
the language of beauty and feeling. It moves us to tears of
compassion for ourselves, for the banality of what we think and
feel.'

The curious thing about 'The Duel' is that this kitsch fantasy
of transgression and forgiveness actually transpires in the course
of the narrative. Atchmianov maliciously leads Laevsky to Mur-
idov's, where Laevsky finds Nadyezhda Fyodorovna in bed with
Kirilin, the police chief. Then Laevsky fights a duel, narrowly
escapes with his life – 'on the right side of his neck was a small
swelling, of the length and breadth of his little finger, and he felt
a pain, as though someone had passed a hot iron over his neck.
The bullet had bruised it' – and is reconciled to his erring
partner and his previously wearisome work. His opponent, Von
Koren, is so impressed by the moral reformation that, before
taking a boat which will carry him away from the Caucasus, he
offers his hand. The element of kitsch is purged by Chekhov
when he gives us a glimpse of Laevsky's thoughts on seeing the
boat which is to ferry Von Koren to the ship. The sea is rough
and the boat moves three yards forward only to be sucked two
yards back. 'No one knows the real truth . . .' thinks Laevsky,
'looking wearily at the dark, restless sea.' It is a pity that
Chekhov should make the equation explicit – 'in the search for
truth man makes two steps forward and one step back' – when
the juxtaposition alone would have told us that the perceived
perfection of the remade life was nothing of the kind, but rather
a bitter struggle of backsliding and romantic recidivism.

These dark notes are not difficult to hear in 'A Dreary Story'
or in 'The Duel', despite the play in both tales of grim comedy.

But what of an apparently innocent, slight story like 'An Incident'? Widely regarded as a charming (if callous) humoresque, it is, in fact, a bleak parable of human cruelty and unconsidered indifference. The children, Vanya and Nina, are a mixture of whimsy ('the cat has got puppies!') and casual cruelty. While we may be charmed by their ingénue playfulness when they decide that the father of the 'puppies' should be the 'dark-red horse without a tail', we can't help registering the truth of the behaviour presented by Chekhov: 'Vanya is watching its movements, and thrusting first a pencil, then a match into its little mouth . . .'; 'he tries to open one kitten's eyes, and spends a long time puffing and breathing hard over it, but his operation is unsuccessful'. This is recognizable childish behaviour, shrewdly seen by Chekhov, and we readers are charmed by its accuracy into overlooking its lack of proper feeling for the kittens. Subtly, we are compromised and go on being morally compromised when we encounter the expected ending – the consumption of the kittens by the dog, Nero. The laughter of the adults and the footman invites us to join in. We can't take the compassion of children too seriously since we have already witnessed the actions they themselves have visited on the kittens. The whole posture of the story encourages us to read it as comedy. Yet it isn't. We have to take into account the ironic moral peroration near the opening of the story: 'Domestic animals play a scarcely noticed but undoubtedly beneficial part in the education and life of children,' it begins. In the midst of an ostensibly idyllic catalogue, this is the first indication of irony: 'birds dying in captivity', an item which is mildly disconcerting and undeniably familiar. The mood of warm indulgence doesn't quite carry off the reference to treading on the cat's tail 'for fun' either. The peroration ends with the assertion that children learn more from animals – about patience, fidelity, forgiveness and sincerity – than they do from the 'long exhortations' of tutors and governesses. In context, those four qualities are tinged with irony because it is the animals who are required to possess them. By the denouement, Chekhov makes it clear that we have learned from animals. We have learned the moral sense of animals. We

are unperturbed by Nero's action – even amused – and our
proper feelings remain immobilized. Basic decency is nowhere in
evidence, only the 'snigger' of the footman. In four pages,
Chekhov has sketched the moral universe of *Lord of the Flies*,
without raising his voice above a deceptively humorous murmur:
'the children expect that all the people in the house will be
aghast and fall upon the miscreant Nero. But they all sit calmly
in their seats, and only express surprise at the appetite of the
huge dog.' *In their seats* is unnecessarily specific – 'they all sit
calmly' would have been enough – but taken with 'Nero' it
ghosts the proceedings with other, bloodier entertainments,
Roman circuses and their equally calm spectators.

In *The Unbearable Lightness of Being*, Milan Kundera
touches on this idea of repetition, of eternal recurrence. The
unbearable lightness of being is experienced when nothing has
weight or importance because nothing is ever repeated: the myth
of eternal recurrence is negated. On the other hand, 'if every
second of our lives recurs an infinite number of times, we are
nailed to eternity as Jesus Christ was nailed to the cross'. This is
the unbearable heaviness of being. Chekhov's characters typically suffer from a mixture of these two myths. Their unhappi-
ness arises out of the sense that their lives are infected with
futility and insignificance – the eternal repetition of actions
whose triviality is suddenly apparent. Life is not life but a
shabby simulacrum: 'I have the feeling,' thinks the professor in
'A Dreary Story', 'as though I had once lived at home with a
real wife and children and that now I am dining with visitors, in
the house of a sham wife who is not the real one, and am
looking at a Liza who is not the real Liza.' For these characters,
very different in other respects, meaning has seeped out of their
lives. Certain protagonists come to terms with their bled existences like, for example, the sterile, cruel egotist Orlov in 'An
Anonymous Story', of whom the revolutionist narrator remarks:
'How early your soul has taken to its dressing gown.' The
majority, however, rebel against their fate, without necessarily
coming any closer to moral redemption. The cry, when it comes,
is standard. The narrator's sister, Kleopatra, in 'My Life',

explodes to her nurse: 'Haven't I wasted my youth? All the best years of my life to know nothing but keeping accounts, pouring out tea, counting the half-pence, entertaining visitors, and thinking there was nothing better in the world! Nurse, do understand, I have the cravings of a human being, and *I want to live* [my italics] and they have turned me into a housekeeper.' Forty pages on, she is unmarried, ill and pregnant: 'I want to act on the stage, I want to live . . .' Her acting comes to grief in the most brilliant account of stage-fright in the whole of literature. It is only a rehearsal: 'she came forward into the middle of the stage with an expression of horror on her face, looking ugly and angular, and for half a minute stood as though in a trance, perfectly motionless, and only her big earrings shook in her ears.'

In 'The Duel', Nadyezhda Fyodorovna shares her plea: 'all this, together with the sultry heat and the soft, transparent waves, excited her and whispered that she must live, live . . .' In 'An Anonymous Story', we re-encounter the formulaic plaint, this time in the mouth of a consumptive narrator: ' "I want to live!" I said genuinely. "To live, to live!" ' And it reappears with undiminished sincerity in 'The Lady with the Dog', where Anna Sergeyevna confesses to her new lover, Gurov: 'I have been tormented by curiosity; I wanted something better. "There must be a different sort of life," I said to myself. I wanted to live! To live, to live! . . .' Collated thus, these heady resolves, identical down to the repetition and aposiopesis, begin to lose a certain potency – and resemble a different illustration of the doctrine of eternal recurrence.

In fact, Chekhov is more repetitive than any great writer has the right to be. The democratic desire to live, live . . . shared among so many characters can be explained as a thematic preoccupation, as can the several discussions of Tolstoyan philosophy which are repeated, more or less unchanged, from story to story to story. 'My Life' and 'An Artist's Story' both address the idea that manual labour should be shared: 'all, without exception, strong and weak, rich and poor, should take part equally in the struggle for existence'. In 'An Artist's Story', this is taken further: the narrator resists social improvement like schools and medical centres, preferring to tackle the 'central' issue of labour. The sharing out of labour would, he argues, free man for his 'highest vocation' – 'the perpetual search for truth and the meaning of life'. This Tolstoyan tosh, advocating communal road-mending as a way to escape from 'this continual, agonizing dread of death, and even from death itself', is thoroughly demolished in 'Ward No. 6' – where Dr Ragin's counsel of philosophic indifference to external circumstances is tested when he finds himself an occupant of Ward 6 for the mentally disturbed. His dressing gown smells of smoked fish; he experiences 'a strange, persistent feeling of irritation', eventually traced to a desire to smoke; beaten up, he survives barely a day: he dies of an apoplectic stroke, in a passage of extraordinarily brilliant writing which utterly transcends the somewhat mechanical debate at the centre of the story. Wittgenstein's irrefutable statement – that death is not an event in life – is somehow refuted by Chekhov:

> At first he felt a numbing chill and nausea; something horrible seemed to be spreading all over his body, even over his fingers, extending from his stomach to his head and flooding his eyes and ears. Everything turned green before his eyes. Dr Ragin realized that his end had come, and remembered that Gromov, the postmaster, and millions of people believed in immortality. What if it did exist? But he did not want immortality, and he thought of it only for a moment. A herd of deer, extraordinarily beautiful and graceful, which he had been reading about on the previous day, raced past him; then a peasant woman stretched out a hand to him with a registered letter . . . The postmaster said something. Then everything vanished, and Dr Ragin lost consciousness for ever.

What an astonishing, lucid, convincing exposition of mental confusion, bringing us, imposing on us with swift authority, the last illusions of a brain able, for once, to be above its circumstances. In death, Dr Ragin's theory is ironically validated.

Elsewhere in Chekhov, a brilliant passage or a brilliant phrase is quite likely to be dimmed by its duplication in another corner of the canon. The dog, Nero, has 'a tail as hard as a stick' in 'An Incident' and so has Som in 'A Teacher of Literature': 'Som was a tall black dog with long legs and a tail as hard as a stick.' In the same story, Varya, the elder daughter, is contrary: 'every conversation, even about the weather, she invariably turned into an argument'. In this trait, she is not unlike Pyotr Petrovitch in 'An Artist's Story', 'who had retained from his student days the habit of turning every conversation into an argument'. Both are remarkably similar to Dr Blagovo in 'My Life', who has 'a habit of turning every conversation into an argument'. 'The Chorus Girl' is one of Chekhov's greatest stories: an enraged upper-class wife bursts in on her husband's chorus girl mistress, while the husband overhears everything in the next room. The physical difference is the first thing to make itself felt. Chekhov is as usual brilliantly laconic: 'Pasha felt that on this lady in black with the angry eyes and white slender fingers she produced the impression of something horrid and unseemly, and she felt ashamed of her chubby red cheeks, the pock-mark on her nose, and the fringe on her forehead, which never could be combed back.' What selection. It is as if Chekhov were holding to the prescription Konstantin formulates for Trigorin: 'Trigorin's worked out his methods, it's easy enough for him. He gives you the neck of a broken bottle glittering against a weir and the black shadow of a mill-wheel – and there's your moonlit night all cut and dried.' Or perhaps he was following the injunction implicit in his story 'The Wolf': 'on the dam, which was covered with moonlight, there was not a trace of shadow; on the middle of it the neck of a broken bottle glittered like a star'. Either way, 'the pock-mark on her nose' is the (beautifully singular) source of the sentence's energy. Both women behave well in the story – the wife according to some consciously noble formula, the tart out of genuine sympathy, tinged with fear. The husband, of course, is more taken by the wife's performance: 'The door from the next room opened and Kolpakov walked in. He was pale and kept shaking his head nervously, as though he had swallowed something very bitter; tears were glistening in his eyes.' *As though he had swallowed something very bitter*. We all recognize the agonized expression of someone trying to hold back tears.

What a pity, then, that, in 'The Duel', Chekhov should recycle the phrase for Von Koren's more conventional, straight-forward disgust when he hears that Kirilin and Nadyezhda Fyodorovna have been caught in flagrante: 'he walked away from Sheshkovsky, unwilling to hear more, and as though he had accidentally tasted something bitter, spat loudly again, and for the first time that morning looked with hatred at Laevsky'. In 'The Lady with the Dog', Gurov arrives at S— in search of Anna Sergeyevna. The provincial hotel is created with a single stroke. 'On the table was an inkstand, grey with dust and adorned with a figure on horseback, with its hat in its hand and its head broken off.' With this resource on call, why is it that Chekhov should redeploy 'a long grey fence adorned with nails' from its previous situation outside Ward 6? Neither is particu-larly distinguished. Nor is the phrase used to describe the English governess in 'A Daughter of Albion' and Gnekker in 'A Dreary Story': both have 'prominent eyes like a crab's'. Similarly, Zinaida in 'An Anonymous Story' shares a tic with Liza in 'A Dreary Story': the former 'screwed up her eyes and looked at me', the latter has a 'way of screwing up her eyes whenever there are men in the room'. Occasionally, the repetitions occur in the same story: in 'My Life', Moisey, the agent, is seen uneasily 'crumpling up his cap in his hands'; then an old servant, gripped by emotion, begins 'crumpling up her apron in her agitation'; lastly, Kleopatra, the sister, is shown 'crumpling up the manuscript' before she fails in the rehearsal. Then there is the character who, in several stories, insists on saying the obvious: in 'The Teacher of Literature' it is Ippolit Ippolititch, who dies, 'but even in his delirium' says 'nothing that was not perfectly well known to everyone': 'The Volga flows into the

Caspian Sea . . . Horses eat oats and hay . . .' In 'An Anonymous Story', Zinaida is silenced by Orlov's complaint: 'don't talk of things that everybody knows'.

In the end, oddly enough, these repetitions matter less than they might in another author. It is easy enough to see why if we return to Moisey, the cap-crumpling agent from 'My Life'. This is the full description in which the gesture plays only a part: 'Moisey, a thin pock-marked fellow of twenty-five, with insolent little eyes, who was in the service of the general's widow, stood near him crumpling up his cap in his hands; *one of his cheeks was bigger than the other, as though he had lain too long on it.*' (My italics.) In *ABC of Reading*, Ezra Pound relates: 'It is said that Flaubert taught De Maupassant to write. When De Maupassant returned from a walk Flaubert would ask him to describe someone, say a concierge whom they would both pass in their next walk, and to describe the person so that Flaubert would recognize, say, the concierge and not mistake her for some other concierge and not the one De Maupassant had described.' Chekhov invariably writes as if this precept were before him at his desk. It is these touches, the swift brush strokes of genius, that neutralize the clichés, the artistic lapses and the argumentative longueurs which disfigure Chekhov's work. Is it likely, for instance, that Dr Ragin will receive Gromov's acute and hostile analysis of his own character with such equanimity? Surely a little ruffle would be in order? Isn't the progress of 'The Darling' just a touch too broadly comic and predictable as she moves from partner to partner, first acquiring then shedding her successive consort's opinions? Can we tolerate (in 'A Daughter of Albion') a silence like 'the stillness of the grave'?

'The Darling' is a good test case. The story begins with such sweet authority that the subsequent variants live in the verisimilitude of the first marriage and her life before it: 'she was always fond of someone, and could not exist without loving. In earlier days she had loved her papa, who now sat in a darkened room, breathing with difficulty.' It is completely convincing, that darkened room and the difficult breathing – as is the nickname given her by the actors, 'Vanitchka and I'. As is the telegram announcing his sudden death: 'Ivan Petrovitch died suddenly yesterday. Awaiting immate instructions fufuneral Tuesday.' No amount of comically stretched plotting could impair these perfect details. In any case, 'The Darling' is a parable like 'An Incident'. Irina in *Three Sisters* speaks for a great many Chekhovian souls when she says: 'Oh, I've longed for love, dreamed about it so much day and night, but my heart is like a wonderful grand piano that can't be used because it's locked up and the key's lost.' Without love, life is without meaning. In 'The Darling' Chekhov shows us this truth comically. Olga Semyonovna has no opinions, no meaning, when there is no love in her life. Sex isn't the issue either, as Chekhov makes clear when the ten-year-old Sasha enters her life and they do his lessons together: ' "An island is a piece of land," she repeated, and this was the first opinion to which she gave utterance with positive conviction after so many years of silence and dearth of ideas.' She is no longer an island.

In 1970, Vladimir Nabokov replied to the contributors whose essays appeared in a special Nabokov number of *Triquarterly*. Of Simon Karlinsky's contribution he had this to say: 'He is right, I do love Chekhov dearly. I fail, however, to rationalize my feeling for him: I can easily do so in regard to a greater artist, Tolstoy, with the flash of this or that unforgettable passage ('. . . how sweetly she said: "and even very much" ' – Vronsky recalling Kitty's reply to some trivial question that we will never know), but when I imagine Chekhov with the same detachment all I can make out is a medley of dreadful prosaisms, ready-made epithets, repetitions, doctors, unconvincing vamps, and so forth; yet it is *his* works which I would take on a trip to another planet.' Actually, the prosaic is an intrinsic and essential part of Chekhov's art. There is something akin to Jane Austen in him, the Austen evoked by Virginia Woolf:

humbly and gaily she collected the twigs and straws out of which the nest was to be made and placed them neatly together. The twigs and straw were a little dry and dusty in themselves. There was a big house and the little house;

a tea party, a dinner party, and an occasional picnic; life
was hedged in with valuable connections and adequate
incomes; by muddy roads, wet feet, and a tendency on the
part of ladies to get tired . . . Vice, adventure, passion were
left outside. But of all this prosiness, of all this littleness,
she evades nothing, and nothing is slurred over.

Of course, 'vice, adventure, passion' show themselves in 'The
Duel' but the length of the story brings its own inevitability to
the duel, the fornications, the fever and the fret: the sensational
is bedded down in the flamboyantly unsensational. There is a
picnic which wouldn't be out of place in *Emma*, except that
Chekhov displays a certain relish for the sordid details: 'as is
always the case at picnics, in the mass of dinner napkins, parcels,
useless greasy papers fluttering in the wind, no one knew where
was his glass or where his bread'. And earlier, when Von Koren
is advocating the extermination of the Laevsky type, Dr Samoy-
lenko interrupts him: ' "With pepper, with pepper," he cried in
a voice of despair, seeing that the deacon was eating stuffed
aubergines without pepper.' For prosaic prose, Chekhov had
perfect pitch. The candidly virtuosic brilliance was beyond him.

In *Speak, Memory*, Nabokov includes this bravura sentence
as a paragraph on its own: 'The tennis court was a region of
great lakes.' No one has caught the aftermath of a rain storm
with the same stylistic panache. It is poetry. Chekhov's speciality, though, was touched on earlier when I quoted his comment
to Suvorin after his brother's death: 'there's not a copeck's
worth of poetry left in life'. Torpor, rather than exaltation, is
his forte: 'on the right came the faint, reluctant note of the
golden oriole'. *Reluctant*. When Nabokov, in *The Gift*, reports
that 'a cuckoo began to call in a copse, listlessly', we note the
adverb is perfect and Chekhov's copyright. In the best of these
stories, there is a Godot provincialism: nothing happens, not
twice, but several times: 'at Dubetchnya they were plastering the
inside of the station, and building a wooden upper storey to the
pumping shed. It was hot; there was a smell of lime, and
workmen sauntered *listlessly* between the heaps of shavings and

mortar rubble. The pointsman lay asleep near his sentry-box, and the sun was blazing full on his face. There was not a single tree. The telegraph wire hummed faintly and hawks were perching on it here and there.' (My italics.)

Some critics find the longer stories deficient in shapeliness. This is a totally misdirected criticism. In the short story, long or short, obvious form is precisely to be avoided. The danger is design and clamorous shape of the kind that threatens 'The Darling' with an excess of pattern. There are two solutions – length and a prodigal generosity with detail. In 'My Life', for example, Tcheprakov is as vivid as it is possible for a minor character to be: 'by way of bravado he used to strip and run about the country naked. He used to eat flies and say they were rather sour.' Generous detail, but still Chekhov doesn't make a meal of his meal. The same thing is true of the railway navvies: 'And more than once I had seen these tatterdemalions with a bloodstained countenance being led to the police station, while a samovar or some linen, *wet from the wash*, was carried behind by way of evidence.' (My italics again.) Only four words – with the weight of a world behind them.

Chekhov's skill is, as it were, to make that Russian month in the country a day-trip, to give his readers a concentrate, without ever creating the impression of parsimony or short measure. His endings are almost always open-ended. 'It began to spot with rain.' 'Two minutes later he was sitting on the sand and angling as before.' 'The sheep were pondering, too.' 'She remembered how three years ago a merchant had beaten her for no sort of reason, and she wailed more loudly than ever.' 'And it was clear to both of them that they still had a long, long way to go, and that the most complicated and difficult part of it was only just beginning.' Were one to attempt an encapsulation of Chekhov's genius, it would centre on this gift for distraction, for what appears in the corner of the eye. Two lovers kiss for the first time. Chekhov imagines them and accepts the suggestion from the corner of his mind: 'we were silent for some time, then I put my arms around her and kissed her, scratching my cheek till it bled with her hatpin as I did it'. Another couple, in a different story, kiss for the first time and Chekhov not only captures the kiss at the lips but also its complicated bodily consequences: 'she turned pale, moved her lips, then stepped back from Nikitin and found herself in the corner between the wall and the cupboard . . . She threw back her head and he kissed her lips, and that it might last longer he put his fingers to her cheeks; and it somehow happened that he found himself in the corner between the cupboard and the wall, and she put her arms round his neck and pressed her head against his chin.' Exactly.

# Pasternak's *An Essay in Autobiography*

Titles mattered to Pasternak. He came to regret as pretentious the title he gave his first volume of poetry, *A Twin in the Clouds*. He always wanted to change Scriabin's *L'Extase* to something less reminiscent of 'a tight soap wrapper'.

Like Lenin, who was born Vladimir Ilyich Ulyanov, Pasternak's *An Essay in Autobiography* started life innocuously enough under a different name. At the instigation of Nikolay Bannikov, his editor at Goslitizdat, Pasternak completed these memoirs in May and June of 1956. At that stage, they were entitled 'Instead of a Foreword' and intended to introduce a one-volume edition of his poetry. By November 1957, Pasternak had corrected the proofs. On 22 November, *Il Dottor Živago* was published in Italy and launched at the Hotel Intercontinental in Milan by the publisher Giangiacomo Feltrinelli. From that moment on, Pasternak's memoir was no longer innocuous. When it eventually appeared in the Soviet Union in January 1967, it was slightly abridged for *Novy Mir* and under yet another alias – like the dangerous character it had become – *People and Circumstances*. In the interval, it had been published worldwide – in America as *I Remember – A Sketch in Autobiography*. Only in Italy, where it was entitled *Autobiografia e nuovi versi*, did the book fulfil Pasternak's original conception – of a volume consisting of newly composed poems and poems which had previously appeared only in periodicals. However, at some stage, Goslitizdat's offer was for, as Guy de Mallac puts it, 'a large volume of Pasternak's poetry (including all the Zhivago poems except "Hamlet")'. Even earlier, Pasternak himself may have intended the essay to introduce his collected works, including *Doctor Zhivago*. At any rate, this joint volume of prose and poetry goes some way towards meeting Pasternak's intention of thirty years ago.

Just as *An Essay in Autobiography* has several *noms de guerre*, so it isn't Pasternak's only attempt at the genre. It has a cloudy twin, the memoir *Safe Conduct*, which Pasternak began in the late twenties and which was published, before appearing in book form, in separate parts from 1929 to 1931 in the journals *Zvezda* and *Krasnaya nov*. Though *Safe Conduct* covers the same period of time and some of the same topics, *An Essay in Autobiography* successfully avoids repetition, is much more readable and quite self-standing. Its approaches are different; it adds a lot of welcome and necessary self-irony; it excises a great many passages of turgid aesthetic speculation, and brings the story, if not up to date, at least to the point where it can briefly bring back to life Marina Tsvetayeva and Pasternak's Georgian friends, Paolo Yashvili and Titsian Tabidze, all three of whom, in their various ways, were victims of Stalin's terror. Pasternak sets down the history of his acquaintance with Tsvetayeva and his feelings of guilt and inadequacy quite frankly, courting neither punishment nor exoneration, in a testimony to the complication of truth that is moving because matter of fact – in the deepest as well as the most obvious sense. We see the Georgian friends toasting Pasternak's black eye at an hilarious, tipsy supper. The nearest Pasternak approaches to the time of composition is in a brief, compassionate reference to the suicide of Alexander Fadeyev in 1956 – an allusion justified by Pasternak's analysis of Mayakovsky's suicide.

But that black eye is important because it illustrates a crucial difference between *Safe Conduct* and *An Essay in Autobiography*. This is Pasternak's increasing indifference to conventional ideas of dignity and a tardy but acute sense of the ridiculous, particularly as applied to himself. In *Safe Conduct*, the young Pasternak is convinced of the importance of being earnest, and the self-importance, too – a common enough tendency in young artists, as Joyce memorably recorded in *Ulysses*, where the young Stephen earnestly bows to himself in the mirror. *Safe Conduct* recalls the visit to Marburg of two sisters, one of whom Boris loved. Seeing off the pair at Marburg station, the young man, convinced his farewells had been inadequate, sprinted down the platform with the departing train and finally clung to it, so that, tear-stained and emotional, he had to be hauled on board by the guard. In cheap lodgings at Berlin, the young Pasternak sits by a table through the night, maintaining a particular posture: 'I have described the position of my body with such accuracy,' he writes, without a flicker of amusement, 'because this had also been its position that morning on the step of the moving train and it had memorized the posture. It was the position of someone fallen from a lofty eminence which had long sustained and carried him but had then let him fall and rushed on noisily over his head, vanishing for ever round a turning.'

There is less of this risibly lofty guff in *An Essay in Autobiography*, where, instead, Pasternak wryly observes himself as a young boy, at a time when he imagined he had once been a girl – 'and that I could regain this earlier more pleasing, more fascinating personality, by pulling in my belt so tight I almost fainted'. In his *Confessions*, Rousseau, that great dealer in the endearingly discreditable, offers his reader a contradictory analysis of his narrative indiscretions. On the one hand, their purpose is to demonstrate the uniqueness of Rousseau, to vindicate his claim that he is 'not made like any of those who are in existence' because, after producing him in an edition of one, Nature broke the mould. On the other hand, Rousseau argues, only a paragraph later, for the concept of human identity and solidarity: will anyone read these memoirs honestly, he asks, and retort, 'I was better than that man'? We all recognize the belt-tightening fantasy element in childhood and cannot say we are 'better than that man'. In *Safe Conduct*, Pasternak is rather too keen on savouring the flavour of his own uniqueness – his sensitivity, his passion, the meniscus of his emotions. *An Essay in Autobiography*, however, is much more aware of human solidarity and silliness.

Pasternak tells us there that he spoke with 'a fake *Berliner* accent' – a piece of absurd vanity which had a humiliating sequel told only by his brother, Alexander, in his memoirs, *A Vanished Present*. The essay also deplores the 'stupid pretentiousness' of calling his first book *A Twin in the Clouds*, a piece of foolishness cognate with the fashionable behaviour of his youth when 'the proper thing was to be insolent and strut about sticking one's nose in the air'. But Pasternak reserves his harshest judgement not for this foolishness, but for his own weak malleability: 'although it sickened me, I tagged along not to be left behind'. He allowed Bobrov to inaugurate and conduct quarrels for him, though his own instincts were pacific. He let himself be talked into writing Gorky 'an idiotic letter, full of ignorance, conceit and affectation'. Pasternak is not out to show himself in a good light.

It is hardly surprising, therefore, that the older, self-critical Pasternak should dismiss his earlier attempt, *Safe Conduct*, as a book 'spoiled by its affected manner, the besetting sin of those days'. More generally, he pronounces damningly on his early output: 'I dislike my style before 1940, just as I quarrel with half of Mayakovsky's writings and with some of Yesenin's. I dislike the disintegrating forms, the impoverished thought and the littered and uneven language of those days.'

Broadly, Pasternak is right. It would be easy to quote from *Safe Conduct* long passages where the 'thought' is little more than syntax in a state of fuddled exaltation. And yet *Safe Conduct* cannot be disowned in the brisk manner Pasternak proposes. It is recognizably the work of the same man who wrote *An Essay in Autobiography* – recognizable in its strengths and its weaknesses, which continue, however modified, into the later work. *Safe Conduct* isn't utterly devoid either of self-irony or self-criticism, though the early work can't match the cool urbanity of the later, whose detachment appears to be modelled on Scriabin's 'worldly manner of putting on a superficial air and avoiding serious subjects'. Not that Pasternak is ever frivolous; only that, in *An Essay in Autobiography*, he is less clenched and frowning, more relaxed and smiling.

The differences exist, then, but so do the similarities. The fake *Berliner* accent isn't so very different, after all, from *Safe Conduct*'s bogus Italian dialect 'made up from earlier attempts to read Dante in the original'. There are, too, moments of characteristically unforgiving self-criticism in *Safe Conduct*: on first meeting Mayakovsky, the young Pasternak feels 'totally bereft of talent' and later on dismisses a quarrel with Mayakovsky as 'a piece of senseless affectation on my part'. *Affectation* – the very word so favoured by the older writer.

*An Essay in Autobiography* has moments of vivid brilliance, yet all of them can be matched by quotations from the rich and wayward pages of *Safe Conduct*. The human observation is of a piece: in the *Essay*, we see and hear the Trubetskoys at the University lecturing 'in imploring accents and in droning, whining voices with an aristocratic lisp'; in *Safe Conduct*, the philosopher Samarin 'arming himself with a dry biscuit, used it like a choirmaster's tuning fork to beat out the logical divisions of his argument'. Pasternak's laconic, unpoetic poetry is also of a piece: in the *Essay*, Venice is portrayed 'swelling like a biscuit soaked in tea', while *Safe Conduct* shows us slush like 'icy kvass-soaked bread' and gives us a Venice whose side canals are dark as offal, 'full of dead rats and dancing melon peel', above which the Milky Way is like a shedding dandelion. In the *Essay*, there is the brilliant metaphoric trope which assimilates old men's grey bald spots to smoke rings; in *Safe Conduct*, the younger writer notices, with equal brilliance, that the smoke from a cigar is like a tortoiseshell comb.

In fact, *An Essay in Autobiography* is economical with its writerly gifts, where *Safe Conduct* is clumsy but prodigal. The later work can give us 'grubby' snowflakes like dropped stitches – a simile at once lucid and just and original – but *Safe Conduct*, for all its faults, is the richer in purely literary terms. A list: 'the heavy capstan of the seasons', 'a reeking gallery' of empty wicker flower hampers 'with sonorous Italian frankmarks', the leather bellows at the joints of a long train of coaches, stations 'like moths made of stone, they rushed by and fled to the rear of the train', Mayakovsky straddling a chair like a motorbike, talking, and leaving behind 'half-eaten cakes and glasses blinded with hot milk'. The gift in *Safe Conduct* is extraordinary – padded cadets learning to fence 'pecked at one another like cockerels in sacks' – and so is the pretentiousness.

By the time of *An Essay in Autobiography*, Pasternak had both more or less under control. There he describes a journey by sleigh with Zbarsky which is a tour de force of accurate observation, in which there are no intricate metaphors to dazzle or distract. Pasternak is less interested in brilliance, more interested in overall success. But a key passage in the *Essay* concerns the death of Tolstoy because it shows clearly how Pasternak has achieved control over his gifts and his susceptibilities. Almost at once, Pasternak yields to temptation: 'Tolstoy's presence filled the room like a mountain – say like Elbrus – or like a storm cloud the size of half a sky.' This is recognizably the febrile mode of the worst of *Safe Conduct* and the worst of the letters exchanged between Rilke, Pasternak and Tsvetayeva. It is followed by an opaque digression about Pushkin and then, just as one fears the worst, Pasternak revokes, in a section of wry, minutely observed realism, everything which has gone before: 'but what there was in the far corner of the room was not a mountain but a wrinkled little old man, one of the dozens of old men invented by Tolstoy and scattered through his books'. And Pasternak drops the evocative to concentrate on the actual – the fir saplings around the bed, the sheaves of light, the shadow of the cross thrown by the window, the local restaurant's brisk trade in 'underdone' beef steaks served to the world's press.

Yet just as we applaud the way in which the dry has overtaken the splashy mode, Pasternak indulges two characteristic weaknesses: the 'poetic' flouting of reality and the glib encapsulation. Both run counter to his gift for the anti-poetic – a gift which he admired in Mayakovsky and which he possessed in abundance himself, though he modestly pretended to amazement when he identified it in the other's poetry: 'I had never heard anything like it before. Everything was there in it: the boulevards, the dogs, the poplars and the butterflies, the barbers, bakers, tailors and locomotives.' The mundane was always a resource for Pasternak, as we can illustrate from *Safe Conduct*, when he compares the endlessly reiterated goodbyes to Scriabin to 'a collar stud that simply refused to slip into its narrow aperture'. Nothing could be further from this gift than the more operatic brand of poetry which tends to turn on some wonky impossibility, as if the impossibility itself were the guarantee of afflatus. In the Tolstoy passage, Pasternak concludes with a cloying poetic fiction in which the heroes and heroines created by Tolstoy unknowingly pass in the train the little station of Astapovo where his body lies dead. For a finale, Pasternak gives in to his weakness for epitome: 'as we might speak of the passionate quality of Lermontov, of Tyutchev's fecundity of thought, of Chekhov's poetry, of Gogol's . . .' It is difficult to take this high-flown Parnassian seriously. The verdicts are served up like *petits fours* in a cloud of hieratic incense. There isn't much of this in *An Essay in Autobiography*, but there is enough of it to show that the author of *Safe Conduct* and the author of the later work are closely related – perhaps even the same gifted, brilliant, simple, down-to-earth person who could be tempted by the noise of sounding generalizations.

The other half of this book is the poetry, about which I am even less qualified to speak than about the prose. I have recently translated several hundred lines of Pasternak's poetry with my wife, Ann Pasternak Slater, who speaks Russian.* The experience encourages me to comment, if timidly, about translation. Pasternak himself was a translator, and *An Essay in Autobiography* includes two asides about translation which are germane and not particularly encouraging. About Rilke, he says, 'In Russia Rilke is unknown. The few translations of him have been unsuccessful. The translators are not to blame. They are used to conveying meaning but not tone, and in Rilke tone is everything.' And of Georgy Leonidze, he says, he is 'the most independent of all poets, the one closest to the secrets of his language and therefore least translatable'. Pasternak is just such a poet –

* See *Boris Pasternak: The Tragic Years 1930–1960*.

a poet from whom we learn that translation is necessary and impossible. Pasternak's sound effects are of paramount importance and virtually unreproduceable in English, or in any other language but Russian I would imagine. Take the poem 'In Hospital'. The first line of the third stanza is a list of what the dying person sees from the ambulance window – *militsia, ulitsa, litsa*. In English, this thickly woven sound pattern is utterly lost: *policemen, streets, faces*. Any attempt to reproduce it and be faithful to the sense is futile. Pasternak's brief lists are one of the glories of his poetry: in the same poem, stanza 6, one encounters *k palatam, polam, i khalatam*, a densely assonantal line which is untranslatable except weakly as 'wards, floors, doctors' gowns'.

Another difficulty with Pasternak is his tendency, like Emily Dickinson, to tell the truth 'but tell it slant'. In one's own language, one can rely on the reader to see the slant and make the correction. In another language, though, the slant can't be reproduced without fatally adding to the confusion: the translator must translate the corrected, adjusted version to some degree, or risk losing the reader entirely. A further difficulty facing the translator is how far to succumb to the foreign idiom of the original. My own preference is to resist absolutely and aim for a poem which is at least English. Yet I can appreciate that readers develop a tolerance for foreign flavours in their translations as a spurious guarantee of authenticity. The 'flaw' actually has a positive effect on the reader. Christopher Logue's marvellous versions of Homer in *War Music* are at once boldly vernacular and yet faintly archaic and more Latinate than is normally permissible in English poetry proper – in a way that affects us as a real taste of Homer.

My mother-in-law's translations of her brother's poetry have their flaws as English poetry, yet they reproduce like no other translations some of the rhythmic complexities of Pasternak's work, and I wasn't at all surprised when Seamus Heaney and the American poet, Tom Sleigh, confessed rather shyly to me in Harvard that they found the versions of Lydia Pasternak Slater, in a curious way, the most authentic versions of Pasternak. In spite of their un-Englishness, I wanted to add at the time. Now, I suspect it was because of their un-Englishness.

The translations here are by Michael Harari and are to be welcomed once again as a brave attempt at the impossible. Having translated some of these poems myself, I am in a position to appreciate his skill and his tenacity and resourcefulness. It isn't enough, of course, but it is the best we can do.

# Pasternak's Poetry in Translation

A couple of years ago, C. H. Sisson sent me a rhyming translation of Valéry's 'Le Cimetière marin'. At roughly the same time, another poet, Alistair Elliot, sent me his translations of the French symbolists, including Mallarmé's 'Brise marine', in which the phrase 'une exotique nature' had been resourcefully but misleadingly rhymed into English as 'different stars' – a true but limiting instance of Mallarmé's proposed exotic nature. Sisson's Valéry was, I felt, open to similar objections, which I communicated to the translator – to be rewarded by a generous, enlightening reply. 'You seem to think,' wrote Sisson, 'that I am one of those who believe translation is possible, whereas I am merely one who translates.' Like Sisson, I am not persuaded that the translation of poetry is possible, though I am sure it is necessary.

The difficulties are appalling in prospect. Even something as obvious as a name can be untranslatable. In his essay 'On Translating Homer', Matthew Arnold took Professor Francis Newman to task for translating the names of Achilles's horses as 'Chestnut' and 'Spotted', 'which is as if a Frenchman were to call Miss Nightingale *Mdlle Rossignol* or Mr Bright *M. Clair*'. Or to call Boris Pasternak *Boris Parsnip*, which is what his surname 'means' in Russian. Some things are better not translated. In fact, one can generalize from this instance of names and say that anything translated runs a severe risk of becoming ludicrous or banal. Pasternak as a Russian name isn't ludicrous,

*Second Nature*, forty-six poems by Boris Pasternak, translated by Andrei Navrozov, Peter Owen.

though Parsnip is – hence Evelyn Waugh's choice of it as one name for his pair of cowardly poets in *Put Out More Flags*, Parsnip and Pimpernell. A droll but inadvertent example of the untranslatability of names occurs, as it happens, on the dust jacket of this book, where Federico García Lorca has been lost in translation but rediscovered as a not quite identical twin, Francisco García Lorca.

The qualifications for undertaking translation are straightforward, if highly restrictive – bilingualism, a feeling for poetry in both languages. The virtual impossibility of anyone fulfilling these preconditions can be illustrated by two famously bilingual writers, Conrad and Nabokov – who, for all their gifts in their adopted tongue, were not exempt from blunders. In *Nostromo*, Conrad writes, with a momentary lapse of concentration: 'This was what said his Excellency, the popular Pedrito . . .' Nor is the lapse unique, as the first sentence of Beerbohm's parody makes clear: 'In the hut where slept the white man . . .' Nabokov's poem 'Pale Fire' evokes Shade's heart attack in Russlish: 'My heart had stopped to beat.' Though Andrei Navrozov is the effortless equal of Conrad and Nabokov in their limitations – 'the quotidian of circumstances' is a Navrozovism not much in general use – this is not the best guarantee that he shares the compensatory largesse of their gifts.

A further indispensable requirement in the translator of poetry is that he should understand the meaning of the line and of the poem in the original language – and not merely money-change the words. Translation must also be interpretation. Let me illustrate this by using a photograph by André Kertész, 'Gologory, July 22, 1915, Poland'. Roland Barthes, in his study of photography, *Camera Lucida*, says of it: 'Here are some Polish soldiers resting in a field; nothing extraordinary, except this, which no realist painting would give me, that *they were there*; what I see is not a memory, an imagination, a reconstitution, a piece of Maya, such as art lavishes upon us, but reality in a past state: at once the past and the real.'

This commentary is eloquent or pretentious according to our inclination, perhaps. However, we have no choice but to call it a mistranslation. Barthes has misunderstood the photograph and in translating its image into words has missed the central point. The soldiers are sitting on a field latrine – a fact which Barthes leaves untranslated. The photograph is taken from a modest angle, so that only the figure on the right, half turned to wipe himself, lets the meaning escape from the photograph's enigmatic custody. The actual photograph defers this meaning – for ever, in the case of Barthes; temporarily, for the rest of us. But the deferment, the slyness of the image, is part of its meaning. Likewise with poetry. But the translator has to understand what has been hidden in order to re-conceal the secret appropriately in the new host language.

The reader must be able to find what has been hidden, rather than anticipate further obstruction from the translator. Robert Frost said that poetry is what gets lost in translation. D. J. Enright wittily rejoined that if poetry isn't translated a great deal more gets lost. I have always agreed with Enright until I read Andrei Navrozov's translations – when I wondered if less would have been lost if he hadn't translated Pasternak. His dotty introduction, where I am mysteriously taken to task for failing to make either my poetry or my opera libretto sufficiently Pasternakian, is incoherent enough in its arguments to be laughably harmless, but the translations themselves are surely misleading. Navrozov has translated his bafflement with Pasternak's early poetry, rather than the poetry itself. His dislike of the later, simple poetry and his inspissated versions of the early poetry are probably best explained by Valéry's jaundiced *obiter dictum*: 'most people have so vague an idea of poetry that the very vagueness of their idea is, for them, its definition'.

Though the press release claims that 'these are the first English translations of previously untranslated Pasternak poems', this is a fib. Other translations exist and can be compared. For instance, my mother-in-law's version of 'Oars at Rest' begins:

> A boat is beating in the breast of the lake.
> Willows hang over, tickling and kissing

> Neckline and knuckles and rowlocks – O wait,
> This could have happened to anyone, listen!

Not only is this translation by the late Lydia Pasternak Slater a more accurate account of her brother's original Russian, it is also lucid and intelligible, whereas Navrozov is virtually incomprehensible without hers as a crib:

> The boat is athrob in the drowsy breast,
> Kissing the clavicles, willows raise
> Oarlocks, elbows: please take a rest,
> It really happens to everyone, always!

My mother-in-law's sense of English poetry was not always perfect. But whatever her limitations, she translated more Pasternak poems than Navrozov and a great deal more effectively. Her efforts count as those of a native speaker compared to Navrozov's pitiful anthology of genteel inversions ('The tendrils and the leaves among'), sheer improbabilities ('That sprinkle the bestrewn'), hilariously obtrusive feminine rhymes ('rippling' / 'Kipling'), antiquated diction (*leman, athrob, knoll, atop, sward, conglobes, atremble, argent, helmed, swipples, spiracles, lea, plaint, sonant*) and continuous obscurity (*passim*).

In everything he writes, Mr Navrozov makes great play with the Cambridge outside his windows, its 'honeycombs of sandstone', notices on the college lawn – so much so that one occasionally thinks that he must be a bedder, rather than the bane of his colleagues in some senior common room. A line of Pasternak in this collection, literal and inept, gives one further pause, however. 'Slant my soul empty! Foam it out entire!' Can Mr Navrozov really imagine some variant of this on the lips of bibulous academics as they 'encirculate' the port and Madeira? 'Splash out my spirit!' would have been a more plausible line in English.

# Bulgakov's Magic Realism

When *The Master and Margarita*, Mikhail Bulgakov's magnificent but flawed masterpiece, finally appeared in Russia in 1966–7, its uniqueness was a provocation to Soviet literary critics. Publication, even thirty years after composition, 'prompted an urgent search for "likenesses"'. With the assistance of the rediscovered writings of Bakhtin, a suitably reassuring and satisfactorily antique analogue was apparently found in the medieval mystery play, whose sacred core is surrounded by an ethos of licence. Lesley Milne records this without irony.

In fact, Bulgakov is the first magic realist, if you except Gogol's excursion into the genre with 'The Nose'. Magic realism is a technique which adds the impossible to the ordinary – trinitrotoluene to the ingredients of a fruit cake, the devil and his entourage to a Moscow straitened by shortages, the transformation of a dog, Sharik, into a man of sorts. It is a genre in which anything can happen, only provided it happens with the inevitability of a dream – and not with the haplessness of what Nabokov, in *Speak, Memory*, calls an 'inept nightmare'.

Everything depends on the detailed presentation of the extraordinary. The satirical import of *Heart of a Dog* is clear enough if one correlates the behaviour of Sharik, as a dog and as a man, with Professor Philip Philipovich Preobrazhensky's diatribe of complaints against the proletariat since 1917 – petty theft, wanton vandalism, filth and the absence of toilet-training. The

*Mikhail Bulgakov: A Critical Biography* by Lesley Milne, Cambridge University Press.

burden of *Heart of a Dog* is that you cannot change an animal into a human being of any worth by engineering. Written in early 1925, the novella is a shrewd assessment of the inertia in the human soul. And it is 'counter-revolutionary', even though the Professor prefers the formula of 'common sense and good advice based on practical experience'.

Lesley Milne, however, finds Bulgakov's barbs 'innocent' and the overall tone 'ebullient' rather than mordant. Her reasons are somewhat confused, since they imply that authorial intention is affected by audience reception. *Heart of a Dog* cannot be 'grim satire' because, she says, 'there was a serious attempt to publish [it] in 1925–6 and a serious offer of a stage adaptation indicates that, from the perspective of the early to mid 1920s, its political aspects were not immediately perceived as breaking taboos'. If the fragments are in front of you, it is not an argument against iconoclasm to say that some people were deaf to the noise of the hammer. Secondly, the performance history of *The Days of the Turbins* – reviled by the official Soviet critics and playing to packed houses night after night – argues that Russian society was more evenly divided in its sympathies than the outcome of the revolution might suggest. Some readers, some editors, even, might be delighted by the counter-revolutionary content of *Heart of a Dog*. Thirdly, Bulgakov's barbs finally proved so innocent and good-natured that his flat was searched and the manuscript confiscated along with his diaries. The novella was first published in Germany in 1968.

In *Heart of a Dog*, Bulgakov proves himself to be a great magic realist by describing the surgical operation in detail. In terms of his allegory, the operation is beside the point. It is only the means to an end – a given, which Bulgakov refuses to accept as a matter of course. Where a lesser author might have *begun* with the successful conclusion of the surgery, Bulgakov lets us hear the scraping of the razor as it shaves the dog's head. We see the odd drop of blood, the soap. We watch the abdominal incision being clipped and staunched. When Preobrazhensky tears out the seminal vesicles, they come 'with some shreds hanging from them'. The trepanning of the skull follows: 'then with an oddly shaped saw, the end of which he inserted into the first hole, he began to saw, just as a cabinetmaker would saw a lady's sewing chest. The skull shook and squeaked.' The operation takes five pages, during which Sharik's 'thready pulse' is revived with camphor injections, before the meninges are replaced and the head sewn up 'in some five minutes, breaking three needles'.

Bulgakov even remembers the boracic powder in the rubber gloves. Chapter 5, which follows, switches to Dr Bormenthal's meticulous notes on the patient. Here Bulgakov brilliantly manages the transition from orthodox medical ('Slight improvement. Pulse 180, respiration 92, temperature 41. Camphor, alimentation by enema') to the purely fantastical ('Today, after his tail dropped off, he enunciated with utmost clarity the word "saloon"'). The turning point, the hinge linking the literal and the licensed, is beautifully masked by a mistake – a deliberate 'mistake' in the dating, which provides a crucial distraction. The entry after 31 December reads: '*December 1 (Crossed out, corrected) January 1, 1925*. Photographed this morning. Happily barks "tsurt", repeating the word loudly and apparently gaily . . .' The word is later deciphered. Of this tour de force, Lesley Milne remarks laconically: 'the actual details of the operation were easily imaginable on the basis of Bulgakov's own surgical experience'.

There was, too, an old school friend in the rejuvenation business, while an uncle of Bulgakov's was a gynaecologist whose living space, like Professor Preobrazhensky's, had been curtailed. These meticulous details might lead you to believe that this critical biography leaned more towards biography than criticism. But this is not the case. Bulgakov's extremely interesting life, the seminal vesicles, as it were, are encased in a large body of dogged literary criticism. Hardly a name is allowed to pass without the statutory examination of its etymology. If Bulgakov mentions the electrically lit cross of St Vladimir in Kiev, Lesley Milne can tell us it was erected in 1853, is 62 feet in height, cast in bronze, with a relief on the pedestal 'representing the baptism of the Russian people'. Aleksey Turbin's dream in *The White Guard* unleashes a four-page essay on the genre from the thirteenth-century fabliau, through Byron's *The Vision of Judgement*, to George Bernard Shaw – 'none of them necessarily known to Bulgakov'. Where heavy industry is required, Lesley Milne seldom lets you down, or lets you off. Though the source for the play *Zoyka's Apartment* is supposed to be an evening edition of *Krasnaya gazeta*, 'a diligent search' has been fruitless. *Evening Moscow*, another paper *not* cited, has provided analogous low-life criminal material, but not the particular story required . . .

And the buried life? Bulgakov was temporarily a morphine addict: as a young medic, he had sucked out a blockage in the throat of a child while performing a tracheotomy; the morphine was used to alleviate the pain of the subsequent anti-diphtheria injection. In 1915, Bulgakov witnessed the suicide of his best-man. These two incidents lend authenticity to the story 'Morphine', particularly the moment of death: 'suddenly Polyakov's mouth twisted into a feeble grimace, like a sleepy person trying to blow a fly off his nose'. Bulgakov married three times and swore his first wife to secrecy about his activities with the White Army. This vow appears to have covered two things. First, his intense commitment to the White cause, as borne out by his first piece of published work – an anti-Bolshevik diatribe in a newspaper. Secondly, his involvement, as an army doctor, with compromising and murderous incidents, about which Lesley Milne is less than clear: 'Bulgakov's first awareness of physical anti-Semitism seems to have been forced upon him in extreme circumstances which rendered absolute both personal responsibility and personal weakness.' Bulgakov, it seems, acted under compulsion, but was to blame. One would like to know if there is more to know. Likewise, one would receive with gratitude more information about Bulgakov's visits to the Moscow casino, his inability to leave the house alone for six months in 1934 and the return of this neurosis in 1937.

The life is exemplary. Although it was lived courageously, it was also lived with cunning and compromise because it was lived in an atmosphere drenched in fear. Lesley Milne makes a brave attempt to detect double-edged, ironical strata in Bulgakov's play for Stalin, but *Batum* is clearly a capitulation in Bulgakov's own terms. The pen is not mightier than the sword. Witness Mandelstam's poem to Stalin, Pasternak's, Akhmatova's. If, as Lesley Milne maintains, the play was mined with hidden criticism of Stalin, why should Bulgakov have been devastated when the tyrant turned it down? Instead, it shortened his life. An ironist would have accepted the risk and expected the consequences. No. Two years previously, Bulgakov was too scared to leave the house. As a young man, he knew about defeat. Later, he knew cowardice at first hand and courageously wrote about it in *The Master and Margarita*.

# Bulgakov's *The Master and Margarita*

Written in the 1930s, unpublished until 1966, Mikhail Bulgakov's great novel, *The Master and Margarita*, has passed from translation to exploitation. Rumour has it that Mick Jagger, Fellini, Lyubimov and Polanski have all acquired, at one time or another, the film rights. The composer Nigel Osborne once told me that Spielberg had the musical rights. In May 1989, the Paris Opéra staged York Höller's opera *Le Maître et Marguerite*. Höller's libretto concentrated, though not exclusively, on the magic realist main plot, in which the Devil and his entourage descend on communist Moscow only to discover that its inhabitants are as venal as ever, unchanged by the revolution and the dictatorship of the proletariat.

This Easter, with a budget of £230,000, Channel 4 will screen *Pontius Pilate*, reversing Höller's emphasis by adapting the novel's sub-plot, which deals with Pilate, Judas and Yeshua Ha-Notsri, the Jesus-figure. The script, by Mark Rogers and Paul Bryers, is, appropriately, religiously faithful to Bulgakov's text – a text which is classic realist, bricks and mortar, a non-divine documentary life, ironically offered as religious proof to a pair of atheists by the Devil. John Woodvine plays Pilate and Mark Rylance takes the role of Yeshua. One day, there will be a film of the whole book, preferably stretched, *Heimat*-like, over twenty-odd hours of television time. Meanwhile, the omens look good for this self-standing extract, though I write this in advance of the shoot.

Less than a week before Take One, I met co-writer and director, Paul Bryers. All film-makers have a thousand things to fret about. Bryers had just had to 'cancel the dwarf' to keep within his tiny budget. He was, he said, 'beginning to get obsessed by flies', even though they are, I learn, the responsibility of the make-up artist. How do you get them to stay on a piece of meat? 'Apparently you cut their wings off and stick them on.'

With all this buzzing in his head, Bryers is surprisingly hospitable to late suggestions. When I point out that the script contains a mistake – confusing the face of the degenerate Tiberius Caesar with the face of the crucified Yeshua – Bryers reflects for maybe half a minute, then concedes the point. For a film director, he is strangely respectful of his source, bringing to it the attentiveness that John Huston brought to Joyce's story 'The Dead'.

We cross Theobald's Road, leaning out of the traffic's slip-stream like bullfighters, and agree that Bulgakov's Yeshua narrative, though ostensibly told by three different narrators, is in fact an unmistakably unified style. Never mind that one narrator, the poet Bezdomny, *dreams* the execution of Yeshua while he is an inmate of a lunatic asylum. The narrative prose is sane, factual, saturated in detail, solid with reality. 'His long sword bumped against his laced leather boot.' Jinking now to the opposite pavement, Bryers laments the lack of nomenclature for this kind of prose – pure protein, thrillingly utilitarian – and is reduced to quoting: 'Early in the morning on the fourteenth of the spring month of Nisan the Procurator of Judaea, Pontius Pilate, in a white cloak lined with blood-red, emerged with his shuffling cavalryman's walk into the arcade connecting the two wings of the palace of Herod the Great.' The unadorned, packed rhetoric here might be called forensic, as if a professional witness – a police officer of genius – were reading a statement in court.

*Reduced to quoting* ... Something odd here. It transpires that Paul Bryers is a writer who became a director in order to stop directors messing around with his writing. He isn't afraid of words, in other words, though we have a longish discussion about how to shoot eight minutes of conversation between Pilate and Arthanius, the head of his secret police. In the novel, this is a masterpiece of sustained irony. Though Pilate appears to order the protection of Judas (from Yeshua's angry followers), he actually insinuates that Judas should be murdered. The aesthetic pleasure is in the very length of the encounter, in seeing how long the ironies can be sustained and refined without once faltering into the explicit. Some of this will be acceptable on screen. All the same, 'it's a hell of a long time without any action and I hate pointless business'. Perhaps, Bryers ventures, flies buzzing around the food will provide an excuse for a few hand movements.

In any case, he associates the head of the secret police with the Devil, basing his interpretation on the Devil's disclosure in Chapter 3: 'The fact is . . . I was there myself. On the balcony with Pontius Pilate, in the garden when he talked to Caiaphas and on the platform, but secretly, incognito so to speak . . .' Arthanius is generally shown as a hooded figure. It is a plausible theory and it also means that, while Pilate is procuring the murder of Judas, any flies will additionally call up the epithet, Lord of the Flies.

When I ask Bryers to isolate the thematic centre of the Yeshua–Pilate story, he picks on the idea of cowardice. Arthanius reports back to Pilate, after the crucifixion, that Yeshua's only words were that 'he regarded cowardice as one of the worst human sins'. At this point, Bryers believes, the Devil–Arthanius is deliberately tormenting Pilate with his sacrifice to political expediency of Yeshua, a man he knows to be fundamentally innocent. In fact, Bryers maintains that Yeshua's words about cowardice have been invented by the Devil as a reproach: 'Stalin's machine was kept going by the ease with which people betrayed each other, casual betrayals in order to get a nice flat once its occupant had been arrested.' Which is exactly what happens in the main plot to the Master. None of which would be possible, according to Bryers, 'without the collusion of middle-rank officialdom' – 'this is the political cowardice of Pilate'.

Here we disagree. While the central subject of the novel is indeed cowardice, Bulgakov's treatment of the theme is more complicated than this summary condemnation might imply. Indubitably, Bulgakov has sympathy for Pilate, whatever his shortcomings. This shines through the narrative. It can also be supported by events in Bulgakov's own life. He knew at first hand what it was like to stand courageously alone, to feel mortally afraid, to swallow the toad-sandwich of compromise, to fall drastically short of the highest moral standards. He was too intimately acquainted with human weakness to condemn Pilate for his pathetic limitations. Bulgakov knew what it was like to defend, even as one concedes it, the high moral ground.

When in 1924, after eleven years of marriage, Bulgakov divorced his first wife, Tatyana, he brought her a bottle of champagne and sealed a pact with her to keep his past a secret. What was he worried about? Boudoir and bathroom betrayals? More likely are two other murky disclosures. The first was decidedly dangerous in 1924. It was that Bulgakov had fought on the White side out of conviction, a loyalty he now wisely chose to conceal.

Bulgakov's first published writing was a splenetic polemic against the Bolsheviks and a rallying call to the disarrayed forces of the White Army. Published on 13 November 1919, in a newspaper whose name is lost to history, the article survives, initialled M.B., as the first item in Bulgakov's cuttings book. His wife was loyal. Bulgakov was betrayed by his own authorial vanity, which led him to preserve, like an unexploded bomb, the incriminating evidence that could have cost him his life. The second secret was also preserved – but in his fiction, where he returns to it again and again. It was an experience during the Civil War which profoundly corroded his self-esteem and left him with an acute sense of the hollowness of man's moral pretensions.

Russian anti-Semitism began to flourish afresh after the assassination of Alexander II and it continued, particularly unabated on the White side, during the Civil War. Isaac Babel was another witness. His story, 'Crossing into Poland', describes, using his own experience with Budyonny's Red Cavalry, a cavalryman being billeted on 'a pregnant woman and two red-haired, scraggy-necked Jews'. Yet another Jew is asleep, huddled against the wall. The cavalryman tosses in his sleep until the pregnant daughter wakes him to complain that he is pushing her father about: 'she raised her thin legs and rounded belly from the floor and removed the blanket from the sleeper. Lying on his back was an old man, a dead old man. His throat had been torn out and his face cleft in two; in his beard blue blood was clotted like a lump of lead.' Despite his plea, he has been killed by Poles in front of his daughter – who now asks, her self-control gone, 'Where in the whole world could you find another father like my father?'

In Bulgakov's first novel, *The White Guard*, Yakov Feldman has his head removed by anti-Semitic Ukrainian troops as he runs for a midwife at the onset of his wife's labour. The last chapter, set in February 1919, begins with the beating to death of a Jew by a cossack sergeant: 'hitting the man over the head with a ramrod. His head jerked at each blow . . .' Another incident occurs in Bulgakov's adaptation of his novel for the stage, though the scene only survives in the English translation made in the 1930s. There, Bolbotun, the commander of the first Cavalry Division of the Petlyura forces, permits his men to torture a Jew by burning his face in an open lantern. This is repeated before the victim is finally shot in the back. Simon Petlyura was a Ukrainian nationalist who briefly controlled the Ukraine between November 1918 and July 1919, when the Bolsheviks took over. He was murdered in Paris in 1926 by a Jew seeking revenge.

Though certainty is impossible, it seems that Bulgakov, a trained doctor, was either working for the Whites or had been forcibly abducted (like Yury Zhivago in Pasternak's novel) by the Ukrainian Republican Army. Whichever, Bulgakov witnessed the torture and murder of a Jew. And did not intervene. Or could not intervene. Several other untranslated stories, apparently, touch on this raw spot in Bulgakov's conscience. In one of them, the doctor kills the murderer (his patient) as an act of retribution – a gesture which looks forward to Pilate's essentially futile act of revenge on Judas. Make believe. In real life, the incriminating taint left by the experience – whatever it was precisely – seems to have persuaded Bulgakov to give up his career as a doctor.

Bulgakov's life is one of unblinking self-assessment. Unfortunate, fortunate, he had faced his limitations. For six months in 1934, his life was so charged with fear that he was unable to leave the house alone. The neurosis returned in 1937. In the end, he was driven to write a play, *Batum*, which eulogized the early life of Stalin. Pure cowardice? Hardly. That confident judgement belongs in the moral laboratory where standards of ethical hygiene are considerably higher than in real life. When Pasternak was expelled from the Writers' Union after the publication of *Doctor Zhivago*, he eventually wrote a letter of retraction to *Pravda* under pressure from his mistress, Olga Ivinskaya. After he had shown so much courage, it is a painful episode. In his biography, the poet's son, Evgeny Pasternak, explains one banal, but easily overlooked cause: expulsion meant Pasternak had no means of earning a living.

In the thirties, when play after play by Bulgakov was rejected by Repertkom, the censorship body of Soviet theatre, the playwright had to repay the advance on unperformed work. Privation is never sufficiently taken into account as we tot up the compromises knowingly undertaken by the wily, courageous and exemplary Bulgakov.

Not a man to condemn Pontius Pilate, therefore, rather a man who would understand and identify with the imperfect Procurator of Judaea – as well as with the imperfect, flinching, yet finally brave Yeshua, whose remark about cowardice was meant to apply to himself as he underwent the ordeal of crucifixion. In the egotism of his guilt, Pilate annexes it as a reference to himself.

In Bulgakov's work, references to the Devil, Faust and Mephistopheles abound. Why? Because Bulgakov's life was one long terrorized pact with the Devil. In Russia, in the thirties, it could not have been otherwise, and there is real moral courage in recognizing the true facts of life – just as there is courage in making one's own cowardice the subject and centre of a novel which, if it survived, Bulgakov must have known, would keep his name alive for ever and also the personal shame encoded there.

# The KGB's Literary Archive

Fear is the most cogent and irresistible of the body's many arguments. In 1905, James Joyce confided to his brother that 'the whole structure of heroism is, and always was, a damned lie'. More recently, a German television documentary showed two boneheads, plaited with muscles, taunting a black man on the Frankfurt subway. The other occupants of the carriage concentrated on the reflective properties of glass, the precise configuration of the floor. Then, amazingly, a young man sat next to the thugs and calmly asked them what their problem was. He suggested they stop – and produced a huge knife.

At which point ... the director intervened and the two skinheads and their black 'victim' rapidly reverted to well-spoken actors. The experiment was over. The young man with the knife regularly rescued people, apparently. Another young man, a body builder, explained that he frequently fantasized the events he had just witnessed – and his own heroic role in them. Theory. In practice, he was shaken to find himself frigid with fear – though there was memorable footage of his bolting eyeballs. Courage, then, isn't utterly impossible, but it's a safer bet to side with the fantasizing body builder. Without a knife, it's balls to think you'll have the balls.

Fear is also one of life's most dramatic surprises. Ask any Russian writer in the hands of the KGB during the thirties or forties. Ask the theatre director Vsevolod Meyerhold, whose

*The KGB Literary Archive* by Vitaly Shentalinsky, translated by John Crowfoot, Harvill.

letter about torture is included in this fascinating and instructive book. Meyerhold 'discovered' he could wriggle and twist like a whipped dog. Exhausted after eighteen hours of interrogation, he was woken up by his own moaning. Not something you could predict in advance. Nevertheless, writers being writers, some attempted to imagine in advance, to prepare. Isaac Babel asked the head of the KGB how to behave after arrest and was told to deny everything. In fact, he confessed to everything and lavishly betrayed his friends – until the end was inevitable. At the final juncture, Babel retracted everything, pained by his scalded conscience – in extremis. Which is where the old lady comes in. On the Frankfurt underground, before the knife was pulled, one old lady gave the skinheads a piece of her mind. The old are frequently braver than the young. Why? Perhaps because they are less prepared to concede to the body's weakened imperatives – either to sex, or hunger, or fear. They care less about themselves and therefore can care more about others. Once the body's battle to survive is over, bravery is possible – without a knife. Finally, the old lady in Isaac Babel spoke and we should honour him for that, even while we weep for his wife, who sprinkled her perfume on the shirts, handkerchiefs and underwear she sent her husband in the Lubyanka prison. To remind him of her.

She had no idea that Babel had betrayed not only his friends but also her – with the wife-to-be of Yezhov, the head of the KGB, who was himself liquidated. Heroism is simple. Life, though, is complicated. And we should respect its complications. Vitaly Shentalinsky's study suffers, I think, from a nostalgia for simplicity. It arose out of a commission set up in the time of Gorbachev's perestroika to locate the lost manuscripts confiscated by the KGB. When Babel was shot, twenty-seven folders of manuscript disappeared for good. On the other hand, an essay by Andrey Bely survived, as did a diary destroyed by Bulgakov after it was returned by the KGB (they kept a copy). Another survival, if the translation is anything to go by, was a terrible epic poem by Klyuev. Mostly what survived are the interrogation files – the transcripts of terror and treachery.

Shentalinsky tries to balance Babel with Nina Hagen-Torn, a woman 'both beautiful and wise' – 'nothing disfigured her soul, broke her spirit or extinguished that smile'. There is nothing quoted here from her file either. Shentalinsky gives us her reminiscences instead. With the priest Pavel Florensky, the files record self-betrayal and betrayal of others, but Shentalinsky prefers to interpret this entirely human behaviour as an example of Christian self-sacrifice rather than as self-interest. I don't see it myself, and I am curiously warmed by a misanthropic note that begins to sound in Florensky's last letters: 'how hateful is human stupidity'; 'with all my being I feel the insignificance of man, his works and all his striving'. Hardly Christian sentiments.

Nor are the operatives of the KGB simple ciphers. Nina Hagen-Torn recalls an interrogator who is preparing for his test on ancient Greece. Another KGB general initially wanted to be an actor, but hadn't the confidence to believe he'd achieve more than minor parts. One interrogator, self-confessedly uneducated, was the author of study aids on how to prepare prisoners for questioning. *Study aids.* These complications are what we go back to history to retrieve – and they survive even the most sentimental archivist.

Take the case of Osip Mandelstam. Though Shentalinsky's account of Mandelstam's treatment at the hands of the KGB depends heavily on Nadezhda Mandelstam's narrative in *Hope Against Hope*, there are significant differences. Mandelstam's wife's memoir gradually secretes the information that her husband told the KGB the names of the people to whom he read his seditious poem about Stalin. She doesn't ignore the danger this put them in: describing Mandelstam's auditory hallucinations after his first release from prison, she says that voices 'blamed him for the ruin he had brought on all those to whom he had read his poem'. Shentalinsky, however, uses the word 'betrayal'. Correctly. In Nadezhda Mandelstam's account, Mandelstam tells his KGB interrogator that everyone who heard the Stalin poem 'begged him to forget it and not bring ruin on himself and others'. The file, on the other hand, details Mandelstam's incriminating analysis of each individual's reaction to the poem. No wonder he heard voices when he was released. It was the old lady bawling him out. And it was to be some time, much closer to the inevitable end, after he had written an ode to Stalin, before his voice and the old lady's voice were one.

Shentalinsky's chapter on Mandelstam is, it seems to me, impossible to reconcile with his later statement that 'Klyuev and Mandelstam alone remained firm and uncompromising'. Mandelstam clearly bent – as Akhmatova bent when she wrote a poem to Stalin in an effort to save her son. As Pasternak bent when he wrote a letter of retraction to *Pravda* after *Doctor Zhivago* attracted the Nobel Prize and incredible opprobrium. As you and I would bend.

But Shentalinsky is partly of the old dispensation – unreliable because nostalgic for heroism. Nadezhda Mandelstam's last letter to her husband is a case in point. Shentalinsky quotes it, very movingly, as if it had been plucked from Mandelstam's file. In fact, it was never sent and comes from the conclusion to *Hope Abandoned*, the widow's second volume of memoirs – where it is longer, undoctored for pathos, less sentimental and more painfully tonic. Here Nadezhda says, 'I never found the time to tell you how I love you.' In Max Hayward's translation, she says, 'Do you know how much I love you? I could never tell you how much I love you. I cannot tell you even now.' Both heartbreaking, but the original, unedited letter has less easy pathos and a more complicated heartbreak.

# The Łódź Ghetto

What is it like to be a witness? Czeslaw Milosz is unequivocal about the lack of clarity: 'Like everyone who lived there and then,' a line of his poetry ruefully confesses, 'I didn't see clearly.'

Why not? In retrospect, evil is often a platform opportunity on which posterity can be indignant and eloquent. At the time, nothing is so simple. When Virginia Woolf was six, her half-brother, George Duckworth, set her on a ledge in order to explore her private parts. Her biographer Quentin Bell comments: 'Eros came with a commotion of leathern wings.' Which is precisely wrong. Eros came, with hideously mixed motives, in the familiar guise of a good-looking half-brother wearing a well-tailored suit. Again, when Frank Burchardt lost his university job for political reasons, he wrote economic articles for the *Frankfurter Allgemeine Zeitung* which were not to Nazi taste – and he adamantly refused to join the Party. One morning, a member of the Gestapo arrived at his house and sat in the hall to await his return. No one was allowed to leave, except the maid, who warned her employer. He left for England immediately, became a fellow of All Souls, and was shortly followed by his wife Arne. I asked her once if she wasn't terrified by the Gestapo man in her hall? No, came the answer, he had been our newsagent for twenty years.

James Stern's *The Hidden Damage* was first published in 1947. An account of the psychological damage inflicted by war

*Łódź Ghetto: Inside a Community under Siege*, compiled and edited by Alan Adelson and Robert Lapides, Viking.

guilt on the German nation, it has recently been reissued – without (alas) an extraordinary appendix written by a survivor of Dachau. This witness describes two camps, not one. The induction camp is essentially a disinfection station – where heads are shaved to prevent lice, fumigated clothing issued and anti-typhus injections administered, using the same needle. Though prisoners were expected to work in the main camp, many longed to enter it because the lavatories and washing facilities were impeccable. The French politician Léon Blum had his own villa within the main perimeter fence.

From Claude Lanzmann's film *Shoah*, one learned that there was no budget for Hitler's Final Solution. It was self-financing. Jewish property was confiscated and the *Reichsmarks* used to purchase railway tickets on the GEDOB (initials meaning east-bound traffic of the *Reichsbahn*). Eichmann's office arranged everything through an ordinary travel agency, the *Mitteleuropä-ereisebureau*. Children under four were free. Children over four were half price. Adults paid full fare. Eventually, group concessions were negotiated. There might be additional bills for filth and damage to stock.

Eichmann and the cattle trucks. These bring us, we think, to the nub of things. In *Łódź Ghetto*, too, there are the expected horrors: men, women and children photographed as the defecated together, perched on a long plank, to demonstrate Jewish degeneracy. 'Frightful scenes in cattle cars – children howling, adults shitting as they stood, some licking at icicles to quench their overwhelming thirst.' This is the image of the holocaust that we know, and it exists – but it doesn't *explain*. In 1962, reporting on the trial of Eichmann in Jerusalem, Hannah Arendt risked an encapsulation – 'the banality of evil'. Ten years later, she was still explaining: 'the phenomenon of evil deeds, committed on a gigantic scale, which could not be traced to any particularity of wickedness, pathology or ideological conviction in the doer, whose only personal distinction was perhaps extraordinary shallowness. However monstrous the deeds were, the doer was neither monstrous nor demonic . . .'

Hannah Arendt is too self-consciously provocative in her

coinage, and her subsequent explanations and modifications confess implicitly to a certain inherent glibness in the phrase, but *Łódź Ghetto* abundantly confirms that her formulation needs only a slight but crucial modification. It should be 'the normality of evil'. The train to Treblinka is timetabled by GEDOB and the tickets come through a travel agency.

*Łódź Ghetto* – a compilation of eyewitness accounts of how only 800 Jews out of 220,000 survived – is a testament to mankind's necessary (and in this case, fatal) ability to adapt to impossible circumstances: 'I made it my goal,' says Chaim Rumkowski, the Eldest in charge of the ghetto, 'to normalize life in the ghetto at any price.' The official record, the *Chronicle* commissioned by Rumkowski, also reports: 'And so, the impossible became possible – real.' Very few inmates resist this deep human impulse. Dr Israel Milejkowski is a rare exception: 'We must not pretend even for a single minute that the Ghetto-form can be adapted to our needs.' But everywhere life itself was conspiring against this passionate outburst.

Everywhere, in a variety of forms, there are examples of ineradicable, illusory, seductive, narcotic normality. There is a party attended by women whose hair is washed in vinegar and waved. One diarist notices lipstick and coloured toenails in open summer sandals. A small orchestra (strings only) performs Beethoven. Oskar Rosenfeld is pleased by the public reading of a chapter of his novel. He reads Schiller and is 'caught up in this blinding storyteller'. Other reading in the ghetto includes Turgenev and Gorki, Heine, Haeckel and Rousseau.

From the very beginning, there is accommodation, preservation and a refusal to accept that justice has gone and left behind it only the law. When the synagogue is burned to the ground, an insurance claim is lodged – and turned down. At first, the Jews welcome the ghetto's isolation since it protects them from casual assault in the street and from demeaning forced labour details which frequently involved cleaning lavatories with their bare hands. When disaster arrives, it isn't kitted out in sackcloth and ashes: 'so that's how a retreating army looks, rather like a regular army passing by'. The occupation even entails a newspaper competition to find a new name for Łódź. In the ghetto, hospital workers strike for an eight-hour working day, as if the old rules still obtained. A department of Garden Cultivation is founded and soon grass is flourishing over the excrement dumps. Ever optimistic, Marxism survives: at a May Day celebration in 1941, a woman speaks 'wonderfully about readiness for action'. The same diarist records: 'I attended a lecture this afternoon on world literature, specifically positivism and decadence.' One could weep for the hardiness of hope.

This is, after all, a world where potato peelings are only obtainable on prescription, where the Jewish police ('muscles') drive children on to the transports ('wedding invitations'), where Biebow the German overseer shoots in the eye a girl he has raped. Yet these terrors coexist with the ordinary knowledge that Biebow was 'a shrewd Bremen business man with a degree', with the order to shave and shine one's shoes on arrival at the Łódź railhead, with the painter Guttmann's inability to suppress his aesthetic ecstacy at 'the beauty of the bleak scenery'. We can summarize with one quotation: 'I thought my heart would break, but it did not. It allowed me to eat, think, talk and go to bed.'

The man responsible for the ghetto, Chaim Rumkowski, is not, I think, the morally ambiguous figure this book implies. He had one survival strategy: to make his Jews economically indispensable to the German war effort. In the short term, he was right, as an extract from an Albert Speer letter shows: Himmler's order to cleanse the ghetto in February 1944 was delayed beause Speer 'made Hitler aware of the production losses that could be expected'. Rumkowski bargained with the Germans – and was able to reduce a transport from 20,000 to 10,000. On the other hand, he had to sacrifice the aged, the sickly and children under ten – the unproductive. For this, he consciously and unflinchingly accepted responsibility: 'one needs the heart of a bandit to ask from you what I am asking. But put yourself in my place, think logically and you'll reach the conclusion that I cannot proceed any other way. The part that can be saved is much larger than the part that must be given away.'

And the part that was given away, flung 'like packages into the wagons'? Let one father speak for all: 'I killed my child with my own hands, I killed Mookha, I am a killer, because how can it be that a father deserts his own child and runs away?' What does it mean to be a witness? At the moment when something heavy jumps on your heart, the witness reaches for pen and paper like Hiroji Kawaguhi, a 52-year-old shipping manager on the doomed Japanese Airlines Boeing 747 in August 1985, who wrote in his company diary to his wife, son and two daughters: 'There is no hope. It was a happy life for me. Thank you all.' The father of Mookha wrote in Yiddish, in pencil, on the back of soup-kitchen records. We will never know what exactly happened – whether he culpably abandoned his five-year-old daughter, or whether, 'simply', his strategy of concealment failed. It isn't clear. For a moment, we are *there* – grieving, confused, trembling, guilty, innocent, greedy for pen and paper, and tragically unclear.

# The Divided Kipling

'Man,' wrote Léon Bloy, 'has places in his heart which do not yet exist, and into them enters suffering in order that they may have existence.'

This bleak, tonic pronouncement is perfectly illustrated in *The Jungle Book*, when Mowgli is expelled from the Seeonee wolf pack: 'Then something began to hurt Mowgli inside him, as he had never been hurt in his life before, and he caught his breath and sobbed, and the tears ran down his face. "What is it? What is it?" he said, "I do not wish to leave the Jungle, and I do not know what this is. Am I dying, Bagheera?"'

And Bagheera the panther replies, 'No, little brother. Those are only tears such as men use. Now I know thou art a man . . .'

In one of Max Beerbohm's nine hate-filled caricatures of Kipling, the coarse imperialist is portrayed raising a tin trumpet to his bristling moustache above a Desperate Dan chin. This image – of crude self-confidence – is belied by a great deal of Kipling's writing and its tender notations of uncertainty. Even so, the brilliant Beerbohm libel continues to command credence across a wide section of the intelligentsia. Kipling is broadly hated.

A truer representation of his gift is the end of 'Mowgli's Song', after his subsequent expulsion from the human tribe: '*Ahae*! My heart is heavy with the things that I do not understand.' This long free-verse line, untypically Whitmanian in its metrical freedom, takes us to the crux of Kipling's psyche. At bottom, he had no idea who he was, or where he belonged, or to whom he belonged.

The reason for this hesitation – rooted, uprooted in his very soul – is not hard to find. In 1871, Kipling and his sister Trix became boarders at Southsea, in what Kipling later called 'The House of Desolation'. It was run by a retired naval officer ('Uncle Harry') and his vindictive wife ('Aunty Rosa'). Kipling was five and a half, his sister not quite three. Their mother sailed back to India and her husband, leaving her young son to a regime of isolation, bullying and persecution. When, five years later, she returned, all-unknowing, Kipling was nearly blind and, when she bent to kiss him goodnight, he raised an arm in bed to ward off the expected blow.

The story of what happened in the five-year interval – half of his life so far – has been told obsessively (or economically) by Kipling in the first chapter of *The Light That Failed*, the short story 'Baa Baa Black Sheep' and his autobiography, *Something of Myself*. The American poet Randall Jarrell has stated, with conscious sensationalism, that Kipling spent six years of his childhood in a concentration camp. Another American, Edmund Wilson, claimed that, as a result, Kipling's art is 'shot through with hatred'.

This testimony is suspect – and, ultimately, sentimental. It is clear that Kipling knew about hatred. Who does not? Look how widely hated Kipling is. It is, however, an unpleasant emotion, like jealousy, and therefore frequently airbrushed out of literature, even while it is a common and intense emotion in life. By writing about it, by writing from *inside* it, Kipling stops the etiolation of literature into the merely respectable. It isn't a question of condoning hatred, understanding hatred or revelling in hatred. It is a question of making us see its chemistry.

Far from being disabled by his Southsea experience, Kipling was granted access to more than the standardized literary emotions. For instance, his sister Trix recorded, in *Chambers Magazine* (1937), that Kipling, when asked if the Southsea house still stood, replied at the end of his life: 'I should like to burn it down and plough the place with salt.'

Readers of *The Second Jungle Book* will recall 'Letting in the Jungle', the story in which Mowgli rescues his putative human parents from the death-threat of their fellow-villagers. After-wards, Mowgli arranges for the jungle to destroy the village itself. His deliberate, applied hatred frightens Bagheera. It is clear to the panther that this cold-blooded, considered hatred is a defining human emotion – one that animals can't share.

This is one parallel between Kipling's autobiography and *The Jungle Books*. There are others – the main one being Mowgli's uncertain identity. Is he a wolf or a man? Who is his mother? Messua or Mother Wolf? This dilemma, central to Kipling, recurs in *Kim*, a boy caught between two worlds, the India of Kim and the Anglo-India of Kimball O'Hara: 'I am Kim. I am Kim. And what is Kim?'

It follows that an opera whose libretto counterpoints the autobiographical 'Baa Baa Black Sheep' with *The Jungle Books* will be lucid and correct in its intuition. As a form, too, it repeats the successful shape of David Malouf's *Voss* libretto for Richard Meale's opera, where the action oscillated between Sydney and the outback.

When Michael Berkeley first mentioned this opera to me at Glyndebourne, I was emerald with envy for David Malouf. It is a great subject – the value of suffering. Let me risk an Australian analogy. In the Flinders, north of Adelaide, each spring the desert suddenly shivers with flowers which evaporate till next year. The reverse happened to Kipling. One minute he was in Paradise – as Mowgli is immersed in the jungle – next minute the vegetation had vanished, leaving behind a bleak grandeur, hard, intricate ridges of hatred, shifting sands of feeling and uncertainty. He was suddenly the little boy who cried down the lane – both lost and lethal. 'Angry as he was at the whole breed and community of Man, something jumped up in his throat and made him catch his breath when he looked at the village roofs.' It could be Kipling. In fact, it is Mowgli. *Something jumped up in his throat* . . . Think of Léon Bloy. Kipling had been enabled by suffering, which, for a writer, is better, truer, than the sentimental pretence of being ennobled by suffering.

# A. E. Housman

In 1972, reviewing Housman's correspondence, W. H. Auden was frankly pleased by the snub to posterity's insatiable prurience. The bawdy letters to Arthur Platt had been destroyed by his widow. No letters survived of those written to Moses Jackson, the (heterosexual) love of Housman's life. Auden's delight in the dullness of the remainder was clearly self-interested. He had already instructed his friends to destroy his own letters. And yet, in the same review, Auden speculates that Housman's sexual tastes were probably 'anal passive'. The contradiction here, between the protective impulse and intrusive instinct, mirrors the contradictions, fissures and fault-lines in Housman's life and work. Housman wanted us to believe that the poet was one thing and that the scholar was another. Poetry was emotion. Textual criticism was devoid of anything but dry ratiocination. But nothing is as neat as it aspired to be. Housman's psychic apartheid impoverishes the scholarship, and fatally flaws his poetry.

Contradictions, complications are everywhere in Housman. Even as he enforced the strictest demarcations. He died in 1936, so it shouldn't be as surprising as it seems that he flew in an aeroplane. 'The noise is great and I alighted rather deaf, not having stuffed my ears with the cotton-wool provided. Nor did I put on the life-belt which they oblige one to take . . .' This intrepidity, bluff and unbending though it is, sits oddly with the

*The Poems of A. E. Housman*, edited by Archie Burnett, Oxford University Press.

poetry, the modernity of the aircraft scarcely compatible with the archaic, stylized pastoral of *A Shropshire Lad*: 'And blithe afield to ploughing / Against the morning beam / I strode beside my team . . .' And the pastoral itself is fractured: it is bitter and unhappy, 'the land of lost content', permeated with tragic ironies, but curiously depleted of anything but timeless details and airbrushed of all emotional complication. Even in 1896, the language had an antique patina. It was aurally distressed. Housman's poetry is profoundly anti-modernist, which may account for the nature of its popularity. Housman isn't a poet's poet. He is the people's poet, carried, according to John Sparrow in 1956, in knapsacks, along with FitzGerald's translation of Omar Khayyám.

Modernism, as practised by Eliot, Lawrence, Yeats and Auden, embraced the intellectual which Housman rejected. More importantly still, the great modernists were committed to the scrutiny of emotions which Housman's poetry embraces so unquestioningly. What passes for current and valid there is likely to be rumbled as a forgery by the alert, sceptical modernist. Impurity, mixed feelings, impacted emotional contradiction, self-dividedness are characteristic of modernism's greater truthfulness. In a note to his *New Year Letter* (or *The Double Man* in America, significantly enough), Auden is a spokesman for the new complication: 'The Devil, indeed, is the father of Poetry, for poetry might be defined as the clear expression of mixed feelings.' Or take Yeats in 'Meditations in Time of Civil War', where he is compelled to count the baby moorhens in order 'to silence the envy in [his] blood' for the Falstaffian warrior – and where he equally prays for peace, even as he envies the man of action. In Housman, emotions are pure, powerful and fatally literary.

Take 'Farewell to barn and stack and tree', his poem of fratricide – in which the cause of the quarrel, the murder's justification or lack of justification, has been edited out by Housman – in the interest of simplified pathos. Protagonist and reader alike can indulge the sentiment of loss, since the murderer must take his leave of the familiar landscape and friends for ever. Regret, guilt, the mother's anguish for her dead son, remorse are all eliminated from the picture, the better to savour self-pity: 'Long for me the rick will wait, / And long will wait the fold, / And long will stand the empty plate, / And dinner will be cold.' Not a whisper of irony or intelligence, merely the swash of poignancy unearned. And the flat bump of bathos in that cold dinner. For this, the murder is only a pretext.

Housman was once visited by Clarence Darrow, an American barrister who specialized in defending murderers. 'He could not return home without seeing me,' Housman wrote, 'because he had so often used my poems to rescue his clients from the electric chair.' Darrow gave Housman a copy of one of his speeches for the defence – 'in which, sure enough, two of my pieces are misquoted'. For Housman, the irony is directed solely against Darrow. The misquotations acquit Housman of any culpable complicity. But the anecdote implicitly indicts Housman's sentimentality – his reflex sympathy for his automatic underdogs. 'There sleeps in Shrewsbury jail to-night / Or wakes, as may betide, / A better lad, if things went right, / Than most that sleep outside.' Tell it to the Criminal Injuries Compensation Board, one is tempted to rejoin. Except that there is something absurd about an appeal to reality when one is dealing with Housman's never-never-land – an ersatz world of arch simplicities, a world where awkward realities are smartly avoided.

Death, for instance. That may seem an odd criticism of Housman, whose poetry is abrim with mortality and yearning for the grave. Strange to say, however, Housman's characteristic way with death is periphrastic: 'the far dwelling'; 'My love rose up so early / And stole out unbeknown / And went to church alone'; 'Ere to a town you journey / Where friends are ill to find'; 'Soldier, sit you down and idle / At the inn of night for aye'; 'The pale, the perished nation / That never see the sun'. The list could be a lot longer. Each example will pass individually, but taken together the trope is facile, almost automatic and dangerously cognate with undertakers' gravestone euphemisms. The real unpleasantness, the ugly, the grotesque, has been politely poeticized. No wonder Housman complained that

'Virgil's besetting sin is the use of words too forcible for his thoughts.'

There is something sanitized about even the best of Housman – which may perhaps account for his enduring popularity. Mr Beebe, the repressed clergyman in Forster's *A Room with a View* (1908), is implicitly condemned when he says, ' "A Shropshire Lad". Never heard of it.' The book is clearly a secret touchstone for Forster – but whenever Forster invokes 'poetry' in his fiction, he invariably means something exalted and simplified. Housman wanted to be very popular, to bypass the intelligentsia and get straight to the box office, though not for mercenary reasons: 'Vanity, not avarice, is my ruling passion; and so long as young men write to me from America saying that they would rather part with their hair than with their copy of my book, I do not feel the need of food or drink.' When his publisher, Grant Richards, doubled the price of *A Shropshire Lad*, Housman pointed out that sales would be diminished. Moreover, the occurrence of a certain circumstance was rendered less likely: 'a soldier is to receive a bullet in the breast, and it is to be turned aside from his heart by a copy of *A Shropshire Lad* which he is carrying there. Hitherto it is only the Bible that has performed this trick.' It is a telling sally – at once waggish, self-ironizing, deprecatory and ingenuous enough under the comic hyperbole. It is also only a whisker away from the romantic world of the poetry, where reality is sufficiently impressionistic to relax the laws of strict plausibility.

Housman reserved his intellect for textual criticism – making scholarship an area where emotion was *streng verboten*. He rejected the emotional content of the texts he scrutinized. Except, of course, that he couldn't completely effect this separation of function, of response, as Archie Burnett's definitive and profoundly helpful commentary shows. In May 1914, Housman shocked his lecture audience by considering his favourite Horace ode 'simply as poetry'. They were accustomed to an analytic process closer to vivisection, a display of brutal intellect and bravura sarcastic wit. 'He read the ode aloud with deep emotion, first in Latin and then in an English translation of his own.'

Pronouncing it 'the most beautiful poem in ancient literature', Housman more or less fled the room. The anecdote appeals to us because it demonstrates the power of emotion, its resistless force. Yet, just as the scholarship needs to take proper cognizance of emotion, so the poetry needs to apply intellect to the easy emotions which are its trademark.

Burnett's commentary demonstrates how much Housman's language trades on reminiscence – of the Bible, Tennyson, Heine, classical literature. It could hardly be bettered, though what it tells us about Housman's diction is ultimately critical. Now and again, it emulates the laconic asperity of Housman: George Watson, Richard Perceval Graves and John Bayley all venture biographically based interpretations of 'Parta Quies'. Burnett dispatches them thus: 'all these interpretations lack is a foundation'. The job has been done well.

In the meantime, what accounts for the durability of this minor poet? Maybe Milan Kundera is right in his play *Jacques and His Master*: 'You are the great Diderot, I am a bad poet . . . All of mankind consists of bad poets! The bad poets who make up mankind are crazy about bad verse! Indeed, it is just because I write bad verse that I shall one day be in the pantheon of great poets!' Housman's poetry speaks to the bad poet in all of us.

# The Short Stories of D. H. Lawrence

What is Lawrence's intellectual context? By 'intellectual context', we usually mean a writer's contemporaries. Yet for major writers, nourishing intellectual allegiances are always significantly anterior. Contemporaries are competitors and a source of friction, as, for example, Joyce is to Lawrence: 'nothing but old fags and cabbage stumps of quotations from the Bible and the rest, stewed in the juice of deliberate journalistic dirty-mindedness'. Hardy and Nietzsche are more fruitful for Lawrence, more formative, than, say, Bennett ('I hate Bennett's resignation') and Strindberg ('I hate Strindberg'). 'Tragedy,' Lawrence complains, 'ought really to be a great kick at misery.' Bennett's 'resignation' is glumly opposed to Nietzsche's more tonic assertion that the tragic artist displays 'precisely the condition of *fearlessness* in the face of the fearsome and questionable'. In 'Border Line', Katherine Farquhar's first husband, the dead Alan Anstruther, is contemptuous of Nietzsche but the beneficiary, in the story, of Nietzsche's doctrine of eternal recurrence. Anstruther 'returns' from the grave, a force sexually potent enough to displace his wife's second husband.

Lawrence's last tale, 'The Man Who Died', published posthumously, is a Nietzschean remake of the central Christian myth, in which the body asserts its rights and superiority over the idealistic imperatives of the soul. The crucified Christ becomes the pagan Osiris, the stigmata become the equivalent of the *disjecta membra*, and the resurrection of the body becomes the erection of the penis. The cock which, in the New Testament, crowed when Peter denied Christ, is here shown to be repressed sexual energy – tethered by its peasant owner when it is really 'but one wave-tip of life overlapping for a minute another, in the tide of the swaying ocean of life'. Nietzsche believed that, in Christianity, 'God degenerated to the *contradiction of life*, instead of being its transfiguration and eternal Yes!' In 'The Man Who Died', Lawrence dramatizes this doctrine: Christ is gradually overcome by 'the necessity to live' and 'the everlasting resoluteness of life'. Nietzsche, then, is a crucial progenitor for Lawrence, but was himself part of a larger ferment about the true nature of feeling, the role of the body and the troubled psyche.

In *Strong Opinions*, Nabokov is characteristically contemptuous of 'the Viennese witch-doctor', Freud, and the efficacy of psychoanalysis – expressing robust incredulity at the idea that a regular application of Greek myths to the patient's private parts can salve the psyche or solve sexual angst. Lawrence shared Nabokov's distaste. In 'England, My England', he jeers at advanced, 'enlightened' thought: 'Let the psycho-analyst talk about the father complex. It is just a word invented.' It is paradoxical, then, that Greek myth should be central in 'Tickets, Please', his very next story, and that Lawrence should analyse the violent revenge of the tram-girls on the philandering (and aptly named) John Thomas Raynor in terms of the Maenads, the female followers of Dionysus. The girls are 'strange, wild creatures', 'with unnatural strength and power', 'supernatural strength' – and their otherwise unrealistic violence is prepared for early in the story by a Greek reference, when the step of the tram is compared to Thermopylae.

Rather than the elegant provision of pseudo-explanatory mythical analogues, however, Lawrence's speciality lies elsewhere. Annie, the conductress who organizes her fellow-Maenads, ends 'as if in torture', rather than requited by revenge. When the cowed Coddy is asked to pick one partner, he chooses Annie, under duress. And, though she repudiates him, her emotion is complicated by his choice. It arouses her love. Her hatred is no longer pure. 'Something was broken in her.' This note of complication sounds through the canon: when March is asked by Henry in 'The Fox' if she *wants* to marry him, she replies, 'Oh, I don't know whether I'm against it, as a matter of fact. That's just it. I don't know'; when Yvette tries to sift her attraction for Joe Boswell in 'The Virgin and the Gypsy', 'she looked at him with clear eyes. Man or woman is made up of many selves. With one self, she loved this gypsy man. With many selves, she ignored him or had a distaste for him.' Yvette's feelings for her father fare no better: 'Under the rector's apparently gallant handsomeness, she saw the weak, feeble nullity. And she despised him. Yet still, in a way, she liked him too. Feelings are so complicated.'

Mixed feelings, psychological contradictions, enigmatic emotions are precisely what interested and engaged Lawrence's genius – as they have engaged every significant modern writer since Arnold. In his 1853 Preface, Arnold defined modernism as 'the dialogue of the mind with itself'. From that moment, Wordsworthian certainties were in retreat. 'The spontaneous overflow of powerful feeling', 'emotion recollected in tranquillity', bluff impostures both, were generally perceived as simplifications – most of all in Wordsworth's poetry itself, which, retrospectively, powerfully contradicts his prose pronouncements. The vague was in vogue.

What did writers feel about feelings?

In *Amours de Voyage*, Clough's Claude was cloudy, querulous, a prey to qualms and the obvious progenitor for Prufrock: 'It is impossible to say just what I mean!' Pater's pretended boldness – 'to burn always with this hard, gemlike flame' – proved in reality to be an abject retreat. His notorious conclusion to *The Renaissance* is more promising in its advocacy of a spurious hedonism than it is real. Christians whose ideas of self-sacrifice were shocked failed to see the clarion call for what it was – a very theoretical pronouncement. 'To burn always with this hard, gemlike flame, to maintain this ecstasy, is success in life.' This famous formulation may have been flourished by the disreputable Wilde, but it amounted to little more than a retreat from life into art. Just as his aesthetic critic specialized in the precise notation of the mental impressions provoked by the work of art – a kind of mental accountancy – so Pater's 'Conclusion' concludes, somewhat bathetically, with an orgy of intellection, as it were, in the National Gallery or the Uffizi: 'Only be sure it is passion – that it does yield you this fruit of a quickened, multiplied consciousness. Of such wisdom, the poetic passion, the desire of beauty, the love of art for its own sake, has most. For art comes to you, proposing frankly to give nothing but the highest quality to your moments as they pass . . .' What a nostalgia here for the quickened heart. What a sense of mere existence, of poor thin experience – a sense that Lawrence's characters share. Yvette, in 'The Virgin and the Gypsy', thinks 'dimly, at the back of her mind', 'Why are we all only like mortal pieces of furniture? Why is nothing *important*?' In 'The Border Line', Katherine Farquhar knows 'the supreme modern terror, of a world all ashy and nerve-dead'. In 'St Mawr', Lou feels 'so unreal, nowadays, as if I were nothing more than a painting by Rico on a millboard'. Her mother, Mrs Witt, failing to find unfallen Pan in modern men (with the belated and unrealizable exception of Lewis), iterates the same complaint: 'Louise, I've come to the conclusion that hardly anybody in the world really lives, and so hardly anybody really dies.' The heroine of 'Sun' is driven to Italy by 'her incapacity to feel anything real'.

Oscar Wilde, with a more lurid and eventful life than Brasenose College or Bradmore Road could provide, nevertheless retreats like Pater into art. Life itself is too intractable, too coarse. Arnold defined art as 'a criticism of life', meaning that art should adopt a moral attitude to life. Wilde, a rogue disciple of Arnold, 'whose gracious memory we all revere', reinterprets the phrase. For him, a criticism of life means the identification of life's obvious imperfections. Life is an artistic failure because it is, we learn from 'The Critic as Artist', 'terribly deficient in form' – a notion borrowed by Henry James in his preface to *The Spoils of Poynton*, where he laments the spectacle of 'clumsy Life again at her stupid work'. Wilde is guilty of strategic withdrawal in the face of overwhelming complication; James, on the other hand, is probably dismayed by life's chronic shortage of intricacy and woeful depletion of ironies. By contrast, Lawrence chooses, in Wordsworth's phrase made famous by Arnold, to see the object as in itself it really is.

In the twentieth century, it is Eliot and Lawrence who take the feelings as their subject. Eliot, in his essay on *Hamlet*, speaks of 'intense feeling, ecstatic or terrible, without an object or exceeding its object'. According to Eliot, 'the ordinary person puts these feelings to sleep, or trims down his feelings to fit the business world'. This is something recorded extremely acutely in Lawrence's stories: in 'You Touched Me', Matilda touches Hadrian by accident as he lies in bed asleep. Both are awakened, literally and figuratively. 'When she was back in her own room, in the light, and her door was closed, she stood holding up her hand that had touched him, *as if it were hurt.*' (My italics.) The next morning, however, 'she tried to bear herself as if nothing at all had happened, and she succeeded. She had the calm self-control, self-indifference, of one who has suffered and borne her suffering. She looked at him from her darkish, almost drugged blue eyes, she met the spark of consciousness in his eyes, and quenched it.' But she is wrong. She cannot control Hadrian's aroused consciousness and, finally, she acquiesces to the marriage. Her merely social self is sapped and succumbs.

Eliot, too, was aware of the dangers presented by the social self. He praises Blake for resisting 'the acquisition of impersonal ideas which obscure what we really are and feel'. In 'Religion and Literature', Eliot returns to the attack: 'knowing what we really feel: very few know that'. Eliot's poetry is true both to life's 'supple confusions' ('Gerontion') and to the chilly certainty of 'Hysteria': 'I decided that if the shaking of her breasts could be stopped, some of the fragments of the afternoon might be collected, and I concentrated my attention with careful subtlety to this end.' Not a breath of compassion, merely controlled, murderous notation. Lawrence's stories are a mine of these steely moments, where the appropriate reaction is resisted in favour of something more honest, truthful and inappropriate. In 'The Fox', Henry, hearing of his grandfather's death, 'did not seem sad, not at all – only rather interestedly surprised'. In 'The

Border Line', Katherine Farquhar, once reunited with her dead husband, ceases to care for her second: 'Afterwards she walked home in a muse to find Philip seriously ill. She could see, he really might die. And she didn't care a bit.' In 'Smile', the presentation is even more radical and perhaps too schematic: Matthew, confronting his wife's dead body in the convent, experiences a reaction rather like the giggles that consume Paul Morel and his sister when they administer an overdose to their dying mother: 'Matthew saw the dead, beautiful composure of his wife's face, and instantly, something leaped like laughter in the depths of him, he gave a little grunt, and an extraordinary smile came over his face.' The merriment is infectious and soon the nuns are shaking with laughter too, trying to disguise it as emotion. By the story's end, Matthew has recovered his sober front. Or, rather, he has lost the Nietzschean joy, 'joy which also encompasses joy in destruction' (*Twilight of the Idols*). The last sentence tells us: 'never was man more utterly smileless'. *Man.* Not 'a man'. Which gives us some idea of the story's allegorical reach.

'In Love' has less obvious designs on the reader, though it, too, has antecedents in Nietzsche's impatience with love ('the state in which man sees things most of all as they are *not*') and his belief that the centrally important institution of marriage would be more durably founded on sexual drive and the desire to own property. Enjoyment of Lawrence's story – one of his funniest and one that gives the lie to Eliot's assertion that Lawrence had no sense of humour – isn't conditional on an acceptance of the arranged marriage and a denial of the love-match. Even so, here and throughout Lawrence's work, love isn't the unquestioned donnée it is in standard fiction. In 'The Ladybird', Lady Daphne's husband, Basil Apsley, is ironized for kneeling to kiss his wife's feet: 'the man religiously worshipped her, not merely amorously'. At first, she is 'thrilled deep down to her soul'. But in short order she is disillusioned: 'To her shame and her heaviness, she knew she was not strong enough, or pure enough, to bear his awful outpouring adoration-lust . . .' Lawrence's 'The Captain's Doll' repeats this idea, more scornfully, when Hannele, Countess von Rassentlow, imagines her lover pledging himself to his wife on their wedding night: 'the man, perhaps in his braces', 'him on his knees, with his heels up'. Typically for Lawrence, it is the woman who enjoys the heightened sense of the ridiculous. The two sisters, Hester and Henrietta, are united by their sense of male romantic fatuity in 'In Love' and eventually Joe drops the pretence and settles for the 'quiet, patient, central desire of a young man' – much as Orlando learns from Rosalind in *As You Like It* to shed romantic excess. The educational process for the man is much more brutal than in Shakespeare: spooning, making love, is described thus: 'as if one were a perfectly priceless meat-pie, and the dog licked it tenderly before he gobbled it up. It *is* rather sickening.'

In 'The Horse Dealer's Daughter' even the classic *coup de foudre* is horribly confused: falling in love involves, as Lawrence describes it, loss of footing, uncertainty, precipitation and a good deal of hurt. 'She was passionately kissing his knees, through the wet clothing, passionately and indiscriminately kissing his knees, his legs, as if unaware of everything.' The passage is too lengthy to quote in full, but Lawrence is true to the reluctance built into this and any transfiguring experience: 'Nay, this introduction of a personal element was very distasteful to him, a violation of his professional honour. It was horrible to have her there embracing his knees. It was horrible. He revolted from it, violently. And yet – and yet – he had not the power to break away.' By the end, Fergusson is referring to his 'newly-torn heart'.

In isolation, 'The Horse Dealer's Daughter' might look like evidence for love as an irresistible force, despite Lawrence's graphic notation of its birth-pangs. 'Monkey Nuts' makes it clear that there is nothing automatic about love and sex. Lest we think of the sexual urge as a reflex, an instinct like blinking or breathing, Lawrence conveys the obverse in a single sentence: 'her arm was round his waist, she drew him closely to her with a soft pressure that made all his bones rotten'. If the sexual experience can be central, it can also be negligible, as Durant's mercenary sex shows in 'Daughters of the Vicar': 'the sordid insignificance of the experience appalled him'. Tom Brangwen's reaction to casual sex in *The Rainbow* leaves him with the taste of ashes in his mouth. 'It's nothing, that's all,' says Joe in 'Monkey Nuts'.

These are all recognizable, if awkward, emotions. On the whole, Lawrence's strength as a writer lies in the manifest verifiability of the feelings he sets down, however inappropriate. Only occasionally do we experience a sense of exaggeration. Then we may feel, like the prosecuting counsel at the *Lady Chatterley's Lover* trial, that there is something ridiculous in, say, a woman 'reverencing' a man's balls. By and large, Lawrence carries his reader and it is astonishing, for instance, that he can ventriloquize the stallion St Mawr's view of modern man without making us guffaw: 'his spirit knew that nobility had gone out of men. And this left him high and dry, in a sort of despair.' A border-line case perhaps.

Lawrence, we feel, has an exceptionally vivid apprehension of life, which is natural and unaffected. His perceptions required no artificial heightening. For him, the lower plane of actual life and the imaginative plane of art were one and the same. In 'Second Best', we read that 'the common, with its sere, blonde-headed thistles, its heaps of silent bramble, its brown-husked gorse in the glare of sunshine, seemed visionary'. Hilda Millership, the Jessie Chambers figure in 'The Shades of Spring', says of the Lawrence-figure, Syson, in comparison with her new lover: 'The stars aren't the same with him. You could make them flash and quiver, and the forget-me-nots come up at me like phosphorescence. You could make things *wonderful*.' Effortlessly, Lawrence saw life in italics. 'The one universal element in consciousness which is fundamental to life is the element of wonder,' he wrote in 'Hymns in a Man's Life'. 'You cannot help feeling it in the glisten of the nucleus of the amoeba. You cannot help feeling it in a bean as it starts to grow and pulls itself out of its jacket.'

That bean undressing itself is characteristic of Lawrence's naked apprehension of nature and the way he discards verbal accoutrement for an unprecedentedly direct gaze which verges naturally on the visionary. When Lou first reaches out to touch St Mawr, the horse 'drifted away from her, as if some wind blew him'. Lewis rides him 'like an insinuation'. The horse *is* a symbol – of a larger, less anthropocentric world, a world of 'old Greek heroes', of the god Pan – but he sustains his symbolic role by virtue of his exceptional actual presence: 'he was grooming the brilliant St Mawr, out in the open. The horse was really glorious: like a marigold, with a pure golden sheen, a shimmer of green-gold lacquer, upon a burning red-orange. There on the shoulder you saw the yellow lacquer glisten.' The acuteness of Lawrence's vision is what makes the visionary plausible.

'A Fragment of Stained Glass' is one of Lawrence's greatest stories, though it is largely ignored by criticism as uncharacteristic. All the same, it incorporates a kind of artistic credo. Mr Colbran, the vicar of Beauvale, says: 'Haven't I told you I was compiling a Bible of the English people – the Bible of their hearts – their exclamations in presence of the unknown?' The tale, however, relates the adventures of a serf on the run, seeking the camp of the outlaws. En route with his girl, he climbs up a cathedral in a blizzard and breaks the stained glass. The terrified monks below are seen by the serf as 'white stunted angels' – their beards and tonsures make them appear two-faced. The carved statuary on the cathedral face is vividly misapprehended: 'I stood higher on the head of a frozen man . . .' The Unknown is not in this case like Lou's sense through St Mawr of 'another darker, more spacious, more dangerous, more splendid world than ours'. It is darker, more dangerous, less spacious, more cruel, lost to historical record and meticulously re-imagined by Lawrence. The serf sets fire to the stables, as revenge for his beating, and the house catches fire, too. 'They cried, all of them when the roof went in, when the sparks splashed up at rebound. They cried then like dogs at the bagpipes howling.' On the run, he sleeps, wakes frozen, but is 'afraid to move, lest all the sores of my back should be broken like thin ice'. In a pig-sty, he joins the farrow and is suckled by the sow, 'guarding my face with my arm'. When he leaves with the miller's daughter, he is still steeped in sleep: 'when I came out into the cold someone touched my face and my hair. "Ha!" I cried, "who now – ?" Then she swiftly clung to me, hushed me. "Someone has touched me," I said aloud, still dazed with sleep. "Oh hush!" she wept. "'Tis snowing . . ." '

This preternatural gift for specific detail never deserts Lawrence, whether it is 'mobs of cattle in an illumined dust', 'the long cornelian talons of the bear', 'the sticky sea-wind', 'the animal onrush of light' at dawn, or a cockerel's 'splitting crow'. No one else, apart from Stanley Spencer, notices women's clothes like Lawrence: 'Yvette in a pale lilac colour with turquoise chenille threading'; 'she dressed very simply, usually in blues or delicate greys, with little collars of old Milan point, or very finely worked linen'; 'Daphne was so beautiful in her dark furs, the black lace of her veil thrown back over her close-fitting, dull-gold-threaded hat.' The professionalism here is both literary and sartorial – yet animated by an undisguised love of clothes, and it is this quality of warm appreciation, of relish, of almost infatuated connoisseurship, which Lawrence brings to the fine-stitching of life in general that gives his fiction its characteristic noumenon. Detail is never inert. It is picked out and worked by Lawrence. Even something so ordinary and familiar to him as a miner washing in front of the fire after a shift underground – a scene the novelist repeats endlessly – never loses its charge of mythopoeia. In the complete tales, it occurs four times, in 'White Stocking', 'Daughters of the Vicar', 'Jimmy and the Desperate Woman' and 'A Sick Collier': 'she felt rather sick, seeing his thick arms bulge their muscles'. In 'Odour of Chrysanthemums', the body being washed is dead but its power to disturb is actually increased.

This scene formulates for the first time a Lawrentian insight that was to become a crucial part of his system of belief. Birkin, in the 'Mino' chapter of *Women in Love*, outlines his theory of male–female relations. It is a theory which has proved difficult for feminists and which, to be fair to Lawrence, is equally difficult for Ursula to swallow. It dispenses with love altogether. Lawrence was shrewd enough to know that this was potentially offensive, actually offensive – and Ursula is, therefore, both hurt, incredulous and mocking. Birkin by no means has everything his own way. Lawrence mocks his self-absorption: 'but he would take no notice of her. He was talking to himself.' As the reader experiences discomfort and embarrassment while Birkin struggles (on Lawrence's behalf) to articulate his thoughts, Ursula is there (on the reader's behalf) to express our discomfiture: ' "What I want is a strange conjunction with you – " he said quietly; " – not meeting and mingling; – you are quite right: – but an equilibrium, a pure balance of two single beings: – as the stars balance each other." She looked at him. He was very earnest, and earnestness was always rather ridiculous, commonplace, to her. It made her feel unfree and uncomfortable. Yet she liked him so much. But why drag in the stars.'

*But why drag in the stars.* Every reader of Lawrence has felt this on occasion – including Lawrence himself. Usually Lawrence is shrewd enough and self-aware enough to incorporate this acute exasperation. The distance between 'Odour of Chrysanthemums' and *Women in Love* can be measured readily enough. In the story, the wife's sense of isolation from her husband's body, more piercingly realized now he is dead, is a source of wondrous horror to her: 'And her soul died in her for fear: she knew she had never seen him, he had never seen her, they had met in the dark and had fought in the dark, not knowing whom they met nor whom they fought.' Thus far it is easy to see what Lawrence owes to Arnold's treatment of moral isolation in 'Dover Beach' and, particularly, 'Sohrab and Rustum'. What in Arnold is dangerously close to an abstract proposition productive of pleasant melancholia is here, in intention at any rate, centred on the inert, immovable presence of the dead body – and its inherent horror. By *Women in Love*, the awesome separation of male and female is less awesome, indeed something to be striven for, rather than inevitably accepted as a condition of life.

In a way, neither works, though each passage fails in a different way. The *doctrine* of *Women in Love* doesn't escape risibility – but Lawrence allows for that, so it succeeds as literature. As for 'Odour of Chrysanthemums', the failure is at the literary level. The enigma of death – Lawrence's subject – is more economically realized in *The White Peacock* when the young boy discovers Annable, his father, under a rock fall at the quarry. The child's incomprehension, confronted with the dead body, is simply a heightened version of everyone's instinctive disbelief in a change so radical, instantaneous and irreversible:

> Sam put his face against his father's and snuffed round him like a dog, to feel the life in him. The child looked at me. 'He won't get up,' he said, and his little voice was hoarse with fear and anxiety. I shook my head. Then the boy began to whimper. He tried to close the lips which were drawn with pain and death, leaving the teeth bare; then his fingers hovered round the eyes, which were wide open, glazed, and I could see he was trembling to touch them into life. 'He's not asleep,' he said, 'because his eyes is open – look!' I could not bear the child's questioning terror. I took him up to carry him away, but he struggled and fought to be free. 'Ma'e 'im get up – ma'e 'im get up,' he cried in a frenzy and I had to let the boy go. He ran to the dead man, calling 'Feyther! Feyther!' and pulling his shoulder; then he sat down, fascinated by the sight of the wound; he put out his finger to touch it . . .

This passage, early in Lawrence's career, remains unequalled. By contrast, 'Odour of Chrysanthemums' is long on philosophy and short on detail. Against the aired cotton shirt, the miner's bound face, the cloths put down to save the carpets, the widow tidying the kitchen 'with peace sunk heavy on her heart', against these details, there is the mechanical classification of mother and wife, as if Lawrence were writing up a laboratory experiment: 'they never forgot it was death, and the touch of the man's dead body gave them strange emotions, different in each of the women; a great dread possessed them both, the mother felt the lie was given to her womb, she was denied; the wife felt the utter isolation of the human soul'. By contrast with the child snuffing his father's body, this is fatally forensic.

And Lawrence does not always succeed in capturing the Unknown alive. Sometimes it is dead on arrival. Given something sufficiently concrete, like a fox, Lawrence can preserve the aura of the incomprehensible intact: 'March stood there bemused, with the head of the fox in her hand. She was wondering, wondering, wondering over his long fine muzzle. For some reason it reminded her of a spoon or a spatula. She felt she could not understand it. The beast was a strange beast to her, incomprehensible, out of her range. Wonderful silver whiskers he had, like ice-threads.' A dead fox, but vividly alive on the page. How beautifully judged Lawrence's repetition is of 'wondering' and also the flat prosaic cul-de-sac of 'the beast was a strange beast'. A lesser writer than Lawrence would not have risked the banal but authentically unresolved comparison of the muzzle to a spoon or a spatula. A few pages on, Lawrence repeats the feat, this time with Henry's heart: 'it was a wonder which made her attend. And then she felt the deep, heavy, powerful stroke of his heart, terrible, like something from beyond. It was like something from beyond, something awful from outside, signalling to her. And the signal paralysed her.' Lawrence here and elsewhere is true to the terror which is inseparable from strong emotion. 'The Fox' is a story central to Lawrence's oeuvre, though one might consider the denouement wished a little melodramatically on the narrative. One's objections, however, are as nothing compared to the flat denial, the absolute negative created by the failure of 'The Ladybird'.

Lawrence initially makes some attempt to build self-criticism into the narrative. As the Nietzschean Count Dionys begins to expound his theory of the dark sun, he asks Lady Daphne, 'Does that interest you at all?' Her reply is, for most readers, a masterpiece of comic understatement: ' "Yes," she said dubiously.' The last seventeen pages, though, are as incautious as Edgar Allan Poe: 'To be gone to the call from the beyond: the call. It was the Count calling. He was calling her. She was sure he was calling her. Out of herself, out of her world, he was calling her.' Next thing we know, the Count is confiding to her (and the smirking, incredulous reader): 'I shall be king in Hades when I am dead. And you will be at my side.' At moments like these, it is difficult not to agree with Eliot's summation of Lawrence in *After Strange Gods*: 'his lack of sense of humour, a certain snobbery, a lack not so much of information as of the critical faculties which education should give, and an incapacity for what we ordinarily call thinking'.

Eliot's final thrust, however, is manifestly misdirected when applied to Lawrence's work as a whole, since Lawrence deliberately repudiated 'what we ordinarily call thinking'. His position was considered. And, as a matter of fact, Eliot himself was aware of the limitations of conventional ratiocination. In 'The Metaphysical Poets', Eliot coined a new theoretical concept – the dissociation of sensibility – a phrase whose success has been extraordinary. We like new jargon. Nevertheless, the idea epitomized in this catch-phrase is not at all new: it is part of the general intellectual context that nourished Eliot as well as Lawrence. The split alleged between thought and feeling is an old Romantic idea – 'wise passiveness' and the elevation of the heart over the brain's 'mere reasoning'. Both Lawrence and Eliot refine this conventional opposition. Why limit feeling to the heart? Eliot includes the digestive tract, Lawrence famously enfranchises the bowels and the blood. Both writers propose a new economy of feeling in which nothing is wasted. Since Eliot and Lawrence are so often opposed to each other as types, it is worth insisting for once on their similarities – similarities that arise out of a shared intellectual milieu and the renewed debate about complex feeling, from which Freud is another major beneficiary. Dissociation of sensibility was Eliot's registered trademark, but his diagnosis was generally accepted – a realignment between mind and body was widely desired.

In his posthumous essay 'Why the Novel Matters', Lawrence attacks the hegemony of mind over matter: 'We have curious ideas of ourselves. We think of ourselves as a body with a spirit in it, or a body with a soul in it, or a body with a mind in it. *Mens sana in corpore sano*. The years drink up the wine, and at last throw the bottle away, the body, of course, being the bottle.

It is a funny sort of superstition. Why should I look at my hand, as it so cleverly writes these words, and decide that it is a mere nothing compared to the mind that directs it?' Lawrence's retrospective conclusion at the end of a full writing life is decidedly benign. Only an ascetic would refuse assent to Lawrence's hospitable inclusiveness: 'Whatever is me alive is me. Every tiny bit of my hands is alive, every little freckle and hair and fold of skin.' Lawrence's sense of wonder is there again, alert as ever, performing its miracle for the hand.

The stories themselves tell a different story – a more difficult story. A minority, it is true, are benign, or broadly benign. In 'Sun', Juliet successfully demotes 'her conscious self' and releases her true self, 'this dark flow from her deep body to the sun'; in 'Blind Man', Maurice's compensation for blindness is immediate access to a richer world of sensation and feeling than is available to his wife's desiccated friend, the merely intellectual Bertie, who ends with his 'insane reserve' broken in after the blind man has handled his head and features. In 'Daughters of the Vicar', at least Louisa achieves real bodily contact with Durant, even if her sister Mary has to put up with the cold, cerebral Mr Massy. Generally, though, Lawrence shows us that the suppression of the body and the disregard of its frantic signals can be fatal. Again, this idea isn't unique to Lawrence. It is clear that, when Emilia Pinnegar writes to Jimmy Frith in 'Jimmy and the Desperate Woman', she is voicing a popular psychological theory: 'I feel I must and will express myself, if only to save myself from developing cancer or some disease that women have.' In her memoir of Lawrence, Frieda Lawrence's daughter, Barbara Weekley Barr, recalls: 'his mother died in her fifties of cancer, a disease Lawrence told me "usually caused by fret" '.

Though Lawrence is generally perceived as a great prophet of sexual liberation, the tales show that he is rather a great poet of repression, like Eliot. The body is capable of ferocious revenge – aided and abetted by Lawrence. In 'None of That', Ethel Cane meets the bullfighter, Cuesta. She is a rich American who believes in the imagination, which, in her case, means the mind: 'Talking of the Mexican atrocities, and of the famous case of

231

raped nuns, she said it was all nonsense that a woman was broken because she had been raped. She could rise above it. The imagination could rise above *anything* . . .' It is a hypothesis that Lawrence tests with off-handed callousness in his final paragraph. After we have learned that Cuesta has inherited her wealth, we learn that she committed suicide. And lastly we learn that when she finally goes to the bullfighter with sexual intentions, he hands her over 'to half a dozen of his bull-ring gang, with orders not to bruise her'. The tale has a gruesome anecdotal cynicism, but it is too obviously a parable freighted with doctrine. Freighted with doctrine when it should be heavy with tension, as the narrative is in one of Lawrence's earliest stories, 'The Prussian Officer'. Here Lawrence is still feeling his way towards a diction capable of accommodating this intractable, instinctual subject matter – of articulating the inarticulate body whose eloquence is in action. The understudy has to be given its own lines and Lawrence has to invent them: 'again the servant's heart ran hot, and he could not breathe'; 'the young soldier's heart was like fire in his chest, and he breathed with difficulty'; 'the flame sprang out of the orderly's heart, nearly suffocating him'. These sentences are taken from several pages, but they indicate Lawrence's struggle to express the constricted and the repressed. And they are recycled when Louisa and Durant push aside their class barrier to make physical contact in 'Daughters of the Vicar': 'He could not bear her to sit there any more. It made his heart go hot and stifled in his breast'; ' "Because I wanted to stay with you," she said suffocated, with her lungs full of fire.' This physical commentary is, as it were, the narrative equivalent of Eliot's theoretical neologism, the dissociation of sensibility. 'Agony', 'torture', 'fuse', 'lapse', 'as if some invisible flame were playing on him to reduce his bones and fuse him down', 'he jumped, feeling as if he were rent in two by a strong flame': Lawrence pastiches the Bible, pillages widely, invents. And repeats his inventions. Repeats them until they feel strangely idiomatic in the context of his own tales.

None of this would work, however, if Lawrence's imagination did not transcend the merely verbal. When Mrs Hepburn, in 'The Captain's Doll', falls from a hotel window and dies, Lawrence imagines it with great bravura: 'Her husband, who was in the dressing-room, heard a queer little noise, a sort of choking cry and came into her room to see what it was. And she wasn't there. The window was open, and the chair by the window. He looked round, and thought she had left the room for a moment, so returned to his shaving. He was half shaved when one of the maids rushed in.' Only a great novelist would invent this comedy of misapprehension, this detour at the crucial moment. When the orderly murders the captain in 'The Prussian Officer', Lawrence is methodical and exact and brilliant: the jargon is there ('a passion of relief', 'exquisite with relief') but more importantly there is 'that hard jaw already slightly rough with beard', the 'little "cluck" and a crunching sensation' when the neck is broken, the 'heavy convulsions' of the body, and then the face in repose. 'How curiously the mouth was pushed out, exaggerating the full lips, and the moustache bristling up from them. Then, with a start, he noticed the nostrils gradually filled with blood. The red brimmed, hesitated, ran over, and went in a thin trickle *down the face to the eyes*.' (My italics.)

Without this greedy detail, this hungry truthfulness, Lawrence's doctrine would go for nothing. In 'The Virgin and the Gypsy', Yvette is another repressed individual, a sleeping beauty, and the flood when it comes is a symbolic release. It is also – and this is what will ensure Lawrence's survival, long after his ideas seem antiquated and his doctrinal certainties are superseded – a real flood, passionately realized. Drowned Granny bobs up, 'spume hissing from her mouth'; Boswell struggles with his 'wet, tight jersey' and his teeth go 'snap-snap-snap, in great snaps'. Lawrence even imagines a *mistake* for an eyewitness: 'The gardener said he was sure that Miss Yvette was not in the house. He had seen her and the gypsy swept away.'

What else, apart from the power and the cold of a flood? 'A wild mill-race of water rushing with refuse, including Rover's green dog-kennel.' Of course, dirt, refuse – and a *green* dog-kennel.

# Primo Levi's Journalism

'My house is characterized by a lack of character,' writes Primo Levi. In the same way, *Other People's Trades* is an important book because it is not an Important Book. This collection of short, occasional pieces, mainly reprinted from *La Stampa*, considers anything from how fleas jump a hundred times their own length, to chess, to literary criticism, to childhood autobiography. It shows us a less familiar Primo Levi. Rather than the level observer and analyst of Auschwitz, the exemplary witness to the holocaust, he is a local writing for locals – exhorting his readers at one point to examine for themselves the incendiary bomb perforations 'in front of No. 9 bis on Corso Umberto'. If he is a provincial, though, he is provincial as Chekhov is provincial. He is not ashamed of being properly worldly and has little time for high-table-mindedness: on the subject of writing for money, he is robust and as practical as Marina Tsvetayeva, who declared in her essay 'A Poet on Criticism': 'Money – how petty, how pitiful, how inglorious, how vain. What meanness. What futility. What, then, do I seek, when I have written something and submit it to someone or other? Money, my dears. As much as I can get. Money enables me to go on writing.' In prose that is less flamboyant and prestidigitatory, but characterized by that 'tough reasonableness' which T. S. Eliot discerned in the poetry of Marvell, Levi concurs: 'I do not understand why some people become indignant or are surprised when they discover that Collodi, Balzac

*Other People's Trades* by Primo Levi, Michael Joseph.

and Dostoevsky wrote to make money or pay gambling debts, or plug up leaks caused by bankrupt commercial enterprises. It seems right to me that writing like any other useful activity should be recompensed.'

Because *Other People's Trades* is at a considerable remove from the harrowing experiences for which Levi is famous, it provides one with a further critical opportunity – to assess Levi as a writer, without the possible danger of applauding, not art, but morality mistaken for art. Even when one is consciously applauding morality – as is proper – there is often the improper sense that one is applauding oneself also. In Western culture, we are unreasonably anxious that our great artists should also be good men. The gap between goodness and greatness, which should surprise no one, is nevertheless the 'enigmatic' paradox which fuels the absurd 'debate' of *Amadeus*. A related tendency – to confuse distinct categories, to regard the giver and the gift as one continuous substance – accounts for Arianna Stassino-poulos Huffington's lopsided study of Picasso. Even in boxing, we yearn for the moral to merge with the muscular, and, confronted with the self-evident niceness of Henry Cooper, the entire community conspires to viva up into a higher class his meagre boxing talent. In the field of literature, the moral stature of Solzhenitsyn, rather than his artistic stature, brought him the Nobel Prize.

An additional difficulty in applauding morality is that moral-ity is not uniform. There is no morality. There are moralities, some of which are sincere and utterly horrible. It is hard to consider the Rushdie affair without concluding that some aspects of Islam are repugnant. Nor is morality stable. Nazi Germany provides us with a conveniently vivid example of a radically unstable morality. We like to think that morality is absolute and that variants are merely short-term distortions, but in reality our morality is a flux, subject to the sway of consensus. Like all things, it is affected by fashion, as Eliot knew: 'And the footman sat upon the dining-table / Holding the second house-maid on his knees – / Who had always been so careful while her mistress lived.'

Levi, too, knows these sudden, fatal fluctuations: 'rules and limitations, being determined historically, tend to change often: the history of all literatures is full of episodes in which rich and valid works were opposed in the name of principles which later proved to be much more ephemeral than the works themselves'. As a moral statement, this is unexceptionable. It is Levi's corollary which shows him to be an extraordinary writer: from the survival of certain initially reviled works of literature, like *Les Fleurs du mal* or *Madame Bovary*, Levi deduces that 'many precious books must have disappeared without leaving a trace, having been defeated in the never-ending struggle between those who write and those who prescribe how one should write'. It is as if Levi has walked out of the world of received ideas and slammed the door behind him. We *know* that great art triumphs against the odds, yet Levi has established not a doubt but a rival certainty. The pessimism is bleak and bracing and, we may as well be frank, exciting. But it is the lucidity with which Levi overturns our certainty that is moving and characteristic of his work as a whole. He is quite without hocus-pocus and writerly pyrotechnics. He is logical, even dry. He presents you with all the steps of the argument – then takes you a step further, so that some given of our world, or world-view, is transformed. For this gift, there is a term coined by Matthew Arnold: imaginative reason.

Everything Levi touches on is changed, re-thought and re-imagined – so that, to take a trivial instance, the kitchen becomes 'the most ancient of workshops and also the most conservative'. Has it ever occurred to you that wood wants to commit suicide? Wood 'is stable only in appearance': 'its mechanical virtues go hand in hand with an intrinsic chemical weakness. In our atmosphere rich in oxygen, wood is stable more or less like a billiard ball placed on a horizontal shelf edged by a border no thicker than a sheet of tissue paper. It can remain there a long time, but the tiniest push, or even a faint breath of air, will be enough to make it go past the barrier and drop to the ground. In short, wood is anxious to oxidize, that is, to destroy itself.' From this, we learn a great deal, too, about the suicidal temperament and its deceptive inertia. Levi, the calm chemist of Auschwitz-Buna-Monowitz, killed himself in 1987.

The entire book might have been more appropriately entitled 'The Book of Strange Data', the title of one of its essays. It is crammed with new, fascinating information. For instance, in praising the adaptation of parasites to the host, Levi considers the intestinal worm: 'they feed themselves at our expense with a food so perfect that, unique in creation together perhaps with the angels, they have no anus'. Levi has a well-developed sense of wonder and a true estimation of its value. In his essay on the first moon-shot, he identifies a growing malaise: 'the rapid succession of spatial portents is extinguishing in us the faculty of wonder, though it is unique in man and indispensable in making us feel alive'. Again, it is the supplementary observation which takes us by surprise. We know that man is becoming blasé. We didn't know that wonder is unique to mankind. A comparable observation might be that pornography is one of the things which distinguishes man from animals, with the corollary that romantic love and pornography issue from the same transfiguring sexual imagination. Levi encourages the mind to adventure forth.

See what he can do with chewing gum: of its 'uselessly excellent performance', Levi has this to say: 'the demand for a gum which resists, which changes form without being destroyed, and can undergo the torment of mastication, which consists in pressure, heat, humidity and enzymes, has resulted in a material which stands up only too well to trampling, rain, frost and the summer sun'. The scientist is here, sifting, sorting, analysing. The poet is also here in one phrase: 'the *torment* of mastication'. The combination makes *Other People's Trades* one of the most continuously interesting books I have ever read – by a great man *and* a good writer.

# Stanley Spencer: Vulgarity and Vision

*The Athenaeum* for 9 May 1919 carried the following anonymous short notice – written by Aldous Huxley – which dispatched a volume of poems called *The Sword*: 'Mrs Warren
writes with the ease and assurance born of literary knowledge.
No lapses of taste disfigure, no flashes of poetry transfigure her
pleasant verse.' More than wordplay links the qualities of
vulgarity and vision. Their symbiosis, necessary and nourishing,
is perfectly illustrated by the great art of Stanley Spencer, whose
aesthetic practice and profession could not differ more diamet-
rically from that of poor, pilloried Mrs Warren.

Like Masaccio – and all the appropriate comparisons are to
the Italian painters of the Renaissance – Spencer was fortunate
enough to have no taste of the conventional kind. In the Brancacci
Chapel in Florence, Masaccio's *Distribution of Alms and Death
of Ananias* is unafraid to show us, in a religious context, the bare
bottom of a little girl, plump on the mother's naked arm. In
Spencer's *Christ Carrying the Cross*, three bystanders watch the
progress of cross and a pair of ladders, at once matter of fact and
transfigured by their new function. Spencer describes the bystanders as louts, because one of them, unaware of the hallowed nature
of the event, which has been depicted a multitude of times, is
actually wiping his nose on the back of his hand.

There is nothing irreverent in this exercise of the artistic
imagination. I am reminded of Joyce, whose hero Stephen
Dedalus finds God 'a shout in the street'. Frank Budgen records

*Stanley Spencer: A Biography* by Kenneth Pople, Collins.

that Joyce had a photograph of a Greek statue of Penelope pinned to the wall of his flat in Zurich. Visitors to Universität-strasse were often asked what she was thinking. ' "My own idea," said Joyce, "is that she is trying to recollect what Ulysses looks like. You see, he has been away many years, and they had no photographs in those days." ' Since Penelope is the byword for fidelity, Joyce's shrewd empathy restores reality to the complacent assumptions of the legend. In his biblical pictures, Spencer did this all the time.

1911 saw Stanley Spencer on a farm near Taunton, from which he wrote, describing a farmworker: 'His face was beaten and cut with the sword of age. You could divide his face up like a [jigsaw] puzzle.' The two sentences are a perfect epitome of Spencer's art. The Authorized Version lies behind the cadence of 'beaten and cut with the sword of age', but the jigsaw puzzle, which is equally eloquent, is as bang up to date as a bus ticket. The timelessness of great art – that hackneyed formulaic phrase – for once means something when you consider the chronological span of Spencer's pictures.

*Christ Delivered to the People* depicts Pontius Pilate in the background, washing his hands as tradition requires, and wearing peculiar headgear, which Kenneth Pople describes as being 'like an inverted light fitting with pendant glass globes'. Pople has written a well-researched, absorbing, corrective, detailed and devoted life of a wonderful man and a great painter. He is anxious to play down the allegedly sensational side of Spencer's life. He provides a calm, balanced and, therefore, quietly horrifying account of Spencer's second marriage to the cold, mercenary Patricia Preece – who teased him sexually, exploited him financially and carried on an imperturbable affair with her companion, Dorothy Hepworth. Pople also names one previously anonymous mistress and reveals another, Daphne Charlton, and her relaxed, complaisant husband. These revelations are properly low-key in tone. Spencer's great love was his first wife Hilda, as all the other women – not many, after all – eventually came to realize. These sad, amorous ghosts have now been definitively laid by Pople.

On the other hand, the pictorial analysis is over-reliant on autobiographical transpositions and the whole notion of solving pictures as if they were detective stories. Pilate's hat is a coxcomb with three balls – like the insignia outside a pawnshop, because Christ is about to redeem our lives by sacrificing his own. Typically, Spencer marries the biblical and the modern. As a child, he was known in the family as 'Tongly', a nickname derived from his childish pronunciation of his proper name: even then he was giving his own inflection to the standard-issue article.

Pople is anxious that Spencer's greatness should be recognized. Those of us who can remember, say, William Feaver's patronizing review of the 1976 travelling exhibition organized by the Arts Council can now be less uneasy. By 1980, Feaver's opinions, like those of several other art critics, had silently deserted to the side which supported Spencer and which was clearly winning the argument. The exhibition about to open at the Barbican, *The Apotheosis of Love*, should only add to the wave of acclaim which began to gather irresistible momentum with the 1980 exhibition at the Royal Academy. In the catalogue then, Hugh Casson described Spencer as 'one of the most remarkable artists of our time'. In fact, Spencer is a painter to equal the Piero della Francesca of Sansepulcro – as anyone knows who has seen his *The Resurrection of the Soldiers* and the accompanying pictures at the Oratory of All Souls in Burghclere.

When, as a student, Spencer was asked what he thought of Picasso, he replied, superciliously (it was thought), that he had 'not got beyond Piero della Francesca'. Pople, from the best of motives, makes nervous connections with the great modernists, Joyce and Eliot, though elsewhere he knows perfectly well that Spencer stands awkwardly and magnificently athwart standard modernism. He is radically old-fashioned. His simplified replicants derive from the readily discernible family likeness one finds in Giotto's figures. Pople would like Spencer to be an obscure painter and therefore modern, but the problem for modern art critics is that, compared to Picasso's analytical cubism, Spencer's pictures are very easy to understand. Even his distortions, in, say, the Beatitudes of Love series, are adequately explained, in my view, by Spencer's staunch assertion that people are like that in reality. They may not be the best specimens Spencer could have painted, given the range of human presentability, but they aren't spectacularly ugly either.

Conventional beauty didn't interest or arouse Spencer, as his great nude paintings demonstrate. The 1942 *Seated Nude* of his first wife, Hilda, is a paean to the palpability of her flesh – the solid scrolls of her belly, the used nipples, the slight breasts. Patricia Preece, the ghastly, gold-digging second wife, has, in the *Leg of Mutton Nude*, her left breast implicitly compared to a lamp chop – the medallion of lean meat echoing her nipple and the streaky remainder assimilated to the stretch marks of her pendulous breasts. Which are in turn echoed by the ticking of the mattress.

This brings us to Spencer's sense of form. In Richard Carline's indispensable 1978 *Stanley Spencer at War*, a letter from Spencer to the recently retired director of the Tate is quoted: in it, Spencer describes a passage of the Burghclere chapel painting as 'a symphony in rashers of bacon' with a 'tea-making obligato'. Spencer was always alert to pattern and always prepared to accept it in its easiest and most obvious manifestations – a series of Sam Browne belts, at once complicated and identical; the endlessly unified ramifications of brickwork, of checks and patterned clothes, of skeins of wool and skeins of hair. Not that sophistication is ruled out: a picture like *Swan Upping* may contain obvious yet pleasing parallels between the long white arms of the boat-menders and the necks of the swans, but the overall form is that of a tree, whose trunk is the tow path with its several branches and its 'foliage' the elaborate ironwork of the bridge.

Kipling has a story, 'The Disturber of Traffic', in which a lighthouse keeper called Dowse is driven nuts by the patterns he sees in the waves, 'like bacon, too streaky'. Not unlike Spencer's 'symphony in rashers of bacon', then. Rescued, Dowse denies being mad, 'but all the time his eyes was held like by the coils of rope on the belaying pins, and he followed those ropes up and up with his eye till he was quite lost and comfortable among the rigging'. Spencer's paintings are like that in their relentless patterning. And the pleasure to be derived by the viewer is not so much in teasing out a hidden pattern as enjoying an ebullient and inventive profusion of the obvious. Kipling is again a useful parallel – Spencer's form generally gives us all the satisfaction of full and frequent rhyme in poetry. Speaking of Henry Lamb's pianism, Spencer said, 'His playing is very good; he gets everything clear.' And of Rupert Brooke, Spencer explained his liking with 'he knows what teatime is'. Spencer wasn't afraid of the clear or of the obvious – and neither should we be.

Here was an artist who could appreciate the 'unexposed-to-the-weatherness' of his wife's leg, whose painting *The Centurion's Servant* is really about the bed rather than the drama of illness and cure – and who, to return to the beginning of this review, once said, 'I think one catches sight of one's own vulgarity when for a moment one gets hold of something vital. I really feel that everything in one that is *not vision* is vulgarity.' Spencer's imagination erected no barriers of decorum, just as his apparent egotism was in fact the expression of a broadcast, seeding, spilling self. Avid for everything, he would have liked to engross pregnancy, labour, motherhood, and he once confided to Hilda, 'You know, ducky, I wish I had the experience of being a bugger. I am sure I would show more real understanding of it.' He had a roving 'I', resistant to the place allotted by convention. Compare, for example, the carpenters with nails in their mouths in *The Crucifixion*, recently sold by Sotheby's for over a million pounds, and this comment of Spencer on Dante: 'When Dante came out of Hell and arrived at the grassy slopes of Purgatory, Virgil placed his hands on the wet grass and washed the grime off Dante's face.' Both artists are linked by their shared ability to imagine accurately and in detail.

# George Orwell

George Orwell was an impostor. An old-Etonian, ex-imperialist policeman, he was desperate to pass for ordinary, to be absolved of social sin, to shed the crime of privilege. To this end, he changed his name and tried to change his character – about which there was always something patrician.

According to a footnote in this welcome, exhausting, enthralling, praiseworthy, imperfect, unaffordable edition, when he arrived in Barcelona to serve with the POUM militia, he pretended to be a grocer. (In fact, he was merely being frugal with the truth: he had resuscitated the meagre shopping facility in his cottage at Wallington.) Doreen Kopp, a relative who married Orwell's commanding officer, accurately commented: 'it was of course very typical of George as he always wanted to be taken for a working man'. However, despite his disguise, that draught-excluder moustache – a door-to-door salesman's centipede of sample bristle – Orwell was a failed transsocial. Hence, though, his particular successes as a writer. The best of Orwell – his journalism, here accounting for fourteen of the twenty volumes – arises from his profound dividedness. His style's polemical effectiveness relies on a preference for deflationary similes and the conflation of the rhetorically plain with a more upper-class idiolect: Orwell's evident courage and authenticity are maximized by the manifest absence of any literary high-style – of *writing* – and the prevalence of a near-Wodehousian comic

*The Complete Works of George Orwell*, edited by Peter Davison, assisted by Ian Angus and Sheila Davison, Secker & Warburg.
*Orwell: The Authorized Biography* by Michael Shelden, Heinemann.

vocabulary ('it was plain eyewash'; 'the pain in my arm was diabolical'; 'damnable inefficiency'; 'the beastly stench', 'the devilish din of firing'; 'a frightful shambles'). His greatest essays, 'A Hanging' and 'Shooting an Elephant', depend on detail for their power, but also on double agency, on Orwell's scrupulous notation of his skewed loyalties: 'with one part of my mind I thought of the British Raj as an unbreakable tyranny . . . with another part I thought the greatest joy in the world would be to drive a bayonet into a Buddhist priest's guts'.

The traitor within suffers the visceral pull of class and nation, while the politically re-educated autodidact exercises his capacity for ethical disgust, the ready rising of the gorge at social injustice. Dividedness was Orwell's element. He suffered it and he recognized it everywhere. It was even there in poetry: '*Prufrock* is an expression of futility, but it is also a poem of wonderful vitality and power.' He saw that Hopkins's Jesuit conformity might have contributed to his aesthetic radicalism: 'he was completely subordinated in one world, that of the Church, and he may have wanted to compensate himself by being a rebel in another, that of poetry'.

In 'My Country Right or Left', written in the autumn of 1940, Orwell explained how his views on the latest war came to change:

> for several years the coming war was a nightmare to me, and at times I made speeches and wrote pamphlets against it. But the night before the Russo-German pact was announced I dreamed that the war had started. It was one of those dreams which, whatever Freudian inner meaning they may have, do sometimes reveal to you the real state of your feelings. It taught me two things, first, that I should be simply relieved when the long-dreaded war started, secondly, that I was patriotic at heart, would not sabotage or act against my own side, would support the war, would fight in it if possible.

In other words, the dream showed Orwell that he was divided – that he thought one thing but felt another.

Previously, he regarded the war not as a war against Hitler, but as a pretext for the English upper class to set in place an authoritarian quasi-fascist regime. With Herbert Read, he conspired to secrete printing presses for the purpose of disseminating anti-government propaganda once the war was under weigh. The war, he then thought, would be a matter of 'wage-reductions, suppression of free speech, brutalities in the colonies etc.'. That etcetera stands for the automatic print-out of the unthinking Spartist faction. But Orwell could be politically stupid more often than one might anticipate. In May 1941, he predicted that 'within two years we shall either be conquered or we shall be a Socialist republic fighting for its life, with a secret police force and half the population starving'. Prediction – vide *Nineteen Eighty-Four* – was never Orwell's strong suit, but this is frankly bonkers, as is his claim in September 1940 that the war was 'manifestly developing into a revolutionary war' – which made him think of 'St Petersburg in 1916'.

Then there is his abiding paranoia about 'direct treachery in high command', his conviction that anti-fascist refugees were jailed because their radical European connections might foment a Bolshevik-style revolution here. Orwell's wife rightly saw that he retained 'an extraordinary political simplicity in spite of everything'. He could see, for example, that P. G. Wodehouse was a political naïf in need of a helping hand. But he couldn't see that his own 'sophistication' was equally risible: the early release of Wodehouse and Nazi permission to let him broadcast, Orwell believed, was 'a minor move' to keep the USA out of the war. Which seems as likely as his contention that the capitalist newspaper proprietors who ran comics like *Gem* and *Magnet* maintained the 'antiquated, conservative tone of these stories ... in the interests of the class structure of society'. Evelyn Waugh, whose summary I quote, pronounced this 'nonsense' when he reviewed Orwell's essays in *The Tablet* in 1946. Which it incontrovertibly is.

So why is Orwell still worth reading? For Peter Davison, he is the precursor of post-colonial studies and anticipates, in his two years at the BBC, the Open University and the Third

Programme. You could also argue that the New Journalism was foreshadowed in the documentary works *Down and Out in Paris and London, The Road to Wigan Pier* and *Homage to Catalonia*, in which the author is half-observer, half-participant – the guinea pig under fire: 'the whole experience of being hit by a bullet is very interesting'. Waugh's review also makes the point that Orwell's essays undermine the concept of literary hierarchy – Dickens and comics are equally proper subjects. You might, therefore, credit Orwell with the postmodern progeny of Barthes and Eco – were it not that Charles Lamb is an even earlier practitioner of the feuilleton, the frisk on any subject.

The real reason we read Orwell is because his own fault-line, his fundamental schism, his hybridity, left him exceptionally sensitive to the fissure – which is everywhere apparent – between what *ought* to be the case and what actually *is* the case. He says the unsayable. Paradoxically, Orwell's own ontological fraudulence confers on him his awkward and appealing honesty. It isn't the gift of the gab. It is the odder bounty of the blurt. Like Whitman, Orwell contains multitudes. Inside him, there is a continuous argument between the convinced socialist, the unregenerate imperialist and his adopted identity of the bloke in the street, George Hairoil. One can never be quite certain what will emerge from these tripartite talks – except that it is unlikely to be safely orthodox. Or even consistent. 'I feel sure that there is quite enough north-country dialect in real life without letting it get into novels,' writes Orwell, only to assert a hundred pages later that literature would be transformed if 'working-class writers will learn to write in their own dialect'. Do I contradict myself? Very well, I contradict myself.

He congratulates Anthony Powell for calling Scotsmen 'Scotchmen' – 'I find this a good easy way of annoying them.' Eleven years later, he changes his mind out of 'the most ordinary politeness'. Provocation is, of course, a tool of his trade: 'one of the surest signs of [Conrad's] genius is that women dislike his books'. Lydia Jackson, a woman he failed to seduce, reports that his 'masculine conceit annoyed' her. Even allowing for coat-trailing, it is clear that Orwell's honesty is rooted in his own conflicted personality. He is litmus to hypocrisy – and to its (rarer) opposite. In March 1936, he is much taken by a man whose mother has 'just died' and is 'lying dead at home': 'she was 89 and had been a midwife for 50 years. I noted the lack of hypocrisy with which he was laughing and joking and came into the pub to have a drink etc.' It might be Camus's Meursault, refusing to lie, refusing to feel more than he feels. This is cognate with the impulse to tell us that the deplorable Oswald Mosley is 'a very good speaker' or that Hitler has 'something deeply appealing about him' – and that his expression reminds Orwell of the crucified Christ. Like Edgar at the end of *King Lear*, Orwell says 'what we feel, not what we ought to say'.

Orwell thought Zola set out 'to symbolize capitalist corruption' in his novels, but that his scenes 'are also scenes'. The balance is crucial and carefully monitored in Orwell's own best epiphanic sketches. In 'A Hanging', the obvious pivotal moment – when the condemned man steps aside to avoid a puddle – is telling in its epitome of the barbarism of capital punishment. It is also commonplace. Its literary antecedents go back to Fagin ('he thought of all the horrors of the gallows and the scaffold – and stopped to watch a man sprinkling the floor to cool it – and then went on to think again') and to Hetty Sorrel in *Adam Bede*: 'she craved food and rest – she hastened towards them at the very moment she was picturing to herself the bank from which she would leap towards death'. Orwell and George Eliot both seize on the logical contradiction – but it is the more insidious contradictions which animate Orwell's sketch. The warders crowd very close to the condemned man – 'with their hands always on him in a careful, *caressing* grip'. (My italics.) The dog that bursts on to the scene is an emblem of all the unruly, improper, well-nigh uncontrollable feelings being repressed, but which Orwell finally steels himself to introduce to his readers. When the condemned man prays, 'each cry [is] another second of life; the same thought was in all our minds: oh, kill him quickly, get it over, stop that abominable noise'. Here, the parable of capital punishment is superseded by the scene itself. And when the hanging is over, the 'moody look' leaves the superintendent's face – and 'one felt an impulse to sing, to break into a run, to snigger'. We are reminded that great art has to articulate fearlessly what it is to be human. What was later to harden into an intellectual mannerism of patrician plain-speaking is here, in this very early work, a dispassionate stare at the existential truth of our unreliable, sluggish, turbid, powerful, meagre emotions.

But Orwell isn't a great prose writer, except in *Animal Farm*, where he accepts the stylistic limitations of his chosen genre – the reverse fairy-tale which ends unhappily ever after. Generally speaking, Orwell's prose is effective journalism, not more than that, and it is only because *Animal Farm* must conform to a narrative of wide-eyed, unseeing somnambulism that he represses his weakness for overstatement and explicit moralizing. For once he forgoes his automatic epithets – 'moth-eaten' and 'flyblown'. But his natural prose style is blunt and emphatic – and disastrous in fiction. Suppose, for instance, this passage from *The Road to Wigan Pier* occurred in a novel: 'Of the five pay-checks I mentioned above, no less than three are rubber-stamped with the words "death-stoppage". When a miner is killed at work it is usual for the other miners to make up a subscription, generally of a shilling each, for his widow, and this is collected by the colliery company and automatically deducted from their wages. The significant detail here is the *rubber stamp*.' Orwell wrote in italics all the time, disfiguring most of his fiction and some of his essays. Orwell's biographer, Michael Shelden, may be impressed by the tabloid quality of the opening of 'Marrakech' but it reads like a parody of Graham Greene at his worst: 'As the corpse went past the flies left the restaurant table in a cloud and rushed after it, but they came back a few minutes later.'

Of *Nineteen Eighty-Four*, Shelden tells us that readers have been 'so absorbed by its riveting story that they have not paid enough attention to the excellence of so many of its passages of prose'. Later he claims that 'the quality of Orwell's prose' is 'a vital part of his novel's originality'. What quality, one may ask? Shelden appears to take the word for the deed, and refers us to the four redactions of the novel – in which, for instance, the inept early phrase 'his bowels seemed to turn over' is improved by Orwell to read 'his bowels seemed to turn to water'. The phrase and its variants are something of a leitmotif in *Nineteen Eighty-Four*: 'Winston's entrails seemed to have turned to ice'; 'suddenly his heart seemed to turn to ice and his bowels to water'; 'with ice at his heart, Winston . . .'. Then there are Orwell's approximations: 'a horrible pang of terror went through him. It was almost gone at once, but it left a sort of nagging uneasiness hehind'; 'with a sort of faded enthusiasm'; 'with a kind of astonishment'; 'with a sort of despairing sensuality'; 'she also stirred a sort of envy in him'; 'a kind of nobility, a kind of purity'; 'with a sort of voluptuousness'. The chancy success of Orwell's dystopia is that the myth contains sufficient imaginative tropes – Big Brother, Room 101, telescreens, Newspeak – to float free of the inferior prose and survive without their cumbersome host.

In 'Reflections on Gandhi', George Orwell wrote that sainthood is 'a thing that human beings must avoid'. He hasn't been wholly successful in his own case and is widely regarded as a secular saint of English letters. A memoir by William Empson, 'Orwell at the BBC', partially explains how this came about. Apparently, the wartime government wished to promote the birth-rate and therefore offered extra rations and free nursery facilities to working parents of new babies. Empson and his wife Hetta 'took advantage of this plan to have two children', and were gleefully explaining the wheeze to Orwell when they noticed 'the familiar look of settled loathing come over his face'. Orwell was known to give away his rations to more deserving cases. He had, as Empson noted, 'a great power to make you feel ashamed of yourself'.

He had, too, an austere charisma, which was recorded by Cyril Connolly, who threw a party during the Spanish war: 'he came along, looking gaunt and shaggy, shabby, aloof, and he had this extraordinary magical effect on these women. They all wanted to meet him and started talking to him, and their fur coats shook with pleasure.' Orwell's moral testosterone, his permanently aroused conscience, is instantly canonized by Connolly, who conjures 'this sort of John the Baptist figure coming in from the wilderness'. In fact, though Orwell's abrasive tweed jacket probably had much in common with the Baptist's camel-hair garb, he more nearly resembles a hybrid figure – St George, the dragon, a moral blow-lamp. Confident declarations of human rights and wrongs are an essential feature of this saint's armoury. Malcolm Muggeridge recalls his friend's facility for generalization, even as he guys it: 'Orwell suddenly announced, "All tobacconists are Fascists," and began to expand on the point as though its truth were self-evident.'

Given this prevailing attitude to Orwell, it is hardly surprising that Sonia Orwell should have been profoundly unhappy with Bernard Crick's authorized biography of her late husband, which demonstrated, a little coolly for some tastes, that Orwell had successfully avoided sainthood. He had been imperceptive about his first wife's illness, about her grief after her brother's death. He had been unfaithful to her. Very shortly after her death, he had proposed marriage in unattractively clinical terms to four different women. On the whole, reviewers shared Sonia Orwell's discomfort with Crick's commendably detached recital of the facts. Ten years on, Crick's delineation no longer looks shocking or chilly, merely full and accurate.

When Orwell met Stephen Spender, it was with regret because he could no longer treat the poet with 'intellectual brutality'. This crucial phrase explains the paucity of personal relations in his life. Integrity and brutality were too closely identified in Orwell's mind to risk the weakness of intimacy. And if he was St George the dragon, the role involved not only intellectual brusqueness to outsiders, but also a complicated loathing of the enemy within, the conformist he spent a lifetime defeating – the man who needed to be loved. 'O stubborn, self-willed exile from the loving breast!' sobs Winston Smith at the end of *Nineteen Eighty-Four*. The Big Brother to whom Orwell succumbed at last, dying and desperate, was Sonia Brownell. In return for everything, his books, his royalties, his reputation, she provided him with the illusion of love. The night he died, she was nightclubbing with her ex-lover, Lucien Freud. Shortly after-wards, she was in France, pursuing another ex-lover, the philo-sopher Maurice Merleau-Ponty. The tough widow and the intellectually brutal author had something in common after all – heartache and longing.

# Ron Mueck

Ron Mueck's *Dead Dad* is an authoritative masterpiece – the equal of Vermeer's *The Lace-Maker* or Hilliard's portrait of Sir Walter Ralegh – and in the Saatchi *Sensation* exhibition at the Royal Academy last year it left Damien Hirst's patched and increasingly shop-soiled shark looking like the *fin de siècle* conversation piece it is. Viewers of the Mueck were held in its force field. It exerted the gravitational pull of great art.

Consider their respective titles. On the one hand, the coffee-bar existentialism of Hirst's *The Physical Impossibility of Death in the Mind of Someone Living*. On the other hand, the blunt, unpretentious, Australian factuality of *Dead Dad*. Physics versus metaphysics, matter versus motor-mouth, attentiveness versus illustration. Whereas the Hirst is grounded in grand guignol, the Mueck confesses the neutral curiosity we all feel about the dead body, as opposed to the dead person. Curiosity, however natural, isn't often the emotion behind a work of art. Given Mueck's subject, you might expect grief.

In fact, the great danger in this subject – the dead father – is sentimentality. Mueck's title is usefully prophylactic. It is also, for all its simplicity, a subtle choice of words. In 'The Wreck of the *Deutschland*', Gerard Manley Hopkins captures the minute gradualism of sand moving in an hourglass by the alteration of only a single letter: 'I am soft sift in an hourglass.' The 'o' alters to 'i'. In Mueck's title, a letter is omitted: the letter 'e', a

*Sensation: Young British Artists from the Saatchi Collection*, Royal Academy of Arts, 1997.

minuscule but resonant change that is cognate with the larger strategy of Mueck's sculpture, the alteration of scale, a reduction which is also a concentration – where nothing is apparently lost, though something is evidently and irretrievably lost.

Wittgenstein said that death is not an event in life – meaning that, therefore, nothing could be usefully said about the experience of death. Damien Hirst's gabby title asserts something similar – that the living can't get their heads around the idea of death, you know what I mean. It is a vacuity on which Mueck wastes no time because he is intent on confronting the deaths of others. Where Damien Hirst offers an illustrational aide-mémoire for his dog-eared proposition – that shark – Mueck sets out to examine, without mystification, the mystery of death, our sense that something vital has vanished, though nothing has changed. Our perspective has shifted – subtly but massively – and Mueck's radical reduction of scale, which yet preserves everything perfectly, mirrors this fundamental experience. No one looking at *Dead Dad* thinks, even for a second, that this is someone sleeping. We *know* the person is dead – despite all the evidence to the contrary, the conspiracy of details, the forensic accumulation of particulars, the calm inventory of flesh. We tot up – the perfect toenails, the hurry of hairs on the calves, the neat hair style which places the subject with such social accuracy, the roseate cock with its prepuce folded close like a link of cold sausage – we tot up and nothing is missing. And everything has been lost. The paradox is there in the sore seepage of pink round the eyes and the helpless hands, palms up. Mueck's sculpture explains why man has felt the need to invent the idea of the soul. Think of Holbein's *Christ in the Sepulchre* or Rembrandt's *Anatomy Lesson* – two great paintings, but paintings which record the absolute aftermath of death and not that long moment when the illusion of life evaporates, when everything is as it was and utterly changed. For this we had to wait for Ron Mueck. And it is more interesting than grief would have been. The grief is taken for granted in the one word, 'Dad'. It is assumed, not indulged.

According to his friend Conrad Aiken, T. S. Eliot was

depressed after he had completed that great *coup* of modernism, 'The Love Song of J. Alfred Prufrock'. He felt he would never write anything quite as good again. *Dead Dad* is destined to be Ron Mueck's *chef-d'œuvre*. Certainly the four new pieces on show at the d'Offay gallery are scarcely a match, though *Ghost*, a gigantified schoolgirl in an unflattering swimming costume, is first-class. Here the scale is exaggerated to record, perfectly, another intense emotion, but one previously ignored by artists – acute self-consciousness. John Updike devoted an entire book to anatomizing the intricate ramifications of his physical shame – largely the result of his lifelong, burgeoning psoriasis – and 'anatomizing' is the *mot juste* for his 245 pages of agonized autobiography, in which he states that he married the first person who would forgive him for his skin. The skin of the adolescent girl is perfectly rendered by Mueck – not pimples, but the pink patches of *healing* pimples, and some dark hairs sleeving her forearms, as well as the awkward eloquence of her angular pose, her monumental feet and hands.

The worry about this piece is in its title, *Ghost*. I fear that Mueck has been badly advised – perhaps by his mother-in-law, Paula Rego. Curiosity, natural, neutral curiosity and self-consciousness are real enough emotions, all the better as subjects for being true as well as neglected, but the art world is sentimentally predisposed to value larger, simplified emotions. Paula Rego's pictures are ingratiating in exactly this way, with their currency of melodramatic innuendo, of trite psychologizing, of sexual naughtiness. Her Balthus–Burra–Tenniel-influenced androgynous figures play with scale, too, but less subtly and more uniformly than those of Mueck. His title, *Ghost*, seems designed to encourage interpretative speculation rather in the Rego manner. In his Phaidon study, John McEwen records two interpretations of her painting *The Cadet and His Sister*, both by the artist. In the first, the cadet is impotent. In the second, 'it's about incest', 'the cock is his masculinity', 'the handbag is her femininity'. McEwen adds: 'in 1992, Paula could not remember ever having described the picture in this latter way. "It's about domination, that's all," she said firmly. But she has let it stand, on the grounds that it is just another story.' Her attitude is shared by her interpreter – the assumption that proliferation of meaning is necessarily a testament to profundity. McEwen writes: 'it is difficult to pin her down on the way one should interpret her pictures. The story she tells one day can be entirely different from the story she tells the next. Her pictures are true to this complexity. Clarity has increased their ambiguity . . .' Complexity? Or merely disguising the trite? A picture like *The Policeman's Daughter* is clearly enough about fist-fucking/masturbation inspired by a fantasy of incest, with the stretching cat barely more than a sexual pun, exhausted by Hockney's use of it in the Tate double portrait of Ossie and Celia Clark, with Percy the cat upright in Ossie's lap.

It would be a great pity if Mueck's unflinching singleness of purpose should become infected by his mother-in-law's whimsy or the general aesthetic sentimentality in the art world. In interview, he has said that the reduction of scale in *Dead Dad* is to encourage the idea that the corpse could be cradled. Fortunately, the bleak factuality of the sculpture resists this lachrymose tendency, just as its uncompromising title tells you exactly what the piece is about. There is, of course, no intrinsic reason why works of art should provide interpretative fodder for the critical industry. Currently, we feel that works of art are strangely diminished if the viewer knows what they are about. You can see this in the umbrella title of the latest Saatchi book, *The New Neurotic Realism* – where the word 'neurotic' is an irrelevant sop to the fashion for psychoanalytical interpretation. No one, however, feels the need to justify a Holbein portrait in terms of its concealed ideas.

Mueck's art, at its very best, is gloriously free of ideas. It can be epitomized by a passage in Vladimir Nabokov's *The Real Life of Sebastian Knight*. Notoriously, Nabokov loathed and despised a whole phalanx of writers whose undeserved reputations rested, as it seemed to him, on high-sounding, hollow ideas – the balsa wood profundities, the papier mâché universal concepts, which he designated as 'bloated topicalities'. Dostoevsky, Balzac, Thomas Mann were his favourite examples.

Nabokov's idea of great art was art in which one could fondle the details – in his famous phrase. He would have adored Mueck's work, though, like me, be anxious for its integrity when faced with *Angel*, a depressed middle-aged man, miniaturized on a paint-flecked studio stool *and equipped with wings*. At first sight, one is charmed by the piece but retrospectively the whimsy of those wings begins to pall. The conceit – that angels might be as anxious as Pope's sylphs in *The Rape of the Lock* and earthy enough to have anal hair – is there to hide a different anxiety, the fear of repetition, to add *content* to what might otherwise look like pure technique, a technical trick. But Mueck's art is not only profligate with details to fondle – it is also savingly secret.

Except in the case of *Mask*, the pieces at the d'Offay and *Dead Dad* preserve the integrity of their illusion no matter how closely you examine them. In the Uffizi, there is a wonderful Holbein of the poet Sir Robert Southwell who has a mouth of Piscean conceit and a scar at the junction of jaw and throat. No scar has ever been better painted. The technique has effaced all trace of itself to leave only *das Ding an sich*, the thing itself – Southwell's scar. But Holbein can do the same thing with the grimy chamois leather of a pair of ducal gloves. As far as I know, no one has complained that this is 'mere' technique, partly because the skill is enigmatic – as it mostly is with Mueck. The exception is *Mask*, where the magnification is so great that the technique yields up its secrets – or some of them. *Mask* is a self-portrait of the early middle-aged Mueck so you can see that his black and grey shaven bristles are in fact made from lengths of nylon fishing line. In literature, there is a term for self-conscious demonstration of methodology – it is known as 'baring the device' and can be almost reflex in the case of certain postmodernist writers. In the past, it was used by Brecht in theatre, when it was called the *Verfremdungseffekt*, or alienation effect: Brecht wanted his audience to be aware that they were in a theatre. As a technique it has its uses but it quickly becomes a mannerism. In the case of Mueck, the charm, the *magic* of his pieces partly depends on the invisibility of his means. Of course, the magic is nothing but hard work and the application of ultra-rigorous standards – who was it said that genius is only the capacity for taking infinite pains? – but Mueck would be wise to keep to himself his working methods because he is likely to spawn a host of imitators. Ideally, his subjects should be obvious and his technique enigmatic. That way Mueck will continue to speak to our need to live in the physical world and his sculptures will simply *be*, in and for themselves, not as vehicles for ideas.

I began this piece with Mueck's great sculptural meditation on death. This is Sebastian Knight's meditation on death in his (invented) novel, *The Doubtful Asphodel*:

'And as the meaning of all things shone through their shapes, many ideas and events which had seemed of the utmost importance dwindled not to insignificance, for nothing could be insignificant now, but to the same size which other ideas and events, once denied any importance, now attained.' Thus, such shining giants of our brain as science, art or religion fell out of the familiar scheme of their classification, and joining hands, were mixed and joyfully levelled. Thus, a cherry stone and its tiny shadow which lay on the painted wood of a tired bench, or a bit of torn paper, or any such trifle out of millions and millions of trifles grew to a wonderful size.

The shadow of the cherry stone. The shadow cast by a nail in the wall behind Vermeer's milkmaid. The sense of questioned scale isn't a technical trick, it is a vision – a way of looking at the world and looking again until you have truly seen it. Mueck has already done this and we are extraordinarily lucky to be alive at the same time.

# Frost the Modernist

I'm going out to fetch the little calf
That's standing by the mother. It's so young
It totters when she licks it with her tongue.
I sha'n't be gone long. – You come too.

This is Robert Frost's *invitation au voyage* at the head of his complete poems – a Yankee murmur, delivered in his best bunkside manner, to reassure his reader that poetry is next to naturalness.

To appreciate it, the only cultivation required is a predisposition to the agricultural – rather than the rebarbative cultural allusions so dauntingly present in the poetry of high modernism. Where T. S. Eliot discusses his art in terms of chemistry, Frost prefers an analogue taken from rodeo: 'the great pleasure in writing poetry is in having been carried off. It is as if you stood astride the subject that lay on the ground, and they cut the cord, and the subject gets up under you and you ride it. You adjust yourself to the motion of the thing itself. That is the poem.'

In fact, Eliot's chemical analogue argues for the same things – the suppression of the poet's personality, the importance of aesthetic form, the relative unimportance of advertised sensibility. Nevertheless, the different choice of analogue is crucial. Frost, apparently, opts for the simple – the direct observation of that (brilliantly vivid) calf, tottering when licked. Notes of a

*Homage to Robert Frost* by Joseph Brodsky, Seamus Heaney and Derek Walcott, Faber.

native son, inveterately veterinarian, and a million miles away from the intimidating accumulation of notes at the end of *The Waste Land* – you can feel easy with Frost.

'Pound down to Eliot they have striven for distinction by a show of learning,' Frost wrote to his daughter in 1934. Significantly, Frost strove to include the robust philistine in his cultural scheme. At Princeton in 1937, he was the spokesman for democratic diversity of excellence: 'when I see young men doing so wonderfully well in athletics, I don't feel angry at them. I feel jealous of them. I wish that some of my boys in writing would do the same thing. I wish they would stop grouching at the athletes – leave them alone and do something as well in the arts.' Frost knew his American audience.

As for Lord Snooty and his pal, Eliot and Pound, not to mention Gertrude Stein, Frost advised his daughter patriotically: 'Claim everything for America.' Even in his earliest days, when Ezra Pound was saluting him as a 'VURRY AMUR'k'n talent', Frost was deeply uneasy about his Europhile supporter. Would his native stateside debut be tainted by Pound's vaunted and vocal hostility to American editors? Frost always had the general reader in mind and, specifically, the American general reader. He was rewarded by being asked in 1963 to recite a poem at Kennedy's inauguration. He was the Voice of America – at last.

Don't believe it. Or the smiling public man. In a dark, complicated sense, Frost did speak for his vision of America – of the land itself, but at the point where geography assumes a metaphysical dimension, where the celebrated wide-open spaces are a metonymy for the cold, black, inhospitable, uninhabited reaches of infinite space. Auden shrewdly pointed out that the deserted homestead is a recurrent motif in Frost's poetry. For Frost as for Hopkins, man is the merest 'spark', a scintilla 'in an enormous dark drowned'. We see this clearly in 'The Census-Taker', where the official confronts an utterly deserted farm and the surrounding waste land, created by clearance and subsequent erosion. The desolation, the last line teaches, symbolizes man's vulnerability, his virtual invisibility against the vastness of the non-human backdrop: 'It must be I want life to go on living.'

'An Old Man's Winter Night' begins with the discrepancy between the human scale and the interstellar vacancy: 'All out of doors looked darkly in at him.' The old man does not return the gaze: 'What kept his eyes from giving back the gaze / Was the lamp tilted near them [his eyes] in his hand.' The poem, though, is acutely aware, conscious without looking directly, of what is tacitly at stake. The old man clomps around 'like beating on a box'. Immediately, the farm shrinks to the size of a coffin. He is, as it were, buried alive, extinction is so close – awesome, threatening and indifferent.

Sometimes it can be attractive, too, and recall the Keats who was 'half in love with easeful death'. Frost's 'Mowing', famous and widely misunderstood, addresses this ambiguous response. The scythe is a traditional symbol for inevitable death. Frost's poem, however, works from a bold pretence that it deals only with country matters – that a scythe is a scythe is a scythe. He insists on actuality more than emblem, specifying the flowers ('Pale orchises') mowed with the grass, just as 'An Old Man's Winter Night' takes pains to secure the old man's mundane actuality – the flicker of thought and its extinction, absent-mindedness, old preoccupations, vacancy. He isn't only Atlas propping up the darkness.

Likewise, Frost affects not to know exactly what the scythe is whispering: 'What was it it whispered? I knew not well myself; / Perhaps it was something about the heat of the sun . . .' The allusion to *Cymbeline*'s famous 'fear no more the heat o' th' sun' represents a consolation Frost takes seriously. Having muted the force of the scythe's traditional symbolism – stark death – Frost offers a death capable of expounding its virtue: 'The fact is the sweetest dream that labor knows.'

'Stopping by Woods on a Snowy Evening' shares this theme – the idea of death as rest after long labour. The final stanza reads:

> The woods are lovely, dark and deep,
> But I have promises to keep,

And miles to go before I sleep,
And miles to go before I sleep.

The last, repeated line is designed to affect us like vernacular repetition, suggesting decision and finality. Yet the line isn't final. The word 'sleep' ripens. It is a euphemism for death. The final stanza, then, doesn't express resignation but instead becomes an account of death's attractiveness – 'The woods are lovely, dark and deep' – so that those 'promises' are obligations which are also obstacles. We find the same idea in 'To Earthward', another (widely misinterpreted) death-wish. Here Keats's vestigial attraction hardens into an unremitting, unrequited passion. Where Keats is 'half in love', Frost is avid:

The hurt is not enough:
I long for weight and strength
To feel the earth as rough
To all my length.

Frost takes an experience we all know – the desperate brute fusion of two bodies – and transfers it to death as a physical need.

'After Apple-Picking', another poem into which Frost secretes his death-wish, alludes to I Corinthians 13:12 and defamiliarizes the familiar 'through a glass darkly': 'I cannot rub the strangeness from my sight / I got from looking through a pane of glass / I skimmed this morning from the drinking trough.' The biblical phrase has been comprehensively rusticated, but its force is still indirectly felt. For all his ostentatious simplicity, Frost uses allusion like any other modernist. Eight years later, in 'For Once, Then, Something', Frost again alludes to a mirror it is possible to see through, the surface of a well: 'I discerned, as I thought, beyond the picture, / Through the picture, a something white, uncertain, / Something more of the depths – ' The allusion – crucial to understanding the poem – comes disguised, the biblical phrase naturalized by prolixity, 'beyond the picture, / Through the picture'.

Frost's best poems seem direct and unpretending and yet they are oblique, indirect, implicit. For all the surface artlessness – the trademark colloquial repetitions of 'What was it it whispered?' or 'You won't believe she said it, but she said it' – Frost was a self-conscious, sophisticated strategist. Even as he denounced Pound and Eliot for 'intimation implication insinuation and innuendo as an object in itself', he was aware that 'all poetry has always said something and implied the rest'. Frost knew that his own poems ripened in the mind and he adumbrates this process in the line: 'My long scythe whispered and left the hay to make.' In a late lecture, Frost said of his poems: 'Oh yea – see. So many of them have literary criticism in them – *in* them.' This is true.

For instance, 'A Hundred Collars' tells how a scholar has to share a hotel room with a drunken stranger. The stranger offers the hundred collars which are now too small for him. Frost is, of course, amused by the enforced, embarrassing intimacy of doctor and drunk. The tale is awash with circumstantial detail. But there is an allegorical undertow. The literary encounters the vulgar, as it must, in Frost's view, if poetry is to benefit from 'the sound of sense' – those cadences, those spontaneous tunes which animate language, and without which it dies.

'The Gum-Gatherer' is another disguised portrait of the artist. The last line's improbability alerts us that this is more appropriate to a poet, say, than an agricultural entrepreneur who could not afford to be quite so dilatory in his marketing:

> I told him this is a pleasant life
> To set your breast to the bark of trees
> That all your days are dim beneath,
> And reaching up with a little knife,
> To loose the resin and take it down
> *And bring it to market when you*
> *please.* [My italics.]

The fast downhill walk, the swinging bag whose neck is wound round his hand – Frost realizes the gum-gatherer so palpably one is likely to miss the literary allusion to *Timon of Athens*, whose poet says, 'Our poesy is as a gum, which oozes / From whence 'tis nourished . . .'

One of the clichés of modernism is that its art is self-aware. The Frost who notoriously compared free verse to playing tennis with the net down, is also the Frost of these deft, hidden allusions, of this modernist self-referentiality. He is, too, a poet whose blank verse is frequently hospitable to lines of completely free verse – despite his disclaimer. In other words, the hayseed hides the highbrow.

Frost is a modernist, masquerading as a naive ruralist. We shouldn't be surprised to discover that 'Maple' is a poem about the meaning of meaning – a cryptic credo of implicitness and its importance for Frost's art. A girl is called Maple, not Mabel, by her mother, just before she dies in childbirth. The intention behind the name casts a shadow. 'No matter,' writes Frost, 'that the meaning was not clear.' It nevertheless affects the girl's life profoundly. Frost here is assuming the most radical theoretical position – the death of the author – so that we will never know exactly what is intended. And yet what is implicit will still project a force field, an aura, a secret agency. One might compare Hemingway's more banal analogue of the iceberg and its visible tip which is the sign only of a more profound, hidden displacement.

Hemingway, like Kipling, like Salinger, like Bellow, is also committed to the vernacular – like Frost. It is easy to mistake Hemingway's stylized patois – where biblical cadence meets bunkhouse drawl – for something naively crude. It is equally easy to write off Frost. In fact, he is part of the modernist strand that descends from Browning – the others are Eliot, Pound and Kipling. Frost had four favourite poems, one of which was Browning's 'Saul'. Frost's temperament was attracted to the portrayal of Saul's depressive gloom. But the deeper attraction is aesthetic. Browning was the first to demonstrate that ostensible linguistic laxity could foster life where before there was only literature. He founded a new poetic economy which favoured speech and was the foe of the oratory that verse is naturally prone to: 'He fell at Gettysburg or Fredericksburg, / I ought to know – it makes a difference which: / Fredericksburg wasn't Gettysburg, of course.' The facts are hazy but the voice is accurate.

Vernacular is a crucial element in modernism. Think of Eliot's Cockney in *The Waste Land*: 'It's them pills I took, to bring it off, she said.' It could be Frost, except that the accent's wrong. Compare Frost's transcription of a telephone conversation: 'I thought I would. – I know, but. Lett – I know – / I could, but what's the sense?' Were Frost the antique pastoralist he sometimes pretends to be, the phone would be quietly banished. Yet this could be David Mamet. It tries to notate the speaking voice exactly. Why? Partly because vernacular is a special effect, its surface sprawl a deliberate calculation, chosen to reinforce modernism's inclination to realism, its anti-poetic bias.

Many of Frost's longer poems feint to offer authentic, verifiable anecdotes out of America. Hemingway uses the same sleight: 'I would like to live long enough to write three more novels and twenty-five more stories. I know some pretty good ones.' That last sentence invokes the tradition of the yarn with its aspirations to truth. Likewise with Frost: the tale about the man who burned down his failing farm and spent the insurance money on a telescope is first mentioned in 'New Hampshire', a poem of ironic chauvinism. It is fully treated in 'The Star-Splitter'. Frost aspires to anonymous oral history, but his narratives differ from Whitman's glancing, encyclopedic album of eloquent snapshots and captioned optimism. Frost's art is more like that of Eadweard Muybridge – the meticulous sequence recording how people really behave, which is also faithful to the difficulty of explaining precisely why. At his best, Frost's black and white, ostentatiously old-fangled photography is full of fugitive colour, of shades, of chromatic subtlety.

'Home Burial' and 'Out, Out –' record two tragedies that turn on the loss of a child's life. In 'Out, Out –' Frost damages a great poem – not by the title's trite allusion to *Macbeth*, but by a weakness for melodramatic chiaroscuro. The boy who has lost his hand to the buzz saw dies of shock under the ether.

Frost can't resist the temptation to accelerate the process of recovery in order to maximize the contrast with the raw tragedy:

> . . . they listened at his heart.
> Little – less – nothing! – and that ended it.
> No more to build on there. And they, since they
> Were not the one dead, turned to their affairs.

Frost intends to show us that life must go on. As it must. But what he succeeds in showing us is that people are implausibly callous. You wonder what their 'affairs' could be. The division of the boy's soup since he isn't at supper?

Whereas 'Out, Out – ' succumbs, with grim Hardyesque relish, in a single line to the coarse ironic contrast between the tragic event and the quotidian imperative, 'Home Burial' is a proper, less laconic examination of grief's after-shock. A couple have lost their first child and the husband has buried the little boy in sight of the house. The wife refuses to come out of the scald of grief: 'Friends make pretense of following to the grave, / But before one is in it, their minds are turned / And making the best of their way back to life.' She is ill with grief. There is something possessive and pathological about her determination to resist any dilution of her feelings. Her husband, on the other hand, believes that grief should have its term, but Frost inflects his rationality with colours of cruelty, of too eager readiness to put the experience behind him – aspects which coexist with sincere tenderness and concern, with self-criticism, indeed. The wife's terrible suffering is inflected with pride, with addiction, with irrationality, with compulsiveness. She protects her pain by refusing to discuss it with her husband. The poem begins by invoking the ghost story topos. The wife is haunted by her lost child as well as mourning him. Her suffering is tinged with terror. She needs help. 'Home Burial' is not a long poem. In only 116 lines Frost gives us the true face of grief, its expression of sincerity and its elements of impurity. He rejects the easy pathos of the standard elegy, just as he rejects, in his image of America, the impulse to airbrush.

Frost prefers the unpalatable, even when it concerns his

country. It isn't patriotism but imaginative precision which produces 'The Vanishing Red', Frost's bleak indictment of America's extermination of its indigenous people. Frost isn't complicit with the affectless racism of his narrative – where the last Red Indian in Acton is casually murdered because he irritates a white man, a miller, who might be killing an insect. Frost is aware, of course, that the 'offence' and the penalty exacted are horrifically disproportionate. Indeed, that there is no offence, merely a murderous whim. The injustice is central to the poem. But he is interested in showing us a mind as alien to us as the Red Indian is to the settler. We can barely comprehend the miller's motivation. Frost dramatizes this sense of distance and immediacy by introducing a reader surrogate: [the miller]

> came up stairs alone – and gave that laugh,
> And said something to a man with a meal-sack
> That the man with the meal-sack didn't catch – then.
> Oh, yes, he showed John the wheel pit all right.

It is one of Frost's most consummate endings – linguistically leaden, flat with pedestrian repetition, fraught with the terrible horror of implication. What isn't immediately heard is the last line's reported speech: I showed John the wheel pit all right. The Red Indian, John, has been drowned, but the euphemism stops us from understanding at once the true horror. The miller's 'laugh' runs through the poem, showing us that the murderer sees himself as a practical joker, for whom genocide is an act of tidiness: 'I hold with getting a thing done with.' And the 'laugh' isn't a laugh at all. Frost's distaste is clear: 'If you like to call such a sound a laugh.' This comment confirms the last line of the unpublished 'Genealogical': 'And I think he explains my lifelong liking for Indians.' 'He' is Frost's Indian-killer ancestor – 'my bad ancestor' as Frost unequivocally designates him in a letter of 1908. Disapproval is one thing. Compelling our imagination so we experience the unthinkable – 'You can't get back and see it as he saw it' – so that the horror only sinks in later, this is the triumph of Frost's implicitness.

A great poet, then, unflinching and oblique, user-friendly and super-subtle; a poet who has influenced Paul Muldoon profoundly and to whom one of the authors under review, Seamus Heaney, owes a great deal. *Homage to Robert Frost* is really a bit of publisher's book-making – three Nobel laureates with a single subject – a coincidence that is saleable. But Brodsky's essay has already appeared, first in the *New Yorker*, then in *On Grief and Reason*. It is, in any case, a prolix performance whose sound enough central perception is swollen with dubious detailed readings, tainted with braggadocio. Derek Walcott's piece is a reprinted review of the Library of America's *Collected Poems, Prose and Plays*: it borrows wholesale from that volume's admittedly useful chronology, from Auden's second fine essay on Frost, and carries over from Brodsky an idea of caesura which is simply wrong. If you like overblown evocations of language itself, you will like this intellectually underpowered essay. The best contribution comes from Seamus Heaney, who attempts to redress the darkly pessimistic Frost set in place by Lionel Trilling in 1959 at the poet's eighty-fifth birthday shindig. It is an interesting endeavour but one that gets too many poems wrong. Heaney's gift for the striking phrase cannot counterbalance one's sense that the poetry is being distorted by the argument. Now and then, too, Heaney indulges his orotundity: 'not a flourish of craft, but a feat of technique' is a fine-sounding but meaningless distinction found in the cave of the mouth without any assistance from the brain.

# Joseph Brodsky

Joseph Brodsky died in January of this year. The general esteem in which he was held was immediately apparent. Seamus Heaney and Paul Muldoon published affecting poems in *The Times Literary Supplement* – a journal whose deputy editor, Alan Jenkins, has consistently promoted Brodsky's work. David Remnick wrote a lengthy eulogy in the *New Yorker* and the most recent number of that magazine carries four elegies by Anthony Hecht, Mark Strand, Carol Rumens and Glyn Maxwell. In person, Brodsky displayed a brusque charm and a winning impatience – a vaunting angularity to which these obituarists paid proper tribute. He was earthy, fond of dirty jokes, warm and often heated. He could also be strangely nervous – the obverse of his more characteristic dogmatic panache which rode on the tidal swell of his reputation. This nervousness may have been connected with the well-nigh inaudible but consistent undercurrent of scepticism that accompanied the noisier acclaim.

Brodsky had a shrewd eye for possible patrons, as any exile must. He arrived in the West with Anna Akhmatova's imprimatur, delivered to Isaiah Berlin and Stephen Spender when she received her honorary degree in Oxford. Asked who were the interesting younger poets, she named Brodsky – as presumably just that, *interesting*. A modest accolade. In a *TLS* review of Purcell's *Dido and Aeneas*, Brodsky dressed up the bare historical anecdote as it has been handed down. He recalled that

*So Forth: Poems* and *On Grief and Reason: Essays* by Joseph Brodsky, Hamish Hamilton.

Spender had sent him the Flagstad/Schwarzkopf recording in the care of Akhmatova. There may be a parallel here between Akhmatova and Auden. Brodsky's tributes to Auden are consistently fulsome – 'the greatest mind of the twentieth century' – and tend to colour Auden's rather guarded endorsement of Brodsky's talent in his foreword to Brodsky's first book of translations. Because he has no Russian and is therefore forced to rely on translations, Auden's considered fall-back position is this: 'I can do little more than guess.' Nevertheless, he is prepared to guess generously: 'after reading Professor Kline's translations, I have no hesitation in declaring that, in Russian, Joseph Brodsky must be a poet of the first order'. *In Russian.* Generous, true, but a guess. Brodsky's declarations of unstinted gratitude to Auden and Akhmatova have blotted out the spectre of reservation haunting both testimonials.

And there have been detractors. As early as 1980, Robert Hass, the American critic, reluctantly lamented the botched English of the poems in *A Part of Speech*. His review appeared under the title 'Lost in Translation'. It assumed that the Russian originals were touched with genius – a verdict which is without weight because Hass does not read Russian. Neither do I. Surely, in that case, the only correct position is that outlined by Wittgenstein? – 'whereof we cannot speak, thereof we must be silent'. In September 1988, I delivered a lecture in which, less reluctantly than Hass, I marvelled at the incompetence of Brodsky's poems in English. In December of the same year, Christopher Reid wrote a judicious and devastating indictment of *To Urania: Selected Poems 1965–1985* in the *London Review of Books*. On the occasion of Brodsky's Nobel Prize, Seamus Heaney, in an otherwise enthusiastic piece for the *New York Times*, entered the caveat that, in English, Brodsky's poetry could seem 'awkward and skewed'. More recently, Gerry Smith, the Professor of Russian at Oxford, has expressed reservations in the *Harriman Review* for July 1995.

Brodsky's death was the result of a chronic heart condition which was exacerbated by a suicidal smoking habit. In Martin Amis's *Money*, the zero hero, John Self, lights up another cigarette with the remark that 'unless I specifically inform you otherwise, I'm always smoking another cigarette'. It was much the same with Brodsky. He underwent serious heart surgery on several occasions – surgery evoked in this cryptic, perplexing, barely decipherable line of Brodsky's English: 'thrice let knives rake my nitty-gritty'. No wonder Christopher Reid confined himself to the comment that this was a 'sentence of baffling obscurity'. The opaque periphrasis is partly forced on Brodsky by the need for a rhyme for 'city' two lines ahead. However, this last, posthumous volume, *So Forth*, and the lumbering, hobbled prose of *On Grief and Reason* demonstrate that, far from being the equal or rival of Nabokov, Brodsky was unable to achieve more than a basic competence in his adopted language.

Brodsky lauds poetry's instinct for economy in an automatic way but his own poetry is the opposite of lapidary. On the one hand, it is Brodsky's proud bardic boast that poetry makes one intolerant of 'any sort of verbosity', that 'being the supreme form of human locution, poetry is the most concise, the most condensed way of conveying human experience'. (Not that it is exactly laconic to follow 'concise' with 'condensed'.) Now consider the opening of the title poem, which Professor Smith judges a successful act of self-translation:

> . . . On the whole, the world changes so fast, as if
> indeed at a certain point it began to mainline
> some muck obtained from a swarthy alien.

The theme of the poem is *tempus fugit*, and here Brodsky is comparing the rapid passage of time with a drug-*rush*. Once crack the metaphor, though, and you are left with Brodsky's garrulous lack of clarity and his prodigal padding. There is the fatally misjudged elaboration and introduction of the drug-pusher, the 'swarthy alien'. But worse are the poetic redundancies, those words which are empty noise: 'as if indeed at a certain point' and 'on the whole'.

On the whole. To say the least. These two phrases, incessantly deployed in Brodsky's poetry and prose, represent nothing except dead air. They are meant to function as colloquialisms that demonstrate ease and familiarity – but in fact demonstrate exactly the opposite by their overuse. They demonstrate not linguistic mastery but foreign ineptitude, to say the least. In *So Forth*, Brodsky uses the phrase 'on the whole' four times in four different poems. In its way, this is just as damning as Brodsky's straightforward mistakes – as when he uses 'solidity' for *solidarity* ('evil is a sucker for solidity'), or when he writes 'puff your nose' for *powder your nose*, or when a woman's face becomes a 'maiden's visage', or a girl becomes 'a belle'. Equally archaic is Brodsky's fearless inversion: 'even metal knows not its fate'. Finally, in the list of irritating mannerisms perhaps one should mention 'not to mention': 'Not to mention a gallery, not to mention a nail'; 'not to mention warmth'; 'not to mention one's features', all from different poems.

It isn't as if Brodsky is unaware of the dangers: 'every experienced poet knows how risky it is to use the same word several times within a short space,' he writes. But then he writes:

> Painted by a gentle dawn
> *one* is proud that like *one's* own
> planet now *one* will not wince
> at what *one* is facing, since
> putting up with nothing . . .

It isn't simply the repetition. It is also those two present participles in ugly proximity ('putting' and 'nothing') and, worst of all, the way in which the rhyme scheme is out of synch with the line breaks. But Brodsky is the boss of the bad line break: 'there. Or standing there, as furniture in the corner'. Everything here is ugly – the repetition of *there*, the ugly assonance of 'furniture' and 'corner'. Then there are the strained rhymes for which Brodsky is always prepared to sacrifice the integrity of the line: 'Manhattan' and 'Man, I hate him'.

For this, Brodsky is to blame. By 1980, he was recklessly reworking the translations of Anglophone poets like Anthony Hecht and Richard Wilbur – to bring them 'closer to the original, though perhaps at the expense of smoothness'. And he was already confident or rash enough to translate himself unassisted and to write in English directly. *So Forth* has only eight assisted translations, none of which is quoted in this review – where Brodsky is on his own.

As a thinker, Brodsky is by turns fatuous and banal. We should choose our leaders according to what they read. Tarzan movies from America probably 'did more for de-Stalinization than all Krushchev's speeches at the Twentieth Party Congress and after'. (Many of Brodsky's *obiter dicta* are designed to flatter his host country with the myth of America's cultural invincibility.) Now address this mature banality: 'For each of us is issued but one life, and we know full well how it all ends.' Pretty idiomatic, to say the least, eh?

As a critic, Brodsky is barely competent and he favours detailed exegeses of particular poems. Here he conducts sustained and methodical acts of vandalism on Hardy's 'The Darkling Thrush' and 'The Convergence of the Twain' as well as Frost's 'Home Burial'. Brodsky is keen on scansion but not consistently accurate. Hardy's two lines 'In a full-hearted evensong / Of joy illimited' are straightforward iambs with an inverted (and allowable) first metrical foot. There is no sign of the 'dactylic undercutting' detected by Brodsky in 'evensong' and 'illimited'. The arbitrariness here is mirrored elsewhere by Brodsky's sightings of caesurae wherever he feels like it.

Brodsky's limitations can be reduced to two. As a thinker, he is fuddled. 'What's unique about [Hardy] is, of course, his extraordinary appetite for the infinite . . . and the infinite is poetry's standard turf.' In other words, what is *unique*, then, is what Hardy has in common with everyone else. Sometimes the nonsense isn't logically contradictory but just indefensibly dotty: 'a conflict within an enclosure – a house, say – normally deteriorates into tragedy, because the rectangularity of the place itself puts a higher premium on reason, offering emotion only a straitjacket'. Exactly.

The second, more serious limitation for a poet, is Brodsky's ear. T. S. Eliot described poetry as 'the intolerable wrestle / With words and meanings'. Matched so unequally with the English language, Brodsky spends most of his time flat on the canvas. For example, he seriously believes that 'dusk' and 'dark' differ 'in just one consonant' – that 'the vowel sound remains essentially the same'. This is consistent with his cavalier 'close' readings: 'you almost see here not so much a thrush as a robin' (or a budgerigar); 'if you want, you may replace "lament" with "repent": the effect will be practically the same'.

If things are as bad as this – and they are – how did Brodsky acquire his inexplicable charisma? Apart from some shrewd career management, not in itself culpable, the central reason is Brodsky's stylistic signature, the characteristic mixture of off-hand 'colloquialisms' and bardic overstatement masquerading as authentic eloquence – slang, then, and what Sir Walter Scott called 'the big Bow-wow'. On his birthday, 24 May 1980, Brodsky ended a poem of grim retrospect, a catalogue of his trials and torments, with these affirmative lines:

> What should I say about life? That it's long and abhors
> transparence.
> Broken eggs make me grieve; the omelette, though, makes
> me vomit.
> Yet until brown clay has been crammed down my larynx,
> Only gratitude will be gushing from it.

Characteristically inept and uplifting. Inept in its allusion to the cliché that you can't make an omelette without breaking eggs. Uplifting in its gratitude for existence, however painful. The grammatical mistake (it should be 'only gratitude will gush from it') is of no importance to that large class of sentimental readers for whom poetry is essentially a matter of bogus operatic attitudinizing – rather than subtle verbal music and hard thought. For them, the self-heroizing is sufficient. And it is no use pointing out that burial after death seldom involves the undertaker in the task of cramming clay (of whatever complexion) down the throat of the deceased. The melodrama is entirely of Brodsky's making.

Granted his ill-health, it isn't perhaps surprising that some of these poems should glance nervously at his posthumous reputation: 'But soon, I'm told, I'll lose my epaulets altogether / And dwindle into a little star.' Odd, you might think, for a Nobel laureate to indulge these neurotic worries. For me, they summon up irresistibly Dickens's fraudulent financier, Mr Merdle – whose tic is to take his own wrists into custody, an act that discloses his deepest fears. Not that Brodsky was a boldly cynical charlatan. He was a nervous, world-class mediocrity – bluffing but aware of his uncertain feel for the English language on which his international reputation was so precariously founded.

# Bruce Chatwin

Bruce Chatwin was a curio. And if you want the authentic flavour of the man, his aura, you could not do better than read Susannah Clapp's excellent, absorbing, affectionate, unillusioned, vivid and affecting memoir. Chatwin was a torrential talker, a bisexual of great beauty, an art dealer with a famous eye for the fake as well as the fabulous bargain, a fastidious cook and a socialite seduced by the austere glamour of the nomadic life in which movement demanded renunciation of personal property. Chatwin was a trafficker in fabulous facts. He always knew something you didn't know.

Not very difficult. In 1812, Napoleon's starved *Grande Armée* entered burning Moscow and was defeated by its over-extended supply lines. The same year, Bryan Donkin patented an invention which might have saved Napoleon's bacon. Literally. It was a tinning process that preserved meat and vegetables. When James Clarke Ross, who discovered the site of the magnetic north pole, was exploring the Arctic, he used the perfectly preserved stores of Lieutenant Parry's previous expedition – and, like other explorers, praised Donkin in his narrative. Which is why, over fifty years later, Joseph Conrad named the demoralizing, whining coward in 'The Nigger of the *Narcissus*' after the inventor. Conrad's Donkin is primarily concerned to preserve his worthless carcass. This isn't an authentic Chatwin riff, but it might have been. It is speculative, spans a huge geographical area, splices together widely different chronological periods –

*With Chatwin* by Susannah Clapp, Jonathan Cape.

and, typically, it concludes with a classic anecdotal twist in which the hero of the North-West Passage becomes the abject and ironized Donkin of Conrad's novella. Chatwin overvalued the sudden *aperçu*, the calculated surprise, and overworked it as a device in his writing.

In conversation, this could be wonderful, as when Susannah Clapp reports his scathing verdict on the pharaohs and their funerals – 'done by Heal's'. Yet if Chatwin could be a hypnotic conversationalist, he could often send you to sleep. Here, Hugo Vickers, another guest of the rich Teddy Millington-Drake, records in his diary as he listens to the violently vomiting Chatwin in the next room, 'Teddy was far from sorry to see him go. He had talked too much and repeated himself a lot.' It could be tiresome to listen to Bruce rehearsing one of his books.

More importantly, the social self flourished at the expense of the writing self, which was increasingly made over to the raconteur. Chatwin relentlessly restaged his material for maximum impact. Susannah Clapp correctly identifies *In Patagonia* as a book 'which was all anecdote and illustration', without quite realizing what a limitation she is pointing up. Chatwin, she says, treated 'each encounter as if it were a short story: shaping it, giving it a turn or twist'. Each encounter, though, is not a short story, but a particular kind of short story – the glibbest, the anecdote. And the anecdotes become formulaic because they were designed to galvanize a table of intoxicated diners into a tableau of astounded theatre-goers, marvelling at the punchline which brought the curtain and the house down. The theatricality of the narrative means quickly palls. Thus Section 96 of *In Patagonia*: 'There is a man in Punta Arenas, dreams pine forests, hums Lieder, wakes each morning and sees the black strait. He drives to a factory that smells of the sea. All about him are scarlet crabs, crawling, then steaming. He hears the shells crack and the claws breaking, sees the sweet white flesh packed firm into metal cans. He is an efficient man, with some previous experience of the production line. Does he remember that other smell? And that other sound, of low voices singing?'

Dramatic pause.

New paragraph.

'Walter Rauff is the inventor of the Gas Truck.'

A cheap theatrical effect can be dramatic without ceasing to be a cheap effect. The power depends on the truth of the anecdote. If it were an invention we would be left with only the undistinguished, automatic evocation of Germany, the journalistic shorthand of Lieder and the *Hochschwartzwald*, the pat irony of the two production lines and the tawdry, sentimentalized epitome of the Holocaust, those 'low voices singing' which are designed to edit out of the picture all the panic, all the pressure that welded bodies in a heap in the centre of any gas chamber – as far away from the incoming gas as possible.

Finally, it is Chatwin's infatuation with the anecdote which flaws his novel, *On the Black Hill*. Susannah Clapp quotes Chatwin's dismissal of Jules Verne: 'the real was always more fantastic than the fantastical'. In his Welsh novel, he holds to this article of faith desperately and destructively. Nearly every death finds him applying the *maquillage*, overdressing the set, bringing magic to the realism and planting the narrative with punchlines. When the twins' mother dies, 'in the morning they hung black crêpe over the beehives to tell the bees that she had gone'. Ready-made for the motion picture it was quickly made into.

When Sam, their grandfather, dies after a long spell of being gaga, the ignominy of death is replaced and redeemed by a demise which is unexpected, touching and downright cute. The old boy gets up and into his wedding-best. He plays his fiddle out of doors for one last time before passing on peacefully. 'There was a high windy sky, and the mares'-tails seemed to dance with the larches.' Did they now. Those larches tend to tap a vein of varicose poetry in Chatwin: 'the larches trailed their black hair over the moon'; 'the golden hair of the larches shone out against a milky blue sky'.

These gooey deaths can be matched by equally anecdotal ghoulish equivalents. When the twins are about to be born, Hannah, the mother-in-law, sits about knitting socks and prophesying doom. But, in the event, babies and mother are fine, and it is the mother-in-law herself who succumbs to anecdotal necessity. 'That night, Hannah rounded off the toe of her second sock and, three days later, died.' What a surprise.

Then there is the death of the Bombardier, the racist survivor of Rorke's Drift, who dies, forgotten in the midst of the celebrations and still clutching his presentation silver cigarette case as he sits in his wheelchair: 'He had ceased to breathe. The man was amazed by the strength of his grip as he prised his fingers from the silver cigarette-case.' Curtain. Or should that be, Close Up and Cut?

Susannah Clapp is not uncritical about Chatwin's work. Some of his expositions are 'graphic, exciting to hear, and not fully graspable'. Of *The Viceroy of Ouidah*, she remarks ruefully that 'it isn't always easy to know what is going on'. *The Songlines*, 'despite its boldness and excitements', 'creaks in trying to make its large statements'. And she finds the character of Arkady 'too transparently a useful device to be persuasive'.

Chatwin was an extraordinarily uneven writer. At his best, he could write like a choir-boy, not like an angel. The poet of *In Patagonia* is swiftly animated and undercut. He has a collection of pet toads and his own bee hives. His desk is 'littered with broken almond shells and his favourite books' – books which are meticulously recorded, just as the shells are specified. The whole is laconic and accurate. The poet is restricted to three brief speeches in this rapid, seemingly free-hand sketch. One of which, the first, comprehensively and irrecoverably undermines him in our eyes: 'Patagonia! She is a hard mistress. She casts her spell. An enchantress. She folds you in her arms and never lets go.' Here the febrile lies entirely in the character. Elsewhere, it can stem from Chatwin himself.

*On the Black Hill* is at its best with children. There is a flawlessly observed school nativity play in which the boy playing the angel Gabriel announces himself 'in a suffocated voice'. Chatwin knows about embarrassment in children. Little Meg manages to say the words 'Emmanuel's veins' but is vanquished by the effort: 'the crushed flowers fell at her feet, and she started sucking her thumb'. *In Patagonia* provides a beetle '*easing*' itself over some stones. Chatwin observes Welsh children playing hide-and-seek among the pews after a chapel service. At Las Pampas, 'the girls wore cretonne dresses and the boys held their partners far away from them' – a sentence utterly simple and saturated in foreignness. The central satisfaction of Chatwin's prose is its accuracy. 'The seats in the compartment reminded them of the texture of bullrushes.'

The central dissatisfaction is its inaccuracy. Similes tend to be disastrous. 'The frozen leaves of the foxgloves drooped like dead donkeys' ears.' Or, 'he was a thin wiry boy with unusually strong hands and ears that stuck out under his cap, like dock-leaves'. 'His ribs stuck out like a concertina.' There is an auctioneer who seems to have strayed from a Bizet opera: 'the auctioneer caught the bids in his mouth, like flowers flying'. This simile is nearly as opaquely subjective as Chatwin's description of a hat lying 'like a slug on the kitchen table'.

When Chatwin isn't being inaccurate, he can be inert or repetitive – and sometimes both at once. An anthology of memorably unmemorable moments: 'his eyes were glued to the young man's every movement'; 'the days were drawing in'; 'all the birds were silent in the stillness that precedes a storm'. The latter sentence crops up again in *The Viceroy of Ouidah*, its compelling essence subtly unchanged: 'one evening she and Cesario were crossing the Sogbadji Quarter in the stillness that precedes a storm'. Susannah Clapp remarks at one point that Chatwin was writing 'like a train' – and it may be that speed was possible because the route was so familiar. Mary Latimer recalls her Eurasian love – 'a streak of a man with syrupy eyes' – which in turn recalls Ali of *In Patagonia*, who has 'enormous syrupy eyes', reminiscent of the 'syrupy eyes' of the Bey in *What Am I Doing Here*, Chatwin's collection of journalistic and occasional writings. A similar coincidence takes place in the sheep-shearing scenes described in his first and third books. *In Patagonia*: 'When the boys tied the animals' legs, all the fight went out of them and they lay, dead weight, till the torture was over. Then, naked and gashed with red cuts about their udders, they bounded wildly into the air as if jumping over an imaginary fence, or jumping to be free.' *On the Black Hill*: 'The sheep lay quietly under the shears, and endured the torture. Then, creamy white again – though with some bloody cuts about their udders – they bounded out into the paddock, jumping in the air, as if over an imaginary fence, or simply to be free.' Almost identical twins, these paragraphs, and both fathered by the cliché, 'with one bound, he was free'.

Susannah Clapp describes Chatwin as 'one of the few authors who seemed actually to enjoy the process of being edited'. This is partly because he clearly owed a great deal to his interventionist editors – and partly because Chatwin was himself a writer whose characteristic strengths were cognate with the editorial process. Writing about Ernst Jünger, he singles out a passage describing an execution by firing squad that Jünger witnessed. In Chatwin's paraphrase, it is almost in note form: 'the trunk of the ash tree riddled with the bullet holes of earlier executions'; 'inside the holes a few black meat flies are sleeping'; 'expensive grey trousers and a grey silk shirt'; 'the medical officer pins a red card over his heart'; 'five small black holes appear on the card like drops of rain'; 'the guard who wipes the handcuffs with a chiffon handkerchief'. It is brilliant. But it isn't Chatwin. And a great deal of the material in *In Patagonia* isn't strictly Chatwin either. According to Susannah Clapp, he said, 'there are books you read for pleasure and books you read for plunder'. Plunder is more romantically self-aggrandizing, more glamorizing than the process really was. It was more like shopping. He bought his ingredients with care and then cooked the books – almost always by reducing and concentrating. In his essay 'The Volga', he borrows freely from Ibn Fadlan's gripping but leisurely account of a Viking ceremonial burial. Chatwin's version contains tiny inaccuracies but crops and clips the original with panache and verve – so that what remains is all headlines and headlights, dazzling but also subtly depleted.

In the end, I think his earliest critics, the teachers at Marlborough, were prescient and correct: 'only the bizarre or trifling really appeals to him,' wrote one master. Another wrote: 'his gift may be slender, perhaps, but it is genuine'.

# The Bible

Chapter and verse – a phrase, derived from the layout of material in the Bible, which has come to mean the minutiae of evidence, the citation of detailed, clinching proof, exactitude, certainty, a sense of truth.

And yet, it was not always so. In the seventeenth century, John Locke was much exercised by chapter and verse – seeing in this arrangement not exactitude, but rather the opportunity for paltering, for equivocation. Ease of reading and of reference were as nothing for Locke, beside the subtle corruption of the Bible's coherence. Sects in search of justification would seize on the discrete fragments and appropriate whatever struck them as appropriate. It was a recipe for theological opportunism. 'This is the Benefit,' wrote Locke with passionate irony, 'of loose Sentences and Scriptures crumbled into Verses, which quickly turn into independent Aphorisms.'

The learned editors of this annotated edition, Robert Carroll and Stephen Prickett, both professors at the University of Glasgow, do not cite this objection of Locke. Nor do they tell us anything precise about the division of the Bible in chapters and verses beyond the statement that the divisions were made in 'late medieval times'. The New English Bible, on the other hand, says 'the conventional verse divisions in the Old Testament are based on those in Hebrew manuscripts'. Of course, these two statements need not necessarily be incompatible. It would be nice to know.

*The Bible: Authorized King James Version*, edited with an introduction and notes by Robert Carroll and Stephen Prickett, Oxford World Classics.

Mind you, the editors are more than covered by their disclaimer at the outset of the endnotes: 'an *adequate* set of endnotes to the Bible would be as long as the book itself, if not longer'. (My italics.) There are approximately one hundred pages of endnotes as against 1,606 pages of Old Testament, Apocrypha and New Testament. What is offered in the way of annotation is interesting, helpful, imaginative, but necessarily glancing. And obviously inadequate – by the editors' own admission. Their introduction contrives to promise a great deal more and strikes one as an impressive series of bold intellectual gestures. They are interested in the Bible as literature.

By 'literature', however, they mean literary theory, in which the Bible is an exemplary indeterminate resource, a text three-quarters of which is borrowed from another religion, Judaism. Add to this theological imperialism the hypothesis that both Christianity and Judaism are themselves derivatives of earlier religions like Zoroastrianism – and the biblical critic comes into his own as arbiter, decoder, architect, archaeologist and (here) playful postmodernist in a state of ecstatic contradiction. The editors are more excited by dynamic possibility than by closure. For them, the Bible is a text like any other text. It is the 'representative' text – intertextual rather than conceived *ex nihilo* – and therefore 'Christianity in effect constitutes a new critical theory'. Christianity isn't so much a religion as another way of reading the Bible. Even an atheist like myself can be irritated by the way a serious belief system is annexed by the untroubled and indolent indecisiveness of postmodernist literary theory. What is a sacred text for some is an intellectual playground for others. Who cares? The editors are happy with either. Or both.

Intellectually, this is consistent with the introduction's take on historical truth – no such thing exists; there are merely competing interpretations. This is a position of profound intellectual complacency. It has not even the cynical pragmatism of the career politician, finessing the truth for tactical advantage, to excuse it. Were it adopted by historians, particularly contemporary historians, it would vitiate an entire intellectual discipline. For discipline substitute torpor and laxity, for truth substitute plausibility and argumentative elegance. No one need decide. No one need weigh the evidence. No one need cite chapter and verse.

The editors are concerned with the Bible principally as 'a classic book of English literature'. The Good Book is, famously, traditionally, a compendium of moral positives, categorical imperatives, calls to duty and angry supernatural rumblings. But, as they hint, it is also possible to read the Good Book as just a good book. Would they had actually done so – but, for them, narrative no longer means narrative. It means something like a reading or an interpretation of the text, designed to make it relevant to a particular set of beliefs. The reader imposes a story on the text, a sequence that makes the text meaningful beyond the purely literal. In the early 1960s, Jan Kott was doing the same thing in *Shakespeare Our Contemporary* – making the text speak to a different historical moment. The editors twice cite Oliver Cromwell's use of Exodus and the occupation of Canaan by the Israelites to justify the Protestant plantation of Ulster. Catholic nationalists, meanwhile, found their sense of oppression in the same book of the Bible – the enslavement of the chosen people in Egypt.

An opportunity has been missed. It is possible to read the Bible as a set of short stories, some of the greatest ever written, where 'narrative' means simply narrative. One of my favourite stories is that of Ehud, the 'judge' who assassinates Eglon the King of Moab. A 'judge' is a chieftain, according to Professor Carroll. The New Scofield Reference Bible is a tad more informative: Judges 'records the activities of twelve men and one woman, designated as judges and raised up by God to deliver Israel in times of declension and disunion after Joshua's death'. Ehud is far from the standard faceless hero of myth. The biblical narrator doesn't so much describe the man as open a file on him: 'the son of Gera, a Benjamite, a man lefthanded'. He is sent to Eglon with the Israelite tribute, but he has also a dagger with him. The dagger has 'two edges, of a cubit length' – 'and he did gird it under his raiment upon his right thigh'. Writers call this technique solidity of specification. Its purpose is, in the immortal words of Conrad, 'to make you hear, to make you feel – it is, before all, to make you *see*. That – and no more, and it is everything.'

King Eglon, Israel's and Ehud's enemy, is 'a very fat man', we learn at Judges 3:17. Five verses more interpose before we discover why this information is important. The tribute is delivered. The bearers return home, but Ehud turns back at the quarries 'that were by Gilgal'. In Eglon's summer parlour, Ehud explains that he has a 'secret errand'. King Eglon sends out his attendants. Ehud says he has a message to the King from God. It is the dagger on his right thigh, its cubit-length now revealed. He thrusts it into the king's belly: 'and the haft also went in after the blade; and the fat closed upon the blade, so that he could not draw the dagger out of his belly; and the dirt came out'. One is tempted to say that this could be Ruth Rendell or Patricia Highsmith – as a way of making the gruesome point – but the narrative certainty here, the unflinching ironic precision is worthy of Evelyn Waugh or Nabokov or Flaubert.

The conclusion has to be quoted in all its tense calmness and black humour:

> Then Ehud went forth through the porch, and shut the doors of the parlour upon him, and locked them. When he was gone out, his servants came; and when they saw that, behold, the doors of the parlour were locked, they said, Surely he covereth his feet in his summer chamber. And they tarried till they were ashamed; and, behold, he opened not the doors of the parlour; therefore they took a key, and opened them: and, behold, their lord was fallen down dead on the earth. And Ehud escaped while they tarried, and passed beyond the quarries, and escaped unto Seirath.

The modern, accurate translation of the much reviled New English Bible explains a narrative opacity, arising out of a delicate euphemism, the phrase 'Surely he covereth his feet'. In the New English Bible, this reads, 'they said, "He must be relieving himself in the closet of his summer palace"'. I prefer the euphemism, murky though it initially is, because it reflects the general reluctance to do more than hover indecisively. Covering one's feet is a phrase full of delicacy and embarrassment. The New English Bible also tells us that the translator responsible for this episode in the King James Version was a writer as well as a translator. The Authorized Version invents a detail absent from the original Hebrew. It is an example of writerly opportunism, the irresistible embellishment which is art's tribute to life: 'and the dirt came out'.

2 Kings 4: 8–37 tells the great story of Elisha and the Shunammite, a story whose art is again pointed up by the more accurate version in the New English Bible. I paraphrase. Unforgivably. Passing through Shunem, Elisha is 'constrained' to eat bread by 'a great woman', who, seeing Elisha is a holy man, persuades her husband to build a little lean-to chamber for the prophet to rest in on his travels. He wonders what he can do in return. The Shunammite replies: 'I dwell among my own people', meaning that she is content as she is. Elisha's servant, Gehazi, tells the prophet she is childless and her husband is old. Elisha tells her she will conceive. She says: 'Do not lie unto thine handmaiden.' It is not a lie.

'And when the child was grown, it fell on a day, that he went out to his father to the reapers. And he said unto his father, My head, my head. And he said to a lad, Carry him to his mother. And when he had taken him, and brought him to his mother, he sat on her knees till noon, and then died.' This is a narrative which proceeds on its way unhurried. It can list the bed, the table, the stool and the candlestick in Elisha's little lodging. It has a vernacular carelessness with pronouns. It is hospitable to tautology: 'And when he had taken him, and brought him . . .' And yet it records, with equal lack of hurry, the quiet swiftness of death, the unremarkable and therefore terrifying repetition, 'My head, my head.' That – and no more, and it is everything. Especially if you are a parent and familiar with those sudden, absolute, everyday eclipses of health in small children. The horror is more telling for the narrative restraint.

We use magic realism as a term to describe a particular potent mixture of the far-fetched, the poetically allowable, in coincidence with the recognizable world. But the term should also apply to those details which sew irrefutability into the weave of the narrative. The story of Elisha and the Shunammite is a brilliant anthology of such charismatic touches. The wife tells her husband that she must go to Elisha. He is baffled: 'it is neither new moon, nor sabbath', occasions when a wish and a prayer would be appropriate. Like us, he expects her to mourn. Her attitude is clear: 'It shall be well.'

Seeing her from a distance, Elisha sends his servant to ask if everything is well with her husband and child. Her reply is not a lie. It is an act of faith. She says everything is well, until she is able to catch Elisha by the feet and remind him of her earlier response to his promise of conception: 'Did I not say, Do not deceive me?' It is not a reproach, it is a recollection of the bargain made between them.

Elisha sends Gehazi ahead. He is to salute no one nor return any greeting. He must lay the staff of Elisha on the child's face. He does so. *It does not work.* Elisha then 'put his mouth upon his mouth, and his eyes upon his eyes, and his hands upon his hands: and he stretched himself upon the child; and the flesh of the child waxed warm. Then he returned, and walked in the house to and fro; and went up, and stretched himself upon him; and the child sneezed seven times, and the child opened his eyes.' A strenuous miracle, yes, worked at by the prophet – and prompted always by the mother's refusal to accept her child's death. It shall be well. Elisha is compelled by her firm extension of his promise not to deceive her – an insistence which is half an act of faith, half an assertion of her rights. Then there are the seven sneezes – absent from the New English Bible and therefore from the original Hebrew – which are put there by a writer touched in his imagination by the power of the incongruous, indecorous detail to deliver life itself to us. The same writer had the taste and judgement to drop the exclamation 'O' from 'O my head, my head' and thus capture for all time the glazed lineaments and flat voice of death, of ordinary death.

All this art is in the Authorized Version. Read it. Read it in this extraordinarily cheap edition.

Imperial College of Science, Technology and Medicine

To: Craig Raine
New College
Oxford

I read with much interest and appreciation your long review of the World's Classics edition of the Authorized Version of the Bible. There is, however, one minor point, coming up twice in your article, on which you are mistaken, and I thought you might like to know. Maybe one of your Oxford colleagues has already told you of it.

In your account, both of Ehud in Judges 3 and of the Shunammite woman's son in 2 Kings 4, you write of a passage in the AV which is absent from the New English Bible 'and therefore from the original Hebrew', and you surmise that the AV translator has used his imagination to 'invent' them. In fact, both translations render what they take to be the original Hebrew text.

Of course one cannot expect you to be able to check the Hebrew text, but you might have been more cautious if you had looked at the footnotes of the NEB and the marginal notes of the standard edition of the AV. In the story of Ehud, a marginal note of the AV gives the alternative rendering 'it [i.e. the dagger] came out at the fundament'. The NEB, translating the alternative more loosely, has '[he] left it protruding behind'. In the story of the Shunammite's son, the NEB translates 'and [sc. Elisha] breathed into him seven times' but adds a footnote giving an alternative rendering of the first words as 'and the boy sneezed'. In both passages each of the two versions is giving a translation of a Hebrew phrase; the AV is not adding or inventing.

I was not familiar with the story of Ehud, but I know the story of the Shunammite woman very well because it is regularly read in the autumn at one of the Sabbath services of the Jewish

287

liturgy. I was surprised to find you saying that 'the child sneezed seven times' is not in the Hebrew text; it sounded familiar to me. So I looked at the Hebrew text and the statement is there quite plainly. It is the NEB which departs from the Hebrew original, perversely in my opinion. I suppose the translator thought that 'the boy sneezed seven times' is fanciful, and that it is more realistic to think of mouth-to-mouth resuscitation. There is, however, no linguistic justification for taking the verb to mean 'breathed'; and, more seriously, this rendering has to ignore the Hebrew word for 'the boy', in a form which requires it to be the subject, not the object, of the verb. The NEB is being too clever by half. In the telling of such a tale, 'the boy sneezed seven times' fits marvellously.

The difference between the two versions on Ehud is more complicated. The Hebrew text has two words. One is a verb meaning 'came out', the other is a long word which occurs nowhere else, so that its meaning is uncertain. The standard lexicon of Old Testament Hebrew suggests that the word may be connected with a short word of three letters (corresponding to the first three letters of the long word in the text) meaning faeces. I suppose that is why we have the suggested translation 'it [the dagger] came out at the fundament', and I also suppose that the AV translators took the unknown Hebrew word to be a corruption and replaced it by the shorter word meaning faeces straightforwardly. The latter move is unscholarly because it does not explain why a simple word (however indecorous) was corrupted to a complex word. The ending of the Hebrew word in the text certainly indicates that it is not a simple noun serving as the subject of 'came out' but adds something like 'at the' to a noun.

Yours sincerely
David Raphael

# The Autobiography of Paul Auster

*Hand to Mouth*. Even the title is a cliché.

'Cliché' is a technical term taken from printing which now denotes phrases and expressions reduced by repetition to what e. e. cummings called 'the mystical point of dullness'. A cliché in printing, as opposed to print, is a cast or mould capable of reproducing its impression more or less to infinity. Recently in Karlsruhe I saw a sign: *Klijschees und Lithographie*. The point of intersection between industrial process and artistic application is the idea of automatic reproduction.

The pen-penultimate episode of Joyce's *Ulysses* is called 'Eumaeus'. Designed to mirror the reader's fatigue after 700-odd pages, the chapter consists entirely and invigoratingly of clichés. Invigoratingly? Yes. Because the cliché's characteristic vacuity depends on its automatic use, whereas Joyce's deployment is considered, at the opposite pole from literary reflex. The chapter is self-conscious. Consider: 'Mr Bloom being handicapped by the circumstance that one of the backbuttons of his trousers had, to vary the time-honoured adage, gone the way of all buttons . . .' Even when the prose is aware that it is clichéd, it registers this in terms of a cliché: 'to vary the time-honoured adage'. By never once deviating out of cliché, Joyce brings virtuosity to vacuity, amplitude to emptiness. The irony is sustained more perfectly and for a lot longer than Swift's *Modest Proposal*.

'Eumaeus' is Joyce's spookiest chapter, haunted as it is so thickly by phrases that were once alive. I am reminded of its

*Hand to Mouth: A Chronicle of Early Failure* by Paul Auster, Faber.

spectral presence because Paul Auster's memoir is poisoned with clichés. Neither are there compensating brilliancies of style. Yet *Hand to Mouth* is described by *Le Monde* as 'one of the most original and audacious autobiographies ever written by a writer'. The author of this dust-jacket puff is not to be trusted. He or she is manifestly one of those by whom language dies. It is meaningless to distinguish between degrees of originality, which, by definition, is incomparable. Notice, too, how the critic relishes the concluding tautological flourish: 'ever written *by a writer*'. Auster's equally redundant 'low-rent dive' matches this.

In fact, autobiographies by writers are relatively rare, so that 'ever written' isn't quite the compliment it seems. The competition is largely spectral. Elias Canetti's *The Play of the Eyes* and *The Torch in My Ear* are less pure autobiography than naked self-aggrandizement. Newman and J. S. Mill are distinguished practitioners of autobiography, but their cultural identities depend on religion and philosophy rather than on pure writing. *The Autobiography of Bertrand Russell* is the work of a philosopher, in which the writing is an admirably clear and sometimes incriminating instrument of exposition, but nothing more. The great literary autobiographies are Gosse's *Father and Son*, Nabokov's *Speak, Memory* and Wordsworth's *The Prelude*. In relation to the scale and stature of these masterpieces, *Hand to Mouth* is barely homoeopathic. 'The details escape me now', 'without rehashing the whole complicated business', 'I can remember what his voice sounded like, but very little of what he said' – these are true but dispiriting observations. Add to local but widespread amnesia a predisposition to autobiographical continence and you create the distance one finds in Coleridge's *Biographia Literaria*, part prose *Prelude*, part intellectual snow-job. In its abstract way, it is an accurate self-portrait – of a man whose quiddity was confined to his private notebooks, of a man whose less private mode was that of the public lecturer, laying down the laws. Coleridge reminds us of Mrs Farrinder, the professional feminist, in James's *The Bostonians*: 'there was something public in her eyes,' writes James in the course of a famous summary paragraph which claims that 'Mrs Farrinder, at almost any time, had the air of being introduced by a few remarks'. Her personal life is relegated to a perfunctory, ironic appendix: 'she had a husband and his name was Amariah'.

We learn almost as little about Paul Auster's private life. He had a wife and her name was Lydia Davis. They were divorced. They had a son and his name is Daniel. *Hand to Mouth* confines itself strictly, decorously, aesthetically and fatally, fatally, to the subject of money. It observes its own unity. Even a disruptive lunatic, H. L. Humes, a forgotten fifties novelist, is cracked about cash, loopy about liquidity. But the real problem is not the subject. James Joyce used to ask his English language pupils in Trieste to write a description of an oil lamp. He believed anything was interesting if described with sufficient lust. The problem is the cliché.

Though Auster initially believed that he was 'a favourite of the gods', he was prepared 'to walk a long, hard road for the rest of his days' in order to be a writer. The idea of having a job 'left him cold'. Being a graduate student was 'a fate worse than death'. He had 'itchy feet'. As a boy, he was aware of his father's natural economy but capable of being glamorized by his spend-thrift mother, who 'swept him up in the whirlwind of another person's enthusiasm'. His parents valued money differently, but Auster developed 'a whole new way of looking at things': 'it's a jungle out there', he thought, and became disgusted 'by the outward trappings of wealth'. His parents finally divorced over money – 'it stands in my mind as the symbolic last straw, the thing that finally knocked the stuffing out of both of them' – and Auster feels 'the slate has been wiped clean'. He enrols at Columbia, goes to Paris for a year, but immediately 'locks horns' with his academic director. He quits school, 'taking the plunge with his eyes wide open'. In Paris, he puts off 'the hour of reckoning'. Determined 'to paddle his own canoe', he quickly finds himself 'clutching at straws'. Back in New York and re-enrolled at Columbia, he encounters the deranged H. L. Humes, who leaves him not only 'dumb-founded' but also 'unable to speak a word'.

Once free of academe, Auster dedicates himself to art and is resolute in 'sticking to his guns'. He fears the draft but has the luck of the draw and 'saves his skin'. He joins the Merchant Fleet, where he reads and is mostly passive, though at one moment 'a demon takes possession of his soul' and he physically threatens a teasing shipmate. After leaving the service, he has trouble 'keeping his head above water', even though he accepts freelance work 'till he is blue in the face'. By chance, he gets employment fixing movie scripts and this leads to a job as amanuensis to a 'larger-than-life' woman whose talents are dissipated by 'a desire to kill too many birds with a single stone'. The atmosphere around this 'larger-than-life' woman is 'cloak-and-dagger'. (The grey prose is lit by tracer-fire of hyphens hereabouts.) Fortunately, Auster gets a $5,000 grant from the Ingram Merrill Foundation, temporary fiduciary salvation arranged by John Bernard Myers, a benefactor who 'wore his heart on his sleeve'. Where else?

Pretty soon, though, Auster's back is 'back against the wall' and his remedy is to try to market a baseball game played with cards. The game is reproduced in an appendix. (It could have been worse. It could have been cricket and then I would have had to have read it.) All this is merely postponing 'the hour of doom'. He writes a detective novel, *Squeeze Play* – also with baseball connections; also reproduced in an appendix. The plot turns on an apparent murder which is actually a suicide (shades of Martin Amis's *Night Train*). Despite its energetic reproduction of the genre's clichés – especially the overextended 'fancy' metaphor – the book flops. And there the memoir ends. In it, there are walk-on-and-off parts for Jean Genet, John Lennon and Jerzy Kosinski. Blink and you'll miss them. Don't blink and you'll miss them anyway.

What changed things? What happened that left Paul Auster moping all the way to the bank? *Laurel and Hardy Go to Heaven*, a failed play also reproduced in an appendix, explains a good deal of Auster's subsequent success, as does *Blackouts*, another failed play, also meticulously preserved. *Blackouts* is the basis for *Ghosts*, the second novella in the New York Trilogy – the work that finally launched Auster as a serious and popular writer. *Laurel and Hardy Go to Heaven* is an abject Xerox of *Waiting for Godot*: the two comedians have to construct a wall in the after-life, according to detailed, absurd and arbitrary instructions. The whey-faced vaudevillians indulge in cross-talk over a metaphysical abyss. This is theatre where the ludicrous meets the Absurd: 'when I think of the wall, it's as if I were going beyond what I think'. Auster's play is pathetically wannabee, but the public invariably prefers the copy to the original, the Complan version to the complex version. This play may have failed, but the idea of using someone else's idea was bound to succeed in the end. And it did.

The *real* trouble with Auster's hero worship of Beckett is that the fan misses Beckett's hostility to his audience and to his art. *Hand to Mouth* is predicated on the absolute value of art and the relative worthlessness of money. Auster's exemplary figures are Beckett and Joyce. He even spends months in Dublin on the scent of his heroes' suffering. But Beckett's oeuvre is founded on the futility of art. There is a punitive element in Beckett which is absent from Auster's imitations. *Waiting for Godot* is a sustained act of theatrical aggression directed at the audience, but the besotted Auster doesn't see this and therefore leaves it out – thus further guaranteeing his eventual success. *Waiting for Godot* depends on a lost theatrical convention, preserved for us by 'The Tragedy of Tragedy', a 1941 Nabokov lecture in which he attacks the 'trick' of promising someone's arrival: 'So-and-so is expected. We know that so-and-so will unavoidably come. He or she will come very soon . . .' And So-and-so is, of course, the most important person in the piece. Beckett, in *Godot*, deprives his audience of the implicitly promised gratification. This frustration is no longer felt by audiences because the non-plot of *Godot* is as well known as *Hamlet*.

Beckett's distaste is catholic and extends to actors and directors: *Play* and *Happy Days* advertise their dislike of theatrical paraphernalia by burying the cast in earth or earthenware to make acting impossible. The medium of drama itself is treated with glazed ennui: Hamm's ironic first words in *Endgame* sum up Beckett's view of drama: 'Me – (*he yawns*) – to play.' The yawn is central to Beckett's fiction, too. The novels are studiously maladroit, considered in their perfunctoriness, and revel coldly in their narrative entropy. Characterization is a black joke when everyone is in a state of ontological deliquescence. We are several pages into *Molloy* before the narrator suddenly remembers his name. Beckett derives real pleasure from bringing an affectless scepticism to the venerated ideas of Western humanism and there are local, droll satisfactions when he is radically offhand with his readers: 'a little dog followed him, a pomeranian I think, but I don't think so'. Beckett can't be fagged. Let the sentence stand – unkempt, unconvincing, insulting.

As a fan, Auster is blind to the insult and therefore doesn't reproduce it. *Ghosts* conflates the thriller's implicit promise of action with the epic eventlessness of the writer's sedentary trade. Nothing much happens. The novella's subject is the writer's need for an audience. A writer hires a detective to watch him. Nothing could be further from the spirit of Beckett, who would gladly dispense with art, let alone an audience. Even so, Auster in *Ghosts* borrows from Beckett the idea of *esse* is *percipi* (to be is to be perceived) – an idea for which Beckett is in debt to Bishop Berkeley. The denouement of *Ghosts* is that the detective eventually attacks and probably murders the writer. In other words, Auster gives us an intelligible parable which argues that the writer has to create his own audience, but that the audience may savage its creator. In Beckett, the opposite is always the case: the author gets in his retaliation first. Might this not be the key to Auster's acclaim? – the comfy familiarity, the greater intelligibility, the determination to succeed with an audience where Beckett was suicidally determined to fail. Beckett is curare. Auster has charm.

# Samuel Beckett

Beckett is a very uneven genius. His dramatic career phutters infallibly to world acclaim with an unbroken series of 'deliberate' duds, plays seething with antipathy to the theatre – *Waiting for Godot, Endgame, Happy Days.* Beckett's truly theatrical, truly human greatness is to be found rather in the dwarf dramas – *Krapp's Last Tape, Not I, Rockaby, Embers.* Alan Schneider, Beckett's chosen director in America, is indiscriminate, an enthusiast who is on for everything. The works meet the perfect works manager. That is the main story of this correspondence.

In the twentieth century, it is axiomatic that to be avant-garde is to be misunderstood. There is no success without prior failure. Instant success entails subsequent failure – think of Kipling, blighted by his perceived blimpishness and his tainted popularity. The true artist's place is well outside the pale. This myth is so potent that it accounts for the most winning moment in these letters. Nixon is being impeached. Schneider sends Beckett a comic revue satirizing Nixon's antics at the White House: *Watergate Classics* parodies Lucky's speech in *Godot* and makes a connection between *Krapp's Last Tape* and the Watergate tapes. Schneider is gleeful. Beckett fastidiously differs: 'Thanks for *Watergate Classics*. I so hate the hue and cry, however obnoxious the quarry, that I'm sorry to be there.' *There* being inside the pale – odiously and invidiously with the majority. This was repugnant to a writer who had spent his life

No Author Better Served: The Correspondence of Samuel Beckett and Alan Schneider, edited by Maurice Harmon, Harvard University Press.

avoiding being caught in the cleft rump of the consensus, with its overpowering odour – not of ordure, not even of sanctity, but of sanctimoniousness. One thinks of Zbigniew Herbert's poem 'The Power of Taste', which explains political dissent not in terms of courage, but in terms of aesthetics – the sense that the regime is, in the end, unacceptably vulgar. Communism is common.

Beckett believed in failure. He courted failure faithfully, assiduously. He snubbed popularity patiently, pointedly, resourcefully: 'success and failure on the public level never mattered much to me, in fact I feel much more at home with the latter, having breathed deep of its vivifying air all my writing life up to the last couple of years'. But surely Beckett *wanted* to be popular in the end? Yes and no. When he won the Nobel Prize in 1969, his wife Suzanne exclaimed, 'Tu as gagné. C'est une catastrophe.' Not an envious cry, I think, but indicative, rather, of an habitual, hardline mistrust of the garlanded – the honoured as harmless, empty, spent forces, plumply sprawled on their laurels, a couple of undone fly-buttons tearfully on show. That quotation about the 'vivifying air' of failure significantly continues: 'And I cannot help feeling that the success of *Godot* has been very largely the result of a misunderstanding, or of various misunderstandings.'

*Godot* is an instrument of sustained torture, of denial. All the audience's expectations and addictions are comprehensively refused – action, sustained dialogue, characterization, basic coherence. When the play first opened, the suspense, the *discomfort*, must have been acute. A glance at the programme would reveal instantly the non-appearance of Godot. The suspense really resides in the play's flaccid, indifferent awareness of its own inadequacy as drama – an attitude encapsulated in these letters by Beckett's set-design specifications for *Happy Days*: 'a pathetic unsuccessful realism, the kind of tawdriness you get in third rate musical or pantomime, *that* quality of *paupier*, laughably earnest bad imitation'. Rather than construction, *bricolage*, make-do-and-mend, routine routines, business as usual, drama with Alzheimers, full of self-forgetful pauses and evaporating connections. The drama lies in whether the play can falter through the next few moments. 'So all things limp together for the only possible' – as Beckett puts it so accurately in *Murphy*. As drama, *Godot* has all the invigorating danger of plunging its audience under a cold trickle of water.

It should be played, wrote Beckett in 1957, 'as *farcical parody of polite drawing-room* conversation'. Beckett the iconoclast, taking his hammer to the French windows and other fixtures of West End drama. Two months earlier, he frets about programming his work in New York: 'I should make it clear that I want *Endgame*, too short (one hour and a half) to provide a full evening's agony, to be followed in NY by the mime (20 minutes) . . .' A *full evening's agony*. It would be a mistake to think Beckett is joking. A year previously, as he puts the finishing touches to *Endgame*, he expresses his preference for 'the desert mime to follow *as last straw*'. (My italics.) The aim is not invention but its opposite, aesthetic exhaustion – not fullness but evacuation, not pleasure but pain. If a thing isn't worth doing, it's worth doing badly. For Beckett, drama at its best is at its worst. Only the cognoscenti can savour the insult of a playwright barely able to bother.

In *Endgame*, the title alludes to chess – a form of play and a ritualized form of conflict – and the moment when, given the paucity of pieces left, a very limited series of moves, of plays, can be predicted. The chess terminology is there emblematically, then, as a guarantee of dramatic dullness. *Endgame* opens with Clov's covert assertion that drama itself, time and the created world, are equally washed-up: 'Finished, it's finished, nearly finished, it must be nearly finished.' A start replete with promise. Joyce, Beckett's greater master and indifferent mentor, applied the term hemiplegia, or paralysis, to the souls of his *Dubliners*, but it would apply more exactly to Beckett's thwarted, hobbling, hampered theatre works. *Endgame* is mined with disaffected innuendo and insulting disclaimers: 'this is slow work'; 'this is not much fun'; 'why this farce, day after day?'; and when one character asks, 'What's happening, what's happening?', the laconic answer comes, 'Something is taking its course'. Each of these torpid reflections is twice repeated. Not so much an economy of scale, as a minginess of scale. Nagg and Nell are pawns at the end of their progress, immobile in their dustbins; Hamm is in a wheelchair, like a King restricted to one movement; Clov limps diagonally across the stage. The two principals sum up the dramatic fiasco: 'HAMM: We're not beginning to . . . to . . . mean something? CLOV: Mean something! You and I, mean something! (*Brief laugh*) Ah that's a good one!' The flickering, exhausted action is the butt of constant disaffected comment: 'Keep going, can't you, keep going!' attempts to keep inanition at bay.

There is something tonic in Beckett's refusal to toady to his audience, in his insistence that the drama is unworthy of applause – utterly clapped-out aesthetically. And his disbelief in the genre curdles nicely with his distaste for its mechanisms: Deirdre Bair's excellent biography has been ostracized by the literary establishment but it is a trove of Beckettian aesthetic brutalities: 'the best possible play is one in which there are no actors, only the text'. Artistically, Beckett is a nihilist. Compare Wilde's doorbell and Beckett's alarm clock. Wilde shares the joke, while Beckett dares you to laugh. Wilde's doorbell is 'Wagnerian', a work of art only because its note is sustained either by a relative or a creditor. In *Endgame*, the alarm clock is there to guy the idea of art and the notion of discrimination, differentiation or development. 'The end is terrific!' says Clov. 'I prefer the middle,' says Hamm.

With this ostentatiously glazed indifference, however, comes a self-regard much on view in these letters. If Beckett turns his back on the world, it is in the manner of Gilbert Osmond in James's *The Portrait of a Lady* – that is, a display of unworldliness that never loses sight of its effect in the world. The dustjacket of *No Author Better Served* promises more disclosure than it actually delivers. Beckett gives less away as the correspondence proceeds. Throughout he sets his face against explication – and sets a fashion for the exegetical oubliette. 'But when it comes to these bastards of journalists I feel the only line is to refuse to be involved in exegesis of any kind. That's for those bastards of critics.' David Caute's biography of Joseph Losey, *A Revenge on Life*, gives us Pinter and Losey facing an audience of college editors about *Accident*. *The Village Voice* reproduces the friction created by Pinter's pretentious perversity with its element of *hommage* to Beckett: 'I'd understand questions about meaning if I knew what the word "meaning" meant.' Losey also took up this 'Trappist ritual' and the critic John Simon accused the pair, with every justification, of insulting their audience: 'I've seldom seen two such consummate phonies on stage at one time.' Remember what a worthy but slight film *Accident* is. Neither was a phoney *au fond* but they had learned two things from Beckett – the trick of treating the audience with contempt and an awareness that an authorial vacuum will suck in hermeneutical interest.

Had this attitude been cynical, it would have been acceptable. In 1967, though, at the time of the Pinter–Losey press conference, the artist was conceived of as fatuously instinctive, a creature of profound intuition. Like the poor, he is still with us. *No Author Better Served* serves up quite a lot of this mystical, self-aggrandizing, pretentious tosh. The explanation in Beckett's case can be found in Deirdre Bair's biography. Beckett was desperate to shake off the shadow of Joyce: 'I am sure that every letter, every syllable, every word, every sentence, every paragraph, every page, every chapter of every book, had meaning, because that is the way Joyce committed his thoughts to paper. In my case, I write because I have to – I don't mean for money, but for my own needs. I don't know where the writing comes from and am often quite surprised when I see what I have committed to paper. Writing, for me, is an entirely different process than it was for Joyce.' What we have here is not truthfulness but territoriality. It is pure pretence when Beckett feigns equality with director, actor and audience in the matter of meaning: writing to Schneider about the gabbling 'dead' woman in *Not I* suffering her after-life of self, Beckett says that she is 'purely a stage entity, part of a stage image and purveyor of a stage text. The rest is Ibsen.' Here Beckett is modishly denying 'the old business of author's supposed privileged information'.

*Supposed*! If it ever came to directorial liberties – that is, assumptions of real equality – Beckett would have none of it.

When he is writing *Happy Days* he confides to Schneider some boldly bogus haruspication as the dramatist investigates the rag-and-bone shop of his brain: 'I don't see the play at all clearly, but a little more so. The figure is a woman as far as I can see . . .' Reading this disingenuous piffle, it is difficult not to quote Paul Valéry on Victor Hugo: 'The very qualities which Hugo thought would make him immeasurably great and rank him with the gods merely make him seem ridiculous. His notion was based on a fallacy. A poet should make no secret of his calling, should talk of versification, own up to his midnight oil, and not profess to hear mysterious voices.' Alas, the example of Alan Schneider, whose half of this correspondence shifts from the devoted to the devout, shows us that Valéry is right to conclude with a rhetorical question: 'But would people have any use for poetry if it did not claim to be oracular?' For 'poetry' read 'drama' and you have the case of Samuel Beckett, sulking formidably in the shadows – waiting perhaps for one of his own stage directions, *Fade-up to dim*.

# Les Murray

Les Murray's long verse novel, *Fredy Neptune*, is all over the place. This considered colloquialism is not entirely negative in its connotations and might conceivably be accepted by the poet himself. Not only because, on the very first page, the narrative shifts from the Australian outback – irrefutably set down in a brilliantly downright opening, 'That was sausage day / on our farm outside Dungog' – to Valparaiso to Singapore to Messina. Thereafter, the hero's picaresque takes him to Turkey, Berlin, Holland, Rio, Buenos Aires, Egypt, Palestine, Australia, Los Angeles, New York, Friedrichshafen, the USSR, Shanghai, Manila, Japanese New Guinea and back to Sydney – in roughly that order. In the course of these travels and travails, Fredy (Frederich Boettcher, an Australian of German extraction) works as a merchant seaman, as a hand on a dredger, in a circus, in the movies, as a Zeppelin operative and as a black-marketeer. At intervals, he also lives off the land and is a hobo in the States.

Without much of interest rubbing off, he rubs against several twentieth-century icons: T. E. Lawrence, Chaim Weizmann, Chaplin, Rasputin's daughter, Johnny Weissmuller, Ross 'Fatty' Arbuckle, Marlene Dietrich and Hitler. Brief encounters. He witnesses the stock-market crash, Nazi book burning, early Hollywood, Zeppelin flights, NKVD atrocities, the Japanese invasion of Shanghai and, even more distantly, newsreels of the atom bomb and the bulldozers at Belsen.

*Fredy Neptune* by Les Murray, Carcanet.

If these events and encounters tend to be hurried, fast-forwarded rather than freeze-framed, headlong rather than honed, at least something happens. Which is more than you can say for Derek Walcott's *Omeros*, an epic of stasis which secured the Nobel Prize. *Omeros* is coma, not Homer. Landscape and Homeric shadowplay supplant psychology, action and interest. By contrast, *Fredy Neptune* is a busy tale of fist-fights and rescues. Every two or three pages, Fredy settles some villain's hash. Eventful, international in its scope and theme, *Fredy Neptune* also answers to more worldly considerations. Its author is aware that the Nobel can only be procured by something substantial enough to tip the scales. As verse, it is, however, astonishingly incompetent in its conduct of the line. One example, from hundreds: 'but I got him a shirt out of my duffel bag, and peeled my / foul-weather jersey off . . .' Which is like hyphenating the word 'hyphen' *hyp-hen*. Structurally, it is without form, too. It is, in fact, all over the place.

Or is this merely 'The Quality of Sprawl' that Murray joyfully embraces in his 1993 poem? That is, an aesthetic which prizes fecund invention over frigid perfectionism, the relaxed over the finicky. The quality of sprawl prefers creativity to culture. It is generous. It won't take crap from anyone. It is Australian and couldn't give a XXXX for rules. It is also extremely personal to Les Murray, whose size is alluded to on the covers of *Fredy Neptune* and his new *Collected Poems* – depicting a Zeppelin and a woman cuddling up to an elephant. Object to sprawl and become a bureaucrat.

And it is true that many of the many enjoyable things here are contingent on Murray's aesthetic of sprawl. They just get included in: 'a tall woman slung cold tea out off the verandah / like cracking a long gold whip'. A woman being wooed sits, mesmerically, 'on the grass with her toes in their stocking webs'. There are 'cannons like enormous kangaroos'. A prostitute tempts: *'take out that brown parcel and part my wet hairs, eh?'* Sprawl isn't prissy. In Shanghai, we learn about human fertilizer: *'You see man with bamboo staff? Imperial official from old times: / he dips and judges, you see? Speed of material flowing*

*down staff. / It tells him quality, whether is water added.'*
Sprawl includes even dip-shit.

It is also determinedly colloquial. Consider the word 'about':
'of course, I'd know all this, as a Reuters man. And about / the
big push that was about to happen (what was he talking
about?)' Only a writer confident of his tonal register could float
that deliberate triple repetition. On the other hand, the aesthetic
of sprawl can lead into, well, sprawl, arhythmical sprawl: 'what
my hiders in Berlin / told me, how the Communists weren't
allowed to help other Left parties // against Hitler made me ask
[a question].' This isn't even good prose. It's barely articulate
speech. It means: people who hid him in Berlin said that
communists were forbidden to assist other radical parties against
Hitler and this made him ask why. Answer: because crisis
precipitates revolution. Worse is better.

Sprawl is also responsible for Murray's way with metaphor.
'Late Snow in Edinburgh' shows the elegant economy of which
metaphor is capable: 'soaped cars, and cars still shaving' gives
us snow as early morning ablutions, leaving us to work out the
windscreen wiper. In *Fredy Neptune*, metaphors arrive carrying
instructions for their assembly. Even the best lack all conviction.
Never explain, never apologize? A man hangs himself: 'I kept
thinking of poor Bulba Domeyko, his thin blond hair / over a
monstrous black boxing glove and his tongue for the thumb.'
Police quell a riot like a combine harvester: 'the upswing of
butts like the screw-boom / of a harvester made of sheriffs, in
their suntans and level-brimmed hats, / mowing the losers.' A
metaphor all fidget and afterthought.

One triumph of sprawl is Hans, a German idiot, saved from
castration by the hero. Murray has an autistic son and this may
account for the tender particularities of inappropriateness when
the narrative tightens its torque. In danger, Hans can be distracted: '*Ick seh mir dat Baby weenen an. I'm watching the
baby cry.*' Out of context, the words in themselves are nothing.
Their force is dramatic. Sneaking out of Rügen harbour and
Nazi control, Hans escapes the story's single-mindedness
because sprawl is a psychological given for him. His thoughts

303

are all over the place: '*All the little lights*, said Hans.' Twice we learn that the boy is sensitive to the strong feelings of others. Once might have been better. But sprawl says otherwise. Sprawl can't count, won't count.

It is the opposite of calculation, selection and exclusion. Hans exemplifies the ethics of sprawl. Nazi genetic theory proposes castration. Sprawl, though, has room for the odd, the bizarre – and the overweight. This is the central theme: Fredy witnesses the burning of Armenian women by Turks and loses all sensation in his body – which becomes a Nothing. Since he feels no pain, the narrative grants him, inexplicably, an excess of strength. At first, this condition is described as leprosy. This is seriously misleading because leprous loss of sensation doesn't entail an increase of strength. It commonly entails endangered extremities – which can be radically damaged without their owner noticing until too late. Murray evidently and erroneously believes that leprosy rots limbs – but perhaps this is poetic licence, the physics of sprawl. Though Fredy's condition is ameliorated mysteriously at various points, it isn't cured until the final two pages: sensation returns when Fredy forgives the Aborigines, then the Jews, then all women.

Clear? Of course not. Let me explain, since the exposition in the text is inadequate. Fredy finally realizes that, exemplary though his conduct is throughout the poem, he shares the general guilt. Atrocities are committed by all nations. It isn't a case of *them*. It's a case of *us*. The final step is the move from *us* to *I*. Inside each of us, there is a Nazi – selecting, choosing, rejecting and hating whatever is different. Thus, though Fredy appears guiltless, he has to acknowledge his guilt, which is part of his humanity. An ex-communist explains to Fredy that Nazism speaks to the bleak facts of life accurately: 'With Marx and old Jesus and the rest, you're always paddling / against the natural flow of blood and shit.' 'Nature,' this Nazi convert assures us, 'is a Nazi.' Contemplating the century's atrocities, Fredy is forced to concur: 'If Russians could do it, my own folk could.' His body chooses numbness rather than acknowledge its shameful kinship with humanity. It isn't simple trauma or repression, it is morality incarnate. We use *humanity* to imply concern and tenderness. *Fredy Neptune* argues that this is sentimental – that *humanity* includes intrinsic, inevitable evil, too. It might be William Golding. It is a forensic, bracing conclusion – or would be, were it clearer – but it is undermined throughout by Fredy's consistently shining behaviour. He may finally accept guilt, but we know there is no case to answer. He is a moral simpleton, invariably on the right side, so the narrative is bled of interest, complication and credibility. The cartoon action and the many plot improbabilities don't help either, and one is left wondering if the quality of sprawl doesn't, after all, need quality control. Otherwise, it's all over the place.

When Les Murray won the T. S. Eliot Prize in 1996, a letter to the *Guardian* immediately denounced him as a fascist, on the basis of four poems: 'The Road Toll', 'On Removing Spiderweb', 'Midnight Lake' and 'The Fall of Aphrodite Street'. The last two were said to gloat over AIDS. The charge is absurd. 'Rock Music' tells us that 'Sex is a Nazi' and so does *Fredy Neptune* – twice. It isn't repetition, it is obsession. As a fat person, Murray must have continuously suffered the sexual apartheid of the ugly, the automatic invisibility of the unattractive. 'Rock Music' asks why the 'beautiful Nazis' are so cruel. Answer: 'to castrate the aberrant, the original, the wounded / who might change our species and make obsolete / the true race . . .' The master race. 'The Fall of Aphrodite Street' isn't specifically homophobic. It deplores a more general hedonistic ideology that locates value exclusively in physical appearance – when 'grace was enslaved to meat', a culture of sensual materialism, 'where people paired or reeled / like desperate swastikas'. A dance of death, in other words. No wonder Fredy Neptune dreams that Hitler's privates are a swastika, 'sallow right-angles of flesh all knobby and stiff // that he wanted me to catch hold of . . .' Moral disapproval isn't the same thing as gloating.

# Elizabeth Bishop

By now, everyone is *au courant* with the symbiotic syndrome of Philoctetes, his incurable wound and his invincible bow. As a psychoanalytical paradigm of the artist – no grit, no pearls – it was first given critical currency by Edmund Wilson in 1941. Those unfamiliar with the theory may relish Alan Bennett's comically Socratic encapsulation, *à propos* Kafka: 'They fuck you up your Mum and Dad, and if you're planning on writing that's probably a good thing. But if you are planning on writing and they haven't fucked you up, well, you've got nothing to go on, so then they've fucked you up good and proper.' How fucked up was Elizabeth Bishop?

In 1964, she wrote to Anne Stevenson: 'Although I think I have a prize "unhappy childhood", almost good enough for the text-books – please don't think I dote on it.' Her father died, aged thirty-nine, and the eight-month-old baby was brought by her mother Gertrude to Great Village, Nova Scotia, where her Bulmer maternal grandparents lived. Gertrude Bishop suffered a series of mental breakdowns, severe enough to require treatment first in McLean's outside Boston (where Robert Lowell was later to shave with a locked razor), and finally at an institution near Dartmouth, Nova Scotia. For the first five years of her life, Elizabeth Bishop was cared for by aunts and her mother's parents.

Aged six, she was taken by her richer paternal grandparents

*Becoming a Poet: Elizabeth Bishop with Marianne Moore and Robert Lowell* by David Kalstone, Chatto & Windus.

to live in Worcester, Massachusetts. She felt 'kidnapped' ('even if I wasn't'). She never saw her mother again and, immediately, suffered an affliction of psychosomatic complaints – asthma, eczema, bronchitis, constipation. On arrival, she had to be carried upstairs by the chauffeur. The next six or seven years were years of prostration – 'lying in bed, wheezing and reading'. At thirteen she began to recover and at sixteen finally went to Walnut Hill boarding school, near Boston, and thence to Vassar.

Still a student, she met Marianne Moore, as she recorded unforgettably in her prose memoir, 'Efforts of Affection': 'the recipient of sixteen honorary degrees (she once modeled her favorite academic hoods for me)'. Though painting was always an enthusiasm, Moore confirmed her in her writer's vocation, and, with Moore's advocacy, *North and South*, her first book, was published in August 1946 with quiet *réclame*.

The grit, you might think, had secreted the pearl – except that Bishop indeed did not 'dote' on her classically unhappy childhood and, in the poetry, it scarcely features at all. 'The crises of our lives,' she wrote, 'do not come, I think, accurately dated; they crop up unexpected and out of turn, and somehow or other arrange themselves according to a calendar we cannot control.' Her prose is a special case. Written in the early sixties, two prose autobiographical pieces, 'Primer Class' and 'The Country Mouse', were published only after her death. The former is idyllic: the dead father and the absent mother are disposed of, painlessly, in a sentence, while other details woo our attention – like her inquiry of other relatives 'if they thought my grandmother could go to heaven with a glass eye'. 'The Country Mouse', though, recounts her reluctant translation south and subsequent Bostonian constrictions on her behaviour and bronchia. She quotes Louise Bogan: 'At midnight tears / run into your ears.' Significantly, the memoir was excluded from her table of contents for a contemplated prose volume. We are lucky to have it, but I don't think she herself would have published it.

'In the Village', her most famous story, touches on her mother's madness, but trades in mystery rather than melo-trauma, and is the more powerful for that: her mother's brief

307

scream never quite disappears, but it comes close to being obliterated by the bluntly imperious claims of village life, like the horse whose 'cloud of . . . odor is a chariot in itself'. The story is exact, not exaggerated.

Knowing she was not quite normal, Bishop preferred to play down her singularity. When a fellow poet, Charles Olson, rented her house in Key West, she had to take his payment to the electricity company: 'a Poet mustn't be asked to do prosaic things like pay bills'. This was just the kind of poet she wasn't. She wrote poems about prosaic things like bills: 'You've left out the decimal points. / Your columns stagger, / honeycombed with zeros.' This wry look at a Brazilian squatter-tenant might be matched by her 'Filling Station', with its oil-soaked domesticity: 'Somebody embroidered the doily. / Somebody waters the plant, / or oils it, maybe . . .' Her poetry makes room for the mundane as if it were a talisman against the abnormal.

To Lowell (of all people), she confessed: 'in general, I deplore the "confessional"'. Temperamentally and aesthetically, her position is identical to Eliot's in 'Tradition and the Individual Talent': 'poetry is not a turning loose of emotion, but an escape from emotion; it is not the expression of personality, but an escape from personality. But, of course, only those who have personality and emotions know what it means to want to escape from those things.' Bishop has one poem only where she confronts this problem directly, 'In the Waiting Room'. Whereas Larkin might improbably conceive of life as 'the million-petalled flower / Of being here', Bishop suddenly perceives life as a miracle, but a repellent one. At the dentist's, she experiences, while reading the *National Geographic*, a moment of human solidarity and individual self-consciousness – which are equally disgusting.

> Why should I be my aunt,
> or me, or anyone?
> What similarities –
> boots, hands, the family voice
> I felt in my throat, or even

the *National Geographic*
and those awful hanging breasts –
held us all together
or made us all just one?
How – I didn't know any
word for it – how 'unlikely' . . .

Yet, if Bishop was to ditch this loathsome, given self, she had to construct a replacement personality. Here, Marianne Moore was a great help and example, since, in her poetry and by her presence, without ever being intimate, she was manifestly informative, agile and interesting. The frisking Lamb-like essayist in Moore is beautifully pastiched by her young protégée. Lowell had given her a cameo carved out of lava:

Sydney Smith speaks somewhere of an Englishman dancing at court in Naples, wearing 'volcanic silk with lava buttons', and I'd wondered what it meant – it sounded slightly Emily-Dickinson-ish for Mr Smith. Now I think I know – perhaps 'volcanic silk' was shot silk, or else just scarlet . . . It makes me think of the Brownings, 'The Marble Faun', 'Roderick Hudson', and my own strange stay in Naples. Did you notice the high point of the carving – that one romantic curl that you can see through? I also like the other cruder curls of the gold, which remind me strongly of sucked dandelion stems; but I'm getting altogether too Marianne-ish about this . . .

As well as these brilliant, recherché reflexes, Bishop also learned to distinguish character from personality, backbone from mere competitive revelation. And yet her poetry avoids Moore's characteristic moral nostrums. 'The power of relinquishing / what one would keep; that is freedom' is a candid moral typical of Moore. In Bishop it becomes an action which is allowed to speak for itself: 'And I let the fish go.' Certainty was always something she could relinquish.

Her poetic personality is strong, but more morally diffident than Marianne Moore's. Intimate in tone, it is never confidential in content. A winning manner had to be compatible with discretion. She would have concurred with Artur Sammler's misgivings: 'one notices most a peculiar play-acting, an elaborate and sometimes quite artistic manner of presenting oneself as an individual and a strange desire for originality, distinction, interest'. She disapproved of self-exploitation. W. D. Snodgrass's *The Heart's Needle* she found self-congratulatory: '"I do all these awful things but don't you think I'm really nice?"' was the subtext for her. She stigmatized as synthetic Randall Jarrell's 'sort-of-over-sympathizing with the lot of women'. And she had hard things to say about Anne Sexton. You would never guess from her work that she was lesbian. When James Merrill, reading 'Crusoe in England', asked why there wasn't more about Friday – 'pretty to watch; he had a pretty body' – she replied that there *had* been much more. On the other hand, perhaps her homosexuality was *faute de mieux*: Crusoe's other wistful comment is 'If only he had been a woman!' Decidedly ungay.

Like Bellow's von Humboldt Fleischer, we are all avid for personal details. Humboldt (modelled on Delmore Schwartz) is obsessed by T. S. Eliot: 'about whom, when he was off his nut, he would spread the most lurid sexual scandal'. In Keats's phrase, his ear was 'open like a greedy shark' – for salacious gossip. Bishop appears to have had only three female partners: Loto de Macedo Soares, who committed suicide in 1967; a replacement from Seattle called Roxanne, who had a nervous breakdown; and Alice Methfessel, with whom she was happy till the end of her life. The late David Kalstone is briskly informative and unprurient, but in a way that necessarily makes one eager for more, if only to clear up doubts raised by the laconic presentation. Why did Loto's relatives successfully contest her will? Why did their mutual friends refuse to speak to Elizabeth? Personally, I'd've preferred more hard information of this kind and less of Kalstone's criticism. If the poem is, so to speak, a handwritten manuscript, you want the critic to set it up in clear, readable type. With David Kalstone, you mostly feel that he is recopying by hand – and that his biro has a piece of fluff in the end, which makes the thing you are trying to read even muzzier. He wants to re-site the poetry to some place he knows – female suffering, depression America, alcoholic dependency – united states all, and far from Elizabeth Bishop's uniqueness and unquestionable greatness.

# William Golding's Imagination

Evelyn Waugh's novels are banquets whose recipes are to be found in his diaries – brief, laconic reports on his inner and outer life which the master chef was later to present as *The Ordeal of Gilbert Pinfold* or the *Sword of Honour* trilogy. Very few scraps were wasted. And Saul Bellow, it is said, refuses to authorize a biography because his life has been amply deployed in his fiction already. These two writers exemplify the symbiosis between life and literature which is common in what we casually call fiction. William Golding, though, is a rarer specimen – the writer in whom imagination operates in a pure, almost helpless way. He belongs with Kafka, who can tell us exactly how it feels to metamorphose into a beetle ('he especially enjoyed hanging suspended from the ceiling'), and with Kipling, who knows what it is like to see a Chinaman for the first time ('he was yellow – not from sickness, but by nature – yellow as honey, and his eyes stood endwise in his head'). In *The Inheritors*, Golding has accurately imagined what it is like to see *homo sapiens* as a Neanderthal man would see him: 'the man had white bone things above his eyes and under the mouth so that his face was longer than a face should be'. These clear and distinct perceptions are not acts of imagination so much as feats of imagination which, though imagined, convince us of their truth immediately, without reflection. All great music, wrote Hans Keller, is distinguished by a single quality – unpredictable inevitability. Golding's art has always had this property: we cannot guess what is coming in advance; nor can we refuse our assent to what he imagines.

WILLIAM GOLDING'S IMAGINATION

Two small examples, both, as it happens, taken from prose essays rather than his fiction proper: in 'An Affection for Cathedrals', there is one sentence which is *echt* Golding, a phrase as authentic as a finger print. He is wondering about vandalism and the curious absence of noses on cathedral statuary. 'It was darkish, I believe, and the cathedral as nearly deserted as may be, when the little man stole out of the shadows with his hammer. Bash! Clitter clatter! and he is away over the downs, *fingering the stung place on his cheek* where a minute fragment of Bishop Poore hit him, but giggling and jerking with a possibly sexual excitement . . .' Figuratively as well as literally, Golding's imagination is here, as ever, *ex cathedra* – unpredictable, inevitable, infallible. The italics are mine, of course, but that intuition, detailed and meticulous, has its own imaginative emphasis, compared to which the work of most other novelists is slackly realized. The thrilling resourcefulness of Golding's imagination differs from their perfunctory records as Technicolor differs from black and white film. As you read Golding, something happens to the print – something which Golding has recorded in another essay, 'The Ladder and the Tree': 'I had no doubt that if one frowned long enough at the page it would brighten and come alive. Indeed, it did. The words and paper vanished. The picture emerged.' And once it emerged, the young reader Golding also became the young writer Golding:

I know something about Odysseus that is not in the text, since I have seen and touched him. When he was washed up in Phaeacia his hands were white and corrugated and his nails bled – not because of the rocks but because he bit them. I saw him, crouched naked beneath the stunted olive, shuddering in the wind, salt drying on his skin, lugging with white teeth at the nail of his third right finger while he peered at the dark, phantom dangers and wondered fearfully what to do. The wily, the great-hearted, the traveller, the nail-biter. These moving pictures in Technicolor lit the underside of the leaves. This place was where I lived.

313

This seminal essay about Golding's adolescence, with its embellishments of Homer, shows us the uncowed artistic temperament that would, in due course, question and invert the fib of childhood innocence that was inscribed like so much pokerwork in Ballantyne's *Coral Island*. Golding is independent, his own man, and 'The Ladder and the Tree' also records a mental disposition which all his fiction has underwritten. While the young Golding espoused science and rationality ('there was no place in this exquisitely logical universe for the terrors of darkness'), he was at the same time profoundly aware that education and sophistication left out of account what, in yet another essay, 'Delphi', he calls that 'dubious, dark quality' which might have something in it – 'for all one's professional disbelief'.

Golding is the master of the imaginative close-up and the mage with a metaphysical overview. His novels are famously various. Yet, from book to utterly different book, these two characteristics remain, brilliantly bifocal. In, say, *Pincher Martin*, he shows us what it is like to be starving and to come on a grain of chocolate: 'the chocolate stung with a piercing sweetness, momentary and agonizing, and was gone'. At the same time, he can explore an egotism so profound that it survives physical death – a futile will, repugnant, heroic, and bitter evidence of a soul which, mercifully, is not immortal.

# The Collected Poems of T. S. Eliot

Modernism, of which T. S. Eliot is a leading proponent, was among other things an assault on sentimentality in literature and in the arts generally. In 1916, Prokofiev's *Sarcasms* were premièred – piano pieces full of ironic lyricism, harsh rhythms and dissonance. The first story of Joyce's *Dubliners* is about a young boy whose mentor, a defrocked priest, has died – a scenario of loss which automatically summons the sentiment of grief. In the event, however, the boy contemplates death with glazed anomie and affectless detachment. The story records instead his fascination with the word 'paralysis'. In other words, in one primary aspect, modernism is an objective inquiry into what we *really* feel – an inquiry in which, post-Nietzsche, the ideal is destined to be supplanted by the real. Even hallowed areas like love. This is Eliot adding characteristically modernist disenchantment to the received view: 'a great deal of sentiment has been spilt, especially in the eighteenth and nineteenth centuries, upon idealizing the reciprocal feelings of man and woman towards each other, *which various realists have been irritated to denounce* [my italics]'. Eliot's own, measured, unsentimental description – 'the coupling of animals', unless analogous to spirituality – is generally thought so reductive as to be unacceptable. But Eliot is a connoisseur of cold sexuality – 'To seize and clutch and penetrate' – a line in which the verbs are verbs of genius, individually, and collectively as they conflate violence, clumsiness and detachment.

In 1916, in *The Dial*, e. e. cummings praised Eliot's 'skilful and immediate violins'. Cummings, though, is a poetic sentimentalist – 'that hugest whole creation may be less / incalculable than a single kiss' – and is, therefore, not a modernist. So he is unlikely to be fully aware of the irony informing some of Eliot's more sumptuous verbal effects, like the eloquent evocation of aridity at the beginning of 'A Game of Chess'. Or the exquisite but ironic verbal music of 'La Figlia Che Piange': 'But weave, weave the sunlight in your hair.' Of course, Eliot could write beautifully, sonorously and unironically: 'What seas what shores what granite islands towards my timbers / And woodthrush calling through the fog / My daughter'. On the other hand, consider the programme implicit in his favourable critique of William Blake. Blake's poetry has, he writes, 'the unpleasantness of great poetry'. In other words, for Eliot, as for Eliot's version of Blake, poetry wasn't to be the usual edited anthology of highlights from life – with a telos of guaranteed, gold-plated afflatus. Eliot was interested in bathos, too. In irony. In complication. In 'unpleasantness'. In realism, in fact. And at this point, modernism is coterminous with all great literature and its relentless critique of the ideal – its determination, in Matthew Arnold's words, 'to see the object as in itself it really is'.

Eliot's version of this credo can be found in *The Use of Poetry and the Use of Criticism* (1933), where he quotes, with approval, from the philosopher T. E. Hulme's essay 'Romanticism and Classicism'. There, classicism is defined: 'the great aim is accurate, precise and definite description. The first thing to recognize is how extraordinarily difficult this is.' Especially if the 'object' being described is the feelings, emotions, sensations. Notoriously, Eliot defined himself in 1928 as 'a classicist in literature' – meaning a writer writing *against* emotional indulgence.

At the end of his career, Eliot's plays present us with a more clearly 'thematized' version of what, in the earlier poetry, was singular and particular. His drama addresses the idea that the real self is hidden under a social construct, or a false self – often we do not know what we really feel; our true self might be elusive even to ourselves. And here, Eliot conjoins with Arnold, who fostered and irritated him in equal measure. Arnold's poem

'The Buried Life' is a seminal text describing the difficulty of articulating our inmost self. In Eliot's early poetry, though, the approach is less theoretical, less general. There are no characters – like Edward in *The Cocktail Party* – who exist primarily as mouthpieces for authorial philosophy, as expositors in the Arnoldian manner of over-lucid expatiation. The early poetry addresses not the Problem of Ontological Insecurity, but the gestalt of murkiness itself. It isn't analysis. It is experience in all its complication, comedy, bathos and actuality. And actuality involves a vigilant scepticism towards the reflex literary prompts – those swift menials who serve our lazy automism, corrupt our alertness with the comfort of the habitual, who anticipate our every need. Take Eliot's sly anti-elegy 'Aunt Helen' – a poem which studiously undermines the expected sentiment, proper feelings, emotional decorum. 'But shortly afterwards the parrot died too.' The poem discovers for us what we sometimes feel at the moment of bereavement – *nothing*. Camus's novella *L'Etranger* records something similar when Meursault, during a nightlong vigil, observes the grief of his dead mother's last wrinkled beau. The tears do not course down but make their way through the intricacies of his facial irrigation system. Without Eliot, without modernism's resolute scepticism, its refusal of the habitual, Camus's Meursault is unthinkable. But the idea that what we really feel may be different from what we *think* we feel grows, too, out the strong social imperatives of Victorianism. E. M. Forster's novels display what one might call ur-modernism – the idea of living a lie, which we find denounced by Ansell in *The Longest Journey*, when he excoriates the false marriage between Agnes and Rickie. After modernism proper, we find something similar to ur-modernism in existentialism's concept of *mauvaise foi* – not being true to oneself. But in central modernism, the problem is not choosing wrongly, but knowing what it is that choice involves. How do we *know* what we really feel?

*The Waste Land* is clearly a poem about the failure of feeling, the sense that the heart-springs are dried up. And the waste land, the desert, is a remarkably candid emblem of the condition

317

of spiritual and emotional *accidie* – of dryness. We can see this quite clearly in 'Choruses from *The Rock*', Eliot's morality play, where we learn that the desert is within us and not a remote geographical landscape – that its topos is psychic for Eliot. It is odd that, after close on a century of academic bafflement and assiduous inquiry, the poem should yield up its secret so equably at last and so simply. Of course, we must be wary. In *The Use of Poetry and the Use of Criticism*, Eliot put 'meaning' firmly in its place – somewhere between the writer's conception and the reader's reception – and in any case secondary to the fusion of content and form. 'Meaning', Eliot wrote, 'is there to satisfy one habit of the reader's mind before the poem gets on with its real work – much as the imaginary burglar is always provided with a bit of nice meat for the house dog.' The 'real work' of *The Waste Land* is its extraordinary dynamic of registers and the assurance with which, for example, Eliot co-opts demotic pub conversation into his poetic enterprise. Lil's false friend's authentic colloquial attack is reproduced by Eliot with towering aesthetic assurance. 'It's them pills I took, to bring it off, she said.' He is stylistically unembarrassed by this flagrant ordinariness because it is, in addition to being realistic, a new and singular sound to add to what is already an astonishingly diverse palette of sounds. Never has such aural richness been brought to the theme of spiritual dryness. The sound-world of *The Waste Land* is gorgeous, sumptuous, anti-selective in its accumulation of registers – and, of course, innovative in its embrace of 'unpleasantness'. It resists aural cliché, just as it resists sentimentality, a narrower, emotional cliché.

*Ash-Wednesday* was written after Eliot's Christian conversion, and is frequently misinterpreted as a poem of belief, when it is, in fact, a poem about the difficulty of religious belief. Incidentally and centrally, it is also a poem about the difficulty of knowing what we really feel. It begins with a statement of manifold despair, of hopelessness – from which the speaker then chooses the way of renunciation, the *via negativa* as a route to God and belief. The speaker sets aside life – its beauties, its temptations: 'Blown hair is sweet, brown hair over the mouth blown.' Yet, at the poem's climax, Eliot shows us the visceral nature of thought. Wishing to believe, willing oneself to affirm, cannot silence the true, unfakable feeling: we 'affirm before the world and deny between the rocks'. *Ash-Wednesday* ends with an involuntary, helpless declaration of love for the already renounced sensual world. It is one of the most moving passages in the whole of English poetry:

> And the weak spirit quickens to rebel
> For the bent golden-rod and the lost sea smell
> Quickens to recover
> The cry of quail and the whirling plover . . .

The Eliotean gift is finally vigilance – an aural vigilance that is intolerant of boredom, an intellectual vigilance that questions everything, that takes nothing for granted. Not even ghosts, that literary staple that continues to be lazily tolerated as an allowable convention. At the beginning of *Burnt Norton*, Eliot re-imagines the ghost as a serious reality – and does this by fastidiously withholding from his readers that stale, familiarizing nomenclature. He never once uses the word 'ghosts' – and this act of verbal continence chimes with the Hulmean credo cited in *The Use of Poetry and the Use of Criticism*: 'but each man sees a little differently, and to get out clearly and exactly what he does see, he must have a terrific struggle with language [which] has its own special nature, its own conventions and communal ideas. It is only by a concentrated effort of your mind that you can hold it to your own purpose.' Eliot, of course, coined the phrase, 'the intolerable wrestle / With words and meanings' – and he was one of the great wrestlers, a specialist in pinning down the object as in itself it really is. Whether it was ghosts, love, the difficulty of religious belief or the difficulty of saying what it is you mean.

# In Defence of T. S. Eliot

'I am not an anti-Semite and never have been,' Eliot insisted. 'It is a terrible slander on a man.' Eliot himself, then, knew precisely what was at stake. Anti-Semitism is a charge of the utmost gravity. It cannot be brushed aside, or evaded. And now there are, as it were, three prosecuting barristers in the field opposed to Eliot – Anthony Julius, the author of *T. S. Eliot, Anti-Semitism and Literary Form*, the Professor of Poetry at Oxford, James Fenton, and the Irish poet Tom Paulin. I think it is fair to say that the substance of Professor Fenton's recent lecture in Oxford repeated a great deal of the matter in Tom Paulin's article in the *London Review of Books* (vol. 18, no. 9) only because both men are essentially representing Julius's material to a larger public. They add their own insights, but the main substance of their argument is taken from Julius's book. Professor Christopher Ricks has also examined the charges of anti-Semitism laid against Eliot in his book *T. S. Eliot and Prejudice* (1988). Ricks found that there were some charges to answer but entered a plea of mitigation because Eliot's poem 'Little Gidding' expressed a general regret for 'things ill done and done to others' harm / Which once you took for exercise of virtue' – lines which Ricks took to be a reference to Eliot's anti-Semitism, obliquely expressed. Julius, Fenton and Paulin will have none of this. Professor Fenton concluded his lecture by denouncing Eliot as a 'scoundrel'. Anthony Julius throughout his book maintains a formal position that he admires Eliot's poetry, but his use of the evidence is candidly adversarial. His Eliot is not simply an anti-Semite but also a racist and a misogynist.

Eliot says of Milton, 'we can certainly enjoy the poetry and yet be fully aware of the intellectual and moral aberrations of the author'. This is my position on Eliot. It is neither necessary nor desirable that one should endorse his every opinion. His mindset can seem unsympathetic and sometimes rebarbative. But anti-Semitism is a special case. The holocaust has made it so. And were the charge proven, the perceived moral blemish would effectively occlude the literary achievement. Time forgives no one for writing well. We have the marginalized genius of Kipling as a sad example before us.

In these circumstances, it is interesting to see what can be said in Eliot's defence. Julius opens his prosecution case by citing a famous instance of anti-Semitism in Eliot's work, from *After Strange Gods*, the 1933 Page-Barbour Lectures given by Eliot at the University of Virginia. The crucial passage is this: 'the population should be homogeneous; where two or more cultures exist in the same place they are likely either to be fiercely self-conscious or both to become adulterate. What is still more important is unity of religious background; and reasons of race and religion combine to make any large number of free-thinking Jews undesirable. There must be a proper balance between urban and rural, industrial and agricultural development. And a spirit of excessive tolerance is to be deprecated.' Though these four sentences are in their entirety an unfortunate collocation, for which Eliot has been properly harried over the years, it is that last sentence which particularly sticks in the craw of Professor Ricks. 'Excessive tolerance' is a subheading of Chapter 2, 'Anti-Semitism'. Ricks interprets this to mean Eliot is advocating intolerance: 'for this allows him to promise a dishonourable pardon to those who act out their intolerance, while not himself being openly inflammatory since his way of putting it maintains nothing'. A covert encouragement to intolerance, therefore, masked by the word 'excessive' which Professor Ricks finds circular or vacant.

But suppose for a charitable moment that Eliot meant exactly what he said. Suppose that the word 'excessive' was neither circular nor vacant, but carried the meaning it normally does. What we readers would be left with then, is this – a sentence which advocated a *degree* of tolerance. Much as, say, both the main parties in this country restrict immigration, while admitting a proportion of cases.

Of course, it is simpler to convict Eliot of anti-Semitism – a verdict which appeals to our sense of *Schadenfreude*, our contemporary instinct for what Milan Kundera has eloquently called 'criminography', by which he means the desire to arraign artists on exclusively moral grounds, the desire to annihilate rather than administer complicated justice, the desire to consider only the faults and ignore the virtues and the achievements. Eliot knew all about what he called 'seductive simplicity' – 'the direct and persuasive appeal to intellect and emotions' that is likely to be 'altogether more plausible than the truth'. My own instinct is for complication.

'And a spirit of excessive tolerance is to be deprecated.' If we read this sentence literally, without prejudice, as *advocating tolerance* on a limited front, it clearly affects the way in which we read the previous troubling sentence – 'reasons of race and religion combine to make any large number of free-thinking Jews undesirable'. This sentence would now mean that Eliot was quite prepared to accept limited numbers of free-thinking Jews.

As it happens, there is another piece of evidence in Eliot's defence which supports my reading of those problematic sentences. It was always been there in the text of *After Strange Gods*, but you would not see it if you were *expecting* to convict Eliot of anti-Semitism. And it is crucial and decisive, in this instance. The Page-Barbour Lectures address the need (as Eliot sees it) to establish or revive 'a tradition and a way of life'. He defines tradition thus: 'all those habitual actions, habits and customs, from the most significant religious rite to our conventional way of greeting a stranger'. These things, Eliot maintains, 'represent the blood kinship of "the same people living in the same place"'. Nowadays of course, even the mention of 'blood kinship' makes us understandably nervous. When Professor Fenton lectured, he drew attention to the quotation marks around the phrase '"the same people living in the same place"'. But he did not know where the quotation came from. He has not read Joyce's *Ulysses*. Or he has not read it recently enough. Nor have Tom Paulin, Professor Ricks or Anthony Julius.

Eliot's definition of a nation comes from the 'Cyclops' episode of Joyce's great and famously tolerant novel. It is Leopold Bloom's definition of a nation, offered to the bigoted Citizen whose rampant anti-Semitism wishes to expel the Semite interloper from the Irish nation. Leopold Bloom is a free-thinking Jew. And his definition, which is also his defence of his right to live in Ireland, is a definition that the allegedly anti-Semitic Eliot is happy to share. This insight should give us pause, both specifically and generally. By consciously alluding to Leopold Bloom, Eliot effectively includes free-thinking Jews in his recipe for a unified culture. Perhaps, after all, reluctantly, we can agree that Eliot's use of the word 'excessive' was neither vacuous, nor circular, but strictly accurate. So that this famous *locus* of Eliot's anti-Semitism in *After Strange Gods* can be seen as nothing of the kind – but rather the equivalent of the Labour Party's immigration policy. If we accept this, I think we should be more inclined to accept also that Eliot meant what he said, when, in correspondence with J. V. Healy, he maintained that he was arguing the undesirability of 'free-thinkers of any race' in large numbers – and that free-thinking Jews are 'only a special case.' By this, Eliot means that, given the diaspora, free-thinking Jews are less likely than free-thinking Christians to retain the vestiges of their religion. This is surely uncontroversial even if arguable. Free-thinking Christians in Europe do live, or did live, in a basically Christian culture.

The general point which arises from the unforeseen intervention of the free-thinking Leopold Bloom is that, just as it is fatal to misunderstand the use of quotation marks in *After Strange Gods*, so, when it comes to a consideration of Eliot's poetry, it is dangerous to pronounce, as Anthony Julius often does, from a position of partial comprehension. These are very difficult poems. Yet Julius is prepared to preface hostile readings of Eliot's poems thus: 'While the poem cannot be reduced to a resolvable riddle, its hostility to Jews is instantly recognizable'; 'whatever its interpretative obscurities. . .'.

323

But Julius has a lawyer's way with evidence. He knows how to present a damaging case. For instance, his book is prefaced with an epigraph which tells us how Eliot was summarily turned out of a house in South Africa when his hostess, a Jew, read the anti-Semitic lines in 'Burbank with a Baedeker: Bleistein with a Cigar'. In his introductory salvo, Julius refers again to the anecdote and says that he hopes 'to keep faith' with it. In a footnote, however, he does no such thing. There, more than two hundred pages away, he tells us that the quotation is, in fact, 'at best, a melodramatic and telescoped version of the truth'. The truth, apparently, is to be found in the correspondence located in the Sarah Gertrude Millin Collection at the William Cullen Library at the University of Witwatersrand. While Julius supplies all this information, he doesn't tell us what the truth is. Perhaps because he didn't know precisely. He thanks a Lavinia Braun for 'this information'. By now, he has probably been to Johannesburg.

As a matter of fact, there is probably an unsinister explanation for this discrepancy between the symbolic epigraph and the bathetic disclaimer in the endnotes. The information arrived as his book was in the press and only an acknowledgement was possible in the notes.

In conceding this, I am aping, sincerely, the opening of Julius's book where he acquits Eliot of two charges of anti-Semitism – the better to prosecute his case elsewhere. Julius would like us to think him adversarial but fair. Actually, I think he is often unfair. For instance, he maintains that Eliot learned from French culture that 'a vigorous anti-Semitism' was 'compatible with cordial salon relations with Jews'. The relevant endnote refers us to Edouard Roditi, whose testimony is pro-Eliot: 'he even suggested publishing . . . one of my overtly Jewish poems . . . he expressed to me on several occasions after 1933 his horror of the anti-Semitic outrages in Nazi Germany'. This, I submit, manifestly exceeds Julius's lukewarm description of it in the main text as hypocritical cordiality.

Or take Eliot on Marx. Julius finds Eliot's evocation of Marx as a 'Jewish economist' an example of 'insulting' anti-Semitism:

'Describing Marx as a "Jewish economist", when he was less than a Jew and more than an economist, is insulting.' Marx was a Jew indifferent to Judaism, if not hostile. Eliot's offending sentence reads in full: 'I never expected that Hegel, having been inverted by a Jewish economist for his own purposes, should come back again into the favour.' The 'Jewish economist' *is* odd but it is odd for a reason which is not anti-Semite. Eliot is relishing an irony. Julius should recognize this because he provides the necessary information thirty pages earlier for a proper appreciation of the irony. Hegel was a noted anti-Semite. For Hegel, 'Judaism is . . . the fulfilment of ugliness.'

I must, reluctantly, leave consideration of details, the proper weighing of each iota of evidence, and come to my general objection to Julius's methodology. Which is guilt by association. His thesis is that Eliot placed his great gifts at the service of anti-Semitism – that he invigorates the stale clichés bandied about by rabid anti-Semites. Inevitably, this places Eliot in criminal, pathological company and assumes an equation between the articulate Eliot and the most cruel excesses of anti-Semitic discourse. I think this unlikely because I believe Eliot to have been proud of his intellectual independence. Remember, it was Eliot who admired Henry James for possessing 'a mind so fine that no idea could violate it'. There are three allegedly anti-Semitic lines in 'Gerontion':

> My house is a decayed house,
> And the Jew squats on the window-sill, the owner,
> Spawned in some estaminet of Antwerp,
> Blistered in Brussels, patched and peeled in London.

Julius prefaces this quotation prejudicially: 'the passage breathes hate, the sibilants hissing scorn'. We are then told that the speaker, Gerontion, *in these lines*, is 'spitting at the Jew in this opening stanza'. Untrue. But Julius arrives at this baseless reading by asserting that 'the word these other words intimate is "spit"'. And he cites Shakespeare's *Merchant* – Antonio's spitting and Shylock's bitter complaint about being spat on. I do not see why. The neutral verb 'squats' does not seem intrinsically anti-Semitic. For instance, Kim habitually rests 'knees to chin': 'said Kim affably, squatting in the shade beside the lama'. Or Tekla in *Under Western Eyes*: 'she had squatted down to put it [a small bowl] on the floor for the benefit of a large cat'. This demonstrably harmless word provokes Julius to cite examples from anti-Semitic discourse in which Jews are forced to squat because they suffer from leprosy. Nor is Julius slow to emphasize the excremental connotations of 'squat'. 'Blistered', 'patched' and 'peeled', in Julius's account of these adjectives, add to leprosy, smallpox, lupus, trachoma, favus, eczema and scurvy. The verb 'spawned', while hardly flattering, hardly supports Julius's extrapolation – that Gerontion's Jew 'emerges as if from the swamp'. But it does permit him to cite, at length, disgusting examples of anti-Semitic discourse which stigmatize Jews as leeches, frogs, 'swamp-life'. But they are not examples from Eliot. Their connection with Eliot is nugatory. Read Eliot's lines again. Here is the central weakness of Julius's thesis about Eliot as the gifted invigorator of anti-Semitic clichés. The lines of Eliot quoted are anodyne, torpid, compared to the anthology amassed by Julius from outside the poetry.

Eliot in an early essay, 'The Function of Criticism', deplored the kind of interpretative criticism which 'is always producing parts of the body from its pockets, and fixing them in place'. This is Julius's method – one of wholesale importation. Moreover, with 'Gerontion', Julius is forced to deny that the poem is a dramatic monologue – which it manifestly is – so that he can attribute the three lines of anti-Semitism to Eliot directly. Julius can be a very inaccurate reader. In 'Gerontion', what interests me is the conflation of house, owner and (possibly) tenant. Eliot is surely touching on the idea of lineage and deracination which encompasses all three.

When Julius comes to the infamous 'Burbank with a Baedeker: Bleistein with a Cigar', he once more, understandably, editorializes Eliot's words. Again, he is anxious to rule out the possibility that the poem is a dramatic monologue, with a loophole therefore through which the anti-Semitic Eliot could escape. On the other hand, he cannot resist the introduction of theatre because it improves his argument against Eliot. 'One *imagines* a pose being struck'; 'one *imagines* the sentence lispingly spoken'. (My italics.) I imagine nothing of the kind. This is a difficult poem to defend. I myself have always thought the crucial lines represented Eliot's anti-Semitism: 'The rats are underneath the piles. / The Jew is underneath the lot.' I have changed my mind.

> . . . On the Rialto once.
> The rats are underneath the piles.
> The Jew is underneath the lot.
> Money in furs. The boatman smiles . . .

There is anti-Semitism here. But it is not Eliot's. It must be Burbank's. The two crucial, middle lines are framed, fatally for Julius's argument, by two incomplete phrases, 'On the Rialto once' and 'Money in furs', whose truncation, were we to encounter it in *Ulysses*, would instantly indicate interior monologue. They would indicate interior monologue anywhere, as a matter of fact, except in Eliot when one reads prejudicially. Basically Burbank's anti-Semitism is a public posture produced by a private derangement – Bleistein's titular cigar, not mentioned in the poem, tells us that he has succeeded sexually with Princess Volupine where Burbank has failed.

There is, I know, a difficulty still awaiting attention in the poem.

> A lustreless protrusive eye
> Stares from the protozoic slime
> At a perspective of Canaletto.
> The smoky candle end of time
>
> Declines.

Following on the stanza describing Bleistein, these lines naturally attach to him, in a way that is morally unacceptable. Julius

envisages Bleistein in an art gallery, *failing* to appreciate Canaletto (my italics, Julius's assumption). I wish to propose a
different reading – a reading which takes 'the smoky candle end
of time' declining as a helpful explanatory gloss on the preceding
lines with their *metaphorical* 'protrusive eye'. We are being
offered not a disgusting example of anti-Semitism, but rather a
description of a sunset – the pale evening sun sinking into the
Venice lagoon and shining on architectural vistas often painted
by Canaletto. In other words, we have not an anti-Semitic poem,
but a poem about anti-Semitism. This new interpretation will
seem implausible for a time, in the way that radical re-readings
do before they become accepted.

It will seem implausible, too, because there are so many
references to Jews in Eliot's poetry and prose and correspondence. It seems a reasonable presumption, given the amount of
evidence assembled by Julius, that Eliot is, at least in some
instances, anti-Semitic. I myself think that Eliot was obsessed by
the Jews at a particular period of his life. And it is possible to
believe this without believing that Eliot was the rabid yet subtle
anti-Semite we find in Julius's reading. James Fenton mentioned
in his lecture that Louis Menand has uncovered a correspondence between his patron John Quinn and Eliot which was anti-
Semitic in places – though the worst offender is clearly Quinn.
Fenton also told me privately that Sir Isaiah Berlin had had a
correspondence with Eliot about anti-Semitism. I should like to
read it, as well as the Quinn correspondence. At the moment,
we have not assembled all the evidence. Julius's book is at best
premature. At the moment, for instance, it is forced to rely on
the assumption that Eliot wrote the review of *The Yellow Spot*
(1936, the first documentary account of mistreatment of
German Jews) which appeared unsigned in *The Criterion*. We
simply do not know if Eliot wrote it. It is inadmissible evidence.
Nor is Eliot responsible for the piece because he was the editor.
Ask any literary editor how responsible they are for the content
of reviews commissioned. In any case, the review is not anti-
Semitic. It exhibits cold pride in its unillusioned pragmatism. It
assuredly 'understates the seriousness of the book's subject

matter, while overstating its defects'. But it is not anti-Semitic: 'certainly no English man or woman would wish to be a German Jew in Germany today'.

The other piece of evidence singled out from Julius by Paulin and Fenton is the tasteless 'Dirge'. 'Dirge' is a parody of Ariel's song in *The Tempest*. It is one of several ironic contrasts with the past. It is dangerously coterminous with anti-Semitism because it is coarsely reliant on caricature. Which may be why Eliot suppressed it. But it is intemperate of Julius to call it an anti-Semitic 'torture fantasy' – especially so when you *contrast* it with the authentic anti-Semitic torture fantasies supplied by Julius for the purpose of incriminating comparison. The manner of Bleistein's death is dictated by literary considerations – the parody – not by a determination to mock Jewish 'stateless transience'. As a misreading, this is as fatuous as Julius finding 'The Love Song of J. Alfred Prufrock' misogynist.

Suppose, however, that when all the evidence is in, posterity convicts Eliot of anti-Semitism. What then? It could be the case. Julius wants to censure, not censor. But my own instinct is to mitigate. If Eliot turns out, in his correspondence, say, to be anti-Semitic, it will not be simple. And I adduce three pieces of evidence, here, of Eliot's pro-Semitism. The first is the attack on the Blackshirts in *The Rock* – an attack which is specifically centred on their anti-Semitism. Here is the relevant quotation:

BLACKSHIRTS: Your vesture, your gesture, your speech
and your face,
Proclaim your extraction from Jewish race.
We have our own prophets, who're ready to speak
For a week and a day and a day and a week.
This being the case, we must firmly refuse
To descend to palaver with anthropoid Jews.

Obviously, this passage presents no difficulty for my case. But it is an embarrassment for Julius and Fenton. To any unprejudiced reader, the passage is hostile to the Blackshirts because they are contemporary examples of anti-Semitic hatred. Julius equivocates: on p. 106 he concedes that here 'anti-Semitism of a kind is repudiated expressly'. Note the reservation: 'of a kind'. Ninety pages later, Julius's argument shifts: 'the rejection of the Blackshirts' anti-Semitism is a rejection of anti-Christian paganism . . . It is not a plea for modern Jewry, it is an endorsement of Christianity . . .'

My second piece of evidence is Eliot's sympathetic account of the persecution of the Jews in the diaspora in 'A Song for Simeon':

> Who shall remember my house, where shall live my
> children's children
> When the time of sorrow is come?
> They will take to the goat's path, and the fox's home,
> Fleeing from the foreign faces and the foreign swords.

Julius knows that this presents a difficulty for his thesis, and he tries to answer it without properly alerting his reader. The crucial question is this: *when* is 'the time of sorrow'? Julius answers: 'not the moment of the dispersion of the Jews but that of the trials of Christ, and of the early Christians'. I think the phrase 'my children's children' means 'posterity', but at the very least it means two generations. Even if taken literally, then, the phrase 'my children's children' is hardly synchronous with Christ's trial and crucifixion. But obviously the phrase is employed metaphorically for a posterity persecuted by 'foreign swords' and 'foreign faces'. Pogroms, in fact.

In the *London Review of Books* (31 August 1989), A. V. C. Schmidt long ago disposed of Erik Svarny's contention that 'Eliot did not repudiate Maurras's anti-Semitism'. Schmidt quoted Eliot's contribution to the *Christian News-Letter* of 3 September 1941, which condemned anti-Semitic policies being introduced in Vichy France:

> What gives us the gravest anxiety, is the statement [in *The Times* article cited] that 'Jews have been given a special status, based on the laws of Nuremberg, which makes

their condition little better than that of bondsmen'. Anti-Semitism there has always been, among the parties of the extreme right: but it was a very different thing, as a symptom of the disorder of French society and politics for the last hundred and fifty years, from what it is when it takes place as a principle of reconstruction . . . *we can only hope that there has been, or that there will be, some organized protest against such injustice* [my italics], by the French ecclesiastical hierarchy: unless we are also optimistic enough to hope that these measures are only taken under the strongest pressure from Germany, and that no French government, once that government was master in its own house, would enforce such measures or keep them on its statutes.

If he repudiated anti-Semitism, Eliot 'in doing so by logical requirement repudiated the anti-Semitism of Charles Maurras', Schmidt concluded irrefutably. Nothing could be plainer than Eliot's explicit recognition of the fundamental injustice of anti-Semitism. Julius will have none of it. He massages the passage perversely and prejudicially like a tyro Deconstructionist until he can conclude *from this evidence* that 'Eliot had the imagination of an anti-Semite in the highest degree. He was alive to anti-Semitism's resources, insensitive to Jewish pain'. Eliot: 'we can only hope that there has been . . . some organized protest against such injustice'. When Julius weighs the evidence, it's as well to solicit a second opinion from a weights and measures inspector. The 'fluid' ounce takes on a changed semantic penumbra.

To these particular examples I would like to add a more general plea of mitigation. Milan Kundera, in *Testaments Betrayed*, one of the century's great and wise books, says that man is not in the dark, but in a fog. 'He sees fifty yards ahead of him, he can clearly make out the features of his interlocutor, can take pleasure in the beauty of the trees that line the path, and can even observe what is happening close by and react. Man proceeds in the fog. But when he looks back to judge the people of the past, he sees no fog on their path . . . their path looks perfectly clear to him, good visibility all the way. Looking back, he sees the patch, he sees the people proceeding, he sees their mistakes, but not the fog.' What a measured and just rebuke to self-righteousness this is. If there prove to be anti-Semitic elements in the record left by Eliot, we should bear this rebuke in mind.

# Evidence in the Eliot Case

What constitutes evidence? In these difficult times for T. S. Eliot's reputation, the answer to this question is crucial – and it is brought into acute focus by this edition of Eliot's previously unpublished early poetry. Recently, the debate about Eliot's alleged anti-Semitism was reopened by Anthony Julius's *T. S. Eliot, Anti-Semitism and Literary Form*. In England, the poets Tom Paulin and James Fenton lent their authority to Julius's cause, summarizing and supplementing his arguments for a wider audience. In America, Louis Menand further supplemented Julius's study in the *New York Review of Books*, excitably headlined 'The Anti-Semitism of T. S. Eliot'.

One interesting shared feature of all these attacks was the centrality given to an unsigned review in Eliot's magazine, *The Criterion*. The book reviewed was *The Yellow Spot* (1936, the first documentary account of the mistreatment of German Jews). It seemed odd to grant so much significance to something anonymous. All four critics, however, were sure that the piece was by Eliot. All four were sure it was anti-Semitic. In this, it should be said, they were in agreement with a longish line of previous Eliot scholars, among them Christopher Ricks, the editor of the book under review. In fact, the review exhibits a cold detachment, pride in its pragmatism, and seriously underestimates the problem, but it is not anti-Semitic: 'certainly no Englishman or woman would wish to be a German Jew in Germany today'.

*Inventions of the March Hare: Poems 1909–1917* by T. S. Eliot, edited by Christopher Ricks, Faber.

Nor was the review written by Eliot, despite the scholarly consensus. In due course, Valerie Eliot, the poet's widow, having examined the financial records of the magazine, identified the author of the contested review as Montgomery Belgion. Julius had written that, if he were wrong in attributing the authorship to Eliot, he would have done him an 'injustice'. His subsequent letter to *The Times Literary Supplement* conceded nothing in the way of apology, but instead complained that scholars were at the mercy of the poet's widow. Why, he wanted to know, hadn't this fact been disclosed before now? Alas for Julius, the very next day a letter was printed in the *London Review of Books* pointing out that Mrs Eliot's research was not strictly necessary since book reviewers were identified in the index of *The Criterion*. All the scholars had to do was consult the index. None of them had done so. Instead, they had used against Eliot an unsigned review for which there was no evidence of Eliot's authorship. The unwarranted prominence given to *The Yellow Spot* review by Julius, Paulin, Fenton and Menand demonstrates a determination to convict the poet of anti-Semitism which itself verges on the prejudicial. Ironically, the 'anti-Semitic' author of *The Yellow Spot* review is the identical Montgomery Belgion who, in the last number of Eliot's *Criterion*, though an admirer of Maurras in certain respects, singled out for specific criticism Maurras's Action Française as 'rabidly anti-Jewish'. There is comedy in the gaffe, of course, but it is profoundly disturbing that four reputable critics should have admitted as evidence in the first place something so demonstrably flimsy. Five if you include Christopher Ricks.

We all make mistakes. Which brings me to Professor Ricks, whose annotations take up 200 pages of the volume under review – adding approximately £15 to the published price. Only days after Professor Ricks's gifted acolyte, Dr Eric Griffiths, had acclaimed his mentor's matchless editing, readers of the *Guardian* were writing in to point out a howler. A bawdy poem, 'There was a jolly tinker', attributed to Eliot by Professor Ricks, had, apparently, been sung by rugger teams since, oooh, 1719, when 'The Ball of Kirriemuir' was first published. [In the *TLS* for 6 June 1997, Professor Ricks mounted his belated defence. Rugby teams had only been singing 'The Ball of Kirriemuir' since 1817. Moreover, he argued that 'Eliot was writing variations, dud ones unfortunately, on a good old theme, and the poem ['Fragments'] is both his and the tradition's'. The authorship controversy could have been avoided had Ricks said this in the first place – i.e., done his editorial job properly and annotated the dirty poems. Why didn't he? His *TLS* piece gave no reason at all. But the reason was probably that permission to include the bawdy poems in his edition was withheld until it was too late for Ricks's customary saturation annotation.]

I don't wish to dwell on this since the bawdy poems are those which, exceptionally for this editor, strike me as under-edited. In the misattributed ballad in question, for example, what is 'hongpronged'? In the King Bolo poems, what *is* a 'pooper'? What is 'Muriatic Acid'? What is 'argyrol'? Are 'whistling chancres' said to be whistling because they are puckered like a whistling mouth, or because they go right through? Professor Ricks is silent on these matters. But his whole approach to these bawdy poems is 'politic, cautious' and not especially meticulous. There is something prim, tepid and spinsterish about his presentation of the poems here. He knows that they will attract 'the wrong kind of volume of attention', but he doesn't defend them. They are there for completeness. Ricks's silence is eloquent. We can hear the dissociation of his sensibility from Eliot's in this area. *Guardian* readers are evidently more robust. Eliot's bawdy poems are scarcely to be compared with masterpieces like 'The Miller's Tale' or 'The Ballad of Eskimo Nell'. Filth wasn't his forte and there are only occasional displays of Eliot's linguistic gifts – 'a big black *knotty* penis'. (My italics.) Generically, these poems are easy to defend against those politically correct readers who object that they are racist, misogynist and, er, dirty. Of course they are. The point of scatological verse is that it *knows* it is transgressive. The true racist thinks he is right. The writer of scatological verse knows he has gone too far. This is what we mean by licence – permission to do so. The alternative is bawdy poetry characterized by its prudence, propriety and moral hygiene. We may be heading for a period when this licence is temporarily revoked, but, seen historically, Eliot's poems are properly improper.

In his introduction, Christopher Ricks professes a desire to be invisible. In this sense – he thinks it editorially improper to interpose his interpretations between the poetry and the reader. You can read the poems without consulting the notes because they are not at the foot of the page. (A procedure unavailable to the reviewer.) The professed restraint obtains in that Professor Ricks seldom tells us what anything means in this sometimes difficult poetry. I for one would have been grateful for more interpretative direction. Otherwise, the annotation is incontinent.

In a recent lecture, I heard Professor Ricks distinguish between notes that helped to elucidate what had gone into the making of the poetry and those which dealt with the meaning. The poet might be unaware of what had gone into the making of his poems. There *are* some excellent notes here: for instance, Ricks's dry observation about the omnibus, 'long a conventionally unconventional poetic setting'. But there are other notes which suggest that Ricks has spent too long combing the English Poetry Database on CD-ROM. If all these alleged echoes come to him unassisted, he should seek medical advice urgently. An example of absurdity fathered by brilliance on diligence: the poem 'Afternoon' contains the following three words well separated over five lines, 'Assyrian', 'perfume' and 'hats'. In Tennyson's *Maud*, scattered over four lines, Professor Ricks has found 'Assyrian' and (contain your impatience) 'Smelling' and 'millinery'. Q.E.D. In his defence, Ricks could quote Eliot on Livingstone Lowes, the critic who traced images and phrases in 'Kubla Khan' and 'The Ancient Mariner' back to Coleridge's voracious reading: 'Lowes showed, once and for all, that poetic originality is largely an original way of assembling the most disparate and unlikely material to make a new whole.' As a defence of Ricks's method, this would be more convincing if so many of his citations did not come from Tennyson and Milton, authors in whom Ricks has famously vested his interest.

And one might quote against Ricks from the same Eliot essay: 'one can explain a poem by investigating what it is made of and the causes that brought it about; and explanation may be a necessary preparation for understanding. But to understand a poem it is also necessary . . . that we should endeavour to grasp what the poetry is aiming to be.' Eliot candidly avowed that one Livingstone Lowes was enough. Now we have another. The additional point to be made about that *Maud* parallel is that it makes no contribution to the meaning of Eliot's poem. If anything, it gets in the way. And it is typical. Ingenious and absurd, an irritating distraction.

'Suppressed Complex' is a rather cruelly ironic poem in which a girl thinks that the ghost she can see in the corner of her bedroom is a figment caused by her neurosis (the 'complex' of the title). Her terror is evoked laconically by her 'stubborn eyes'. Even in her sleep, she is 'very pale and breathe[s] hard'. However, the poem is narrated by the ghost: 'I passed joyously through the window', having amused itself in the torment of the girl. Ricks's two and a half pages of notes tell you nothing of this. The self-denial seems perverse – as perverse as the unwarranted assumption commonly made by editors that their readers are all fluent French speakers and therefore require no translations. You will need a good dictionary here.

Another poem, 'Hidden under the heron's wing', begins with an evocation of the beloved's presence somehow in natural phenomena. The meniscus of lyricism ('With evening feet walking across the grass / And fragile arms dividing the evening mist') ruptures swiftly and radically, thus: 'I lie on the floor a bottle's broken glass / To be swept away by the housemaid's crimson fist.' Such is Ricks's continence that he doesn't tell us that the broken glass is a skewed and therefore powerful emblem of a broken heart, or perhaps of a nervous breakdown, and certainly of a relationship gone smash. It could be that Professor Ricks successfully resists the temptation to tell us all because such explanations strike him as reductive – that poetry itself is too simple for him and he is irritated into complicating it.

At the lecture I mentioned earlier, Professor Ricks also

touched on the furore surrounding Eliot's anti-Semitism. It was a characteristic intervention. 'There are those,' he claimed, 'who have argued that Eliot chose the word "estaminet" [in 'Geron-tion'] because it is an anagram of "anti-Semite".' Broad brief grin. He soon disposed of this fatuous ingenuity. Apart from anything else, 'estaminet' is one letter short. At the same time, however, he could see that Eliot had encoded *Polonius* in the line from 'Prufrock', '*Poli*tic, cautious, and meti*culous*'. No doubt he will correct me, but I find it hard to expel the suspicion that no one except Professor Ricks has suggested 'estaminet' is an anagram of 'anti-Semite'. [I was wrong. Ricks in the *TLS*, 14 March 1997, cited David Spurr in *PMLA*, 1994.] He has chosen to disown his insight before defusing it. The encoding of 'Polon-ius' is just as ludicrous but only a really clever man in full flight from the obvious could have thought of either.

No wonder, therefore, that in his *T. S. Eliot and Prejudice*, when he came to consider Eliot's notorious comment about 'free-thinking Jews', Ricks should have rejected the obvious meaning – like countless others, before and after him. Consider this sentence: 'Excessive consumption of alcohol is to be dep-recated.' Does this imply a need for total prohibition? No. It implies that alcohol should be consumed in moderation. Eliot's much quoted collocation reads: 'The population should be homogeneous; where two or more cultures exist in the same place they are likely either to be fiercely self-conscious or both to become adulterate. What is still more important is unity of religious background; and reasons of race and religion combine to make any large number of free-thinking Jews undesirable.' 'And a spirit of excessive tolerance is to be deprecated.' Professor Ricks sees this as a covert encouragement to intolerance. He is wrong. It is rather a passage which allows for limited numbers of free-thinking Jews. The wording is unfortunate, but the intention behind it is not inflammatory. It is moderate. As for restrictions on immigration, both major political parties now accept their necessity.

In Louis Menand's essay-review of Anthony Julius, Eliot's qualification, '*free-thinking* Jews', went missing by the end of the piece. It became 'the direct reference to the undesirability of Jews'. Menand's attack was the most temperate so far, conceding that anti-Semitism was 'a relatively minor aspect' of Eliot's thought: 'part of the reason it was so half-baked even as anti-Semitism was that Eliot didn't give much attention to it, and in most of the poetry and almost all of the literary criticism it fades into insignificance'. Nevertheless, Menand's methodology proved to be remarkably like that of Julius – guilt by association. Menand tells us that Julius is heavily dependent on Leon Poliakov's four-volume *History of Anti-Semitism* – a rabid context which, on the face of it, looks a mite improbable for T. S. Eliot, O.M. and Nobel Prize winner. Menand's essay is devoted to showing us how Eliot comes to be of this company and in what way. Where Julius cites verbal echoes with as little evidential rigour as Professor Ricks, Menand cites the incriminating company Eliot kept: Pound, John Quinn, Charles Maurras and Viscount Lymington (Gerald Wallop, later the Earl of Portsmouth). The evidence here is circumstantial in the main. And it carries conviction only in so far as you believe that friendship and/or association entails the friend in sharing the opinions of his close circle in their entirety.

When I tell you that I am a close friend of James Fenton and that we disagree about Eliot's anti-Semitism, you will know how risky I consider this method of argument to be. Let me start with Viscount Lymington's *Famine in England*, a book which (Menand tells us) Eliot praised in *The Criterion* 'at some length, though in vague terms'. Menand quotes a Lymington passage denouncing immigrants and 'the foreign invasion of London' which goes on to invoke Arthur Lane's classically anti-Semitic book, *The Alien Menace*. There is no evidence that Eliot read *The Alien Menace* or that he approved of it. Certainly, the Viscount Lymington is no social democrat, but Menand seriously misrepresents his book, its analysis and its probable appeal to Eliot. Lymington argues for an agricultural revival, the stock-piling of a year's food, the abolition of death duties on land – anything, in fact, that will make England more self-sufficient and avoid a famine in the war he regards (rightly) as

339

imminent. *Famine in England* undoubtedly spoke to the agrarian
sentimentalist in Eliot whom we see in *After Strange Gods*
praising unified, rooted culture, settled on the land and opposed
to deracinated cosmopolitanism. Eliot's Commentary (October
1938) draws these conclusions from Lymington: 'What is fundamentally wrong is the *urbanization of mind* of which I have
previously spoken . . . It is necessary that the greater part of the
population, of all classes (so long as we have classes), should be
settled in the country and dependent upon it.'

Lymington *can* sound like Rachel Carson as he deplores
'reckless use of sulphate of ammonia, nitro chalk, potash and
other salts' which kill off the natural soil bacteria. He invokes
dust-bowls, deserts and deforestation caused by mismanagement
of the land – and you begin to see that, for Eliot, the waste land
was not merely an emblem of spiritual aridity ('The desert is
squeezed in the tube-train next to you, / The desert is in the
heart of your brother'). It was also a literal fact to be feared.
Lymington invokes 'the old fertility legends of Adonis and
Tammuz' as versions of good agricultural practice – the cycle of
life, decay and renewal, of earthworms and bacteria creating a
healthy humus. Lymington, too, tries to show us fear in a
handful of dust. We think of Eliot as the quintessential urban
poet but he is also a poet who finds the City 'unreal'. Several
times in this volume, Eliot touches on our impoverished commerce with the natural world: 'We hibernate among the bricks /
And live across the window panes.' This nostalgic disposition is
Arnoldian and nineteenth-century, and it allows us to see how
attractive aspects of Lymington's programme might be to Eliot.
Lymington actually uses the phrase 'merry England' as he
invokes 'the unhurried cycle of the soil' far from 'the noise,
restlessness and rootlessness of towns'. It is the antithesis of the
rootless transients in *The Waste Land* who 'go south in winter',
whose nationality is uncertain ('Bin gar keine Russin . . .')

Politically, Lymington is well to the Right: he fears communists, mistrusts foreigners, disapproves of Italian and German
dictatorships yet approves of leadership, but his assertion that
'blood and soil rule at last' isn't a declaration of solidarity with

German fascism's 'Blut und Boden'. Though he had an audience with Hitler, his faith in English breeding stock and English soil is a landowner's patriotism. In any case, Eliot is not responsible for Viscount Lymington's political opinions on the evidence adduced by Menand.

Perhaps Eliot's correspondence will tell a different tale. As it may in the case of Charles Maurras, the anti-Semitic leader of Action Française, who was convicted of collaboration and treason after the war and whose views, some of them at least, Eliot found in 1955 'exasperating' and 'deplorable'. Which views we do not precisely know, since Eliot does not absolutely repudiate Maurras. Some ideas of Maurras he still finds 'sound and strong'. The Eliot scholar Ronald Schuhard told me a research student had written to the Maurras family and been sent copies of Eliot's side of the correspondence. Letters exist, then, and will be published in due course. Till then, we must be patient and work with the evidence we have. For now, let us bear in mind Montgomery Belgion's clearly demarcated admiration for, and disavowal of, Maurras. And, of course, Eliot's condemnation of anti-Semitism in 1941: 'we can only hope that there has been, or that there will be, some organized protest against such injustice' (the *Christian News-Letter*).

The most obvious attraction of Maurras for Eliot is literary. He was one of several bickering French critics who espoused classicism as against romanticism – that is, the superiority of sense over sensibility, of reason over emotion. In 1930, Eliot commissioned for Faber a history of these intellectual tendencies, *Tradition and Barbarism*, by P. M. Jones, a French scholar from Cardiff. Jones's title tells us how much the movement had in common with Arnoldian precepts – Culture and Anarchy, obviously, but also Arnold's opposition of Attic to Asiatic. Maurras was one way Eliot could agree with Arnold without acknowledging his awkward father-figure. In essence, these French thinkers, Maurras, Benda, Lasserre, were opposed to the exaggeration of emotion – their rallying cry was that, since Rousseau, literature was effeminate, overvalued the individual personality, originality and excessive emotion. Jones is quite clear that within the movement there were disagreements – Benda, for instance, accused Maurras of 'the Romanticism of Reason'. Exactly where Eliot stood isn't clear. The participants were diverse, and Eliot, for example, praised Benda's *Belphégor* but gave his *Trahison des clercs* a tanking. Menand thinks *Belphégor* is misogynist. If it is, it is because it uses 'the female temperament' as a synecdoche for emotional incontinence. Yet these ideas lie behind Flaubert's great treatment of Emma Bovary's death by arsenic poisoning. She thinks, 'I shall go to sleep, and it will all be over.' Which is how it might be in conventional literature – feminine literature. George Eliot's 'Silly Novels by Lady Novelists'. But Flaubert gives us the poisoning as it would be: prolonged, painful, retching, vomiting blood, tasting ink, brown spots on the body, dilated pupils, convulsions, a million miles from romantic preconceptions, in fact. Eliot, like Joyce (another writer of classical temper), chose the Flaubertian, Maurrasian way. Whether this entailed the assumption of Maurras's anti-Semitism also we cannot say as yet. It does not necessarily follow.

In the meanwhile, we have Eliot's unpublished poetry of 1909 to 1917, excluded, with impeccable judgement, by Eliot from his published oeuvre, but profoundly fascinating to anyone interested in the work of a great poetic master. We have, too, richly informative drafts of 'Prufrock', 'Portrait of a Lady', 'Gerontion', 'Whispers of Immortality' – and Christopher Ricks's editorial work, carried out not wisely but too well.

# Conrad and Prejudice

'Joseph Conrad was a thoroughgoing racist.' This quotation is taken from 'An Image of Africa: Racism in Conrad's *Heart of Darkness*', a lecture delivered by the Nigerian novelist Chinua Achebe at the University of Massachusetts, Amherst, as long ago as 1974 and now collected in *Hopes and Impediments*.

In *City Without Walls*, W. H. Auden included this squib:

> Even Hate should be precise:
> very few White Folks
> have fucked their mothers.

A valid point, except that, in a sense, Auden's plea for precision is vitiated by his perfectly understandable misapprehension that 'mother-fucker' is an epithet exclusively applied to whites by blacks. Auden's experience here – that of a slightly decrepit, nervous WASP on the Lower East Side – is eloquent in its way and perhaps explains his decision to return to Oxford and Christ Church: but it did not inform him (obviously) that blacks might use the word of each other. The general point, nevertheless, remains good. Only a theoretician with a propensity to automatism would cite it as an example of 'unexamined discourse' – a holier-than-thou formula usually invoked by moral pedants attentive not to the intended meaning but to their own narrow (if important) agendas. Let us count it a bonus that Auden's

*Hopes and Impediments: Selected Essays 1967–1987* by Chinua Achebe, Heinemann.

particular encapsulation has the additional benefit of warning against the identification of one's own point of view with objectivity. And, thence, with authority.

When Christopher Ricks's *T. S. Eliot and Prejudice* was published in 1988, it attracted more than its fair share of dim-witted commentary, but perhaps the most stupid moment occurred in an otherwise well-meaning review by Dannie Abse in the *Listener* (1 December 1988). Dr Abse, usually the most modest of men, was, in this instance, adamantine in his Jewishness, and could be seen enjoying the access of authority which had accrued to him by virtue of his race and his presence, as a witness, when Emanual Litvinoff charged Eliot with anti-Semitism and was rewarded by hearing the 'contrite' Eliot describe Litvinoff's awful denunciatory poem as 'a good poem'. One might trust Dr Abse's assessment of Eliot's inner turmoil at this moment, were it not that elsewhere he shows himself capable of the most brusque judgement: 'Leonard Woolf once remarked that T. S. Eliot was "only slightly anti-semitic". I am reminded of that wise physician, Sir Adolph Abrahams, who, on his ward-rounds at Westminster, forbade medical students to utter the word "slightly". "Either a woman is pregnant or not pregnant," he would say. "She cannot be slightly pregnant, boy."'

I have two objections to this argument. First, Sir Adolph is surely wrong about pregnancy. 'Slightly pregnant' tells us immediately that the pregnancy is not advanced. As far as I know, the terms 'early' and 'late' are commonly used of pregnancy by gynaecologists, and I cannot see that 'slightly' is such an objectionable alternative to 'early'. Secondly, the analogy is false. There are clear differences of degree in anti-Semitism. No one, except Dr Abse, and possibly Sir Adolph Abrahams, 'that wise physician', is going to be unwise enough to deny a difference between the anti-Semitism of Hitler and the more complicated case of Eliot, which Christopher Ricks sifts and unpicks with his customary nimble scrupulosity.

Reviewing Peter Ackroyd's biography of Eliot (*LRB*, vol. 6, no. 20), Professor Ricks began: 'Peter Ackroyd has written a benign life of T. S. Eliot. Given the malignity visited on Eliot, this is a good deal.' I turn, deliberately, from this last sentence to George Steiner – who, on a television programme in November 1988, discussed the case of Eliot and that of Ezra Pound with Professor Ricks, Annie Cohen-Solal and Clive James. Professor Steiner began by discomfiting Ricks: there were, he remarked humorously, two attacks in the *TLS* which Professor Ricks, fresh from his transatlantic flight, would not have had time to come to terms with. A wan smile from Professor Ricks. And Steiner concluded, in a general attack on 'feline caution', that, while he could forgive Pound's 'crackerbarrel' prejudice, others who had been more guarded deserved to 'sizzle in hell'. The application to Eliot was unmistakable – as unmistakable as the adjective 'crackerbarrel' applied three times to Pound.

At the heart of the argument, Steiner completely flummoxed Professor Ricks by referring to a footnote in *Notes Towards the Definition of Culture*. The context of Professor Steiner's remarks was the culpability of silence after the holocaust – a context in which Steiner's sense of outrage harnessed Eliot to Heidegger:

> We are now after Auschwitz, and I, reading Christopher's book with immense profit, I was deeply disappointed that the great question – a text which does not appear in it (correct me if I've overlooked it) – it's when all the photographs, the whole world is looking at the photographs of Auschwitz and Belsen in '47, '48, the man addresses himself centrally to what is culture, what is society, not only, like Heidegger, the only comparison I know, after '45, the most terrible silence, a silence which I find intolerable, but a footnote for which we don't have time, page 70 in the standard edition of *Notes To*, which kind of waffles about Jews and Christians perhaps having lived too close to each other so that the borderline got kind of messy and problematic. 1948 and there, I must say, I don't know what to think. [My punctuation.]

Ricks didn't know what to think either. Hardly surprising, given Professor Steiner's syntactically amoeboid insinuation, delivered in that inimitable tone – pitched somewhere between utter conviction and feline regret. Ricks confined his reply to the more coherent argument that we cannot expect everyone to be a saint. Hardly surprisingly, too, because the footnote to which Steiner so confidently, if incoherently, appealed is, in point of fact, two footnotes. The footnote to which Steiner draws our attention here appears in the first edition of *Notes Towards the Definition of Culture*: 'Since the diaspora, and the scattering of Jews amongst peoples holding the Christian Faith, it may have been unfortunate both for these peoples and for the Jews themselves, that the culture-contact between them has had to be within those neutral zones of culture in which religion could be ignored: and the effect may have been to strengthen the illusion that there can be culture without religion.'

Of this footnote, several months before the television programme, while reviewing in the *LRB* (vol. 10, no. 9) *Visions and Blueprints: Avant-garde Culture and Radical Politics in Early Twentieth-century Europe*, Professor Steiner remarked with more clarity and more hostility: ' "Old Ez" spouted venomous, crackerbarrel Jew-baiting and lunatic Fascist economics while continuing to help individual Jews wherever he could. Nothing in Pound's black silliness equals the footnote in the *Notes Towards a [sic] Definition of Culture* in which Eliot, after Auschwitz, suggests, with feline caution, that the Jews did have some historical responsibility for the fate just visited upon them.' For all their similarities, the two Steiner glosses have unaccountably different emphases. In print, Steiner maintains that the burden of Eliot's footnote is partial Jewish responsibility for the holocaust. On television, Steiner's drift is that Eliot was culpably silent about the holocaust – a recycled view more cogently expressed in 1971, when Steiner only considered Eliot's footnote 'oddly condescending', though he found Eliot's general silence 'acutely disturbing'. The analysis given *In Bluebeard's Castle* (1971) was temperate enough and therefore ignored. Steiner's subsequent suicidal intemperateness should surprise no one. It is a cry for attention.

Let us start with the accusation of silence. However much

Steiner may want to prescribe an agenda for Eliot – in order to proscribe him – Eliot is not obliged to confine himself to Professor Steiner's preoccupations, however important they unquestionably are. I can hardly see how Eliot's silence can be advanced quite so confidently as evidence of guilt. Objectively, silence looks like absence of evidence either way. As it happens, Steiner's prescriptive instinct isn't without parallel. In his second published essay on Auden, Randall Jarrell denounced his former poetic hero in tones of scalded outrage. Auden, he wrote, was a moral solipsist: 'the universe is his own shadow on the wall beside his bed'. And Auden's offence? He had urged parents to read to their children a new edition of *Grimm's Tales* – as salutary, anti-rationalist and, in effect, politically incorrect. Jarrell invoked the camps, fire-bombing, Hiroshima, Nagasaki, and professed amazement at Auden's advice 'within months' of these events. Had Auden not considered whether 'the SS men at Lublin and Birkenau had not been told these tales by their parents'? The disproportion is all Jarrell's. His affront is a non sequitur.

It isn't difficult either to project on the footnote the ghost of Steiner's other accusation – the allocation of blame to the Jews, carried out with 'feline caution'. Yet it depends on the idea not only that Eliot was malignant but also a complete fool: no one would say such a thing in 1948, even with 'feline caution'. Steiner should 'know what to think'. Only a fool – or a bigot – wouldn't.

It is an even less likely interpretation of the footnote when you realize – as Steiner quite evidently does not, referring as he does to the 'standard' edition – that Eliot rewrote this very footnote to clarify his meaning and rule out the possibility of a misinterpretation like that of Professor Steiner. This change was not secretive. It is openly advertised by Eliot in his preface to the paperback edition in 1962. The revised footnote makes Steiner's original dubious interpretation completely untenable:

> It seems to me highly desirable that there should be close culture-contact between devout and practising Christians and devout and practising Jews. Much culture-contact in

the past has been within those neutral zones of culture in which religion can be ignored, and between Jews and Gentiles both more or less emancipated from their religious traditions. The effect may have been to strengthen the illusion that there can be culture without religion. In this context I recommend to my readers two books by Professor Will Herberg published in New York: *Judaism and Modern Man* (Farrar, Straus & Cudahy) and *Protestant-Catholic-Jew* (Doubleday).

No one can say of this that Eliot is suggesting the Jews were historically responsible for their own fate. In the light of this clarification, it is possible to say that the original wording was inept – as Eliot's emendation implicitly acknowledges – but it scarcely justifies the sentence pronounced on television with so much relish by Professor Steiner. If inept phraseology is to be punished by sizzling in hell, Professor Steiner should reconsider the transcript of his television remarks.

How does one explain Steiner's ignorance of this revised footnote? For one so engaged, he might have been expected to check. He didn't, I suggest, because the first footnote, while it appalled him, also gratified his (perfectly understandable) sense of unappeased grievance and his desire to identify a culprit. The same instinct – to punish – is at work in Chinua Achebe's essay on Conrad. Both men, Steiner and Achebe, are so vividly conscious of the pain they feel that they cannot conceive it has not been inflicted by the perpetrator they have in mind.

Achebe is not without his own careless prejudice, however. He argues, for instance, that even when allowance has been made for contemporary attitudes, there is in Conrad 'a residue of antipathy to black people which his peculiar psychology alone can explain'. A 'residue' is importantly different in degree from the 'thoroughgoing' racism imputed by Achebe when he cites Conrad's account of his first encounter with a black man. 'A certain enormous buck nigger encountered in Haiti fixed my conception of blind, furious, unreasoning rage, as manifested in the human animal to the end of my days. Of the nigger I used to dream for years afterward.' Achebe's source for this quotation is Jonah Raskin's *The Mythology of Imperialism*. Clearly, he has no idea that it comes from the preface to *Victory* or he would know that there is no indication that this is Conrad's *first* and, by implication, traumatic encounter with a black. It could be his fiftieth encounter – since Conrad is not addressing himself to the colour of skin but to the idea of brute rage, as manifested not only by the 'buck nigger' but also by a Nicaraguan, on both of whom the figure of Pedro is based. One of Achebe's complaints about *Heart of Darkness* is that the blacks are 'deprived of human expression' and 'in place of speech' make ' "a violent babble of uncouth sounds" '. But it is not only blacks who are so singled out by Conrad: Pedro and his brother Antonio sit by the camp-fire 'grunting a word or two to each other now and then, hardly human speech at all'. Nicaraguans have at least as much ground of complaint as Nigerians.

Let us look at the full quotation from the preface to *Victory*.

My contact with the faithful Pedro was much shorter and my observation of him was less complete but incomparably more anxious. It ended in a sudden inspiration to get out of his way. It was in a hovel of sticks and mats by the side of a path. As I went in there only to ask for a bottle of lemonade I have not to this day the slightest idea what in my appearance or actions could have raised his terrible ire. It became manifest to me less than two minutes after I had set eyes on him for the first time, and though immensely surprised of course I didn't stop to think it out. I took the nearest short cut – through the wall.

So much for the first prototype of the awesome Pedro. The quotation continues: '*This bestial apparition and* a certain enormous buck nigger encountered in Haiti *only a couple of months afterwards, have* fixed my conception of blind, furious, unreasoning rage, as manifested in the human animal, to the end of my days. Of the nigger I used to dream for years afterwards. *Of Pedro never. The impression was less vivid. I got away from*

*him too quickly.*' The omitted phrases I have italicized complicate Achebe's simple analysis of Conrad's 'residue of antipathy
to black people' – even if only by extending Conrad's prejudice
to certain Occidentals, in this case Spanish Americans.

In fact, the quotation proves nothing of the kind. Conrad
wishes to illustrate violence, and it is plainly a matter of
indifference to him which race is responsible – his fictional
character is based on two individuals, not two representative
racial types. Achebe, though, is keen to contrast 'the enormous
buck nigger' with Conrad's portrayal of an Englishman. Accordingly, he quotes from *A Personal Record* the passage in which
Conrad remembers seeing his 'unforgettable Englishman'. Achebe selects from Conrad's description and writes off the whole
episode as 'irrational love' to balance the 'irrational hate' for
the 'buck nigger'. Actually, it *is* an exalted portrait, touched
with comedy. But Conrad is aware that his 'unforgettable
Englishman' is not a typical figure – certainly not the representative figure Achebe implies he is. The compliment to the English
race is withheld from the majority of Englishmen. 'One does not
meet such an Englishman twice in a lifetime,' Conrad ruefully
concludes.

On the one hand, we have Achebe's assertion that *Heart of
Darkness* is 'a book which parades in the most vulgar fashion
prejudices and insults'. On the other hand, we have Conrad's
clear testimony to the evils of colonialism inside and outside the
story itself. In 'Geography and Some Explorers' Conrad unambiguously states that 'the discovery of Africa was the occasion
of the greatest outburst of reckless cruelty and greed known to
history'. In the same essay he describes his feelings of disgust on
arrival: he experienced 'great melancholy' as he absorbed 'the
distasteful knowledge of the vilest scramble for loot that ever
disfigured the history of human conscience and geographical
exploration. What an end to the idealized realities of a boy's
daydreams.' Inside the story, Marlow, Conrad's moral mouth-
piece, is equally unambiguous: 'It was just robbery with violence, aggravated murder on a great scale, and men going at it
blind – as is very proper for those who tackle a darkness. The

conquest of the earth, which mostly means the taking it away from those who have a different complexion or slightly flatter noses than ourselves, is not a pretty thing when you look into it too much.' This quotation fails to find its way into Mr Achebe's essay: since it sits awkwardly with Conrad the 'thoroughgoing racist' and completely undermines Achebe's conclusion that 'Conrad saw and condemned the evil of imperial exploitation but was strangely unaware of the racism on which it sharpened its iron tooth.'

Not that Achebe doesn't comment witheringly on Marlow's 'advanced and humane views appropriate to the English liberal tradition', when Marlow is shocked by the grove of death. Marlow's inconvenient indignation is brushed aside as 'bleeding-heart sentiments' which avoid what is, for Achebe, the central issue – 'the ultimate question of equality between white people and black people'. In other words, Achebe doesn't want charity and pity, he wants respect and equality. Reasonably enough, if he wants them for himself. It is less reasonable, however, to demand unconditional blanket approval for all the activities of the black inhabitants of the Congo in the middle of the nine-teenth century. For instance, Achebe is offended by the presence of cannibals in Conrad's story. But cannibals existed. Conrad did not invent them. Norman Sherry quotes W. Holman Bentley's *Pioneering in the Congo* on the joyfully cannibalistic Bangalas, one of whom said, when asked if he ate human flesh: 'Ah! I wish I could eat everybody on earth.' The choice facing Achebe is straightforward at this juncture: either he exonerates cannibalism and discounts criticism of it as Eurocentric, or he has to accept the uncomfortable fact of its existence when Conrad journeyed up the Congo. In *Heart of Darkness*, Conrad commends the inborn moral restraint of the hungry cannibals. But Achebe is unable to appreciate this, since he profoundly resents Conrad's racially ambiguous gift of English speech to a cannibal – who can then condemn himself, as a cannibal, out of his own mouth.

Achebe's other source of resentment is a single sentence of Conrad's: 'sometimes his fixation on blackness is equally interesting as when he gives us this brief description: "A black figure stood up, strode on long black legs, waving long black arms" – as though we might expect a black figure striding along on black legs to wave white arms! But so unrelenting is Conrad's obsession.' Achebe may have a point here – but in context the repeated adjective makes perfect narrative sense, because Marlow is pursuing Kurtz only 'thirty yards from the nearest fire' and he wishes to illustrate the proximity of danger by emphasizing how much detail he can see. Significantly, Achebe does not include a further detail – 'It had horns – antelope horns, I think – on its head' – because it serves the vividness so essential to the narrative at this juncture, yet cannot be read as racist in any way.

The nub of Achebe's anger is understandable but irrational. The blacks in *Heart of Darkness* are shown by Conrad to be primitive and savage. For Achebe, this is a racial libel, even when Conrad specifically approves of the savagery.

> Now and then a boat from the shore gave one a momentary contact with reality. It was paddled by black fellows. You could see from afar the white of their eyeballs glistening. They shouted, sang: their bodies streamed with perspiration; they had faces like grotesque masks – these chaps; but they had bone, muscle, a wild vitality, an intense energy of movement, that was as natural and true as the surf along the coast. They wanted no excuse for being there. They were a great comfort to look at.

From this, Achebe divines only a bigoted desire to confine the black man to an inferior position, masked by 'romantic' enthusiasm. The evidence, both for and against, is bound to be problematic. Henry Morton Stanley's *The Congo and the Founding of Its Free State* (1885) isn't quite the ugly imperialist tract one might expect it to be: 'In the management of a bargain I should back the Congoese native against Jew or Christian, Parsee or Banyan, in all the round world. Unthinking men may say cleverness at barter, and shrewdness in trade, consort not with their unsophisticated condition and degraded customs. Unsophisticated is the very last term I should ever apply to an African child or man in connection with the knowledge of how to trade.' Yet, while Stanley blazons this commercial sophistication, he also notes that in 'the basin of the Congo there is a vast field lying untouched by the European merchant and about three-fourths unexplored by the geographical explorer. For the most part it is peopled by ferocious savages, devoted to abominable cannibalism and wanton murder of inoffensive people but along the great river towards Livingstone Falls there dwell numerous amiable tribes who would gladly embrace the arrival of the European merchant.' So if Stanley identifies cannibalism he also identifies other 'amiable' tribes. In less optimistic moods, however, he gives a gloomier, more backward picture, when the professional adventurer takes over from the professional propagandist for trading opportunities: 'If they have a bad dream, some unfortunate is accused, and burnt for witchcraft, or hung for being an accessory to it. A chief dies from illness, and from two to fifty people are butchered over his grave. When the chief of Moye – the next village above our station – died, forty-five people were slaughtered, and only a short time before Ibaka strangled a lovely young girl because her lover had sickened and died.'

I cut Stanley's catalogue short, but that last item is reminiscent of suttee – another barbarity which still has not completely disappeared and which, for a long period, was repressed in India by just that Eurocentric certainty that Achebe deplores. Though in another essay, 'Named for Victoria, Queen of England', he concedes that alien Christianity had the merit of outlawing for converts the widespread practice of exposing newborn twins, he does so grudgingly and, in the Conrad essay, is so beleaguered that, foolishly and unnecessarily, he will concede nothing at all to Conrad.

Naturally, Achebe's picture differs fundamentally from that of Conrad and Stanley. His inhabitants of the Congo are not savages – Conrad's testimony is dismissed as 'jaundiced', as 'traveller's tales'. These people are ur-Cubists, actually in advance of European modern art. According to Achebe, 'European art had run completely out of strength' and was only saved by an 'infusion of new life' from African art. This is a partial, simplified account of Cubism. It ignores, for instance, the preparatory example of Cézanne, analytic Cubism's subsequent spatial discoveries, and the argument that only a strong art is capable of ingesting new influences without itself being swallowed. It is easy enough to accept that the Fang people are 'masters of the sculptured form'. But Achebe's corollary does not necessarily follow – that, therefore, these 'savages living just north of Conrad's River Congo' could not have been savages after all. The history of art and the history of savagery in Europe show clearly enough that sophistication in the first hardly impinged on the sophistication of the latter – from thumbscrews, choke-pears, pressings and rackings to brandings, beheadings, hangings, drawings and quarterings.

Conrad's argument in *Heart of Darkness* is that the savagery in all men is never quite tamed, can never be safely discounted. Everyone, European nationals included, has emerged from savagery, at different times – a view I find uncontroversial – and is capable of reverting at any time. Achebe is insulted because he thinks that Conrad is saying that only blacks are savage – but Conrad's condemnation is more inclusive than that. No one is spared. You cannot 'answer' Conrad, as Achebe seems to think, by listing European imperfections.

Isn't there, all the same, something racist in Conrad's use of the adjective 'black' and the noun 'nigger'? Achebe thinks so. It is quite possible that, whatever his conscious anti-colonial position, Conrad was disturbed unconsciously by negritude. But does this mean that 'Joseph Conrad was a thoroughgoing racist'?

In *Typhoon*, Conrad gives us in the callow Jukes an obviously ironized example of racism: 'he was gruff, as became his racial superiority, but not unfriendly'. Jukes is a fool and his foolishness is manifest in his lack of talent for foreign languages, the way he mangles 'the very pidgin-English cruelly', and in Conrad's implicit contrast between his coarseness and the evident refinement of the patronized Chinaman: 'the Chinaman, who concealed his distrust of this pantomime under a collected demeanour tinged by a gentle and refined melancholy, glanced out of his almond eyes'.

On the other hand, there is the problematic instance of James Wait in 'The Nigger of the *Narcissus*', whom Conrad presents as 'calm, cool, towering, superb', six foot three of self-possession, disdain and articulacy. His 'superb assurance' is evident later: his girl 'would chuck – any toff – for a coloured gentleman'. At this, Donkin is 'scandalized' and shows his 'unrestrained disgust' – but Conrad does not share Donkin's feelings and has already shown him to be morally nugatory, as reliable, say, as Iago. Nevertheless, Conrad's initial introduction of Wait concludes thus: 'He held his head up in the glare of the lamp – a head vigorously modelled into deep shadows and shining lights – a head powerful and misshapen with a tormented and flattened face – a face pathetic and brutal: the tragic, the mysterious, the repulsive mask of a nigger's soul.' This final phrase is replete with offence and hurt – not just now, but then.

However, given Conrad's overall presentation of Wait's physical nobility ('The nigger seemed not to hear. He balanced himself where he stood in a swagger that marked time'), I do not think the phrase is racist, but rather a narrow (and hurtful) Eurocentric aesthetic standard. The Black is Beautiful movement in the sixties was inaugurated to counter – in whites, but also in blacks themselves – something like the general proposition assumed by Conrad when he writes that Wait's features are an imperfect version of a white man's. Wait himself – I think to Conrad's credit – is conscious only of his superiority: 'he was naturally scornful, unaffectedly condescending'.

As for the word 'nigger', Achebe comments: 'His inordinate love of that word itself should be of interest to psychoanalysts.' Again, this isn't the simple matter one might believe it to be. On the one hand, Norman Sherry in his *Life of Graham Greene* can remark parenthetically that 'in 1935 it was common to call blacks "niggers" ', thus excusing Greene's use of the word in his story 'The Basement Room'. There again, it is noticeable that

Stanley never uses it once in the two volumes of *The Congo*, preferring more elaborate epithets, like 'ebon-hued servitors'.

According to Frederick Karl's biography, Faulkner used 'nigger' in an entirely neutral way. Yet Max Müller's 'Three Introductory Lectures on the Science of Thought' makes it clear that 'nigger' had negative connotations in 1888: 'in India the earliest grammarians asked the question, which we have asked but lately, namely, what is language made of? and they found, as we have found, that it consisted of those material elements or roots, and of a certain number of formal elements, called suffixes, prefixes and infixes. This was a wonderful achievement, particularly for men whom certain people even now would call savages or niggers.' *Even now.* 1888.

Nomenclature is a notably fraught area of subjectivity. Updike's invented Jewish novelist Bech finds himself in trouble at a high-class girls' college in Virginia where he is guest speaker. At dinner, a black student asks him if he isn't 'somewhat racist' for calling one of his characters 'a negress' – a word which, for her, has 'distinctly racist overtones'. Bech argues that he uses the word without prejudice: ' "negro" designates a scientific racial grouping, like Caucasian or Mongolian'. The black woman responds to this: 'How do you feel then about "Jewess"?' Updike beautifully identifies the chasm which opens between logic and reflex subjectivity: 'Bech lied; the word made him wince. "Just as I do about 'duchess'." ' The black woman concludes by rejecting the love of the white man and asking instead for his respect. Which is Achebe's position, too.

I respect him sufficiently to tell him something he knows already as a novelist but which, as a spokesman, he chooses to ignore. All 'minorities' will treat representations of themselves as typical, whereas art deals with actualities, and not necessarily with truth and justice. But Achebe, in these essays, places art at the service of propaganda and social engineering because they are, in his view, appropriate to the African context. In 'The Novelist as Teacher', he writes: 'for the moment it is in the nature of things that we may need to counter racism with what Jean-Paul Sartre has called an anti-racist racism, to announce not just that we are as good as the next man but that we are much better'. This is a disastrous statement for an artist to make, but no worse than this mixture of threat and abject surrender of authorial independence, which occurs in 'Colonialist Criticism': 'There are clear signs that critics and readers from those areas of the world where continuing incidents and recent memories of racism, colonialism and other forms of victimization exist will more and more demand to know from their writers just on whose ideological side they are playing. And we writers had better be prepared to reckon with this questioning.' What a chilling last sentence, prophesying the purely political evaluation of literature and the fatal restriction of subject matter. One cannot serve art and write with big brother in mind. One cannot even serve art and write with, so to speak, one's mother in mind. 'Speak what we feel, not what we ought to say' is a serviceable formula.

Just the same, one wishes that Achebe had felt less and thought more. He has leapt to his conclusions but badly misjudged the distance. That noise you can hear is the noise of the bigger splash – very different from the splash envisaged by Achebe when, with the authority of his own suffering, he set down the attention-grabbing sentence: 'Joseph Conrad was a thoroughgoing racist.'

357

# Conrad's *Heart of Darkness*

In his 1921 essay, 'Geography and Some Explorers', Conrad recalls his school atlas, published in 1852: 'one day, putting my finger on a spot in the very middle of the then white heart of Africa, I declared that some day I would go there'. And, in 1890–91, he did so – as an employee of the Société Anonyme Belge pour le Commerce du Haut-Congo. The literary booty from this experience was the short story 'An Outpost of Progress' (1896) and the novella *Heart of Darkness* (1899).

Conrad shrewdly brought the element of reportage in both works to the attention of his readers in separate author notes. He claims 'An Outpost of Progress' is 'true enough in its essentials', if only for the mock-modest reason that 'the sustained invention of a really telling lie demands a talent' he claims to lack. *Heart of Darkness* is prefaced by a note which, while it indicates departures from strict documentary truth, allows us to understand that the substantial residue is factual: '*Heart of Darkness* is experience, too; but it is experience pushed a little (and only very little) beyond the actual facts of the case for the perfectly legitimate, I believe, purpose of bringing it home to the minds and bosoms of the readers.' Conrad, in other words, has artistic as well as factual responsibilities. Thus forewarned, readers of *Heart of Darkness* should not expect a plodding transcription of actual events. There is truth and there is artistic truth.

This seems obvious enough, yet it is at odds with the obtuse, fundamentalist approach of Norman Sherry, our most indefatigable Conrad expert, the author of *Conrad's Western World* and *Conrad's Eastern World*, books to which anyone who is even marginally interested in Conrad owes a debt of some kind. It is from Sherry that we know, for instance, that although Conrad's experience mirrors that of Marlow when he secures his appointment by the intervention of an influential aunt, in other respects their histories differed radically. In pedestrian reality, Conrad was not the captain of *Le Roi des Belges* when it steamed upriver to bring back Klein, an agent who was sick with dysentery at Stanley Falls. Conrad's own steamer, *Ville de Bruxelles*, was damaged two days before his arrival and on this trip he had the role of observer, learning navigational intricacies from a more experienced skipper. Though Klein died on the journey downstream, he was not the model for Kurtz, despite the similarity of their names. Sherry has discovered that Conrad probably based Kurtz on Arthur Eugene Constant Hodister, an idealist who was killed in an uprising of local inhabitants, leaving behind a native wife and children – though it hardly matters, since art is seldom explained by the location of sources in real life. On the other hand, alterations to the original reality may provide us with a glimpse of the artist's intention. Sherry tells us, for instance, that this trip, far from being the slow progress of 'a grimy beetle', was completed in record time. He tells us, too, that the waterway and its various stations were thriving and bustling, quite different from the primitive, lonely, oppressive environment presented in *Heart of Darkness*. The authorial intention revealed for Sherry is little more than a vulgar determination on Conrad's part to light his story melodramatically.

So alert is Sherry for authorial mendacity that he is prepared to accept even very dubious evidence. For instance, the manuscript of *Heart of Darkness* (but not the finished text) has a long description of Boma, the seat of government where Conrad stayed one night: 'I had heard enough in Europe about its advanced state of civilization; the papers, nay the very paper vendors in the sepulchral city were boasting about the steam tramway and the hotel – especially the hotel. I beheld that wonder. It was like a symbol at the gate. It stood alone, a grey high cube of iron with two tiers of galleries outside, towering above one of those ruinous-looking foreshores you come upon at home in out-of-the-way places where refuse is thrown out.' The vaunted trams run only twice a day. Against this disenchanted accuracy, Sherry sets the tainted newspaper source already discredited by Conrad, a glowing account in *Mouvement Géographique*, the Société Anonyme Belge's house paper, in effect, and concludes that Boma was 'a well-established, well-organized seat of government'. It is odd of Sherry to give credence to the understandably biased report rather than to Conrad's dispassionate and appealingly ironical epitome. But Sherry feels he has uncovered a pattern of deliberate, cynical distortion by Conrad – of which this is only another example.

Sherry's failure as a critic is a failure to look beyond the literal. Because Conrad's own experience seems an obviously adequate source, Sherry does not realize that *Heart of Darkness* is set chronologically in Henry Morton Stanley's time, 1883, when the waterway was really deserted, oppressive and slow, and based equally on Conrad's experience (1890) and on Stanley's as told in *The Congo and the Founding of Its Free State: A Story of Work and Exploration* (1885). Sherry cites Stanley as the source for 'An Outpost of Progress', adduces a speech of Stanley's (published in *The Times* of 4 October 1892) as the source for the philosophical speculation at the opening of *Heart of Darkness*, and is prepared to credit Stanley as 'never far from the sidelines of Conrad's Congo experience' – yet he remains obstinately and exclusively wedded to Conrad's own experience as the source for the rest of *Heart of Darkness*. In fact, Stanley's book contains the hints for many sensational details in Conrad's story, like ritual sacrifice, for example: 'heads unfleshed by boiling, that the skulls might decorate the poles around the grave'. There is even the germ of Kurtz's atavistic behaviour in Stanley's account of the Bolobo rebellion, when, for a moment only, Stanley suspects the station chief of tampering 'with these savages from a sinister design of his own'. Conrad's suggestibility requires literary understanding rather than Professor Sherry's prim, affronted vigilance. The ideal reader of fiction is not the lie detector.

*Heart of Darkness* needs tactful intelligence more than the dogged detective work of the intrepid Sherry. It is a story which advertises its difficulty: 'the yarns of seamen have a direct simplicity, the whole meaning of which lies within the shell of a cracked nut. But Marlow was not typical . . .' The earlier tale, 'An Outpost of Progress', is simpler, coarser and more bluntly ironical than *Heart of Darkness*, yet it can, by virtue of these very limitations, give us the rough dimensions of Conrad's moral architecture. 'An Outpost of Progress' is based on Stanley's disappointment with the settlement of Vivi and describes how two men, Carlier and Kayerts, exist in Platonic indolence until a crisis is forced on them by the arrival of marauders from the coast – who abduct into slavery native company employees and a few local tribesmen, paying with ivory, in a deal arranged by the black manager, Makola. As a result, the local tribe totally ostracizes the two white men and their supplies dwindle. They have a small amount of sugar for medicinal emergencies. When Carlier wants to use some for a decent cup of coffee, a quarrel ensues, which results in a chase, which results in Kayerts shooting Carlier. At which point, too patly, the steamer arrives, before Carlier can be buried (and passed off as a casualty of fever), so Kayerts commits suicide. The Stanley figure

> stood and fumbled in his pockets (for a knife) while he faced Kayerts, who was hanging by a leather strap from the cross. He had evidently climbed the grave [of the previous, deceased station incumbent] which was high and narrow, and after tying the end of the strap to the arm, had swung himself off. His toes were only a couple of inches above the ground; his arms hung stiffly down; he seemed to be standing rigidly at attention, but with one purple cheek playfully posed on the shoulder. And, irreverently, he was putting out a swollen tongue at his Managing Director.

Conrad is so expert at the macabre, coldly gruesome details normally associated with thriller writers, that one might almost believe 'An Outpost of Progress' existed merely as the pretext for this grim finale – or that *Heart of Darkness* was written to provide a context for the shockingly measured, Hitchcockian notation of Kurtz's sacrificial heads. 'Then I went carefully from post to post with my glass, and I saw my mistake. These round knobs were not ornamental but symbolic; they were expressive and puzzling, striking and disturbing – food for thought and also for the vultures if there had been any looking down from the sky; but at all events for such ants as were industrious enough to ascend the pole.' The power here is all in the restraint, in the gradual, methodical disclosure, in the refusal of melodrama: 'They would have been even more impressive, those heads on the stakes, if their faces had not been turned to the house. Only one, the first I had made out, was facing my way. I was not so shocked as you may think.' What follows is deliberate, clinical, ironical: 'there it was, black, dried, sunken, with closed eyelids – a head that seemed to sleep at the top of that pole, and, with shrunken dry lips showing a narrow white line of teeth, was smiling, too, smiling continuously at some endless and jocose dream of that eternal slumber'.

*Jocose.* Not 'funny', no7t 'amusing', not 'diverting' – but *jocose*, with its suggestion of something willed and artificial, an adjective of genius.

To this local brilliance, Conrad attaches his larger issues in both stories. For most of its length 'An Outpost of Progress' is an ironic examination of the idea of progress as exemplified by the ineffable complacency of two ignorant Europeans. Conrad clearly dissociates himself from their crass insularity, just as the narrator of *Heart of Darkness* can evaluate the attitude of the seafarer to foreign shores: 'the foreign faces, the changing immensity of life, glide past, veiled not by a sense of mystery but by a slightly disdainful ignorance'. Kayerts and Carlier consume fiction like chocolates, in a state of dreamy torpor, ignore their surroundings, and pore over old newspapers of the kind dear to Professor Sherry:

They also found some old copies of a home paper. That print discussed what it was pleased to call 'Our Colonial Expansion' in highflown language. It spoke much of the rights and duties of civilization, of the sacredness of the civilizing work, and extolled the merits of those who went about bringing light, and faith and commerce to the dark places of the earth. Carlier and Kayerts read, wondered, and began to think better of themselves. Carlier said one evening, waving his hand about, 'In a hundred years, there will be perhaps a town here. Quays, and warehouses, and barracks, and – and – billiard rooms. Civilization, my boy, and virtue – and all.'

The local chief, Gobila, is the recipient of their cultural overtures, the beneficiary of their civilization: 'Carlier slapped him on the back, and recklessly struck off matches for his amusement. Kayerts was always ready to let him have a sniff at the ammonia bottle.'

The mockery here is directed not at Gobila but at the limited human material supplied by the Europeans as they attempt to stretch it over the chasm which opens between the ideal of Progress and the pathetic actuality of their circumstances. On the one hand, Civilization: on the other, the bathos of billiard rooms, the benison of smelling salts, and a squalid affray over fifteen sugar lumps. This, too, is a central subject of *Heart of Darkness* – in which the colonial ideal is economically imaged in all its benighted idealism by Kurtz's portrait of his fiancée, blindfolded but bearing a torch into darkness.

Yet the scope of *Heart of Darkness* isn't restricted to Conrad's disapproval of colonialism, even though colonialism's commercial and racist motivation is clearly identified and denounced explicitly by Conrad on several occasions. When Marlow's aunt is tempted to see her nephew as 'something like an emissary of light, something like a lower sort of apostle', Marlow ventures 'to hint that the Company was run for profit'. The humbug of civilization, 'the philanthropic pretence', is anathema to Conrad and Marlow. As it is put in the frame aboard the *Nellie*, 'the conquest of the earth, which mostly means the taking it away from those who have a different complexion or slightly flatter noses than ourselves, is not a pretty sight when you look into it too much'. And Conrad is scathing in 'Geography and Some Explorers': 'the discovery of Africa was the occasion of the greatest outburst of reckless cruelty and greed known to history'.

In the same essay, however, Conrad touches on the larger, metaphysical nub of his argument. Having reached the destination picked out on the map so many years before, he experiences disillusionment: 'A great melancholy descended on me. Yes, this was the very spot. But there was no shadowy friend to stand by my side in the night of the enormous wilderness, no great haunting memory, but only the unholy recollection of a prosaic newspaper "stunt" and the distasteful knowledge of the vilest scramble for loot that ever disfigured the history of human conscience and geographical exploration. What an end to the idealized realities of a boy's daydreams!' Despite this outcome, is there anything to be said for the idea? Not the idea of colonialism *per se*, but the idea itself?

This is the question asked by *Heart of Darkness*. And asked most directly immediately after Conrad's most wholesale denunciation of colonialism: 'the conquest of the earth, which mostly means the taking it away from those who have a different complexion or slightly flatter noses than ourselves, is not a pretty thing when you look into it too much. What redeems it is the idea only. An idea at the back of it; not a sentimental pretence but an idea; and an unselfish belief in the idea – something you can set up, and bow down before, and offer a sacrifice to . . .' No wonder Marlow breaks off. The aposiopesis represents Marlow's awareness that his words are equally applicable to Kurtz's as yet unmentioned, barbarous, primitive rites.

But Marlow's encounter with Kurtz isn't a simple instance of straightforward disillusionment. In this respect, *Heart of Darkness* is very different from 'An Outpost of Progress'. When the natives steal the carcass of the hippo he has shot, Carlier talks about 'the necessity of exterminating all the niggers before the country could be made habitable' and we are reminded of Kurtz's scrawled imperative at the end of his report to the International Society for the Suppression of Savage Customs – 'exterminate all the brutes'. Nevertheless, Kurtz is not dismissed from consideration in the way that Carlier is. This is because Kurtz has two Ideas – one which is bogus, one which is bitter, but tonic and real. The bogus idea is outlined in Kurtz's seventeen-page report: 'The peroration was magnificent, though difficult to remember, you know,' Marlow reports in his turn. 'It gave me the notion of an exotic Immensity ruled by an august Benevolence.' It is the idea of supernatural supervision that Conrad finds laughable. The aspiration to bring European benefits to the indigenous population is fair enough, if futile.

Conrad intends this balanced pairing ('Immensity' and 'Benevolence') to recall an earlier formula, much scorned by F. R. Leavis as merely 'adjectival insistence' – 'it was the stillness of an implacable force brooding over an inscrutable intention'. In fact, shortly after the death of Kurtz, there is a less orotund formulation of this proposition: 'Droll thing life is – that mysterious arrangement of merciless logic for a futile purpose.' That is, far from being overseen by an 'august Benevolence', the earth obeys its complicated physical laws to no end at all.

If natural selection isn't the 'inscrutable intention', what is? The problem evaporates if one substitutes Conrad's alternative phrasing – 'a futile purpose'. As far as he is concerned, and as far as Kurtz is concerned, the issue is not a scientific theory to which man is not central – but the utter futility of existence. When Kurtz exclaims in his famous whisper, 'The horror', Marlow offers this approving commentary on a man whom, in many respects and with good reason, he despises: 'This is the reason why I affirm that Kurtz was a remarkable man. He had something to say. He said it.' A few pages earlier, Marlow has offered this proleptic gloss on 'The horror': 'No eloquence could have been so withering to one's belief in mankind as his final burst of sincerity.' What, for Marlow, is so positive about this negation of mankind and its works?

*

Seen twice, even the most original notion looks less forbidding and enigmatic. Louis-Ferdinand Céline's *Voyage au bout de la nuit* (1932) is a beneficiary of *Heart of Darkness* whose very title is a conscious homage to Conrad. (In English: *Journey to the End of the Night*.) In Céline's novel, Conrad's central idea is re-presented, along with much else – particularly an episode in the Congo, in which the random absurdities of Conrad's narrative become a comprehensive, frankly absurdist vision. Thus in *Heart of Darkness*, one encounters the 'objectless blasting' of non-existent obstacles for a railway, the murder of Captain Fresleven in a quarrel over two black hens, a fire bucket rendered useless by a hole, a dearth of rivets in the place where they are needed and a plethora in the place where they are not. In *Voyage au bout de la nuit*, the narrative is a series of mere contingencies, frankly meaningless, registered resignedly by the novel's morally comatose anti-hero, Bardamou, whose sensibility is as impermeable as a rubber mackintosh. It is he who witnesses the daily drilling of native troops by Sergeant Alcide: 'Newly emerged from a vigorous, near-by Nature, an apology for khaki shorts was all they wore. Everything else had to be imagined, and was. At Alcide's peremptory "Attack!" these ingenious warriors put down their make-believe packs and dashed wildly forward, to lunge imaginary bayonets at imaginary enemies. Then, making as if to unbutton their tunics, they would stack their rifles and at another sign from Alcide become passionately absorbed in abstractions of musketry.' Like Marlow, Bardamou is anxious for information about the person he is to succeed upriver: 'But time went by and not one of my companions could tell me what sort of an odd person the man I was going to replace at Bikomimbo was. "He's an extraordinary chap," they informed me, and that's all I could get out of them.

The extraordinary chap is probably Léon Robinson – Céline's narrative is somewhat perfunctory and indecisive at the crucial juncture – a man who appears and reappears in the narrative of Bardamou's life. At the end of *Voyage*, Robinson is shot three times by his girlfriend, Madelon. She is provoked by Robinson's credo, which is a version of Kurtz's brief summary, 'The horror':

'Why, it's every darn thing that repels me and disgusts me now,' Robinson explains to Madelon. 'Not only you! Everything! . . . Love especially . . .' Robinson's garrulous psychic grimace at everything the world conventionally values elicits frank admiration from the narrator, Bardamou: 'I hadn't acquired one single good solid idea, like the one he'd had to get himself severely manhandled like that.' Bardamou is impressed by Robinson as Marlow is impressed by Kurtz – by the bleak sincerity which spares nothing, particularly not the speaker himself.

Contrary to one's expectation, Marlow admires Kurtz for having looked into the heart of darkness – not Africa, but the self and its possibilities – and pronounced truthfully. This is an issue – an Idea – larger than the evils of colonialism, important though those are. Kurtz's achievement, like Robinson's, is to have not merely endured life, but to have made sense of it while seeing it, in Matthew Arnold's phrase, steadily and seeing it whole.

But where does this leave the Russian harlequin, the mysterious son of an arch-priest, a survivor who has twice nursed Kurtz, a man he fears and admires in equal proportions? This minor character is a key to the overall pattern of *Heart of Darkness* – as minor characters, when properly placed, often are in literature which deploys form and symmetry. His patched clothes, of course, make him as memorable as Diggory Venn, the reddleman, in Hardy's *The Return of the Native*. He is so striking, in fact, that one is inclined to overlook his extreme functionality – he is a piece of literary mechanism we should be lost without; abolish him from the narrative and how is the history of Kurtz's demeanour and misdemeanours to be reconstructed, given that Kurtz's half-caste assistant is banished, wordlessly, from the narrative? One is tempted to believe that Conrad has disguised such an obvious *ficelle* by the bold expedient of making this thread, this narrative thread, a thing of threads and patches. In other words, by disguising a narrative patch as itself – just as the Negro in the Father Brown story 'The God of the Gongs' escapes the country in the disguise of a nigger minstrel. This is an elegant hypothesis but unlikely – as is the temptation to relate the Russian to Carlyle's *Sartor Resartus* (the tailor patched), the autobiography in which Carlyle argues for, as it were, 'an exotic Immensity ruled over by an august Benevolence'. The Carlyle is pleasingly pat, but it is literary and academic as a way of stating Conrad's meaning – in a story which emphasizes time and again the importance of the immediate experience, the moment's gestalt: 'No, it is impossible; it is impossible to convey the life-sensation of any given epoch of one's existence – that which makes its truth, its meaning – its subtle and penetrating essence.' The writer who believed that is hardly going to trust his meaning to a second-hand literary allusion.

Everything we know about Conrad suggests that we should admire this harlequin seaman who so ostentatiously embraces the English work ethic and implicitly, therefore, the idea that the immediate task can often save a man from fatal introspection about reality. As Marlow says, 'when you have to attend to things of that sort, to mere incidents of the surface, the reality – the reality, I tell you – fades. The inner truth is hidden – luckily, luckily.' Towser's or Towson's or Tower's *An Inquiry into Some Points of Seamanship*, the 'not very enthralling book' carried around by the Russian, appears to belong with this group of ideas, in which duty is more important than self-indulgent philosophizing. Its virtue is the 'honest concern for the right way of going to work'. And yet . . . What would be more absurd in this jungle than to annotate this dull, irrelevant text in Cyrillic? The manual may *seem* 'unmistakably real' to Marlow and the Russian harlequin – but actually the book is nothing more than a fetish, a thing invested with magical, protective properties. It is significant that when the Russian takes his leave, he is protected by Martini-Henry cartridges in one pocket and this fetish in the other. The irrational importance of a book devoid of any utility in the jungle is a perfect illustration in miniature that even the most apparently well adjusted of us – Marlow, the Russian, the Kurtz who set out for the Congo – are in thrall to our own primitive superstitions.

Nor should we be surprised to learn that the model for the

Russian is Conrad himself. The clue (overlooked by the intrepid Sherry) is there in 'A Personal Record', where Conrad divulges that he took into the Congo the manuscript of his first novel, *Almayer's Folly*: 'And the MS of *Almayer's Folly* carried about me *as if it were a talisman* [my italics] or a treasure, went *there* too. That it ever came out of *there* seems a special dispensation of providence . . .' Conrad's list of possibly fatal accidents – particularly upset canoes – is largely duplicated by the Russian in *Heart of Darkness*.

The patching is another example of fetishism – an act important beyond its immediate utility. Conrad has already touched on the primitive magic of clothing when, at the grove of death, he links by zeugma the dying black with 'a bit of white worsted round his neck' and the ludicrously spruce company accountant, decked in his own absurdly inappropriate finery, whose function is to ward off the evils of Africa. The other key to the young Russian's survival – against all odds – is that his drive is pure and utterly uncontaminated by ulterior motives: 'if the absolutely pure, uncalculating, unpractical spirit of adventure had ever ruled a human being, it ruled this be-patched youth'. He is a human being untouched, untainted and unredeemed by the Idea.

# Toni Morrison's *Paradise*

What confers authority on a writer? Toni Morrison's seventh novel, and her first since the 1993 Nobel Prize, raises this question in an acute form. *Paradise* is an account of an all-black township, Ruby, established in rural, isolated Oklahoma after the Civil War and the migration of ex-slaves north. The time-span extends to the Watergate hearings. It is the last of a trilogy begun with *Beloved* (1987), a slave-era narrative, and continued with *Jazz* (1992), a post-liberation story set in twenties Harlem. Toni Morrison is a writer whose coverage aims to be comprehensive, who wishes to engross virtually every aspect of black experience – from slavery to the aftermath of Vietnam and beyond. Is her ambition overextended? Will she prove to be the African-American Solzhenitsyn – worthy, courageous, essential to a particular historical moment, a crucial consciousness-raiser, but a novelist of only average talent, with a weakness for over-writing and a tendency to Gothic melodrama?

What is really possible for a writer who wants to represent her race in literature? The first sentence of *A Tale of Two Cities* deals, definitively, with those writers who profess to deal with the Zeitgeist, or 'The Period' as Dickens calls his chapter: 'It was the best of times, it was the worst of times . . .' So much for those hilarious caricatures – historical periods – which Virginia Woolf was also to send up in *Orlando*, where 1800 inaugurates a century of rising damp, where better drainage and improved

*Paradise* by Toni Morrison, Chatto & Windus.

lighting have their effect (somehow) on literary style – a synec-doche for every alleged modification of art by social conditions.

But if a period is impossible, what about the culture of a particular place, the spirit of the deep South, say? This is Ken Tynan on the essentially mythic topos, at once torpid and inflamed, of another Nobel Prize winner, William Faulkner: 'End of another day in the city of Jefferson, Yoknapatawpha County, Mississippi. Nothin' much happened. Couple of people got raped, couple more got their teeth kicked in, but way up there those faraway old stars are still doing their old cosmic criss-cross, and there ain't a thing we can do about it.' How swiftly the authentic, the first-hand, begins to look second-hand, inauthentic and vulnerable to parody. What seemed an objective report on a region suddenly shrinks to the merely solipsistic.

Consider, for example, the treatment of sex in *Beloved*. One danger for a black writer is, I believe, the temptation to unique-ness – to say, implicitly, of your neglected subject matter that it is *sui generis* and to ground your claim to authority there. As a student in the all-black Howard University, Toni Morrison noticed that lighter-skinned Negroes had more éclat. Her early novel, *The Bluest Eye*, writes about black self-hatred in a way that now seems unavailable to any white writer. The white South African dramatist Athol Fugard told me once that his play *The Blood Knot* attracted considerable black criticism for touch-ing on this problematic subject. That was in 1961. Now no one is going to credit a white writer's version of black experience. In *Paradise*, the inhabitants of Ruby operate a reverse discrimina-tion against those townsfolk with lighter skins. Only a black writer can thus correct an excess created by the black power movement.

Sex, however, is an area of equal rights, of common experi-ence. While the slaves at Sweet Home are waiting for the fourteen-year-old Sethe to choose one of them as her partner, their sexual frustration is such that they spend their time 'fuck-ing cows, dreaming of rape'. Paul D., moreover, doesn't think that the difference between a girl and a calf is 'that mighty'. I don't imagine that black men were happy with this ludicrous libel. Masturbation, that common valve against fornication, has been erased by Toni Morrison from the black male experience. Here her authority is manifestly forfeit. Fatally, *Beloved* becomes fodder for ripe parody. Behind the mistake is the impulse, strangely enough, to glamorize. D. H. Lawrence identified the temptation in 1927: 'one likes to cherish illusions about the race soul, the eternal negroid soul, black and glistening and touched with awfulness and mystery'. This temptation isn't restricted to white outsiders. You can see it implicitly in Paul D.'s assertion about 124, the haunted house in *Beloved*: 'as he stepped through the red light he knew that, compared to 124, the rest of the world was bald'. Those horny black slaves are engorged not by normal sexual frustration but by a curious kind of racial pride in mythic black potency.

And behind this is the more general impulse to redeem some of the genuine horrors of black experience by embracing their dramatic richness, against which the ordinary world can too easily look 'bald'. The writer is likely to exaggerate rather than enrich.

It is very difficult to be a writer and a spokeswoman. Toni Morrison's *Paris Review* interview shows her alert to danger: 'it's important not to have a totalizing view. In American literature we [blacks] have been so totalized – as though there is only one version. We are not one indistinguishable block of people who always behave the same way.' This is well said. But it contains its own dangers. One is that, avoiding the representative, you over-favour the bizarre. Secondly, taken to its logical conclusion, this insistence on distinction will destroy the solidarity which was its starting point. In *The Voyage Out*, Virginia Woolf plants a little speech in the mouth of Terence Hewet, an aspiring novelist. He is aware that, although literature is full of women, 'it's never come from women themselves'. The black experience has obvious affinities with what he calls 'this curious silent unrepresented life' of women. Immediately, however, that life – so oddly singular – becomes *lives*. 'The lives of women of forty, of unmarried women, of women who keep shops and bring up children . . .' It is an interesting list – its individualistic,

even quirky third item already beginning to escape the confinement of category altogether. Literature differentiates, politics
tends to classify.

To an embattled black writer, this teleological view must look
like an unaffordable luxury. Literature and politics seem inseparable rather than intrinsically opposed in their tendencies. Toni
Morrison, like George Eliot, is a writer bent on making her
readers hear 'the roar which lies on the other side of silence'.
For George Eliot, literature practised its own segregation: 'insignificant people, whom you pass unnoticed on the road every
day, have their tragedy too; but it is of that unwept, hidden sort,
that goes on from generation to generation, and leaves no
record'. The difference between George Eliot and Toni Morrison
is that Morrison's characters are scarcely ever ordinary, sometimes incoherently conceived, and frequently at the mercy of
sensational plot requirements, of the novelist's desire to insist on
her unique access to experiences more vivid than any the reader
could possibly know. In another context, Saul Bellow called this
'event-glamour', and it is a thing novelists should be wary of. It
is Toni Morrison's stock-in-trade.

*Paradise* begins dramatically with the massacre of five women
in a convent, and the rest of the novel is an explication of how
these innocent women became the victims of respectable killers.
However, nothing we are told about the murderers makes the
outcome in any way probable – not even remotely. In fact, the
responsibility appears to rest on Toni Morrison's weakness for
grand guignol – on that and on her weakness for religious
allegory. The occluded metaphysics of *Paradise* strongly hint
that spirit and body, good and evil, are inextricably bound up
in each other. Just as Christianity overlays a pagan foundation,
so the convent was previously the mansion of a worldly embez-
zler. Its faucets were formerly full sets of male genitalia. Likewise, one woman, the *louche*-est, has two names – Gigi and
*Grace*. She is initially drawn to the place by rumours of a
natural sculpture of an endlessly copulating couple – clearly
a pagan version of the Adam and Eve creation myth. The
very architecture of the convent is bullet-shaped in a coarsely

proleptic way. Should you wish to apportion responsibility for the murders, Symbolism is a prime suspect, even if Allegory is the actual culprit.

This black hole where the motivation should be is the major weakness. In addition, the narrative method is a form of torture – a kind of demonic pass-the-parcel, a trance of the seven veils, common to *Beloved* and *Jazz*. The basic set-up is given, but the novelist deliberately conceals the information that might explain it. You are meant to see – but only gradually, very gradually. In practice, this means a large quota of sentences which are candidly unintelligible because they precede the information necessary to explicate them – often by hundreds of pages, so the solution may arrive when the puzzle has been forgotten. For instance, on page 189 we learn that Big Papa has been shot through the foot. On page 302 we are told how this came about. Similar, if less absurdly sustained, aporia abound in this novel. *Paradise* is a bungled nightmare of deferral which can only be resolved by a second reading. What was previously a mannerism has matured into a dismaying narrative incompetence. This isn't helped by the cast of hundreds. *Paradise* is a muffed *Middlemarch*, thronging with richly individualized characters. In theory. Actually, it is like trying to read a telephone directory. Big Papa, to take only one example, is really called Zechariah Morgan, or Coffee Morgan – a name which is probably a corruption of Kofi Moyne. It is hard to keep track. The proliferation of names underlines the central theme of *Paradise* – that our very identities are palimpsests – but the local effect is unambiguous unreadability.

# Speaking Up for Dickens

Volume 8 of the magnificent Pilgrim Edition of Dickens's letters covers the years 1856–58 – the years of fame and misfortune, of *Little Dorrit*, of lucrative and lauded reading tours, of the scandal surrounding his separation from his wife, Catherine.

Despite his friend Forster's feeling that there was something demeaning and ungentlemanly about going on the stump, the reading tours were warmly received. There was only one really hostile notice (in Plymouth). Warm in every sense. 'I get so wonderfully hot in my dress clothes, that they positively won't dry in the short interval they get, and I have been obliged to write to Doudney's to make me another suit, that I may have a constant change.' Apart from that, the main problems seem to have been exhaustion (at the peak, eight readings in a week in five different towns) and audiences so crammed that, in Belfast, someone stood on the flexible pipe and extinguished the gaslight.

Dickens, however, must have been as hungry for privacy as he was voracious for popularity. Most of the time he was buoyed up by acclaim, but one letter shows us (comically, of course) the down side: Dickens was at the theatre in Doncaster (to see Ellen Ternan and therefore maybe hoping to be incognito) 'behaving excessively ill in the way of gaping and rubbing my head wearily', 'with my hands in my pockets and a general expression upon me of total want of dignity', when the cry went up, 'Three cheers for Charles Dickens Esquire!' He was public

*The Letters of Charles Dickens. Volume 8: 1856–1858*, edited by Graham Storey and Kathleen Tillotson, Clarendon Press.

property. In Dublin, prior to readings at Cork and Limerick, Dickens describes his manager, Arthur Smith, sitting atop a bag of silver. 'It must be dreadfully hard,' Dickens appends with characteristic comic asperity. As an emblem, it will do for these years – for the rewards of fame and the price of fame, for advantages inseparable from disadvantages, a paean in the arse.

The public and private intersect comically when the Revd Chauncy Hare Townshend pays a visit with his dog, Bully: 'Bully disconcerts me a good deal. He dined here on Sunday with his master, and got a young family of puppies out of each of the doors, fell into indecent transports with the claws of the round table, and was madly in love with Townshend's boots. All of which, Townshend seems to have no idea of, but merely says "Bul-ly" when he is on his hind-legs like the sign of a public house.' In Volume 5, Dickens's own dog, Timber, exhibited 'frightful and horribly unnatural tokens of virility, in connexion with an insignificant, drivelling, blear-eyed little tame rabbit of the female sex.' One of the questions prompted by this volume is concerned with Dickens's sexuality. Was he a randy old dog? Clearly, his malicious contemporaries were inclined to think so. Volume 8 details Dickens's desperate and necessarily public attempts to counter the inevitable gossip provoked by his separation. We have here Dickens's 'Personal Statement' (published in *The Times* and *Household Words*, his own magazine). Also reprinted is the so-called 'Violated Letter', intended by Dickens for private circulation but subsequently published too. In *The Invisible Woman*, her study of Ellen Ternan, Claire Tomalin invokes the Dickens public relations machine as 'unrivalled' – with the presumption that Dickens had everything to hide, rather than a blameless reputation to defend against gossip. Was it a snow-job?

Since Michael Slater's impressive *Dickens and Women*, the balance of scholarly opinion has been sceptical about Dickens's account of his marriage and its breakdown. I'm not so sure. Of course, any defensive statement is bound to have self-serving aspects, but Dickens's marital summaries aren't quite the protests of outraged innocence that his detractors claim. To Miss

Burdett Coutts, Dickens admits to 'impulsive faults'. Nevertheless, he wishes to justify himself, as who wouldn't? One of his justifications has gone down particularly badly – that Catherine Dickens was a poor mother whose emotional links with her children were very weak. But the counter-evidence, for her warmth, largely consists, as it happens, of long letters from Dickens, detailing for her the exploits of their children – letters, it is argued, that presume her interest.

On the other hand, Georgina Hogarth, Catherine's sister, who stayed to look after the children when the separation occurred, wrote a letter to an American friend in 1872 when Sydney Dickens died at sea. It said that Catherine felt her son's death 'as much as she can feel anything, but she is a very curious person – unlike anyone else in the world'. This strong corroborative testimony, two years after Dickens's death, is dismissed by Michael Slater because it is corroborative. Georgina, he writes, 'seems to have been inclined to keep up Dickens's 1858 line about her sister'. The present editors see the comment merely as demonstrating Catherine's reticence in front of her sister. There is another interpretation – that Catherine was indeed deficient.

Several things incline me to the view that the marriage was flawed even before the advent of Ellen Ternan: a letter to Miss Coutts in January 1854 in which Dickens criticizes his wife's 'indescribable lassitude', and a letter of October 1857 to De La Rue which alludes to marital dissatisfaction as a long-standing grievance, with which De La Rue was already familiar from old. Neither letter could be described as part of Dickens's unrivalled PR machine. And they precede the actual break-up.

The editors also reinforce the current consensus that Dickens lied when he said that his eldest son Charley decided to live with his mother at Dickens's request. The letter of Charley's, copied by Dickens, just as easily bears the interpretation Dickens himself gives it – that is, he asked Charley to reside with his mother in her new home at Gloucester Terrace, but, of course, left the final decision to his son's judgement. Far from being an act of defiance, the son's reply – why else would Dickens copy it out?

– is merely anxious that, having decided to accede to Dickens's wish, his father shouldn't imagine that he preferred his mother to his father. A related criticism is that Dickens, not Catherine, was indifferent to the children. Why, then, should he have sought custody of all except Charley? And I don't accept that his desire to find them employment in the colonies is necessarily an indication of hatred.

It is difficult, despite these reservations, to praise the editors highly enough. Here are two footnotes taken from many. Dickens recounts to Forster the macabre details of a murder in the Champs-Elysées – a reclusive duchess done in by her coachman. The editors supply a touch unaccountably overlooked by Dickens – that the murderer strangled his mistress 'with hands heated by brandy'. Later, Dickens writes a fan letter to Professor George Wilson. The footnote tells us the title of his book and adds, well beyond the call of duty, that 'the book fully justifies CD's high opinion of it'.

The editors fall below these high standards only three or four times: I wanted to know *how* the snowcloth worked in *The Frozen Deep*, not just be fobbed off with the assertion that it was a 'device for producing snow'. Also an item of gossip touched on fully in this volume is the rumoured affair between Dickens and his sister-in-law Georgina. Colin Rae Brown was threatened with a libel action by Dickens for spreading the rumour that Dickens had three children by his sister-in-law. This is surely the place for a footnote retailing the evidence (admittedly rather hearsay) put forward by Michael Slater that perhaps Georgina was examined by a doctor and given a certificate of virginity. Of course, there is no certainty here either – though Slater's tentative hypothesis has typically become a hard fact in Ackroyd's biography.

Dickens's genius was popular, so the animus of his contemporaries, Trollope and Thackeray, isn't hard to understand. Thackeray believed that 'the Great Moralist', as he sneeringly designates Dickens, was capable of encouraging a journalist to smear his rivals. Trollope despised Dickens ('Mr Popular Sentiment') for his reduction of government to the travesty of the

Circumlocution Office. Now, following the impulse to reinstate Dickens after the demotion initiated by F. R. Leavis, criticism is at the full once more, poised between the hostile and the sceptical.

But whatever his behaviour, Dickens is fluent with genius, even in these hastily penned letters. We encounter 'beehives of excellent manure' and several examples of his 'fanciful fidelity' – Allonby described as 'very much what Broadstairs would have been if it had been born Irish, and had not inherited a cliff'. In Paris, Dickens saw a production of *Comme il vous plaira*: 'Nobody has anything to do, but sit upon as many grey stones as he can. When Jacques had sat upon seventy seven stones and forty two roots of trees (which was at the end of the second act), we came away.' Every theatre-goer knows what he means.

# Ackroyd's *Dickens*

About halfway through this comprehensive yet uncomprehending life of Dickens, Peter Ackroyd quotes Copperfield on his marriage to the dead Dora: 'trifles make the sum of life'. It is a truism to which Ackroyd returns on his penultimate page – unsurprisingly, because all biography is not unlike the trifle itself, *zuppa inglese*, the dish that uses up damaged fruit, stale cake, dregs of wine, orts and leftovers. Dickens combed his hair in public. Simple vanity? Taken in conjunction with Dickens's obsessive punctuality, the habit is evidence of existential guilt – according to Ackroyd. But the biographer has to unify the odds and ends of life's detritus as best he can – so there will always be wobbly argument and gelatinous links.

For example: orifices. In the course of this new but nevertheless largely familiar biography, orifices occur frequently enough to provide a pseudo-theme. As a young boy in London, Dickens saw a tape worm with 'ears like a mouse'. Recovered from the stomach of a human being, it must have entered by one of two orifices. While writing *Barnaby Rudge*, Dickens suffered an operation to remedy an anal fistula – 'a gap in the rectal wall through which tissue had been forced'. The surgeon was Frederick Salmon, who, thirteen years later, wrote *A Practical Essay on Stricture of the Rectum*. There was, of course, no anaesthetic: 'the rectum would be opened up, and then held apart by some kind of surgical appliance, while the tissue was cut away and the sides of the rectal wall then sewn together'. One's eyes water

*Dickens* by Peter Ackroyd, Sinclair-Stevenson.

just reading about it. Recuperating, Dickens was forced to write the pressing instalments of *Barnaby Rudge* while lying on the sofa. At the end of his life, massive discharges of blood issued from 'his old complaint, piles' – one symptom of his eventually fatal vascular trouble. Another pathetically human anecdote, located in the same region, is retailed by Ackroyd: Dickens once stayed in the same hotel as the actor, Charles Kean, and, when he went to the lavatory, heard 'a man's voice (of tragic quality)' crying out, 'There is somebody here.'

Under the same spurious category, one might include the interesting fact that the morally prudish Dickens once told Daniel Maclise that he knew where the tarts lived in Margate – female orifices. Equally fascinating is the gynaecological exam-ination allegedly undergone by Georgina Hogarth, Dickens's sister-in-law, after Dickens separated from his wife, Catherine. His mother-in-law was convinced, apparently, that the cause of the break-up was her other, unmarried daughter, who had lived in the Dickens household for most of their married life. Georgina was found to be *virgo intacta* – and the in-laws were compelled to sign a legal document repudiating all rumours to the contrary.

Ackroyd is fulsome in his praise of the Pilgrim Edition of Dickens's letters – which is only proper, since virtually every 'new' fact in his biography comes from this source. *Dickens* is an intermittently conscientious trawl through the scholarship of others. Ackroyd's contribution is the sensibility of the novelist. However, since Ackroyd is a novelist whose speciality is pas-tiche, the sensibility on view is primarily that of Dickens. The style is the man. Orifices. The reason I chose this single word is that Dickens famously begins *Bleak House* with a one-word sentence. 'London.' Ackroyd's text, by the time it has passed the 1,000-page mark, is so slavishly imitative that almost every word in the English language, it seems, has been quarantined off from the others. Isolated. Not just the trouble-makers like 'Neglect' or 'Ruin', but even the patently harmless words. For instance: 'Expeditions'. 'Theatre'. 'Dust'. 'Water'. 'Blue'. 'Scar-let'. 'Lilac-green'.

In addition to being written in a prose style which resembles that of Dickens as waxworks in Madame Tussaud's resemble their real-life counterparts, Ackroyd also splices into his narrative a series of excursions. In these, T. S. Eliot, Oscar Wilde and Chatterton (old Ackroyd subjects) chat with Dickens; Dickens is shown encountering in 'real' life his imagined creations – thus illustrating an Ackroyd contention, tediously maintained over a thousand repetitive pages, that, for Dickens, nothing was real until written, and that he felt more deeply about his fictions than about actual people. In yet another interlude, Ackroyd meets the subject of his biography: Dickens, to one's surprise, doesn't denounce the misappropriation of his prose style.

None of these ornamental episodes is important. They are like the moustache and goatee which Marcel Duchamp pencilled on a cheap chromo reproduction of Leonardo da Vinci's *Mona Lisa*. Duchamp called it a 'combination readymade and iconoclastic dadaism'. (It was entitled *L.H.O.O.Q.* – 'letters which, pronounced like initials in French, made a very risqué joke on the Gioconda'.) That was in 1919. In 1965, invitations to a Duchamp retrospective showed the *Mona Lisa* untouched – but entitled *L.H.O.O.Q. Shaved*. Under the modish top-dressing, *Dickens* is equally conventional.

In one respect, however, it breaks with biographical procedure. There are no footnotes. Instead, there are notes about footnotes – short essaylets about Ackroyd's sources, which are calculated to madden anyone bent on checking either his facts, or the emphasis he puts on them. For instance, he accuses Dickens, at the time of writing Little Nell's death, of mocking Forster's grief when Macready's three-year-old daughter, Joan, died. The truth isn't quite so callous. Here, as elsewhere, Ackroyd has summarily travestied the detail of the Pilgrim Edition, flattened its intricate commentary beyond recognition. Dickens wrote to a mutual friend, Maclise: 'It is impossible, I am sure, that any people can more truly sympathise with the affliction of others, than we do for the sorrows of those to whom we are so strongly and ardently attached – and so I know you will say and feel. But I vow to God that if you had seen Forster last night, you would have supposed our Dear Friend was dead himself –

in such an amazing display of grief did he indulge and into such a very gloomy gulf was he sunk up to the chin.' When, in 1869, Macready's grown-up daughter, Kate, died, Dickens noted the same competitive mournfulness in Forster: 'I *cannot* get over the mania for proprietorship which is rampant at Palace House.'

Ackroyd includes none of this explanatory detail. It is squeezed out by a display of bland critical flourishes – a preference that might have astonished one less, had Ackroyd's preface been in the usual place, rather than page 892. There, in a general discussion of his biography, while boasting he has read everything Dickens wrote 'at least three times', he lets slip the following: 'Eliot was a breeze in contrast – you can get through his collected works in the course of a long weekend.' You can *get through* them indeed – but you can't read them, much less think about them. 'Reading' of this order is bound to produce criticism of this order: the 'peculiar chemistry of genius'; 'that strange alchemy of his genius' (twice); 'the crucible of young Dickens's imagination'; 'the alembic of his imagination'; 'sudden lance of wit'; 'the novelist of a thousand moods', unlike Tolstoy, George Eliot, Sterne, anyone. For Ackroyd, Chesterton is still the best critic of Dickens.

Every example of fudging, of trifling, follows from that allegiance. In case after case, Ackroyd assembles a few facts about each fiction – more or less interesting – and lazily pronounces the ritual formula, 'Everything comes together.' The phrase is applied twelve times, at a rough count, commencing with *The Pickwick Papers* and ending with *Our Mutual Friend*. Originally, for once, Ackroyd argues that *The Pickwick Papers* isn't a shapeless, improvised ragbag. Rather, it comes 'close to incorporating the rhythm of life itself', because it is without 'the conventional inhibitions of ordinary fiction' – which makes it sound implausibly Umberto Eco-like and ludic, or, as Ackroyd so poetically puts it, 'a shout of pure creation that rings out like the laughter of a child on a frosty day'. Or the guffaw of a reviewer. I do hope this fotherington-thomas school of criticism doesn't catch on.

*Dickens* has its virtues. It is commendably restrained in its speculations about Ellen Ternan and concludes, plausibly enough, that there were no sexual relations between her and Dickens. Dickens called her 'The Patient' – not a medical allusion, I think, but because she was waiting, patiently, yet in vain, for the death of Catherine Dickens, which would free the novelist for marriage. Ackroyd is good, too, on Dickens's racism. He believed blacks should be free, but the idea of granting them the vote struck Dickens as self-evidently absurd. Ackroyd attempts no alibi. Nor does he flinch from quoting letters to Miss Burdett Coutts which appear to advocate genocide in India, by way of reprisal.

Nevertheless, this is a bad, exhausted biography. Fat. Scant of breath. Too long. Too long for Ackroyd. On page 413, he tells us that Dickens did not invent Christmas, 'as the more sentimental of his chroniclers have suggested'. Including Ackroyd, on page 34: 'in view of the fact that Dickens can be said to have almost single-handedly created the modern idea of Christmas'. On page 583, Ackroyd adopts a tone of scalded affront: 'And there are still those who accuse Dickens of melodramatic exaggeration.' Indeed there are. One of them is Ackroyd on the next page: '*A Child's History of England* is in many ways a melodramatic and theatrical account.' As early as page 255, Ackroyd comments on Dickens's Hogarthian procedures: 'of his exaggerations there can be little doubt'.

This biography is bloated with contradictions, literary-critical baloney and suspect generalizations. How can Ackroyd maintain that Dickens was uninterested in psychological exploration or social realism? Nancy, the victim who connives in her fate? Fagin in the condemned cell? Peter Ackroyd has read everything, thought about precious little, and written blindly, hoping that everything will somehow 'come together'. It hasn't. Even that would be forgivable if he didn't write like Mantovani: 'Wasted. His heart laid bare.' Leave over, Mr Ackroyd. You done to Dickens what a stage hand said that Fechter did to *Hamlet*: 'Mr Kean was great. But with 'im *'Amlet* was a tragedy, with Mr Fechter it's quite another thing. He has raised it to a mellerdrama.'

# A Book that Changed My Life

> Not so much a book as a page. Not a page, even, more a
> paragraph. Not a paragraph so much as a word.   – *Lolita*

At my boarding school in 1959, when I was fourteen, another,
older boy, now I daresay happily married, his generosity not
untinged by homoeroticism, presented me with the first English
edition of Vladimir Nabokov's great novel. Inside the chastely
inscribed book – whose austere 'to' and 'from' gave nothing
away – the donor had thoughtfully underlined this passage in
Nabokov's ruminative postscript: 'But after all we are not
children, not illiterate juvenile delinquents, not English public
school boys who after a night of homosexual romps have to
endure the paradox of reading the Ancients in expurgated
versions.' Poor Nabokov. How could he know that his majestic
disclaimer would provide titillation for two of those very public
school boys?

I settled to read this dirty book – undeceived by the international tributes to Nabokov's art which were anthologized at
the back – and was at once *bouleversé* by the first paragraph,
which had, as it turned out, a particular personal message from
Nabokov to me. It was this: the word has a life of its own, a
sound of its own and a shape of its own. It isn't simply a
harmless drudge, it is also a monarch with a retinue of associations. It lives in the kingdom of the mouth and the mind. If it is
to obey you, you must cherish it as an individual and respect its
unique powers and properties. Every word is irreplaceable, as
Roget paradoxically but invariably demonstrates.

Nabokov told me this by concentrating on a single word, by telling me what it felt like in his mouth, by endowing it with the charisma of Fred Astaire tap-dancing down a flight of stairs: 'Lolita, light of my life, fire of my loins. My sin, my soul. Lo-lee-ta: the tip of the tongue taking a trip of three steps down the palate to tap, at three, on the teeth. Lo. Lee. Ta.' Not so much a word, then, as three syllables, an incantation. Not a sound but articulated sounds, achieving a kind of music – a tango.

At that point, deep down it was decided I would be a poet rather than a novelist. James Joyce is another writer who realized the magical power of words – words whose spell can so easily be dispelled by being mispelled. In *Ulysses*, Leopold Bloom remembers asking a young amateur in Meath to say a dirty word: 'All the dirty things I made her say all wrong of course. My arks she called it.' Bloom's discovery and my own discovery (thanks to Nabokov) are the same – *this* word and no other; anything else is simply inert. Coleridge's definition of poetry still holds: 'the best possible words in the best possible order'.

# Nabokov: The Russian Years

To the less gifted members of the literary body politic, great writers arrive among us like new diseases – threatening, power-ful, impatient for patients to pick up their virus, irresistible. Time, of course, will render them harmless. But in the meantime, no one is immune. Take the case of Nabokov, whose poised, profuse, exact, poetic style has proved to be a particularly virulent strain across the entire spectrum of talent.

Timofey Pnin has been to the dentist for an extraction that has radically altered the ecology of his mouth: 'his tongue, a fat sleek seal, used to flop and slide so happily among the familiar rocks'. It should come as no surprise to find a frank echo in Martin Amis's *Other People*, because Amis is a virtuoso fear-lessly open to influence and a notably generous celebrant of Nabokov's extraordinary talent: 'uselessly, like a sick old seal, Trev's tongue flaps round among the rock-pools and barnacles of his mouth'.

*Lolita* famously begins: 'Lolita, light of my life, fire of my loins. My sin, my soul. Lo-lee-ta: the tip of the tongue taking a trip of three steps down the palate to tap, at three, on the teeth. Lo. Lee. Ta.' It is risky and brilliant. But what if your heroine's name happens to be Bernadette? As it is in this bungled homage from Melvyn Bragg's *A Time to Dance*: 'How I loved saying your name to you in those early days. The three syllables, softly clacking my tongue against my palate. Bern – how urgent, how hot! A – the pause, a sigh, the fulcrum of anticipation; dette –

*Vladimir Nabokov: The Russian Years* by Brian Boyd, Chatto & Windus.

the stab, the claim.' It could have been worse. She could have been called Clothilda.

It could have been worse, too, because the echo could have been unintentional, as it is in John Updike's *Rabbit Redux*. There, Jill provides Rabbit Angstrom with 'the upside-down valentine of a woman's satin rear'. Updike could be indebted to Bellow's *Humboldt's Gift*: 'You have a bottom like a white valentine greeting.' But this trope has already had an outing in Nabokov's *Bend Sinister*: 'her rump, which in those days of tight skirts, looked like an inverted heart'. The coincidence of genius, perhaps – except that Updike is another reliable admirer, so much so that, when you learn of Nabokov's psoriasis (brought on by a serious adultery), you almost wonder if Updike's more famous psoriasis wasn't acquired in the spirit of emulation. After all, Samuel Beckett crushed his feet for years because he worshipped Joyce and his infatuation extended to the strikingly small footwear of the maestro. The disease can manifest itself in a multitude of ways – some of them silly.

Andrew Field's biography of Nabokov earned him the unstinted hatred of the family, and one of its most irritating features was the way the disciple persisted in purloining the manner of his master. Roll over, Beethoven. Shove off, Nabokov. Brian Boyd is not an authorized biographer, but he has been given the run of the Montreux archive and the freedom to dislike whichever of Nabokov's works he chooses. (His favoured mode of negative criticism is sweeping *complimenti* hotly pursued by equally sweeping reservations.) Boyd is more restrained than Field, but isn't above a little stylistic emulation himself. If he avers that Nabokov's head 'felt like a bowling alley' as he reworded his play *The Tragedy of Mr Morn*, be warned by the brilliance that the phrase comes from *Look at the Harlequins*: 'the left side of my head was now a bowling alley of pain'. Nabokov's 'chick-fluff of mimosas' from *Speak, Memory* is twice misappropriated. And, on one occasion, Boyd actually sounds more like Nabokov than Nabokov. In his story 'Perfection', Nabokov describes 'those transparent little knots that swim diagonally in the vitreous humour of the eye'. Boyd's scientifically Latinate version reads with authentically Nabokovian relish in the technical – 'ocular infusoria rolling across our field of vision' – and is probably stolen, too.

When Boyd introduces Nabokov's first love, he does so in a nimble pastiche of *Lolita*'s opening page: 'She was Valentina Evgenievna Shulgin on the dotted line, "Tamara" in his autobiography, "Mary" in his first novel, but on his lips she was always "Lyussya".' This quotation tells you a lot about Boyd's biography and the way in which, inevitably, it is tied to the authorized text and doctored pretext of Nabokov's autobiography, *Speak, Memory*. The material is no longer fluid. The picture has been sprayed with fixative. Norman Sherry faced the same problem with Graham Greene's pre-edited autobiography, *A Sort of Life*. Footnotes are possible. Boyd adds some meaty and indigestible tracts of Russian history, which one supposes are necessary but which Nabokov shrewdly did without – concentrating instead on the detailed foreground of a childhood whose vividness is conveyed to us with a directness unparalleled in literature. Certainly, no biographer could begin to rival it.

And it continues into the thirties and Berlin. When it stops, Boyd is honest enough to admit that biography is really bibliography, since Nabokov is at his desk, writing hard. Critical exposition, therefore, shares the honours with biographical data. There is sufficient, though, of the latter to divert the reader: for example, that desk was sometimes a suitcase over the bidet, so poor and cramped were the Nabokovs. We see how Nabokov inherited sang-froid from his father who, at his trial, corrected proofs, and later, imprisoned in St Petersburg's Kresty jail, had a collapsible rubber tub and ample hot water – and the determination to use his incarceration to catch up on his reading. Something of this cool poise is shown by the young Nabokov submitting a blank sheet of paper for the essay topic 'Laziness', or when he challenges his tutor to a bet that Dickens was not the author of *Uncle Tom's Cabin* – and wins a knuckle-duster.

At Trinity, Cambridge, he screwed the local girls, fought the local boys, took a first in part one of the tripos, broke furniture and street lamps, failed to pay his tailor or to locate the university library. He was 'any lively trilingual boy', who began as a poet and continued as the novelist Sirin.

Boyd tells us enough about Nabokov's love life to show that his right nostril, whose cartilage he damaged while boxing, was no handicap. He had three women in 1916, as part of an admittedly futile scheme to feed his art. Boyd has read *drafts* of some love letters – which suggests that Nabokov was always a conscious and painstaking writer, whatever the context. No mystery here – except to non-writers. In Greece, en route from Sebastopol and the Red Army, Nabokov conducted three affairs in three and a half weeks. In 1932, at a reading in Paris, a mistress from 1919 turned up to haunt him, 'reeking unbearably of sweat'. Then he married Véra. Throughout their married life, they slept in separate rooms, since Nabokov was insomniac. Nabokov's only serious infidelity was with Irina Guadanini, an émigrée who worked as a poodle-trimmer. Boyd's account of this is unprurient and touching. No one comes out of it badly, though Nabokov sees himself as a 'scoundrel'. The denouement is a sad, torn encounter on the beach at Cannes, where the loved but rejected mistress watches Nabokov with his beloved family from a distance – then vanishes, as asked.

In the impersonal world, history blunders brutally on. We learn about the patchy way in which state anti-Semitism could work: Véra, a Jew, applies for a job at the chancellery of a German minister and is told 'we pay no attention to such things'. At the same time, 1933, state power humiliates a non-Jew, Ivan Bunin, the first Russian Nobel Prize winner, who is fed castor oil by the Gestapo and made to squat over a bucket, in case he is smuggling jewels.

From this everyday unpleasantness, Nabokov's mother was relatively safe in Prague. On page 220, Boyd describes her arrival in 1923. It is an account I can add to because my late friend, Georgy Katkov, also an émigré, was the Nabokovs' landlord. According to him, the mother was grand and pitiful. Shown the cooker, she looked through her lorgnette and said: 'I know what *that* is for. You burn wood in it.' Despite warnings, she bought a second-hand *madame récamier* on which to recline with her son's poems. It was infested and the bugs bounced to the ceiling, where Volodya smashed them with a fly-swat. The commotion attracted my friend from the floor below. 'I thought you were a lepidopterist,' he remarked mischievously. Thirty years later, at a dinner in New York, Nabokov was still not speaking to him, although they had been seated next to each other.

This unforgiving streak was part of Nabokov's prose style as well as his personal style. He is ironical, not self-ironical – except in small doses. Not everyone admires Nabokov's prose without reserve and not everyone will be convinced by Boyd's rather contradictory and muddled justification of its candid artfulness. The expository style is central to his achievement. In the drama, as Boyd justly remarks, Nabokov plays chess without his queen. Otherwise, his style is incapable of self-effacement. Nabokov is a great *writer* – full of baroque brio and light years removed from a windowpane style. The prose is naturally cold – ideally suited to romping in the cruel situations that Nabokov's fiction contrives and punishing the nasty casts of characters he assembles.

Finally, though, Nabokov compels it to serve him in tender areas of human experience. The key moment comes with his first, early attempt at autobiography, an account of his French governess. Nabokov is significantly uneasy: the governess is ridiculous, but she is not morally grotesque. In fact, he is touched by her, without conceding one iota of accuracy: 'she surrenders her bulk to the wicker armchair, which, out of sheer fright, bursts into a salvo of crackling'. Even extreme consciousness, eternally vigilant and fluently expressive, can include kindness. The man himself was nicer than his rhetorical gift, as all his dealings with his dear ones show. On the third anniversary of his father's assassination, he wrote to his mother: 'we will see him again, in an unexpected but completely natural heaven ... He will come towards us in our common bright eternity, slightly raising his shoulders as he used to do, and we will kiss the birthmark on his hand without surprise.'

# Nabokov: The American Years

Nabokov 'had a flypaper feel for words', according to Alison Bishop, who knew him at Cornell when she was a child. He might, therefore, have relished his biographer coming mildly unstuck in the course of this otherwise tenacious, intricately argued, judicious account of Nabokov's life in the States, and, post-*Lolita*, in Montreux. Disposing of Andrew Field, his predecessor in the field, Brian Boyd cites his insolent, perfunctory response to one of Nabokov's factual corrections. Told an event had taken place in July and not on 'a wet autumnal day', Field amended the phrase to 'a wet autumnal day in July' – a covert imputation and rebuke of pedantry, not without a certain Nabokovian brilliance. The brilliance is unconsciously acknowledged by Boyd from forty pages later when his own phrase, 'a wretched autumnlike spring', revisits the trope.

Sometimes Nabokov's own flypaper feel betrayed him in the same way, though it is often difficult to distinguish between allusion, homage and degrees of debt, direct or indirect, to other writers. For example, he was a lifelong admirer of E. B. White and his correspondence indefatigably quotes White's colourful definition of a miracle: 'blue snow on a red barn'. (In *Lolita*, Humbert speaks of 'one humble blue car and its imperious red shadow'.) Of course, Nabokov was abnormally sensitive to colours – sounds and letters arrived in his ear colour-coded – and this may account for the depth of his response to White's

*Vladimir Nabokov: The American Years* by Brian Boyd, Chatto & Windus.

oxymoronic accuracy of observation. Is it fellow-feeling or emulous study which produces an earlier variant on the plausible mismatches of nature's palette? 'Brown woolly smoke arched and dipped over the green shadow it cast on the aquamarine lake.'

White matters less than Joyce, about whom Nabokov, on occasion, could be unruefully generous. In one interview, he gave out this undeniable admission: 'my English is patball to Joyce's champion game'. Mostly, though, Nabokov was inclined to minimize the influence of Joyce on his work. He held by his stern avowal that his mature style was formed long before he read *Ulysses* with any attention. That flypaper feel, however, means that Nabokov is, consciously and unconsciously, an aural retentive. A conscious example: 'bizarre, tender, salivating Dr Humbert, practising on supremely lovely Lolita the Third the art of being a granddad'. Here Nabokov presents us with an allusion to an allusion. In the library episode of *Ulysses*, Mr Best does his best to insert an allusion to Victor Hugo into the torrent of Stephen's Shakespearean speculation. ' – The art of being a grandfather, Mr Best gan murmur. *L'art d'être grand . . .*' But the title of Hugo's volume of verse for children is carried away on the cataract of eloquence.

On the other hand, consider the transmogrified, involuntary progress of Bloom's kidney, 'the moist tender gland' he purchases at Dlugacz's shop. In Humbert's parody of *Ash-Wednesday*, which he makes Quilty recite prior to his murder, the adjectives suddenly obtrude: 'Because you took advantage of a sin when I was helpless moulting moist and tender . . .' And when the young Nabokov is attracted to Tamara in *Speak, Memory*, his *tendresse* resorts to the same paired adjectives, appropriately relocated: 'the tender, moist gleam on her lower eyelid'. A Humbert would draw the jury's attention not only to the two familiar adjectives, arm-in-arm, but also to the swift glissando of 'gland' to 'gleam'. *Enormous Changes at the Last Minute.*

In *The Gift*, there is a more generalized debt to Bloom's shopping. Godunov-Cherdynstev's purchase of shoes – an epic of hypnotic banality retailed with rapt pedantry – is inconceivable without Joyce's prior example:

> A young woman in a black dress, with a shiny forehead and quick, wandering eyes, sat down at his feet for the eighth time, sideways on a stool, numbly extracted a narrow shoe from the rustling interior of its box, spread her elbows apart as she slackened the edges, glanced abstractedly aside as she loosened the laces, and then, producing a shoehorn from her bosom, addressed Fyodor's large, shy, poorly darned foot. Miraculously the foot entered, but having done so, went completely blind: the wiggling of toes inside had no effect on the exterior smoothness of the taut black leather. With phenomenal speed the salesgirl tied the lace ends and touched the tip of the shoe with two fingers.

She is, of course, fondling the details, as if she were a student of Nabokov: 'in reading one should notice and fondle the details,' he adjured his class at Cornell. As a writer, Nabokov is a fanatic for detail, his mimesis rivalling that of nature itself: 'when a butterfly had to look like a leaf, not only were all the details of the leaf beautifully rendered but markings mimicking grub-holes were generously thrown in'. Nabokov consciously competes with this luxuriant, exuberant generosity: 'I discovered in nature,' he writes in *Speak, Memory*, 'the non-utilitarian delights that I sought in art.' There is something gloriously otiose in, say, Humbert's discovery, after he has murdered Quilty and passed unmolested through the guests congregated downstairs, that his car is likewise in a tight spot from which it, too, will negotiate an escape unscathed: 'two other cars were parked on both sides of it, and I had some trouble squeezing out'.

When Humbert initially arrives at Ramsdale, it is to stay with the McCoo family, but, on the day, the McCoo house burns down and Mr McCoo brings the bad news to Humbert's hotel

– 'distraught' and *'in wet clothes'*. (My italics.) The prodigality reminds me of Emily Dickinson:

> As if I asked a common Alms,
> And in my wondering hand
> A Stranger pressed a Kingdom,
> And I, bewildered, stand –

Then there is the little, optionally extra dog taking 'rapid chords with his front paws on the resilient turf'. Or the quarrel between Humbert and Lo about their pursuer which she suddenly interrupts with eloquent irrelevance: 'If I were you – Oh, look, all the nines are changing into the next thousand. When I was a little kid . . . I used to think they'd stop and go back to nines, if only my mother agreed to put the car in reverse.'

All this is a long way from the prose commonly associated with Nabokov, poetic prose whose oppressiveness Virginia Woolf reluctantly stigmatized in 'Impassioned Prose', where she evokes Laurence Binyon's remark that 'poetical prose has but a bastard kind of beauty, easily appearing overdressed'. Nabokov, it should be said, is not entirely immune to sartorial excess. Now and then the odd sentence flourishes like Dickens's Dickensian signature – a towering whirlwind of inky underlinings. For instance, it is dismaying to learn from Boyd that a particularly tiresome sentence in *Speak, Memory* was not a temporary lapse, but a considered substitute for a shy piece of nomenclature which wouldn't reveal itself even after extensive inquiries. Nabokov wanted to know what the concertina connections between railway carriages were called. No luck. He settled for 'intervestibular connecting curtains as black as bat-wings'. At his best, though, he is superseded only by Joyce: the E. B. White-ish 'maroon morons near blued pools'; 'the beaded tracks of a wagtail'; 'a cuckoo began to call in a copse, listlessly'.

A great deal to fondle, then. But, with all this fondling, how much feeling? Critics have always had their doubts. Ronald Hingley maintained that Nabokov's work in general 'secretes about as much milk of human kindness as a cornered black mamba'. Nabokov responded by putting Hingley into the translation (heavily revised) of *King, Queen, Knave* as a department store mannequin – a literal blockhead. The odd thing is that, in addition to a critical study, Hingley was reviewing *Speak, Memory*, a book which, like *Pnin*, displays Nabokov's humanity at its most engaging.

His private manner was utterly winning, particularly his comic mode. Boyd includes two anecdotes, both innocently revealing. In the late sixties, Nabokov asked Alfred Appel if student unrest was disrupting his lectures. The only demonstrations were demonstrations of affection: 'I told him about a nun who sat in the back row of one of my lecture courses, and who one day complained after class that a couple near her were always spooning. "Sister," I said, "in these troubled times we should be grateful if that's all they were doing." ... "Ohhh," moaned Nabokov, mourning my lost opportunity, clapping his hand to his head in mock anguish. "You should have said, 'Sister, be grateful that they were not forking.' "' No problem with the man. When *Lolita* was scaling the bestseller list and before Nabokov became wary of the spontaneous interview, a reporter from *Sports Illustrated* accompanied the Nabokovs on a butterfly-hunting trip. Nabokov kept up a running commentary. When the car wouldn't start, he explained it was 'nervous'. When the expected butterflies didn't materialize, Nabokov lugubriously narrated: 'And then I saw that strong man put his head on his forearms and sob like a woman.' Another blank search produced another parodic cliché: 'his face now a tear-stained mask'. But the books, what do they reveal?

According to Christopher Ricks, the notes to *Eugene Onegin* have a tone of 'patiently patrician calm' whose 'coolness can easily become the condescending heartlessness which so attenuates Nabokov's fiction'. D. J. Enright found Nabokov 'rich in what is given to few writers and poor in what is given to most men'. Martin Seymour-Smith, reviewing *Laughter in the Dark*, described Nabokov as 'a kind of Satanic Mantovani, coming into cruel close-up on your screens at the end of the compelling torment to ask (the question mark ironic) "You have been distressed by my music, you worms?"' All three critics, with their very different abilities, share the comforting belief that, *au fond*, the artist is great because he is morally commendable. This is sentimental in two important respects. It undervalues skill and giftedness. And is goodness so commendable if, like beauty, like grace, it, too, is a gift well beyond most of us? By goodness I mean something more than the mere negative exercise of virtue. But even arid virtue would be something, were one able to discern it on any scale in the annals of history. Anyone who, like Nabokov, had survived Nazi Germany would be unlikely to leave unquestioned Enright's accusation that Nabokov was 'poor in what is given to most men'. Most men when? Enright's review begins (an hilarious category mistake) by comparing Nabokov to Peter De Vries: 'whereas De Vries despairs of his fellow beings *without ceasing to love them* altogether'. [My pop-eyed italics]. The friend of the world is nigh. But love is an exclusive emotion. Loving mankind is a logical contradiction, produced by too much treacle in the blood. Duty is a different matter.

Edmund Wilson considered Nabokov cruel, too. But if we reconsider that hemmed-in car at the end of *Lolita*, we can see the fidelity of Nabokov's record. Experience will never endorse the simplified democracy of emotion desired by Enright, or the heartiness that Ricks would oppose to Nabokov's 'condescending heartlessness'. Experience is never unmixed with irony. You commit a murder, but this doesn't alter the eternal parking problem, the presence of the trivial, always soliciting attention. Flaubert, who climbed the great pyramid only to discover the card of a French polisher from Rouen on the top (put there by his friend Maxime DuCamp), knew the indestructible irony that plays around life and death: he had seen his surgeon father park a cigar between the toes of a stiff.

Nabokov shared the same knowledge. In hospital with chronic diarrhoea and vomiting, he not only observed his own throes, but also an old man dying: 'all very interesting and useful to me'. Boyd quotes a newspaper report of a student who killed himself at Evanston. Answering the last question of his French paper, the student wrote, in French, 'I am going to God. Life does not offer me much.' Nabokov pounced on it: 'Adopt him. I see the story clearly. Combine him with notes of Jan 26 . . . Make him make some pathetic mistake in the last sentence. Change it, of course . . . Probe, brood.' This is only superficially hardhearted. One word, 'pathetic', gives us the key to Nabokov's vision – the way it fuses pathos and pitiable ineptitude. It is the admixture of the absurd, the touch of verisimilitude, which ministers, in the end, to the pathos. It is something Martin Seymour-Smith reports quite accurately, without understanding the least particle of Nabokov's method: 'yet such is Nabokov's casual power that he causes the reader to suffer with the ridiculous Albinus as he loses his daughter, his sight, and his money, actually to wish to plead with Margot on his behalf, and to loathe the villainous Rex'. Quite so. Nabokov's tragedy wasn't reserved for the noble. It could encompass and engulf the ignoble too.

Artistically, the point is that we readers should see, with fascinated gratitude, the mixed truth of experience as it actually is. In Nabokov's world, you are either an ironist or a simpleton. Consider *Lolita*, for example, a book denounced by Enright as 'his most distasteful, arch, affected, and perverse' work. Enright's disgust is less shocking now than it once would have seemed. We know about child abuse. But Nabokov is interested in both child abuse *and* romantic love. He brings the two together the better to explore pathos and pitiable ineptitude. Boyd, after a brief nod towards *Lolita* as 'a passionate and poignant love story', as 'an unformulaic novel', then goes out of his way to underscore Nabokov's moral disapproval of Humbert. He is correct, but only up to a point. 'Dolores Haze,' Humbert avers self-inculpatingly, 'had been deprived of her childhood by a maniac.' This verdict – *maniac* – may comfort readers by its fundamentalism, but it isn't accurate.

Truer to the book, though, is Humbert's constant reference to the myth of beauty *and* the beast, with its princely outcome. If having fondled Nabokov's details, we allow them to copulate, we can see a theme pregnant with interest for Nabokov in several books. *Laughter in the Dark* gives us the helpless passion of Albinus for the unworthy object, the tawdry Margot. Pnin is in abject thrall to an equally unworthy object, Liza Wind, his former wife: 'to hold her, to keep her – just as she was – with her cruelty, with her vulgarity, with her blinding blue eyes, with her miserable poetry, with her fat feet, with her impure, dry, sordid, infantile soul'. One thinks of Stanley Spencer's Beatitudes of Love, a series which reminds us that, seen truly, the body is rather more grotesque than we usually imagine. In *Transparent Things*, Hugh Person is locked to Armande after one display of tenderness – unique, as it turns out, but curiously binding: 'He loved her in spite of her unloveableness.' *Lolita* surely began as another novel of this kind, with this difference – that the object of the love is not 'unworthy', rather that the love-object can never be commensurate with the love. This is the disparity it shares with *Pnin*, *Laughter in the Dark* and *Transparent Things*.

Nabokov's interest in *Lolita* is in the indestructible myth of the indestructible passion – the categorical imperative that overrides all other categorical imperatives. We see it in Racine, in *Wuthering Heights*, in Graham Greene, in *Les Liaisons Dangereuses*, in *Love in a Time of Cholera* – love as a terminal illness. In contrast, we may consider the *nous* of Auden: 'We meet romantically passionate engaged couples, but never a couple of whom we can say that their romantic passion will not and cannot change into married affection or decline into indifference.' Auden is right, but the myth endures and, in *Lolita*, Nabokov's strategy is to lend it the only plausibility possible: it is credible, this obsessive love, only if it is perverse. Nabokov finds the perfect carrier of the romantic virus in Humbert – biologically doomed to a select sexual sliver of the female spectrum, laceratingly intelligent at the same time, and therefore capable of abject attachment and supreme detachment. The rhetoric of sarcasm, the deliciously heartless observations ('a man having a lavish epileptic fit on the ground in Russian Gulch State Park') are all apparently opposed to the mythos, but actually underwrite it, therefore.

399

In the meantime, comedy is the Nabokovian additive to the romantic mythos. Humbert reports the fusion of feeling and fatuity, faithful to the actuality of his first act of intercourse with Lolita. The account isn't edited by passion: Humbert's heels are 'stone-cold', the sleeping Lo has an 'unfair amount of pillow', Humbert has no place to rest his head and 'a fit of heartburn', his thoughts are preoccupied with sleeping pills ('in the glove compartment – or in the Gladstone bag?'), his ears occupied with the surrounding chorus of lavatories, once or twice he catches himself 'drifting into a melancholy snore'. At the same time, Humbert and Nabokov can make us feel 'the aura of her bare shoulder'. The peculiar, brilliant Nabokovian gift is to make us feel equally the force of Humbert's claim to be 'burning with desire and dyspepsia'.

Nabokov brings fresh enervation to Ovid's acute observation that post-coital sadness isn't rare. 'With the ebb of lust, an ashen sense of awfulness, abetted by the realistic drabness of a grey neuralgic day, crept over me and hummed within my temples.' Mood established, Nabokov can now let the external detail speak for itself, a little huskily in the aftermath: 'a touch of rosy rash around her swollen lips'; 'I was unbathed, unshaven, and had had no bowel movement'. Lastly, there is frank panic, not unmixed with lust: 'This was a lone child, an absolute waif, with whom a heavy-limbed, foul-smelling adult had had strenu-ous intercourse three times that very morning. Whether or not the realization of a lifelong dream had surpassed all expectation, it had, in a sense, overshot its mark – and plunged into a nightmare. I had been careless, stupid and ignoble. And let me be frank: somewhere at the bottom of that dark turmoil I felt the rising of desire again . . .' No one is better than Nabokov at reporting the thing which did not happen – that non-existent bowel movement or the assertion of Lo that Humbert has 'torn something inside her', which proves not to be the case, despite the awesome power of the adjective 'strenuous' when coupled with 'intercourse'. The attentiveness here, so crucial to the complex truth of the event described, is the same attentiveness that gave us the shoe purchase in *The Gift* and the X-ray machine's vision of every phalange on the foot. The method is methodical, unhurried, meticulous, forensic and inspired.

For Brian Boyd, *Lolita* is 'the radical, repulsive inversion of the whole theme' of parental love for children. I'm afraid I find this a reductive reading, in which a great many details go unfondled in the interests of protecting Nabokov's reputation for humanity. One could cite Nabokov's afterword to the novel: 'despite John Ray's assertion, *Lolita* has no moral in tow'. I prefer, too, Nabokov's aesthetic as it emerges from a discussion of Gogol's 'The Overcoat': 'the diver, the seeker for black pearls, the man who prefers the monsters of the deep to the sunshades on the beach, will find in "The Overcoat" shadows linking our state of existence to those other states and modes we dimly apprehend in our rare moments of irrational perception . . . At this superhigh level of art, literature is of course not concerned with pitying the underdog or cursing the upperdog. It appeals to that secret depth of the human soul where the shadows of other worlds pass like the shadows of nameless and soundless ships.' His aesthetic, then, is not prescriptive, but descriptive, exploratory, unafraid – certainly unafraid of the Humbert he can locate within himself and, therefore, within us, his readers.

Asked in 1962 by Peter Duval-Smith in an interview, Nabokov addressed the charge of cruelty directly. The question was: 'It sometimes seems to me that in your novels – in *Laughter in the Dark*, for instance – there is a strain of perversity amounting to cruelty.' Answer: 'I don't know. Maybe. Some of my characters are, no doubt, pretty beastly, but I really don't care, they are outside my inner self like the mournful monsters of a cathedral façade – demons placed there merely to show that they have been booted out. Actually, I'm a mild old gentleman who loathes cruelty.' It's a curiously unthreatened credo, but also an admission that the monsters were inside and have been 'booted out'. In these self-righteous times, it is a brave, considered affirmation of all those negatives, all those black potentialities, which only age can efface – if then – and which age now and then actually uncovers. Unsurprisingly, Golding, a novelist given to unflinching self-criticism, picks up and literal-

NABOKOV: THE AMERICAN YEARS

izes Nabokov's metaphor in *The Spire*: 'he would stand, thinking with what accuracy and inspiration those giants had built
the place, because the gargoyles seemed cast out of the stone,
burst out of the stone like boils and pimples, purging the body
of sickness, ensuring by their self-damnation, the purity of the
whole'.

Boyd evidently loves Nabokov – not uncritically, but protec-
tively, and this is a quality to be cherished in a biographer when
the general tendency seems to veer towards iconoclasm (in
Humphrey Carpenter's case, towards a good-natured, philistine
vandalism). So one applauds his defence. And yet one is still
unsettled when it comes to what Boyd calls, in his closing pages,
'the superficially heartless worlds of many of his books'. One
absolutely convincing explanation of Nabokov's apparent lofty
indifference is Boyd's demonstration that Nabokov believed, like
Pnin, 'dimly, in a democracy of ghosts. The souls of the dead,
perhaps, formed committees, and these, in continuous session,
attended to the destinies of the quick'. With such a belief, you
can see why even the most oppressive circumstances can be
considered with authorial equanimity. Nevertheless, there is
something which asks to be explained at the end of *Bend
Sinister*: 'Twang. A good night for mothing.' Updike, in a review
of *The Defence*, tentatively offered lepidoptery as a key to
Nabokov's psyche: 'the lepidopterist's habit of killing what it
loves; how remarkably few, after all, of Nabokov's characters
do evade the mounting pin'. Perhaps, though, 'The Ballad of
Reading Gaol' isn't the poem we want at this juncture. Might it
not rather be a case of gathering things into the artifice of
eternity? Isn't it, too, a refusal to accept, even for a nanosecond,
the sentimental fiction that fiction is anything more than fiction,
however real the novelist strives to make it? Nabokov was
imperiously testy about Forster's notion ('as old as the quills')
that characters could 'take over' a novel. 'My characters are
galley slaves.'

In Volume 1, Brian Boyd referred to a short story, 'Breaking
the News': 'those who have called Nabokov cold and inhuman
have not read this story'. In fact, the story is not obviously

compassionate. Most readers would find elements in it that are grotesque, macabre and a little pitiless. The plot is easily summarized: 'Eugenia Isakovna Mints was an elderly émigrée widow, who always wore black. Her only son had died on the previous day. She had not yet been told.' This is Nabokov's opening paragraph in its entirety – so neutral as to verge on the summary, though there may be a hint of pathos in her continued mourning.

To the basic situation, Nabokov adds a dangerous, destabilizing, comic ingredient – Eugenia Isakovna's deafness. She is 'ideally deaf' as Pnin is 'ideally bald'. Boris Chernobylski, a friend, is the person with the responsibility for breaking the news. Having arranged the son's job (in Paris), he is the person who has been informed, by telegram, then airmail letter, of the death: 'the poor young man had fallen into an elevator shaft from the top floor and had remained in agony for forty minutes: although unconscious, he kept moaning horribly and uninterruptedly, till the very end'.

At this point, the deafness is introduced by Nabokov and, with it, a whole train of wincing ironies. Synchronized with the fatal telegram is the delayed arrival of a postcard from the dead man to his mother. A comic masterpiece of mangled idiom, it is gruesomely proleptic: '*My darling Moolik* [her son's pet name for her since childhood[, *I continue to be plunged up to the neck in work and when evening comes I literally fall off my feet, and I never go anywhere* – ' As the widow goes out shopping, she is observed with a kind of Joycean 'scrupulous meanness': 'one also noted that her feet seemed disproportionately large and that she set them down draggingly, with toes turned out'. Her friends, meanwhile, consult on the telephone and foregather at the widow's apartment. The difficulty for them is her deafness, which precludes tact and gradualism. 'Shuf suggested they write on bits of paper, and give her to read, gradual communications: "Sick". "Very sick." "Very, very sick."' The thriving comedy already challenges the pathos. Nabokov's imaginative alertness treats us to a superb digression into Chernobylski's egotism, helpless, harmless, utterly human in its bizarre insistence: 'And to think it was *I* who got that job for him, *I* who helped him with his living expenses!' Nabokov further assaults the purity of his tragic donnée by the comically maladroit English of the émigrés, by their authentic mixture of sadness, sympathy and self-importance. They are dismayed, but enjoying the drama. Not that the drama excludes the little, irrelevant, ironical sartorial soliloquy as Chernobylski dresses to go out: 'fiercely and agonizingly baring his teeth and throwing back his fat face, he finally got his collar fastened'.

At the apartment, the widow misreads the situation. For her, the sudden confluence of friends seems the opportunity for an impromptu lunch and, deafly, she busies herself to that end, until a 'warm-hearted' (i.e., tactless) pianist lodger at the Chernobylskis *shouts* 'to her that nobody, nobody would stay for lunch'. The widow, still unconscious of anything amiss, turns instead to making snacks . . . More and more friends arrive, form oppressive groups, and gradually a contagious sense of doom begins to affect the widow. 'Somebody had already walked away to the window and was shaking and heaving there, and Dr Orshanski, who sat next to her at the table, attentively examined a gaufrette, matching it, like a domino, with another.' Finally, Chernobylski, sobbing, roars across the room: 'What's there to explain – dead, dead, dead!' 'But she was already afraid to look in his direction' is the final sentence of the tale.

How do we read it? It has the resourceful ingenuity of a gifted torturer and a kind of grim gaiety: 'Madame Chernobylski and the warm-hearted pianist had been waiting there for quite a long time. *Now the execution would start.*' (My italics.) Is it possible to relish the ironies and cherish the injuries? The answer is clearer if one considers the two biographical sources for this story (neither picked up by Boyd, oddly enough). The story was written circa 1935 but its twin germs occurred almost simultaneously a decade earlier. In mid-December 1921, Nabokov, en route from Cambridge, visited his former governess, Cécile Miauton. She was almost completely deaf. Nabokov bought her a hearing aid, on the assumption that she was unable to afford one. The result is recorded in *Speak, Memory*: 'she adjusted the clumsy thing improperly at first, but no sooner had she done so than she turned to me with a dazzled look of moist wonder and bliss in her eyes. She swore she could hear every word, every murmur of mine. She could not for, having my doubts, I had not spoken.' Mlle Miauton lives with Mlle Golay, 'my mother's former governess', 'with whom she had not been on speaking terms when both had been living under our roof'. (In 'Breaking the News', the widow has not been on speaking terms with Frau Doktor Schwarz, her landlady, for a week.)

If this is the comic germ of the story, the tragic germ occurred only a few months later, in March 1922, when Nabokov's father was assassinated, as he defended a political rival. The assassins didn't even know who Nabokov's father was. This inept tragedy goes some way towards explaining Nabokov's artistic predilection for fatal farce. Eliot said memorably that when 'a poet's mind is perfectly equipped for its work, it is constantly amalgamating disparate experience'. Nabokov's biography supplies a classic case history – mating a deaf governess and a political assassination. Nabokov's diary provides a complete account of the latter event, the centre of which is the difficulty of breaking the news, both to Nabokov and to his mother.

Hessen conceals the full truth from Nabokov when he telephones: 'Something terrible has happened to your father.' A car is dispatched for mother and son. Nabokov informs his mother and *invents* an accident: 'Father hurt his leg, rather seriously Hessen said.' When the car arrives, Yakovlev tells Nabokov: 'Keep calm. Shots were fired at the meeting. Your father was wounded.' Nabokov, knowing the truth has been softened, passes on to his mother that her husband has been 'badly' wounded. When they reach the Philharmonie where the meeting has been, they are met by Hessen and Kaminka. 'Avgust Isaakievich, Avgust Isaakievich, what has happened, tell me, what's happened?' Nabokov's mother begs. Neither man can bring himself to utter the absolute truth. 'He sobs, cannot finish.' And the widow at last makes it out for herself. The police will not allow them into the room where the body lies. The whole passage is an extraordinary feat of memorialization. Nabokov misses nothing. Not the way Hessen, appealed to for the truth, 'spreads out his hands'. Not the way 'their teeth chatter' and 'their eyes dart away'. Not the way 'from one door a black-bearded man with a bandaged hand came out, and *somehow helplessly smiling* muttered, "You see I . . . I am wounded too." ' [My humbled italics.] Nabokov was twenty-three. What a writer.

The egotism of the bearded marginal figure finds its way into 'Breaking the News', where it is transposed into Chernobylski's protestations. More surprising perhaps is the physical detail which Elena Nabokov shares with Eugenia Isakovna Mints: both have 'twitching eyebrows' and when Nabokov's mother first hears of the unspecified accident, she exclaims, 'My heart will burst, simply burst if you are hiding anything.' When the Chernobylskis are wondering how to break the news, their words are identical: 'Her heart will not bear it, it will burst, her poor heart.' Nabokov knew about the impurity of experience at first hand and was faithful to its farce as well as to its tragedy.

In August 1954, Nabokov wrote to his *New Yorker* editor, Katharine White, about the second chapter of *Pnin*, which she had rejected five months previously. 'Let me say merely that the "unpleasant" quality of Chapter 2 is a special trait of my work in general; you just did not notice in Chapter 1 the same nastiness, the same "realism" and the same pathos.' The protest of Katharine White, faced with the selfish absolutism of the Winds' exploitation of Pnin, its banal evil, is the protest of Nahum Tate when he rewrote *King Lear*. It represents the desire in all of us to close our eyes, to give the retina a rest, and love our fellow beings en masse – to see evil as aberrant rather than intrinsic. Tell it to Gloucester.

From 1940 or so, Nabokov's life gradually settled and simpli-fied itself, after a promising zany beginning in America – where customs officers, on his arrival, donned the boxing gloves they found in his luggage and staged some impromptu sparring on the wharf side. At his naturalization ceremony, the language test and the history test dissolved into an extended rally of kidding

between Nabokov and his examiner ('of Italian origin apparently, judging by his slight accent'). Teaching, lepidoptery and
writing devoured his time and attention. The Nabokovs were
poor but indifferent to the ugly furniture of their rented surroundings. Volodya would serve local port in jam-jars to his
guests and sit outdoors reading in the two feet of unmown grass.
Teaching was a matter of persuading his students to fondle the
details. 'Describe the wallpaper in the Karenins' bedroom' was
a typical examination question. Listening to the hobbled Russian
of his students, he would remark, 'So good to hear Russian
spoken again! I am practically back in Moscow.' The denouncer
of Dostoevsky, *Doctor Zhivago*, Thomas Mann, Faulkner,
George Eliot, Klebnikov, *War and Peace*, Stendhal and Cervan-
tes, 'he particularly liked reading bad literature aloud – "I can't
stop quoting!" he would chortle with glee'. His ebullience and
self-delight were clearly a trial to Edmund Wilson, who, though
a generous supporter of the unknown genius, was always irked
by Nabokov's independence. As a writer, he was completely
sure of his own worth and we believe Véra's diary when it says:
'There hardly ever was an author as indifferent to praise or
invective as V – "I have too high an opinion of myself to
mind."' With *Lolita*, publishers suddenly came running, only to
cool as subsequent sales proved less sensational. Then McGraw-
Hill offered wholesale prestige publication of more or less
anything Nabokov wanted in print. He was to be their flagship
author – until 'economic changes made him seem almost unaffordable and corporate changes eliminated his editors'. The
infatuation lasted six years, a long time in the world of fickle,
philistine publishers.

# Lolita

Robert Bridges, to the dismay of his correspondent Gerard Manley Hopkins, once described Matthew Arnold as Mr Kidgloves Cocksure. It sounds like one of Nabokov's hilarious, candidly transparent pseudonyms – Miss Opposite, Insomnia Lodge, Taxovich, Professor Chem – and it has some relevance to Nabokov's imperious, icy, unfaltering, acid, unimpressed public persona. Kidgloves Cocksure. Writing to his mentor Edmund Wilson, sometime in the forties, Nabokov appends a P.S.: 'P.S. I have read your Faulkner. You are pulling my leg.' This perfunctory postscript is pseudo-humorously pseudo-baffled, but in fact contemptuously downright in its certainty. Behind that amiable, indulgent chuckle, there is affronted taste and indignant critical chastisement.

This forthright, unforgiving side to Nabokov's personality was a facet foreign to his domestic circle. He was a tender son, an affectionate sibling, loving husband and generous parent. Nor is it central to his novels, though *minor* characters find their nastiness matched by their author's exacting genius for the punitive. 'Never trust the artist,' said D. H. Lawrence, 'trust the tale.' Despite Nabokov's entirely external denunciation (in *Strong Opinions*) of Humbert Humbert as 'a vain and cruel wretch who manages to appear "touching"', the novel itself offers us something less dogmatic. The same thing is true of Lolita, the recipient of an equally external unqualified testimonial to her sterling qualities: she was, observed Nabokov, second only to Pnin in the list of his characters he most admired as people.

Humbert, however, is no simple pervert, whatever these strong opinions may suggest. Nor is Nabokov's strategy that adumbrated by his biographer Brian Boyd – to compromise his readers' sympathy for Humbert by finally confronting us with the sordid truth, the haggled-over handjobs, the pricing of fancy embraces, the nymphet's nightly weeping, the tawdry actuality of Humbert's paedophilia. Great novelists write out of division, uncertainties, borderlines, complication, rather than moral wall-charts and the charge-sheets of crude common law. They explore their characters. They do not arraign them. As a matter of fact, Humbert arraigns himself.

The imaginative, cellular division which sustains *Lolita*, nourishing and enriching it, begins in the novel's Foreword by John Ray, Jr, Ph.D. (described in Nabokov's afterword as a 'character', significantly enough). Dr Ray represents the conventional moral viewpoint we are sometimes urged to attribute to Nabokov. Ray is the spokesman for a world of papier mâché pieties, as exemplified in his final auto-ironic flourish: '*Lolita* should make all of us – parents, social workers, educators – apply ourselves with still greater vigilance and vision to the task of bringing up a better generation in a safer world.' The authentic intonation of a man finding his mouth full of conventional solemnities. No wonder Nabokov specifically disowns him: 'I am neither a reader nor a writer of didactic fiction, and, despite John Ray's assertion, *Lolita* has no moral in tow' – in tow, one is tempted to add, like 'the huge fat house trailer weaving in front' of the Haze sedan. (*Weaving!*)

Another, subversive voice is audible in the Foreword, which, while condemning Humbert, confides and coerces: 'how magically his singing violin can conjure up a tendresse, a compassion for Lolita that makes us entranced with the book while abhorring its author!' When the Foreword refers to 'the robust philistine' or asserts that 'a great work of art is of course always original, and thus by its very nature should come as a more or less shocking surprise', we distinguish between these authorial apothegms and the simplicities of the psychiatrist. As we are intended to do. The effect is not unlike Humbert's double-take on his first encounter with the darkened, drunken Quilty on the porch of The Enchanted Hunters, immediately prior to Humbert's seduction of and by Lolita. Just as Quilty's name deliberately evokes the word 'guilty', so their conversation is, as it were, tuned to two stations at once – the conventional signal and the singular signal. ' "Where the devil did you get her?" "I beg your pardon?" "I said: the weather's getting better." '

Dog Latin, suave French, fluffed French, 'a perfect love song of wisecracks', inarticulate American ('Why do those people guess so much and shave so little?'), fatuous Fauntleroy ('One summer noon, just below timberline, where heavenly-hued blossoms that I would fain call larkspur crowded all along a purly mountain brook, we did find, Lolita and I, a secluded romantic spot'), the psychodrivel of Miss Pratt, the telephonic *tendresse* of Charlotte Haze – these are a few samples of the exact polyphony preserved in *Lolita* by Nabokov's exacting ear.

Nevertheless, the two central voices, dominating all others, belong to Humbert Humbert. At first they are indistinguishable – like his Christian name and surname – but eventually they too divide and we recognize them for what they are, the imperative and the accusative, the sexually romantic and the sated regret. It takes Humbert the length of the novel to realize what Nabokov has known all along – 'fulfilment's desolate attic', to adopt Larkin's bleak insight. The key passage comes early in the novel: at the end of Chapter 5, Humbert recounts an emblematic episode:

> It happened for instance that from my balcony I would notice a lighted window across the street and what looked like a nymphet in the act of undressing before a cooperative mirror. Thus isolated, thus removed, the vision acquired an especially keen charm that made me race with all speed toward my lone gratification. But abruptly, fiendishly, the tender pattern of nudity I had adored would be transformed into the disgusting lamp-lit bare arm of a man in his underclothes reading his paper by the open window, in the hot, damp, hopeless summer night.

It is a passage executed with great bravura by Nabokov and alluded to much later at the beginning of Chapter 27 (Part Two), some 240 pages later – and it encapsulates the Humbert erotic experience, from concupiscent cooperation (or the illusion of it) to dirty old man, from romance to self-revulsion, from reciprocation to the sordid solipsism of sperm on the hand. Humbert Humbert – the name a mirror of the inescapable self he is stuck with. 'We had been everywhere. We had really seen nothing.'

Nabokov's subject and Humbert's affliction is the discrepancy between the dizzy desire and the dingy truth: 'we all admire the spangled acrobat with classical grace meticulously walking his tightrope in the talcum light; but how much rarer art there is in the sagging rope expert wearing scarecrow clothes and impersonating a grotesque drunk! *I* should know.' The polarity expressed here is extreme, as is the sudden shuttle from desirable damsel into dirty old man – a radical transformation whose symbolic usefulness subtly betrays the matted and meshed complications of reality, the Siamese twinning and the intricate surgical separation performed over the length of *Lolita*. Humbert Humbert: two people, the same person. There is more to it than Humbert's abrupt anguished emblem: 'Eve would revert to a rib, and there would be nothing in the window but an obese partly clad man reading the paper.'

We must resist remorseful Humbert's final reversion to simple stereotype. For most of the novel, he is not an unreliable narrator to be distrusted, and his distortions, when they occur, are acknowledged. Retailing the substance of Charlotte's declaration of love, he admits 'there is just a chance that "the vortex of the toilet" (where the letter did go) is my own matter-of-fact contribution'. Nabokov's *galère* of unreliable narrators (Hermann in *Despair*, Kinbote in *Pale Fire*) represent unreliability in its most extreme form. They are reliably unreliable. They get nothing right. Humbert, on the other hand, is a paragon of exactitude, a miracle of meticulousness, who misses nothing, be it a 'solemn pool of alien urine with a soggy, tawny cigarette butt disintegrating in it' – or his own duality, compounded of adoration and disgust, fused into one genuine whole, before the final separation. In The Enchanted Hunters hotel, Humbert *is* enchanted, though even there he records the ironic impurity of experience: 'Humbert resting his head on his hand and burning with desire and dyspepsia'. Later, of course, things begin to look different. Miss Pratt, the headmistress, with a Freudian slip, reverses the title of Quilty's play to *The Hunted Enchanters* – and we pick up an inkling of Lolita's beleaguered, badgered existence, particularly when the malapropism is swiftly followed by a 65¢ handjob performed in the classroom by Lo as Humbert eyes up one of her coevals.

The sordidness is there. It is there all the time. It is there when, in Kasbeam, Humbert buys 'a bunch of bananas for my monkey' – an allusion to Lo's adored monkeyish feet which carries with it the cunning innuendo that Humbert is an organ-grinder. As he is: 'I would lead my reluctant pet to our small home for a quick connection before dinner.' As he is when, confronted with the fevered girl, he performs cunnilingus before contacting a hospital. Nabokov's main symbol for this purely physical gratification is the motif of mutilation. Nabokov disliked symbols and symbol-chasers – so we should be careful. He once rebuked a critic publicly – not to 'answer' him, Nabokov explained, 'but to ask him to remove his belongings'. The hapless William Woodin Rowe was particularly chastized for the third part of *Nabokov's Deceptive World* (1971), entitled 'Sexual Manipulations': 'no less ludicrous is his examination of Lolita's tennis and his claim that the tennis balls represent testicles (those of a giant albino, no doubt)'. (Those vicious Nabokovian parentheses.)

Fortunately, however, we take the hint from Humbert, who, observing a window-dresser at work among 'a cluster of three slender arms', remarks: 'Is not that a rather good symbol of something or other?' Two of the arms happen 'to be twisted and seemed to suggest a clasping gesture of horror and supplication'. The hint is dropped – then dropped. But it is picked up again when Frank of the final motel frankly removes the glove he usually wore over his crippled left hand: 'and revealed to the fascinated sufferer not only an entire lack of fourth and fifth fingers, but also a naked girl, with cinnabar nipples and indigo delta, charmingly tattooed on the back of his crippled hand, its index and middle digit making her legs, while his wrist bore her flower-crowned head. Oh, delicious . . . He noticed the direction of my gaze and made her right hip twitch amorously.' We recall that Valeria, Humbert's first wife, was to be nothing more than 'an animated merkin' – and wonder what has become of Humbert's love for Lolita. Finally, there is one-armed Bill, friend of Mr and Mrs Richard Schiller: 'it occurred to me that her ambiguous, brown and pale beauty excited the cripple'. Well, it *would* occur to Humbert.

This is the Humbert who, while consoling himself for Lolita's loss with brandied Rita, wakes up one morning *à trois*. Beside them in bed is 'a young fellow with white eyelashes and large transparent ears, whom neither Rita nor I recalled having ever seen in our sad lives': 'sweating in thick dirty underwear, and with old army boots on, he lay snoring on the double bed beyond my chaste Rita'. The man is amnesic. He is hospitalized and given the name Jack Humbertson. The bizarre quiddity of this event is pungent enough to conceal its emblematic implications – particularly because it is transposed to Rita and Humbert. They may not recall this person, but the reader does, alert to the 'thick dirty underwear' – in this case, of a dirty *young* man. The point being that, inexplicably, alarmingly, something unknown has entered the bedroom and sullied the sheets – someone all body and no mind, *Humbertson*.

There is, then, ample evidence, actual and symbolic, to garner up against the voracious Humbert as he abuses the *appetitlich* Lo. But it does not cancel out the love. It coexists with love. It coexists with the cultured precedents conjured up by Humbert to justify his paedophilia, the central defence witness being Edgar Allan Poe, who married his cousin Virginia (Vee) when she was only thirteen. The other precedents are Dante and Beatrice and Petrarch and Laura. Poe, however, is crucial – and evoked on the very first page: 'Ladies and gentlemen of the jury, exhibit number one is what the seraphs, the misinformed, simple, noble-winged seraphs, envied. Look at this tangle of thorns.' The reference is to Poe's poem, 'Annabel Lee':

> It was many and many a year ago,
>    In a kingdom by the sea
> That a maiden there lived whom you may know
>    By the name of ANNABEL LEE;
> And this maiden she lived with no other thought
>    Than to love and be loved by me.
>
> *I* was a child and *she* was a child,
>    In this kingdom by the sea,
> But we loved with a love that was more than love –
>    I and my ANNABEL LEE –
> With a love that the winged seraphs of heaven
>    Coveted her and me.

In Poe's poem, a chill wind sent by the envious angels comes and kills Annabel Lee. In *Lolita*, Humbert's first love, Annabel Leigh, dies of typhus, aged thirteen. Though, appropriately enough, the young Humbert has given her to hold 'in her awkward fist the sceptre of my passion' in that princedom by the sea – the affair is never consummated and Humbert is condemned to spend the rest of his life in a state of sexual aporia, until he achieves the postponed climax with Lolita. In other words, Humbert's starting point is the purest love. Its endpoint is the death in childbirth of Dolly Schiller at Gray Star – the capital town of the book, according to Nabokov's afterword. In between is 'this tangle of thorns', the pain of realized passion, its awful and inevitable entropy – practice making imperfect. As Humbert ruefully notes in Chapter 31: 'the beastly and the beautiful merged at one point, and it is that borderline I would like to fix'. At what point was the vision displaced by the ghastly presence of something else in the bedroom – the merely physical, garbed in its grimy underwear? When did the rapt become the wracked?

For a good deal of *Lolita*, the two are inextricably mixed.

The notations of love – 'the aura of her bare shoulder', 'scratches like tiny dotted lines of coagulated rubies', 'the crenulated imprint left by the band of her shorts' – live with the threats of the reformatory and the withholding of coffee until Lo's morning duty is done. Gradually, 'her sobs in the night – every night, every night' make themselves heard to Humbert but ecstasy holds them at bay – and then physical necessity. It is the mixture which is the heart of the novel and which is best served by Nabokov's particular genius. In 'The Critic as Artist', Oscar Wilde unwittingly mapped out Nabokov's singular, truthful territory – singular because horribly plural: 'for life is terribly deficient in form. Its catastrophes happen in the wrong way and to the wrong people. There is a grotesque horror about its comedies, and its tragedies seem to culminate in farce . . .' Think of Quilty's bloody-minded sabotage of Humbert's serious murder scenario.

Think too of Lolita herself. By the end of the novel, Humbert wholly regrets not having taken the 'angelic line of conduct' at The Enchanted Hunters. He sees himself as a 'maniac' who has deprived Lolita of her childhood. He has forced her into 'a world of total evil'. He realizes, finally, that 'the hopelessly poignant thing was not Lolita's absence from my side, but the absence of her voice from that concord' – that concord being 'the melody of children at play'. Isn't there something false and sentimental in Humbert here making its appeal to the reader? And doesn't Nabokov stand back from it and maintain a critical distance between himself and his creation? If you believe, as some readers do, that Humbert is a classically unreliable narrator, then you may conclude that the portrait of Dolores Haze, as given in the bulk of the book, is false – that we only have Humbert's word for her undeceived toughness and the way it verges on the callous. You may prefer Humbert's revised portrait in Chapter 32 and agree that she is really sensitive and only distorted by her sordid circumstances: 'she would mail her vulnerability in trite brashness and boredom'. This previously unseen Lo is founded on one smile losing its light at the spectacle of a proper father–daughter relationship in action, and on one stray overheard remark: 'You know, what's so dreadful about dying is that you are completely on your own.' The profundity of this aphorism would be greater were it not lifted from Pascal's *Pensées*: 'we shall die alone.' (I am reminded of the early moment when Nabokov slyly ironizes Humbert's poetic pretensions to any kind of equality with Dante and Poe by setting out his verse as prose: 'Oh Lolita, you are my girl, as Vee was Poe's and Bea Dante's, and what little girl would not like to whirl in a circular skirt and scanties?')

Lolita is neither a saint nor a slut. Like everything else in the novel, she is a complex mixture – an uncrazy mixed-up kid. If she has lost her virginity to Charlie Holmes behind a bush at summer camp, this hardly constitutes Experience if Experience arrives polarized with Innocence. Nevertheless, it undermines Humbert's lachrymose longplayer of 'the melody of children at play'. Shouldn't that be the *rhythm* of Charlie at play? Equally, though Lo definitely seduces Humbert, even that isn't wholly straightforward. True, she has had some unspecified dealings with Quilty before the advent of Humbert – hence the poster in her room of the playwright smoking Dromes. But her apparent experience is held in balance by a simultaneously disclosed piece of innocent behaviour. Humbert pretends that adults don't fuck, thus procuring from Lo a demonstration of what she now believes to be a practice limited to children. She believes his lie and thus betrays her profound innocence.

Unlike Humbert, Lolita never gussies things up. Were it not that Nabokov hated the very sound of the word, one might describe her as existentially truthful – sometimes callous, but always authentic. And this, I suppose, is what Nabokov so admired in her. Early in the novel, Louise, the Haze maid, discovers something dead in the basement: 'little Lolita was not one to miss such a tale'. After all, death *is* interesting, as Nabokov records later in the novel: Humbert and Lolita silently stare, 'with other motorists *and their children* [my italics], at some smashed, blood-bespattered car with a young woman's shoe in the ditch (Lo, as we drove on: "That was the exact type of moccasin I was trying to describe to that jerk in the store")'.

There is no reason to disbelieve this, nor to deplore it conventionally. It might be Meursault speaking. It might be anyone – anyone uncensored, that is. Nor does she indulge in false emotion when told her mother 'may have to undergo a very serious operation'. She doesn't like her mother. Her reply: 'Stop at that candy bar, will you.'

It is precisely this startling, shocking unsentimentality which saves her in the end. She isn't traumatized, she is matter-of-fact. Nabokov signals it when Humbert receives his first letter from 'DOLLY (MRS RICHARD F. SCHILLER)': 'letter began talking to me in a small matter-of-fact voice'. During their final interview, Lo keeps up this resilient calm in the face of Humbert's urgent demand for a reprise of events. Of Quilty: 'he was the only man she had ever been crazy about'. She went to him forewarned by Edusa of Quilty's liking for little girls. At the Duk Duk Ranch, she won't take part in his orgies because she loves him – and he kicks her out. Her refusal of rancour is astonishing but credible. She hasn't a shred of self-pity. And so she survives – by not recognizing she is a victim. She refuses the role of outraged innocence. If Humbert is greedy for *fruit vert*, Lo isn't exactly bereft of knowledge herself: think of that 'glistening plum stone', that brown apple core by the fender, and, less symbolically, the unchildlike kiss she gives Humbert before she leaves for summer camp and the unfussed familiarity with the word 'incest' at The Enchanted Hunters hotel. Before 'incest' takes place.

Incest brings out the intricate side of Nabokov. At the hotel, the room number is 342 – the number of the Haze house in Ramsdale and also the number of hotels (Chapter 23) at which Humbert has registered in his travels with Lo. 'We had been everywhere. We had really seen nothing.' From 342 to 342 via 342. The mirror image of the trapped numeral is perfect for incest – the coupling of identicals. And therefore the hotel room is a wilderness of doubles: 'There was a double bed, a mirror, a double bed in the mirror, a closet door with a mirror, a bathroom door ditto . . .' Etc. . . .

The coincidence of numbers sends further tremors through

the reader. The triple coincidence is a pattern which is drawing attention to itself. We feel the presence of the writer – as Nabokov intends. He was always impatient with the realistic convention: ' "reality" (one of the few words which mean nothing without quotes)'. But there is the further innuendo that Humbert is being written by Quilty. Nabokov's first nudge towards this complication occurs in the summary of Quilty's play (Chapter 13): the six enchanted hunters are informed by the seventh, 'a Young Poet', that they and everything else are his invention. As Humbert attempts to retrace his travels, clues from Quilty (cues from Cue) keep cropping up in motel registers, nearly all of them literary and ministering to Humbert's growing suspicion that he is not the author of his own fate but the subservient pawn of Quilty's narrative ebullience. 'N. Petit, Larousse, Ill.' The issue isn't resolved by Nabokov but left undecided, like so much else in *Lolita* – poised between *Verfremdungseffekt* and a malicious tease.

Of course, in some sense, Quilty is Humbert, or Humbert's *Doppelgänger*. The mannerisms and pretensions they share, as well as their common depravity, are too obvious to list. By killing Quilty, Humbert kills the dirty old man in himself, his grubby reflection in the moral mirror. Which is why, after the murder is accomplished, Humbert drives on the wrong side of the road – 'that queer mirror side'. He passes through the image of the molester to the other side – where nothing but remorse awaits him for what he thinks he has done to Lolita.

Quilty's murder takes us back to the opening page and one particular, puzzling sentence: 'You can always count on a murderer for a fancy prose style.' Why? The statement has the gnomic irrefutability of Eliot's 'April is the cruellest month'. In fact, Nabokov has begun with a sleight of hand. His non sequitur is so brilliantly bizarre that we do not recognize it for what it is – a diversion while Nabokov palms off on us the basic information that Humbert is a murderer, avoiding clumsiness and (importantly) concealing the identity of his victim. It could be Charlotte Haze. More likely, given Nabokov's intensive allusions to *Carmen*, with Humbert doubling as Don José, it could be Lolita herself. Nabokov's novel, unnaturally enough, is now so well known, it cannot be anyone other than Quilty. We should be aware, nevertheless, of the novelist's original intention – to deploy brute suspense on his readers, relieving them only at Chapter 29: 'I could not kill *her*, of course, as some have thought. You see I loved her. It was love at first sight, at last sight, at ever and ever sight.' Hardly the words you'd expect if you thought 'Humbert Humbert is without question an honest-to-God, open-and-shut sexual deviant' (Martin Amis). It has to be more complicated than that. Why would a writer as great, and as contrary, as Nabokov want to spend his time bolstering the consensus?

Unlike Taxovich-Maximovich, Nabovok was incapable, in the intellectual sphere, of 'agreeing his frame with the anatomy of the flat'. His prose style is completely individual too, and not only because of Russianisms and Gallicisms like the one just quoted. (To which one could add, from *Lolita*, the following eerie solecisms: 'the human females I was allowed to wield'; 'I quietly suggested she comment her wild talk'; 'the anything but distracted swimmer was finishing to tread his wife underfoot'; 'How smugly would I marvel that she was mine, mine, mine, and revise the recent matitudinal swoon'; 'it was then that began our extensive travels all over the States'; 'I really did not mind where to dwell'; 'in result of this venture'; 'I cannot well explain . . .') Nabokov, these slips apart, is often described as a master of English – an accolade too bland to mean very much. I prefer to think of him as a valet of English – constantly attentive to the nap of his high-quality material, tweaking here, arranging there, burnishing every button, leaving nothing to chance, devoted to every detail. *Conscious.* Consider his car doors: 'how matter-of-fact, how square that slam sounded'; 'the car door was slammed – was re-slammed'. Consider the *red* candles of Charlotte Haze, the harlequin glasses of artistic Jean Farlow, the letter from Lo ('I [crossed out and rewritten again] I . . .'), the 'prompt' fly on her young knee, her 'beautiful, young bicycle'.

And then consider the following two extracts, the first of

which shows why Nabokov falls short of Joyce, the second of which shows why he is an honourable *proxime accessit*.

Now and then the valet fusses. We think of George Moore accusing Kipling of describing a sunset like a detective: 'Beyond the tilled plain, beyond the toy roofs, there would be a slow suffusion of inutile loveliness, a low sun in a platinum haze with a warm, peeled-peach tinge pervading the upper-edge of a two-dimensional, dove-gray cloud fusing with the distant amorous mist.' Here the valet has been overtaken by the fashion writer's pastel prose, by the wine-writer's winsome 'precision'. On the other hand, there is this passage evoking Humbert's farewells to the Farlows, a passage which pretends to succumb to the stream of consciousness, but which floats one poisoned parenthesis, all irony and intelligence, on the flickering surface:

And presently I was shaking hands with both of them in the street, the sloping street, and everything was whirling and flying before the approaching white deluge, and a truck with a mattress from Philadelphia was confidently rolling down to an empty house, and dust was running and writhing over the exact slab of stone where Charlotte, when they lifted the laprobe for me, had been revealed, curled up, her eyes intact, their black lashes still wet, matted, like yours, Lolita.

That truck. That mattress.

One last, irresistible detail: 'two professors of English, tweedy and short-haired Miss *Les*ter and fadedly feminine Miss Fa*bian* . . .' My applauding italics.

# The Stories of Vladimir Nabokov

For many of today's best writers, Vladimir Nabokov's prose is exemplary, perfection itself. He was a poet – but a poet who wrote in a prose economy as if it were a poetic economy. It isn't. Felicities and flaws alike arise from this fundamental misprision. Poetry permits high intensity, linguistic brilliance, whereas prose is more casual, more laissez-faire.

When is a street like an epistolary novel? The answer occurs in *The Gift*, where Nabokov offers this elegant formulation: when the street begins with a post office and ends with a church. This natty simile is a narrative aside, an offhand observation, but its casualness is studied. And it doesn't quite match its surroundings. We aren't persuaded that this Fabergé egghead sentence can sit comfortably with the surrounding clutch of spattered, drab, less dandified examples in the narrative.

When is a Henry James novel like a back flip? When it is *The Ambassadors* – in which the hero, Lambert Strether, sets out to persuade Chad Newsome to leave the flesh-pots of Paris, only to conclude by begging him to stay. This ironic inversion takes three hundred densely intuitive and analytically clairvoyant pages to realize convincingly and unobtrusively. Now you see it, then you don't. In other words, James disguises his essentially anecdotal form. The twist is in the tail. At the very point when the short story was beginning to banish the anecdote for its narrative triteness, its predictable unpredictability, James took it over for the shape it could offer. The short story,

*The Stories of Vladimir Nabokov*, edited by Dmitri Nabokov, Chatto & Windus.

though, had no place for it: Maupassant gave way to open-ended Chekhov and Joyce. The classic anecdote thrived only in Saki.

Vladimir Nabokov's stories situate themselves in the tradition of high modernism as exemplified by Joyce's *Dubliners* – stories which are purged of anecdote. 'Ivy Day in the Committee Room', Joyce's unforgiving, stony look at sentimental Irish politics, is a tale that peters out rather than tapering to the traditional sting. Joyce's stories were written in a style of scrupulous meanness, and he replaces anecdote by form of a more implicit kind – intrinsic to each story and applied to the whole collection. With Nabokov, too, plot is in a state of entropy – but what supplants plot is the sentence itself. The pleasure of prose. There are, of course, stories here. A professor frightens his wife to death by secreting a skeleton in the marital bed; a GPU officer is kidnapped and imprisoned by two exiled White Russians behind their tobacconist's shop in extraordinary ironic luxury; a rank-smelling, furry angel seduces a girl with 'translucent' shoulders in her hotel room (obviously a moth magnified imaginatively; the brutal brother of Elizabeth Bishop's timid 'man-moth'); a salesman with a cold-sore on his lip makes a pick-up on the train but ejaculates prematurely; another man shoots his estranged wife through her 'fat' shoulder before being knocked out by a waiter wielding an iron ash-tray. But these plots – some of them preposterous, some of them *noir*-ishly banal – are the merest pretext for the exercise of Nabokov's prose style. The sentence itself is strangely self-sufficient, transcending individual stories. It is rich and voluble while the human characters appear before us precarious in their ontology, exemplars of Sylvia Plath's 'thin papery feeling'.

But perhaps the short story isn't the place for profound characterization. What else is the novel for? And Nabokov's sentences have their rich rewards. Birds 'fidget' in their cages; a ticket collector on the last tram moves like a drunk; a man 'coddles' the flame as he lights his pipe; the face of a fallen skier is covered with 'moist sparks'; later, he steps into 'the deafening cone of an ice-cold shower'; later still, with Euclidean decorum, he watches someone exhale 'a megaphone of smoke'; a barber fusses over a client's 'waxy bald spot'. *Waxy.*

In this command economy where the sentence rules, there are dangers too. The barber in that last sentence isn't a barber, for example. He is a 'tonsor'. This one word may stand for many other recondite alternatives, winkled out of the dark of the dictionary by Nabokov and beckoned, blinking, into the limelight of his prose. After these abrupt introductions, words like 'fatidic' and 'conformance' return to their accustomed neglect. This is a minor blemish. But it does indicate an instinct in Nabokov for fancification. Rather than write 'smelling of', he prefers 'emanating the aromas of'. Fancification also explains Nabokov's irritating repertoire of poetic diction to which he incessantly repairs as if unaware of the irreparable brokenness of these words: 'vernal', 'steed', 'dappled', 'auroral', 'cloudlet', 'darkling', 'leathern', 'girt', 'tarried', 'volupty'. I could finger a few more, but these are the ones to which Nabokov resorts like a helpless recidivist. Diction as addiction. The poetic economy instantly conjured.

And if you treasure the sentence, if you have, in the words of *Speak, Memory*, tested words on your tongue 'with the glazed solemnity of a tea-taster', well, then you are likely to reprise your perfected prose. There is a lot of repetition in this collection. In 'Cloud, Castle, Lake', 'the locomotive, working rapidly with its elbows, hurried through a pine forest'. The sentence was strangely better, though strangely identical, in the earlier story, 'Perfection': 'then the train, its bell ringing, its elbows working ever so rapidly, straightened out again to enter a beech forest'. Then there is the collage-effect portrait of Tolstoy made out of a 'framed chapter of *Anna Karenina*'. This stolen property reappears in a later story as 'a portrait of Tolstoy, entirely composed of the text of one of his stories printed in microscopic type'. Elsewhere a piano raises 'its lacquered wing' only to be copied later by another piano's plagiarized and 'upraised wing'. I could bore you.

All this would be forgivable – after all, great artists make up their own rules – were it not that this collection makes you wonder if the author of the superb *Lolita* and the immeasurably greater *Pnin* isn't a much more uneven writer than one had previously thought. Again and again the prose self-destructs as Nabokov fatally over-elaborates, aiming perhaps for a Proustian dimension of complication. Thus: 'a wagtail, like a blue-gray wind, quickstepped across the sand'. A brilliant sentence, the better, the *quicker* for losing the hyphen in the crucial 'quick-stepped'. Nabokov then adds, pointlessly, painfully, patroniz-ingly: 'A pause, two or three steps, another pause, more steps.' Consider, too, this stammer: 'I stammer so badly that any attempt on my part to tell Dr Shoe what I thought of him would have sounded like the explosions of a motorcycle which refuses to start on a frosty night in an intolerant suburban lane.' This is *Nabokov*? This orotund and pitifully prolonged simile wouldn't pass in ordinary conversation.

Nabokov's excess baggage in this collection is the result of two things. The first is his fidelity to the ironic impurity of experience. In the lecture 'The Art of Literature and Common-sense', Nabokov remembered 'a cartoon depicting a chimney sweep falling from the roof of a tall building and noticing on the way that a sign-board had one word spelled wrong'. Nabo-kov adds: 'these asides of the spirit, these footnotes in the volume of life are the highest forms of consciousness'. No wonder he was a master of parenthesis. Given this credo, there is always the temptation to indulge an after-thought, to finick with colour – and run the risk of pedantry. This is especially so when you consider how central to Nabokov's art the acts of memory are. In 'The Doorbell', we read: 'an unexpected recol-lection virtually scalded him'. In 'The Fight', the noticing narra-tor commits 'to memory' the detail of an electrician's hand, down to the blackened and broken thumbnail. Nabokov was expelled from paradise young and the rest of his life was spent in search of total recall. Expect, therefore, that he should sometimes give us too much. In *Speak, Memory*, Nabokov speaks of his memory's 'almost pathological keenness'. All the prose, even the fiction, has this stamp of pathological recollec-tion. Every sentence recalls something to be relished. Nabokov had a rich consciousness and, if it sometimes seems under-peopled in these stories, we have *Pnin* and *Lolita* to remind us that this was not inevitable. And here we have 'Signs and Symbols', a story utterly true to the ugliness of heartbreak.

# Seamus Heaney's *The Spirit Level*

'He was hard as nails', 'bald as a coot', 'safe as houses', 'rain or shine': why is Seamus Heaney's latest trim, efficient, pleasing volume so hospitable to cliché?

It isn't because his gifts are on the wane. There are two or three superb poems in *The Spirit Level* and characteristic examples of the Nobel laureate's *sprezzatura* everywhere. Even though the opening poem, 'The Rain Stick', explores the condition of aridity, it finds there a beautiful, palpable, audible illusion of liquidity and plenitude – which, paradoxically, is more heartening than the real thing. The poem describes the noises produced by seed-grit moving down a length of dry cactus – drip drop drop drop, cold flushes, gifts of rain. The process proves inexhaustibly various and the application to a poet in his mid-fifties is obvious, as well as optimistic. One is reminded of Elizabeth Bishop's great sestina 'A Miracle for Breakfast', where sunlight in a dry crumb of bread provokes a vision of a heavenly villa, all white galleries and marble chambers – the equivalent of my father's house with many mansions and a miracle of pure imagination. In Heaney's poem, 'You are like a rich man entering heaven / Through the ear of a raindrop'. And this is the crucial, repeated moment in the majority of poems – the movement from the mundane to the mystical.

Heaney began as a 'bullockbefriending bard', to borrow Buck Mulligan's (attributed) ironic epitome of Stephen Dedalus – a poet almost unprecedented in his ability to reproduce the reek of rural Derry on the printed page, a writer whose mimic gifts rivalled those of his great mentor, Ted Hughes. Clive James once wittily summed up this achievement by parodying Eliot: 'I will show you fear in a tinful of bait.' Heaney himself describes this phase in his Nobel lecture, *Crediting Poetry*, as reposing in what Dr Johnson called 'the stability of truth'. Meaning the ungainsayable pleasure of perfect mimesis. Peter Ustinov is a renowned mimic whose repertoire extends beyond the merely human to encompass, for example, the Wagnerian intensity of the electric bell. Heaney's dialogue is always authentic, but his way with pure sound can be awesome: 'the sibilant penumbra of close-down' on the wireless; 'a kind of dry, ringing / foreclosure of sound' in a punted soccer ball. These are virtuoso effects. It is odd, therefore, that the sounds evoked in 'The Rain Stick' should arrive in the ear as relatively insubstantial and underpowered rather than as convinced renditions: 'diminuendo runs through all its scales / Like a gutter stopping trickling.' The deliberate mistake (two present participles in succession) is there to mimic the announced, interminable diminuendo. (Compare the last line of 'Keeping Going', which repeats the title, conflating grammatical repetition with a double dying fall, matching continuity with conclusion.) Nevertheless, compare this perfunctory sound world with the unchallengeable precision of 'A Drink of Water' from *Field Work* (1989): 'The pump's whooping cough, the bucket's clatter / And slow diminuendo as it filled . . .'

There are other moments, too, of faltering here: 'Weighing In', a poem about the tentative (and now broken) truce in Northern Ireland, has a wonderful evocation of a 'well-adjusted, freshly greased weighbridge' – 'everything trembled, flowed with give and take' (*flowed*!) – but is otherwise rather lumpen in its allegorical procedures and laboured exposition, especially at those moments when Heaney's once-impeccable sense of line has forsaken him. Compare the inspired intuitive risk of 'But *bog* / meaning soft' (from *North*, 1975, and still his best book, by some distance) with the coarse calculation of the infinitive split across stanzas in 'And bearing out, just having to // Balance the intolerable in others.' Elsewhere in this poem, the line breaks are either bluntly obvious, or merely occur, counter-intuitively – heavy-handed or haphazard. The sestina of 'Two Lorries' is marred also, by the reliance on exclamation to accommodate the required, crucial initial repetition. There is padding here as there is in 'To a Dutch Potter in Ireland', a translation from the Dutch which subtly exploits an implicit parallel between post-war Holland and post-Troubles Ulster.

On the whole, though, *The Spirit Level* is a welcome and ambitious attempt to further Heaney's disciplined development beyond the literal to the transcendent. 'I began a few years ago,' he writes in *Crediting Poetry*, 'to try to make space in my reckoning and imagining for the marvellous as well as for the murderous.' The marvellous began with the Dantean visitants of *Station Island*, whose insinuations into existence first manifested Heaney's talent for treating the supernatural: 'Something came to life in the driving mirror.' Their fadings from the world of flesh were exquisitely managed, too: 'he trembled like heatwave and faded'; 'the downpour loosed its screens round his straight walk.' The biographical poems in *The Spirit Level* make it clear that the phenomenal world of Heaney's childhood was always ghosted by the noumenal – ominous with omen, sodden with superstition ('Piss at the gable, the dead will congregate'; 'When the thorn tree was cut down / You broke your arm. I shared the dread / When a strange bird perched for days on the byre roof'). And the title of the book sets Heaney's poetic agenda by its punning ambiguity: on the one hand, it indicates the practical, the straight, the straight-forward, the level-headed; on the other hand, it gestures towards existence at the level of the spirit. It is appropriate, then, that the book's bricklayer should also be representative of the Red Hand of Ulster, one of this volume's many and on the whole benign hauntings.

Heaney is particularly interested in the marvellous, but, shrewd poet that he is, he knows that without the actual, the visionary is without a launching pad. Larkin had much the same programme himself in 'High Windows' where the transcendent conclusion is unthinkable without the deliberate and foul-mouthed *actualité* of the poem's opening. And Larkin's exemplar is the Yeats of 'Beautiful Lofty Things', where Maud Gonne is 'at Howth station' in all its prosaic particularity – and also

'Pallas Athene in that straight back and arrogant head'. Those clichés I drew attention to at the head of this review are Heaney's necessary declarations of earthiness, his equivalent of Howth station or Larkin's 'When I see a couple of kids / And guess he's fucking her . . .' Clichés establish the ordinary with economy, just as it is about to metamorphose into something else, or disclose a larger template disguised by the veil of the usual. Larkin may seem a peculiar poet to cite, were it not for his appearance in *Seeing Things* (1991), where he appears as a tutelary shade, quoting Dante, and also, *necessarily* so, as 'A nine-to-five man who had seen poetry'.

In *The Spirit Level*, not every attempt to refract from the temporal to the supernatural works uniformly well. Quite often, you feel that Heaney is forcing his material out of the phenomenal into the realm of the merely rhetorical. 'Two Lorries' would be my example. Here, Heaney's mother is a convincing revenant because he brings before us the bus station at Magherafelt with its 'cold-floored waiting room'. The figure of death, though, is less convincing because Heaney presses 'a dust-faced coalman' into service, fussily switching his coal-sacks so that they become 'body-bags' – so that the poem seems rigged, implausible and leaking conviction. There is another reluctant mating of the worldly and the other-worldly in 'The Butter-Print', where the breastless St Agatha shades into the young Seamus – an interface rather woodenly engineered in line 4, where the butter-print is credited with a *'breast'* 'scored with slivered glass'. Triumphs, however, include 'The Swing', 'A Dog was Crying Tonight in Wicklow Also' and 'A Call'. This last poem describes the poet telephoning someone, a male friend, who is in the garden, weeding – weeding in a way which suggests the day of judgement and also the breaking of last links. This implicit tone, the subtlest innuendo of mortality, leads Heaney to evoke the hallway where the phone is waiting, waiting, as time calmly passes:

> Then found myself listening to
> The amplified grave ticking of hall clocks

Where the phone lay unattended in a calm
Of mirror glass and sunstruck pendulums . . .

*Grave* tickings. Yes, but also of a scene perfectly written, perfectly realized actuality. The subtext and the impeccable reality both allow Heaney his next extraordinary but risk-free move: 'This is how death would summon Everyman.' And then something even more extraordinary happens: 'Next thing he spoke and I nearly said I loved him.' Either Heaney is surprised by the strength of his feeling – which would make it a very good poem. Or the person he is telephoning is his father – and it is a great, tragic poem of regret for the unspoken love we all of us carry in our breasts. Someone, an Irish poet, said anonymously once that Heaney would win all the prizes, including the Nobel, but that he would never write a great poem. 'A Call' is, I think, a great poem, great also because it is short and so swift to break your heart. And well worth the Nobel Prize.

# Edmund White's Prose

Edmund White can't write. In the normal way, this chiming, rhythmically awkward, ugly little sentence might be enough. Edmund White's prose, however, is a special case. It is bad by choice. It is considered. *The Farewell Symphony* is not a novel, but what White calls 'autofiction', dealing with two decades of gay hedonism and the subsequent scourge of AIDS. We know from White's Oxford Amnesty lecture of 1995 that, for him, autofiction is 'a convergence of two very different literary traditions, realism and the confession'. In practice, though, *The Farewell Symphony* reads as thinly disguised autobiography: like White, the narrator is HIV positive, lives in Paris, owns a basset hound and so on. It is a work of considerable self-consciousness, not least with regard to its own prose style: White knows he is given to 'over-elaborated, arthritic conceits'; Christopher Isherwood, he remembers, advised him to write 'more simply and directly'; critics, he complains, praise prose which plays safe, prose there is nothing '*against*'. He admits to the deliberate cultivation of a Baroque style. In an earlier work, *A Boy's Own Story* (1983), this produced phrases like 'the torso flowering out of the humble calyx of his jeans'. In *The Farewell Symphony*, it produces sentences like this: 'we were dismissed with a shrug of a pretty bare shoulder rising out of a calyx of ivory silk'. We can identify a certain consistency in the prose.

In March 1926, T. S. Eliot wrote an anonymous, unfavourable essay-review in *The Times Literary Supplement* of Arthur

*The Farewell Symphony* by Edmund White, Chatto & Windus.

Quiller-Couch's *Oxford Book of English Prose*. Eliot divided good prose into two kinds – writers like Defoe who favoured an impersonal idiom based on the genius of the language, and those like Henry James who invent their own inimitable personal idiom. I want to divide bad prose into two kinds. The first kind of badness goes against the genius of the language in a flawlessly inept way. For example, this is the worst sentence ever committed to paper by a reputable writer in full possession of his faculties: 'I thought – if it is possible to think retrospectively simultaneously with thinking actually – I might have thought that I would have preferred you as you had been before.' This isn't so much a sentence as a pile-up on the page. The author's *taxis* – the structural 'arrangement' of the words – is in collision with itself. Though the sentence seems hideously memorable, the syntactic trauma is so great that it is in fact impossible to memorize.

Edmund White is sometimes bad in this way. He is capable of beginning consecutive sentences with 'whereas' (twice), of using a cliché like 'a deafening silence' or 'suddenly the intervening years melted away', or a gussied-up cliché like being 'left arctically cold' by something intended to impress. There are some dire tautologies: 'tireless assiduity'; 'like a somnambulist I sleepwalked'. Is 'an upholstered couch with sprung springs' an example of further redundancy, or merely a broken couch, where 'sprung' means 'unsprung'? There are some startling repetitions: 'our words weren't plucked from vocal cords but rather were the spontaneous condensation of thoughts precipitated out of the cloud of smoke hanging in a dense haze over our table'. The ecologist in White recycles this trope 200 pages later: 'we'd confide without much urgency thoughts that collected like condensation and formed, slowly, irregularly, into one drop of language after another'.

On the other hand, *The Farewell Symphony* is not without its rudimentary art. White's marked recourse to the 'Stone Guest', Mozart's Commendatore from *Don Giovanni*, is no accident, given White's subject matter. The penultimate page provides a convenient credo: 'in a masterpiece the whole network of impulses could be isolated in any paragraph throughout the book, a monad containing all the important features in miniature'. This, I fear, is the explanation for an over-lavishly rendered traffic light in Chapter 1, burning in snow-bound New York 'demented red beneath an old man's heavy white eyebrow'. We are looking at a symbol. Transgress. Don't transgress.

The over-dressed prose here, its chosen purple, is White's speciality and rather different from the routine incompetences so far cited. And it brings me to the second kind of bad prose, not the lavish, but the slavish. Eliot anticipates in the Quiller-Couch review: 'only a weak-minded or characterless writer would condescend to imitate, or even be influenced by, anything so little his own as the personal idiom of another writer'. Edmund White has, I think, confused the extension of a prose tradition in gay writing with copying a characteristic manner. The writer I have in mind is also the writer that Edmund White has too much in mind – Proust. The second kind of bad writing is work in regress, the gimcrack copy of the unique manner, pure reproduction, the unreal thing.

Proust is a constant reference point in *The Farewell Symphony*, as well he might be for the anatomy of a world where sexual partners come so thick and fast that they are frequently forgotten. White attempts to bring a Proustian quality of recall to a world of often deliberate anonymity. One character is prepared to pay a small fortune to satisfy his obsession with one young man – 'a hundred thousand dollars just to sleep beside his naked body' – until the narrator tells him that he has already had the object of his desire via a hustling agency, and has simply forgotten. White estimates that between 1962 and 1982 he must have 'fooled around' with 3,120 men. Of this cast of thousands, many are memorable only for their genitalia or their sexual preferences. Inevitably, the crucial moment of any encounter in this world is liable to be the twin of another crucial moment elsewhere in the novel. 'He exploded with anxious alacrity and I swallowed it all down like a cat licking its bowl clean'; 'he exploded in my hand after a single thrust'. Only ten pages separate these quotations.

In Haydn's 'Farewell Symphony', the players leave the platform one by one until only a violinist is left – a perfect metaphor
for AIDS and White's own position. His novel is an attempt to
reconstitute the orchestra – not only its principal players, the
soloists with whom he fell in love, but also members of the
chorus, bit players in the string section. Unsurprisingly, the
novel succeeds best with White's family – his mother, his sister,
his nephew and his nephew's girlfriend, Ana, who, while they
too are sexual beings, are less exclusively so than Edmund White
and his anonymous, intimate circles. Not that the homosexual
material doesn't have real anthropological value. White's candour is exemplary even if his experience is probably not representative. My gay friends tell me that White was on the
dangerous edge of things.

Here you can learn what a 'top' is, what a 'bottom' is, and
that the gay world has an imbalance between the two types.
'Peaceful, reciprocal love-making' is known as 'vanilla sex'. You
can discover what the initials C.B.T., T.T. and V.A. stand for,
but not an increasingly common cluster in gay personal columns,
G.S.O.H. On offer here are cock and balls torture, tit torture,
verbal abuse and great sense of humour. For this lost time,
White sees himself not as the historian 'but rather an archeo-
logist of gossip'. Proust might have said the same.

Edmund White is less well advised to emulate Proust's plush
metaphorical idiom – an act less of emulation than hopeless,
helpless infatuation. Five hundred pages of trying yields only
a scintilla of success – a man's aureole 'elliptical as Saturn'
because he is stretching. Otherwise, the writing is insufferably
periphrastic ('skin that looked as though he'd swallowed a
light bulb' signifies a shining complexion, not a sickening tumour)
or metaphorically overextended until accuracy declines into
descriptive pedantry: physical description is particularly prone
to this over-elaboration, as in 'his biceps looked like veined
gooseberries [packed in snow]' or 'the shoulders like boulders
[in cream]' (my editorial square brackets). Again, 'a line of black
hair crept up his pale, ridged stomach like a trail of ants [across
tablets of white chocolate]'. Sometimes the root image isn't far-

fetched in itself, but far-fetched in its exposition: taking a water-taxi to Venice from the airport, White notices 'pylons bound together like asparagus', which would have been enough. Except that he is anxious to convince the reader of the justice of his metaphor: 'like asparagus held upright in the steamer so that the stems cook faster than the tender heads'. Worse is the initially misjudged but nevertheless kindled spark of comparison: 'huge eyes, liquid as oysters, floating between lids as black as mussel shells'.

Worse still is the utterly arbitrary metaphor, prolonged to the point where any putative pleasure has long ago become vividly painful: 'as soon as I was back in my room I plunged down through warm, brackish tides to wrest one small yellow pearl from the depths but it was poison, the sea heavy, my oxygen supply compromised. For a long time I was dragged across the shingle, my battered body wound and unwound on a bobbin of white water.' I think this is a description of hepatitis-induced fever. But the white water looks like so much froth.

It is a pity Edmund White ignored Isherwood's advice. His plain style scores at least one notable success: 'a thick-thighed Diana drew an arrow from a quiver on her shoulder. The tip of her cement bow had broken off and the exposed metal armature dripped rust stains down her gathered hunting skirt.' This really works – because it is concrete . . .

# Nicholson Baker

'U' stands for John Updike, whom Nicholson Baker has met only twice, fleetingly and faintly farcically. Ardent, adoring, emulous, as Martin Amis is to Saul Bellow, so Nicholson Baker is to John Updike. *U and I* is a saga of shared psoriasis, of hero-worship from afar, of authorial superstition, of omen and fetish – a brilliant essay in self-examination whose starting point and competitor is Updike's autobiography, *Self-Consciousness*. Baker's self-scrutiny, however, is conducted under exam conditions, unlike Updike's. Baker allows himself no access to the Updike texts he has, in any case, often only half read, or less than half read. Wonderfully, honestly inaccurate and partial, he nevertheless emerges from the ordeal with extraordinarily high marks – for mental agility, moral probity ('who will sort out the self-servingness of self-effacement?') and sheer originality.

Baker's title arrives in the ear snugly, like something quasi-erotic – the wishful, ironic intimacy of 'you and I' – but another extended image captures better the touchingly ragged imperfection of the relationship: 'I *am* friends with Updike – that's what I really feel – I have, as I never had when I was a child, this imaginary friend I have constructed out of sodden criss-crossing strips of rivalry and gratefulness over an armature of misremembered quotation.' Ignore for a moment the distraction created by Baker's virtuoso transfiguration of that familiar figure, the 'model friend'. Forget that this endearing whine is couched not

U *and I: A True Story* by Nicholson Baker, Granta.

in adult prose ('I *am* a friend') but in the idiom of primary school ('I *am* friends with'). Think instead what the passage reminds you of. *Exactly*. Though Baker believes he is after a buddy, the image indicates his defiantly argumentative desire to adopt a parent. It summons, like a sad, shuffling queue at Lourdes, every skewed papier mâché model, every deformed drawing, every heartbreakingly halt work of art that was ever laid in tribute before the eyes of an adoring parent by a child in the grip of his gift.

But how like Updike *is* Baker? Both writers share with Nabokov what Baker calls a 'louped scrutiny' (alluding to the magnifying glass a watchmaker works into his eye) or 'hyper-receptivity'. Loupe in place, Updike in *Couples* twice describes pubic hair as 'watchsprings'. It is a technique which, in another context, Baker calls 'up-to-the-minutiae'. Baker's version is more instruction-manual in tone: 'the outriggers of Updike's admirably quilled eyebrows would alter their tangential angles under the subdermal bunch of a frown of momentary consideration'. At this juncture, following up the hint in Baker's title, one can't help pointing out the appropriateness of his own initials. N.B. Few writers note things better than Nicholson Baker, whether it be his baby daughter's pudendum in *Room Temperature* – 'her captivating little coffee bean' – or, in *The Mezzanine*, 'the beautiful Ms and Vs' left by vacuum-cleaner wands on carpet pile.

Babies call forth differing precisions from both writers. In *Room Temperature*, Baker's second novel, his baby daughter holds her bottle in one hand, 'like a screech trumpet player', while in Updike's 'Wife-Wooing' a baby 'sucks at his bottle with frowning mastery'. So far, so similar. However, when the Updike infant finishes, 'with a sizzling noise like the sighs of the exhausted logs', he drops the bottle 'with its distasteful hoax of vacant suds'. Baker is more technical, noting, forensically, ecstatically, that his daughter, in order to suck and breathe, has to manage two separate vacuums, 'a lung vacuum for inhaling, and a mouth vacuum for sucking'. When the vacuum is released, air, 'with its faint squealing cries', enters the bottle and 'takes its

437

place in neat semicircular bubble-rows'. Baker's prose is exact, perfectly sterile and very sharp.

Neither writer, though, is capable of comparing a new-born baby's face to 'the color of an inner-tube', as Nabokov does, with necessary 'cruelty'. Updike would be too worried by his own coldness, which he discusses in *Self-Consciousness*; Nicholson Baker is evidently anxious, if only intermittently, not to offend against certain democratically elected ideas. Baker has his presidential candidate profile, though he doesn't present it often. Nabokov, by contrast, took whatever imagery was required because he was fearlessly confident of his own humanity: the conscience he consulted was his own. He wasn't kissing babies for votes and approval. Exactitude will always offend against decorum.

The one dud section in *U and I* occurs when Baker comments on Nabokov's 'uncharitable streak' and the way his 'reflex contempt' momentarily infects Updike. Here, Baker's tough clinician's tone turns to tepid chit-chat: 'we don't want the sum of pain or dissatisfaction to be increased by a writer's printed passage through the world'. See the blue rinse and the burly handbag? Shamefully, Baker is rescued from these desperate pieties by his mother, who, correctly, believes her son's art will be harmed by self-censorship: 'I should try, she said, to do more as Updike did by telling the bad and not worrying about the hurt.' Right on, lady. Hereabouts, too, Baker confesses that in 1984 he was homophobic. Now he affects to believe that, unlike gays and women, heterosexual males are intrinsically disadvantaged as novelists. This is ingratiatingly affirmative, but entails the conclusion that *Ulysses*, *War and Peace* and *Pnin*, though great, are 'oddities'. Like *Madame Bovary*, *The Master and Margarita* and the whole of Dickens, presumably?

Wrong about this, Baker is also wrong about his literary parentage. The *real* father is Henry James. Baker shares, of course, contemporary candour with Updike. One can't imagine James placing Piet Hanema in a lavatory so he can suck the nursing breasts of his mistress. And one can easily imagine James's dismay at Baker's paean to nosepicking: 'an innocent forgetful pick of what you thought was a simple tab of dry material would draw out with it a deep horrifying oyster'. *But*, consider that eyebrow again: 'admirably quilled eyebrows would alter their tangential angles under the subdermal bunch'. Retune, and what seems at first like the super-close-up pop-realism of Roy Lichtenstein is more accurately identified, by one word, as the indefatigable explanation of Henry James. The one word is the orotund but otiose adverb, 'admirably'.

Now that Baker has turned from the study of things to the consideration of his own mind, the responsibility for these superb microepics can be seen to rest with James. A possible rival candidate is Laurence Sterne, whose great anti-travel book, *A Sentimental Journey*, takes twenty-odd pages to hire and enter a carriage – just as, in *Room Temperature*, the twenty seconds it takes a puff of breath to cross a room takes twenty-eight pages of prose. Sterne believed that 'a large volume of adventures may be grasped within this little span of life by him who interests his heart in every thing'. In *Room Temperature*, Baker floats a remarkably similar credo: 'with a little concentration one's whole life could be constructed from any single twenty-minute period randomly or almost randomly selected'. Henry James, too, believed that everything was visible from 'the window of a wide, quite sufficiently wide, consciousness' – and references to 'King Henry James' are seeded everywhere in *U and I*. If the method is to work, what has to be attended to is the stream of consciousness playing over the randomly chosen, intrinsically worthless pebble of pretext – a lunch hour, a baby's feed, the debt one doesn't owe to Updike. In Baker's case, the flux and reflux of the mind is more like a seething jacuzzi of consciousness.

When Baker fantasizes about partnering Updike on the golf course, he is as alert to the psychological ramifications as any of James's 'centres of consciousness' which, in the interests of verisimilitude, James had to hobble with perceptual imperfections, lest they seem too brilliant to be true. (I hope Baker will stick to first-person and thus avoid the problem facing James and Updike, of how to lodge their own fabulous intelligence in some ordinary, cramped bedsitter of a brain.) Worried about having the golfer-novelist steal or pre-empt his ideas, Baker imagines a similar conversational wariness on Updike's part also: 'our very guardedness and mutual suspicion, or at least my suspicion (or hope, rather) that the suspicion was mutual'. It is difficult here not to be reminded of James's comic *regressus* in *What Maisie Knew*: 'while they sat together, there was an extraordinary mute passage between her vision of this vision of his, his vision of her vision, and her vision of his vision of her vision'.

Just in case this sounds too finicky to be funny, consider Baker on our differing attitudes to contemporary literature and literature of the past: 'to show our sophistication across time, we laugh politely whenever we sense, say in Sheridan, that a dead person is trying to be funny, although seldom with the real honking abandonment that the living can inspire'. Some of Baker's best riffs resemble the joke definitions in *The Meaning of Liff*, the great masterpiece of home anthropology by Douglas Adams and John Lloyd – which classifies into conscious existence things and circumstances which previously slumbered in a penumbra of routine. Take crapping. Lloyd and Adams define *Great Wakering* (participial vb) as 'Panic which sets in when you badly need to go to the lavatory and cannot make up your mind about what book or magazine to take with you.' *Room Temperature* dilates on this and related issues at length. Nor is it the only area of coincidence.

*U and I* is a fine, funny book by a very clever writer – a kind of *Portrait of the Young Man as a Writer* which risks maximum complicity. Where Joyce, in *Ulysses*, writes 'you bowed to yourself in the mirror', Baker writes 'I lay awake two nights planning the acceptance speech I would make when my novel won the National Book Award.' *You* bowed. *I* lay awake. The shift is significant. Joyce is insured by irony. Baker is unprotected and thrillingly open – the bare forked writer – a touch ridiculous, therefore, but ridiculously talented. Soon the mediocre, the untalented and the envious will be advising him to do something different, something relevant, compassionate, committed, something more like them.

# Auden's Prose

As a convinced thirties socialist, W. H. Auden had a vested interest in believing that environment was a more powerful influence than heredity: 'But, in the transition from parent to child, the whole pack of inherited genetic characters is shuffled.' He also believed that blank verse eliminated the possibility of individual characterization because everyone sounded the same. Lear? Othello? Iago? He believed that man needs mental escape the way he needs sleep.

All these are recurrent ideas. Others are almost improvisations – like his concurrence with Gide that friends are people with whom you do something disreputable. Which is merely a dramatization of a banality: our friends are those we trust. Auden has buffed and brightened, back-lit and emboldened the commonplace till it sparkles attractively and seems more profound than it is. Typical. He also believed that asthma was the child's attempt to resist the demands of life.

He was a writer for whom ideas had allure, glamour, seductiveness. He was easily infatuated. *Prose 1926–1938*, impeccably edited by Edward Mendelson, is a detailed record of his intellectual peccadilloes. He fell for ideas again and again – like a ton of tricks. Oscar Wilde, on the other hand, flirted with ideas. His great dialogue 'The Critic as Artist' brings the fictive to aesthetics, willing suspension of disbelief – and literalness to the idea of *entertaining* an idea. To exposition, Wilde brings

*W. H. Auden: Prose 1926–1938 (Essays and Reviews and Travel Books in Prose and Verse)*, edited by Edward Mendelson, Faber.

wit: clarity is less important than surprise, than paradox; the outré more engaging than the truth. Everything is said for effect. Thus it is that Gilbert flourishes and flounces a catwalk of spectacular ideas, only to have Ernest finally and fatally point out, in a single summarizing sentence, that these ideas are unfitted for everyday wear:

> You have told me that it is more difficult to talk about a thing than to do it, and that to do nothing at all is the most difficult thing in the world; you have told me that all Art is immoral, and all thought dangerous; that criticism is more creative than creation, and that the highest criticism is that which reveals in a work of Art what the artist had not put there; that it is exactly because a man cannot do a thing that he is a proper judge of it; and that the true critic is unfair, insincere, and not rational. My friend, you are a dreamer.

Or an intellectual flirt.

Auden is different – more like the besotted Professor Unrath in Von Sternberg's film *The Blue Angel*. Even as he protested to Louis MacNeice that he was 'too fed up with prose generalizations to do an article', or complained that Herbert Read failed to persuade him that Shelley had ever 'looked or listened to anything, except ideas', he was indulging his weakness for notions. He took them to heart. He bedded them in the back of his mind. Henry James, however, was a famous intellectual celibate, as T. S. Eliot remarked in the *Little Review* (January 1918): 'he had a mind so fine that no idea could violate it'. Eliot's compliment is often read as an irony at James's expense. It isn't. As the preceding sentence makes clear: 'James's critical genius comes out most tellingly in his mastery over, his baffling escape from, Ideas; a mastery and an escape which are perhaps the last test of a superior intelligence.'

Nabokov is another writer of pronounced intellectual continence: 'Mediocrity,' he said, 'thrives on "ideas".' And he clarified his contempt: 'general ideas, the big, sincere ideas which permeate a so-called great novel, and which, in the inevitable long run, amount to bloated topicalities stranded like dead whales'. Compare Milan Kundera: 'IDEAS. My disgust for those who reduce a work to its ideas. My revulsion at being dragged into what they call "discussions and ideas". My despair at this era befogged with ideas and indifferent to works.'

Eliot and Arnold had their own reservations about topicalities. In *Culture and Anarchy*, Arnold declares for the established Church because the innovatory ideas of the dissenters have not stood the test of time. Eliot, in *After Strange Gods*, proposes an equally traditional culture in opposition to the cult of Romantic individualism, where idiosyncrasy replaced authority. Both men preferred to make it true rather than make it new. Novelty was risk.

Henry James's position is more radical than Arnold's or Eliot's, because it refuses all endorsement. Their ideas, however hallowed by time, have evanesced like the established religion they were tied to. They are no longer part of a living tradition. They are items in the history of ideas. They were conservative ideas and now they are passé. The same is true of Freud, though generations of intellectuals – including Auden – were taken in by the charm and elegance of his theorems. They survive not as science but as curios in the history of thought.

How many ideas do survive, in fact? Very, very few. Marxism looked plausible for a while. Saussure's equation of thought and language – their inseparability, their interdependence, their simultaneity – was neatly dispatched in Steven Pinker's *The Language Instinct*. Pinker offered a blunt but unanswerable refutation of Saussure: everyone knows what it is to write down something, then cross it out because language, what you wrote, doesn't express what you really thought. Super-string theory in physics is notably silent. Black holes are undergoing a refit. This is a doctor in *Lady Chatterley's Lover*: 'the nerves of the heart a bit queer already . . . You're spending your vitality without making any.' I wonder which of our fluent medical formulae will sound comparably quaint in eighty years' time. Remember when the dinosaurs were wiped out by a change in climate? And

444

when they were wiped out by a storm of meteorites? In Auden's day, there was a different idea. 'Called on Gerald to hear the latest news about the Dinosaurs. Apparently they suffered from arthritis.'

Gerald is Gerald Heard, described thus in P. N. Furbank's biography of E. M. Forster: Heard 'was reputed to read two thousand books a year and had an extraordinary flow of information about hygiene, sex, paranormal phenomena, and the probable destiny of mankind'. Though initially impressive, the portrait is significantly modified when you suspect that, for Heard, ideas were held for effect, as fashion accessories: 'he was a dress-fetishist, favouring purple suede shoes and leather jackets with leopard-skin collars, and he had his eyelids painted with what looked like mascara (actually a specific against conjunctivitis). Strangers thought of him, nervously, as a sort of Wellsian supermind . . .' In Eliot's essay, Wells and G. K. Chesterton are invoked in contrast to Henry James: 'Mr Chesterton's brain swarms with ideas; I see no evidence that it thinks.' Heard and Auden share a determination to dazzle, a sense that the only ideas are bright ideas, whose shine and newness substitute for the tried, the tested and the dully true.

Though Auden never achieved the high plateau of dottiness mapped out by Yeats, he had plenty of daft ideas: thieves differed from other criminals because their crime was 'an attempt to recover the lost or stolen treasure, love'. Primitive peoples, apparently, 'have very little idea of death, only a very strong sense of the life of the tribe which of course never dies'. This idea of surpassing silliness is accounted for by Auden's exaggerated respect for anthropology: 'one of the main differences between the Victorians and ourselves is that we have one more science, the science of anthropology'. Two, actually. There is also psychology, which seeds several of Auden's more manic extrapolations. 'Early mental stimulation can interfere with physical development.' 'Everything we do, everything we think or feel modifies our bodies': one can lend credence to hysteria and to the reality of psychosomatic symptoms without accepting that absurd 'everything'. 'The sense of guilt under which every human being suffers was not, of course, lessened by the fading of hell. It was only transferred to medicine. The hospital and the asylum became the punishment for moral offences, particularly the sexual.' This is clever, close to the exercise of wit, fun even, and fatuous. Compare his assertion that athletics are a substitute for religion in schools. Or his claim that rhyme began with the marching songs of Roman soldiers. Or his consistent return to the idea of artist as neurotic: 'Pope knew what it was to be flattered and libelled, to be ambitious, to be snubbed, to have enemies, to be short, and ugly, and ill, and unhappy, and out of his knowledge he made his poetry.' Eventually, not only artists, but all intellectuals fall into this damaged category.

I prefer the commonsense Auden with no time for this twaddle: poets 'are people with a particular interest and skill in handling words in a particular way which is extremely difficult to describe and extremely easy to recognize'. No ideas but in the thing. This is awkward but accurate. Compare this: 'curiosity is the only human passion that can be indulged in for twenty-four hours a day without satiety'. This is forceful, pithy, elegant and utterly mistaken. Curiosity isn't a passion. Think how often the adjective 'curious' is coupled with 'mildly'. Even were it a passion, the claim would apply only to chronic insomniacs. It is no accident that Auden edited *The Faber Book of Aphorisms* in 1964. He was a lifelong addict of the genre's features – exaggeration, authority and brevity verging on arrogance. 'Aphorisms,' he wrote, 'are essentially an aristocratic genre of writing.' Aphorism has a take-it-or-leave-it air which defies you to spoil its laconic effect by a display of pedantry. Meredith's 'Modern Love' points out the human ache which is soothed by aphorism: 'Ah, what a dusty answer gets the soul / When hot for certainties in this our life!' The aphorist and the pedagogue are professionally certain – and Auden was both.

Life is complicated. Ideas are simpler. That is their appeal. We like to make up an attentive audience, to listen to those who, if they are neither wise nor knowledgeable, are at least in the know. Auden broadcast for the BBC in favour of gossip ('remember, never hesitate to invent') and many of his ideas have the air of gossip. We may be humble before anyone with a full set of shining answers, yet we are also suspicious of ideas and their volatility. Auden knew this:

> Joyces are firm and there there's nothing new.
> Eliots have hardened just a point or two.
> Hopkins are brisk, thanks to some recent boosts.
> There's been some further weakening in Prousts.

Warily, we know that certainty is a desirable but temporary state. And so we tend to look for the latest thing – as least likely in the short term to be superseded. This explains a lot of Auden's thinking. 'Called on Gerald to hear the *latest news* on Dinosaurs.' (My italics.)

Auden insisted that the artist should also be a journalist. This is partly because, in his ideas, Auden overvalued the latest thing, where fashion fades into the avant-garde. Partly, though, he is showing us his salvation as a writer: 'The first, second and third thing in cinema, as in any art, is subject.' Subject matter saved him because the emphasis was not on the new but on facts.

In his poetry, aphoristic complacency, 'assured of certain certainties' (in Eliot's phrase), is repudiated. What remains is the aphoristic technique of point-blankness, of counter-banal assertiveness, of context-free éclat. Never apologize, never explain, could have been invented for Auden's most characteristic enigmatic, assertive poetry:

> remember the doomed man thrown by his horse and
> crying
> *Beautiful is the hillside. I will not go,*
> the old woman confessing *He that I loved the*
> *best, to him I was worst.*

In the prose, the best writing is the least given to pronouncement and pontification. 'Sat in a café in the market square listening to Hitler shouting from Hamburg. Sounded like a Latin lesson.' From China, there is a definition of war which is far removed from Auden's habitual tic of definition and categorization. It isn't analysis. It is example on example. 'War is bombing an already disused arsenal, missing it and killing a few old women. War is lying in a stable with a gangrenous leg. War is drinking hot water in a barn and worrying about one's wife . . .'

That 'hot water' is worth a thousand ideas. Ideas, though, are inevitable. They are indispensable. They are what, imperfectly, we live by. But they come infected with entropy. Human progress is like the rook in chess – for every step forward, there are two steps sideways, often into absurdity. And sometimes three steps backwards, into barbarism. We need ideas, but not in our art. Just think what an old lie the idea of freedom is, and how useful it is, and how we treasure it.

# Kipling's Prose

We need to think again about Kipling. He is our greatest short-story writer, but one whose achievement is more complex and surprising than even his admirers recognize. When the talkies arrived in Hollywood, Charlie Chaplin ruefully considered the future: 'It would mean giving up my tramp character entirely. Some people suggested that the tramp might talk. This was unthinkable, for the first word he ever uttered would transform him into another person. Besides, the matrix out of which he was born was as mute as the rags he wore.' There is no evidence that the patchily read Chaplin ever glanced at Kipling. If he had, he might have realized that Kipling, in his different field, had already wired a silent world for sound. The centre of his achievement is that he made talkies out of the mute matrix he shares with Chaplin. He is our greatest practitioner of dialect and idiolect – a writer whose ear for inflection and accent is not just ebullient technique, a prose virtuosity, but the expression of a profoundly democratic artistry, however eccentric that claim may appear to those for whom his politics are repugnant and his transcriptions of demotic speech condescending.

In his best work, Kipling exends the literary franchise to the inarticulate. The mute are given a say in things – and this generosity extends even to those machines which Henry James found so distressingly preponderant in Kipling's later work. In *Ulysses*, Leopold Bloom meditates in the typesetting room of a newspaper: 'Sllt. The nethermost deck of the first machine jogged forwards its flyboard with sllt the first batch of quire-folded papers. Sllt. Almost human the way it sllt to call attention. Doing its level best to speak. That door too sllt creaking, asking to be shut. Everything speaks in its own way. Sllt.' In Kipling, too, everything speaks in its own way, not just people. *Kim* gives us 'the sticky pull of slow-rending oilskin' and 'the well-known purr and fizzle of grains of incense'. In 'Through the Fire', there is the charcoal-burners' fire: 'the dying flames said *"whit, whit, whit"* as they fluttered and whispered over the white ashes'.

Kipling's eye was extraordinary right from the beginning. There is no shortage of brilliant local detail in his work. One has only to remember the corpse in 'The Other Man', 'sitting in the back seat, very square and firm, with one hand on the awning-stanchion and the wet pouring off his hat and moustache'. One thinks of the water in 'At Twenty-Two' which floods a coal mine – 'a sucking whirlpool, all yellow and yeasty'. Or of the unforgettable, bloated, two-day corpse of Hirman Singh, from 'In Flood Time', which the hero uses as an improvised life-jacket. Kipling's ear, though, was initially less perfect – in particular the sometimes excruciating Irish of Mulvaney, which isn't properly perfected until ' "Love-o'-Women" ' in *Many Inventions*. This faultiness is detectable, too, in the narrator's voice of *Plain Tales from the Hills*, where it is occasionally unclear whether Kipling endorses the tough moral pokerwork with which several stories begin. In 'Beyond the Pale', Kipling clearly uses the story to ironize the flat fiat of his opening sentence: 'A man should, whatever happens, keep to his own caste, race, and breed.' The tale illustrates the dangers, but the Kipling who interprets the object-letter of Bisesa so ably cannot possibly underwrite the statement that 'no Englishman should be able to translate object-letters'. (An object-letter being a collection of objects by which the illiterate communicate with each other since they cannot write.) On the other hand, there is no indication that Kipling dissociates himself from the repeated notion that callow young men are like colts who need violent use of the bit. Indeed, his last work, *Something of Myself*, reiterates the advice *in propria persona*.

But Kipling's own voice, overconfidently confident, is always less plausible than the alien voices he chose to assume. The latter make a long list. 'The Dream of Duncan Parrenness' is a faultless pastiche of Bunyan's *Grace Abounding*. 'On Greenhow Hill' is narrated in Learoyd's Yorkshire accent, ' "Love-o'-Women" ' in Mulvaney's Irish, 'Dray Wara Yow Dee' in Indian–English, 'The Wish House' and 'Friendly Brook' in broad Sussex. The prose of 'The Bull that Thought' is delicately tinged with French idiom and 'The Judgement of Dungara' and 'Reingelder and the German Flag' exploit the German accent and word-order, perhaps a trifle crudely, but comedy is always Kipling's least successful mode: 'We will him our converts in all their by their own hands constructed new clothes exhibit.' As Kipling reaches maturity, his mastery of dialect comes to depend less on orthography. Fenwick, the lighthouse-keeper who narrates 'The Disturber of Traffic', is given a circling delivery that is naturally conversational. His prose isn't good in the conventional sense, but it is dramatically appropriate: 'those streaks, they preyed upon his intellecks, he said; and he made up his mind, every time that the Dutch gunboat that attends to the Lights in those parts come along, that he'd ask to be took off.' Kipling's ear at this stage was perfect. And later, like Joyce's 'Clay' and 'Counterparts', Kipling in 'The Gardener' deploys disguised interior monologue for a story which appears to be impersonally narrated. Just as Joyce's leaden, ponderous style in 'Counterparts' mirrors the mental process of its alcoholic protagonist, so the Home Counties accent of Helen Turrell informs 'The Gardener': 'She learnt that Hagenzeele Third could be comfortably reached by an afternoon train which fitted in with the morning boat, and that there was a comfortable little hotel not three kilometres from Hagenzeele itself, where one could spend quite a comfortable night and see one's grave next morning.' Those three 'comfortable's' in the same sentence, like the three 'that's' in Fenwick's, are artfully calculated to convey to 'one' the stifling propriety of Helen Turrell's protective carapace. They are designed to make 'one' feel 'uncomfortable' about her version of events – and to show that her lie has infected her very thought-processes. She doesn't just act a lie – that her illegitimate son is her nephew – she *thinks* a lie even to herself. And Kipling conveys this without external, explicit comment.

' "The Finest Story in the World" ' explains why Kipling chose to use such a bewildering number of different narrative voices. In it the clerk, Charlie Mears, like Jonson's Dapper, has literary aspirations: 'He rhymed "dove" with "love" and "moon" with "June", and devoutly believed that they had never so been rhymed before.' His confidant, the narrator, is necessarily sceptical until Charlie tells him the fragment of a story about being a galley-slave. The details are extraordinary and vivid: 'When that storm comes . . . I think that all the oars in the ship that I was talking about get broken, and the rowers have their chests smashed in by the oar-heads bucking'; 'he's on the lower deck where the worst men are sent, and the only light comes from the hatchways and through the oar-holes. Can't you imagine the sunlight just squeezing through between the handle and the hole and wobbling about as the ship moves?' These details are, in fact, not imagined at all. Charlie is merely remembering, in a completely unliterary way, two previous existences – a hypothesis Kipling somewhat clumsily corroborates by a fortuitous meeting with Grish Chunder, a Bengali acquaintance with whom the narrator can discuss metempsychosis before he is dismissed from the story as summarily as he was introduced into it. The baldly functional Grish Chunder isn't the story's only flaw. There is also the melodramatic detail of dead rowers being cut up at their oars before they are 'stuffed through the oar-hole in little pieces' – evidently, but unconvincingly, to terrify the living remainder. Here we feel Kipling's design on his reader. He means to shock us, but we can see the electrodes in his hands.

More vivid, and more germane to Kipling's preference for dialect, is the description of seawater topping the bulwarks. Here Kipling offers us two versions of the same event – the educated and the demotic, the cooked and the raw. Charlie's version ('It looked just like a banjo-string drawn tight, and it seemed to stay there for years') is far more graphic than the more decorous alternative ('It looked like a silver wire laid down along the bulwarks, and I thought it was never going to break').

'"The Finest Story in the World"' is, in its way, an expression of Kipling's artistic credo. It explains his commitment to dialect – largely by its frontal attack on the conventionally literary: when Charlie Mears gets his head into Literature, his power is fatally diminished, his memories become tarnished and second-hand. 'Again I cursed all the poets of England. The plastic mind of the bank-clerk had been overlaid, coloured, and distorted by that which he had read . . .' Kipling knows that Charlie Mears could never do justice to his own story, because he is incapable of telling it in his own words. Only a genius like Kipling could do that, the most unliterary of literary men.

'"Love-o'-Women"' makes the same point – makes it initially in exactly the same way as '"The Finest Story in the World"' – by a considered use of quotation marks around the title. Here the story is given to Mulvaney, his brogue tuned down just the requisite fraction from its earlier appearances in *Soldiers Three*. It is still broad, but acceptable – an evocation rather than a phonetically pedantic transcription. The art, of course, is there in the powerful frame, which parallels the sexual vagaries of Larry Tighe, the gentleman-ranker, with those of Mackie (who is shot by a distressed husband) and with those of Doctor Lowndes, who 'ran away wid Major – Major Van Dyce's lady that year'. That hesitation over the name is typical of Kipling's prodigious attention to detail: it is less flamboyant than the justly famous description of Mackie's blood on the barrack-square, dried 'to a dusky goldbeater-skin film, cracked lozenge-wise by the heat', but it carries weight all the same.

Larry Tighe is suffering the final stage of locomotor ataxia brought on by syphilis: '"Love-o'-Women" was cripplin' and crumblin' at ivry step. He walked wid a hand on my shoulder all slued sideways, an' his right leg swingin' like a lame camel.' By the end of the story, Tighe has 'shrivelled like beef-rations in a hot sun' – and one cannot read this distressingly powerful simile without recalling that banjo-string of Charlie Mears. The demotic opens on reality like an oven door. We feel the unmiti-gated blast, rather than a literary effect. Mulvaney is no Giga-dibs. When Tighe is being diagnosed by the army doctor, Kipling carefully prepares for his boldest stroke in this non-literary milieu – a quotation from *Antony and Cleopatra*. He establishes Tighe's superior social status and, therefore, the likelihood of such a quotation, by what might seem a gratuitous detail: ' "Thrate me as a study, Doctor Lowndes," he sez; and that was the first time I'd iver heard a docthor called his name.' The immediate gain in verisimilitude is enormous: Mulvaney, Tighe, and the social gulf between them are measured as if by a micrometer screwgauge. But this detailed record of Tighe's sangfroid and social politesse also means that we are able to accept his final words to the woman he has ruined: ' "I'm dyin', Aigypt – dyin'," he sez.'

Dialect, the filter of Mulvaney's accent and ignorance, is crucial here. Kipling uses it to distinguish between the effect Tighe intends and the one which is achieved. It is a gesture towards the tragic, which is typical of the man, yet the reader is left with a more bitter, less literary effect – the desperate pathos of Tighe's borrowed gesture, denuded of its false nobility by Mulvaney's coarse rendition of the line. As a straight quotation, it would have been sentimental. In dialect, it is redeemed, rough and powerful. Kipling manages to keep the force of the words and to place the literary gesture.

'Dymchurch Flit' is one of Kipling's greatest stories. Largely told in Sussex dialect, it bears comparison with Frost's 'The Witch of Coös' and probably surpasses it. Again, the use of dialect is crucial. Both Frost and Kipling renew the ballad tradition where the kind of supernatural subject matter they treat would have naturally found expression. The alterations are simple but profound. Both abandon rhyme and literary dialect-equivalent, Frost choosing real American and a flexible blank verse, Kipling going to prose and authentic Sussex speech. When Wordsworth wanted to renew the ballad, he chose to eliminate the sensational event that had been its staple. Kipling and Frost retain the macabre event, but naturalize the form.

In 'Dymchurch Flit', Widow Whitgift is a psychic and, therefore, a possible channel of communication for the fairies or Pharisees who have been driven into the Romney Marsh as

Henry VIII's Reformation gets under way, tearing down 'the Images'. The Pharisees wish to escape to France where the atmosphere is more congenial, where they will be less 'stenched up an' frighted'. After a typically oblique and powerfully elusive exposition of the groundwork, much like Frost's sidling approach to his narrative subjects, the tale suddenly simplifies and accelerates:

> Now there was a poor widow at Dymchurch under the Wall, which, lacking man or property, she had the more time for feeling; and she come to feel there was a Trouble outside her doorstep bigger an' heavier than aught she'd ever carried over it. She had two sons – one born blind, an' t'other struck dumb through fallin' off the Wall when he was liddle. They was men grown, but not wage-earnin', an' she worked for 'em, keepin' bees and answerin' Questions.

Has any writer ever used capital letters with more authority or to greater effect? Kipling not only reproduces the dialect exactly and with complete conviction, he also, as it were, reproduces an authentic dialect of thought – which barely distinguishes between the relative importance of 'man or property' or between 'keepin' bees and answerin' Questions'. Picasso once said that Van Gogh invented boots: 'Take Van Gogh: Potatoes, those shapeless things! To have painted that, or a pair of old shoes! That's really something!' In the same way, Kipling extends the literary franchise. To the speaker, Tom Shoesmith, himself a covert Pharisee, bees and Questions are equally natural and the reader is persuaded by his matter-of-factness. Without dialect, there can be no entrée to his mind and the story is literally inconceivable, except in the terms in which Kipling frames it. The voice provides its own inherent conviction. Its accent and tone brook no questions.

In almost every way, Kipling is the opposite of Henry James, his devoted but not uncritical admirer – and not only in the way he so frequently opts for dialect. The sophisticated author has the burden of explanation, the transcriber of dialect has the different burden of accuracy, however much both are, finally, inventing. T. S. Eliot, in his essay on Milton, brilliantly observed that 'the style of James certainly depends for its effect a good deal on the sound of a voice, James's own, painfully explaining'. Kipling never explains. He asserts. On political and moral issues this assertiveness is often irksome to contemporary taste, but in matters of description Kipling leaves James agonizing at the starting line while he has breasted the tape. 'Deep away in the heart of the City, behind Jitha Megji's *bustee*, lies Amir Nath's Gully, which ends in a dead-wall pierced by one grated window.' In fictional terms, the place-names mean everything. They are authoritative and unarguable. Contrast the beginning of *The Spoils of Poynton*: James sets out to establish the vulgar taste-lessness of the Brigstock family seat. As often, he is fabulously wordy and relies on the transmitted opinions of Mrs Gereth rather than on direct evocation. The tone is comprehensively Jamesian. We take on trust the fiction that Mrs Gereth is the actual source:

> What was dreadful now, what was horrible, was the intimate ugliness of Waterbath, and it was of that phenom-enon these ladies talked while they sat in the shade and drew refreshment from the great tranquil sky, from which no blue saucers were suspended. It was an ugliness funda-mental and systematic, the result of the abnormal nature of the Brigstocks, from whose composition the principle of taste had been extravagantly omitted. In the arrangement of their home some other principle, remarkably active, but uncanny and obscure, had operated instead, with conse-quences depressing to behold, consequences that took the form of a universal futility. The house was bad in all conscience, but it might have passed if they had only let it alone. This saving mercy was beyond them; they had smothered it with trumpery ornament and scrapbook art, with strange excrescences and bunchy draperies, with gimcracks that might have been keepsakes for maid-

servants and nondescript conveniences that might have been prizes for the blind. They had gone wildly astray over carpets and curtains; they had an infallible instinct for disaster, and were so cruelly doom-ridden that it rendered them almost tragic.

There is a pleasing, if tasteless, asperity in the reference to the blind, but essentially this is James painfully explaining kitschiness in the abstract. What *are* 'strange excrescences'?

This style is wonderfully adapted to the exploration of intricate cul-de-sacs in the minds of his 'super-subtle fry', but it is frankly embarrassed by anything more concrete than a perception. Kipling, however, can arrest kitsch in a sentence of brisk description: 'Besides fragments of the day's market, garlic, stale incense, clothes thrown on the floor, petticoats hung on strings for screens, old bottles, pewter crucifixes, dried *immortelles*, pariah puppies, plaster images of the Virgin, and hats without crowns.' This isn't one of Kipling's great lists like the remorseless, tragic inventory of childish things to be burned in 'Mary Postgate', but it serves to show how little Kipling needed to explain. To the objection that James has the more difficult task of describing *expensive* kitsch, as opposed to Kipling's vulgar kitsch, one might cite James's evocation of the butler, Brooksmith, fallen on hard times:

There was a great deal of grimy infant life up and down the place, and there was a hot moist smell within, as of the 'boiling' of dirty linen. Brooksmith sat with a blanket over his legs at a clean little window where, from behind stiff bluish-white curtains, he could look across at a huckster's and a tinsmith's and a small greasy public-house. He had passed through an illness and was convalescent, and his mother, as well as his aunt, was in attendance on him. I liked the nearer relative, who was bland and intensely humble, but I had my doubts about the remoter, whom I connected perhaps unjustly with the opposite public-house – she seemed greasy somehow with the same grease . . .

Certainly, this is better, but there is something desperate in his reliance on the adjective greasy. You feel that James made seeing difficult for himself by allowing himself to wrinkle his nose so floridly.

But, then, James was a natural novelist and suffered agonies of introspective dieting when *The Spoils of Poynton*, promised as a short novella, proved after all to be a novel. With James's tirelessly greedy appetite for complication, every snack turned out to be a banquet. Kipling, on the other hand, was a natural short-story writer, whose inborn instinct was for economy and limitation. Even in his most successful novel, *Kim*, he doesn't explain. Take Lurgan, the healer of pearls: we hear of him first, not by name, but by his title. When we meet him, Kipling is both intensely specific and ultimately baffling. Having created in the reader an itch to know what a healer of pearls *is*, Kipling successfully refuses to scratch the itch properly. Just as ghost-daggers are mentioned but never explained, so the healer of pearls meditates on his art:

> 'My work is on the table – some of it.' It blazed in the morning light – all red and blue and green flashes, picked out with the vicious blue-white spurt of a diamond here and there. Kim opened his eyes. 'Oh, they are quite well, those stones. It will not hurt them to take the sun. Besides, they are cheap. But with sick stones it is very different.' He piled Kim's plate anew. 'There is no one but *me* can doctor a sick pearl and re-blue turquoises. I grant you opals – any fool can cure an opal – but for a sick pearl there is only me. Suppose I were to die! Then there would be no one ... Oh no! *You* cannot do anything with jewels. It will be quite enough if you understand a little about the Turquoise – some day.'

It is a brilliant sleight of hand. Kipling has done what the short-story writer must do: he has convinced us that *he* knows, so that, for a moment, we believe we do, too.

Kipling, of course, *could* explain the arcane. He explains the way an object-letter works in 'Beyond the Pale':

A broken glass-bangle stands for a Hindu widow all India over; because, when her husband dies, a woman's bracelets are broken on her wrists. Trejago saw the meaning of the little bit of glass. The flower of the *dhak* means diversely 'desire', 'come', 'write', or 'danger', according to the other things with it. One cardamom means 'jealousy'; but when any article is duplicated in an object-letter, it loses its symbolic meaning and stands merely for one of a number indicating time . . .

And so on, until the meaning is spelled out and the reader has learned something he never knew before. It is a process which is instantly gratifying, but it is also deliberately misleading: it promises explanation everywhere, whereas Kipling's point is that the whole tale is exactly like its setting – a blind alley leading nowhere. So that, when the denouement comes and Bisesa displays her 'nearly healed stumps', Kipling refuses to enlighten us: the circumstances remain unclear and 'one special feature of the case is that he does not know where lies the front of Durga Charan's house. It may open on to a courtyard common to two or more houses, or it may lie behind any one of the gates of Jitha Megji's *bustee*. Trejago cannot tell.'

The balance, in this early story, between the rigorously specific and the rigorously withheld, is a mode which Kipling discovered right at the beginning of his career and maintained thereafter. The short story is like Iago – whose final words are: 'Demand me nothing: what you know, you know: / From this time forth I never will speak word.' 'Beyond the Pale' is, in its way, as difficult as any of the more notoriously obscure late stories.

'The Wish House', for example, is described by Eliot as a 'hard and obscure story'. To Eliot, every reader of Kipling owes a great debt. Most of us came to Kipling via Eliot's finely judged recommendation. All the same, I think cautious dissent is the appropriate reaction in the case of 'The Wish House'. The meaning of the story is never in doubt for a minute: Kipling allows one of the inarticulate to speak, Grace Ashcroft, a widow who, for love, has taken on the burden of her ex-lover's physical pain. Kipling's theme, as in much of his late work, is the undying, secret passion which persists even in old age and which is prepared to sacrifice its life for another. This is the theme, too, of 'A Madonna of the Trenches', in which the disturbed Strangwick pretends to be haunted by memories of thawing corpses in a trench-wall. In fact, their creaks terrify him less than the proof he has of an all-consuming passion between his 'uncle', John Godsoe, and his aunt Armine – 'an' she nearer fifty than forty'. It is a passion for which death is no obstacle, merely the opportunity to meet freely at last beyond the grave. The force of the feeling is achieved by Kipling's judicious contrast, by which the corpses facing the trenches are as nothing, and by Strangwick's struggle to express the inexpressible: 'It was a bit of a mix-up, for me, from then on. I must have carried on – they told me I did, but – but I was – I felt a – a long way inside of meself, like – if you've ever had that feelin'. I wasn't rightly on the spot at all.' The broken speech is at once banal and brilliant, like Charlie Mears's banjo-string.

In 'The Wish House', Kipling again rejects a conventional literary treatment in favour of something more authentic. The supernatural machinery is fantastic, but the details sustain our belief – from the adolescent sapphism of Sophy Ellis ('But – you know how liddle maids first feel it sometimes – she come to be crazy-fond o' me, pawin' and cuddlin' all whiles; an' I 'adn't the 'eart to beat her off . . .') to Grace's 'waxy yellow forehead' and her cancerous leg with the wound's edges 'all heaped up, like – same as a collar'. All this, and more, is rigorously specific. It is only the Token which is unexplained and, therefore, 'hard and obscure'. Even here, though, Kipling volunteers the information that a Token 'is the wraith of the dead or, worse still, of the living'. In this case, the Token is a wraith of the living – which is why Sophie's and Grace's accounts differ, each being a version of the teller: a 'gigglin'' girl and a 'heavy woman' who walks with difficulty. This partial explanation, of course, did not satisfy Eliot, nor does it satisfy us. But I do not think Kipling means it to. He knew that the Token's potency in the story is dependent on its precise obscurity.

> I turned into the gate bold as brass; up de steps I went an'
> I ringed the front-door bell. She pealed loud, like it do in
> an empty house. When she'd all ceased, I 'eard a cheer,
> like, pushed back on de floor o' the kitchen. Then I 'eard
> feet on de kitchen-stairs, like it might ha' been a heavy
> woman in slippers. They come up to de stairhead, acrost
> the hall – I 'eard the bare boards creak under 'em – an' at
> de front door dey stopped. I stooped me to the letter-box
> slit, an' I says: 'Let me take everythin' bad that's in store
> for my man, 'Arry Mockler, for love's sake.' Then, what-
> ever it was 'tother side de door let its breath out, like, as if
> it 'ad been holdin' it for to 'ear better.

Should Kipling have given more information than this unaspirated, compelling, methodical account?

The answer must be negative. In fact, the hypothesis can be tested: 'In the Same Boat', a tale of drug addiction, shows two protagonists haunted by appalling hallucinations. They exchange horrors. Conroy's involves 'a steamer – on a stifling hot night'. Innocuous details – like rolled-up carpets and hot, soapy swabbed decks – are interrupted by the hooting of scalded men in the engine room, one of whom taps Conroy on the shoulder and drops dead at his feet. It is a powerful scenario, but perhaps less so than Miss Henschil's: she walks down a white sandy road near the sea, with broken fences on either side, and men with mildewy faces, 'eaten away', run after her and touch her. For a time, these horrors retain their undisclosed power and rank with Hummil's vision, in 'At the End of the Passage', of 'a blind face that cries and can't wipe its eyes, a blind face that chases him down corridors'. One thinks, too, of 'A Friend of the Family', in which we hear briefly and inexplicably of 'the man without a face – preaching' on the beach at

Gallipoli, before and *after* his death. It is a parenthesis which lurks in the mind long after the rest of the revenge tale has been forgotten. And it remains there because Kipling never explains. 'In the Same Boat', however, provides a joint explanation of the scalded engineers and the mildewy faces: their respective mothers, while pregnant, have brushed against an engine-room accident and a leper colony. Under the influence of their addiction, Conroy and the girl relive these traumas which have penetrated the womb. The pat psychology is an artistic blunder, and the tension in the tale, palpable as a blister, leaks away uncharacteristically. The reader is left with the thing that Kipling, miraculously often, managed to avoid – mere writing, Wardour Street psychology in which the mystery is plucked, trussed and oven-ready.

Normally, the exigencies of the form prevent anything more than necessary assertion. Soon it will be over – the secret of the short story is known to everyone. From the moment it begins, it is about to die and the artist knows that every word, therefore, must tell. Digression is a luxury that must pay its way tenfold. As it does in 'The Gardener', when Mrs Scarsworth begins her confession with the observation, 'What extraordinary wallpapers they have in Belgium, don't you think?' It is bizarre, yet convincing psychology – a last-minute reluctance to proceed with her embarrassing disclosure. But whenever Kipling is literary, he falters, as in the self-conscious reference which flaws 'The House of Suddhoo': 'read Poe's account of the voice that came from the mesmerized dying man, and you will realize less than one-half of the horror of that head's voice'. This is a rare failure.

Kipling, more than any other writer, except perhaps Chekhov, mastered the stipulated economy. His openings are packed: 'The house of Suddhoo, near the Taksali Gate, is two-storeyed, with four carved windows of old brown wood, and a flat roof. You may recognize it by five red hand-prints arranged like the Five of Diamonds on the whitewash between the upper windows.' In 'The Limitations of Pambé Serang', Nurkeed is instantly established as 'the big fat Zanzibar stoker who fed the second right furnace'. In that 'second right', what might seem an embellishment is actually a stringent economy.

Because the short story is always haunted by the sense of its ending, there are things – convoluted plots, ambiguous motivation, extended histories – which it should not attempt to tell, as well as those it must retail with the maximum efficiency. In the course of a long writing career, from 1890 to 1936, Kipling both abides by this principle and subtly violates it. The oeuvre of any good writer exhibits two opposite, but perfectly consistent tendencies: certain features will persist throughout ('in my beginning is my end') and there will also be a trajectory of change and development. So far, we have considered Kipling from the first point of view – that of consistency. His arc of change more or less follows the development of the short story itself. This can be roughly summarized by the difference between, say, Maupassant's 'The Necklace', with its notorious trick ending, and, say, Hemingway's 'The Big Two-Hearted River'. Admirers of Maupassant claim that 'The Necklace' is untypical of him, but actually even his best work is essentially anecdotal: 'Boule de suif', despite its length, has little particular characterization and is designed merely to expose the hypocrisy of the French upper and middle classes; 'The Trouble with André', 'The Piece of String' and 'My Uncle Jules', to take a broad sample, are all anecdotes. 'The Piece of String' is the story of a peasant who is unjustly accused of theft, exonerated by the facts, yet sent into a rather implausible decline by the refusal of the community to believe him. He has parsimoniously picked up a piece of string, not the wallet he is accused by an enemy of taking. Maupassant's talent is to dress up this amusing but thin tale with a vivid opening that describes the Normandy peasants going to market. 'Boule de suif' shows a prostitute sharing her food with her fellow passengers, whose hunger conquers their moral repugnance. Yet when, to oblige them, she has slept with an occupying Prussian officer who is holding up the coach till she complies, they refuse to share their food with her. The irony is typically pat and not unlike that of 'The Necklace', in which the lost diamond necklace, replaced after years of scrimping, turns out, after all, to have been paste. Hemingway's 'The Big Two-Hearted River', on the other hand, avoids this fearful symmetry by abjuring plot: Nick Adams goes angling, but does not feel able yet to fish in the swamp. In terms of plot, a meal is a big event. The story's power resides in its brooding implications which, though never made clear, involve the attempt to regain the simple life after the trauma of war, symbolized by a fire which has razed the whole area about the river. In other words, the short story moves away from anecdote, the neat tale, to a plotless genre of implication. This, of course, is a generalization and Hemingway's 'Fifty Grand' shows that the anecdote, if brilliantly enough handled, will always continue to have a life. There the Irish boxer has to lose a fight because he has bet on his opponent. However, in a double-cross, his opponent has bet on him. The upshot is that, in order to lose, Jack Brennan is forced to call on enormous reserves of courage by going on after he has been hit low. The narrator, his trainer, puts this down to Brennan's meanness in money matters, which he overemphasizes throughout: Hemingway, though, is more interested in the paradox by which Brennan's cynical decision to throw the fight has to be sustained by brute heroism. The 'cowardly' route proves to be its opposite.

'Fifty Grand' is an exception. More typical of the short story in this century is 'The Killers', in which two gangsters take over a café in order to murder a customer, who doesn't in fact appear. The dialogue we hear is full of menace, but we never discover why the men are after Andreson. The modernity of the story can be gauged when you consider how like Pinter's *The Birthday Party* this dramatic vignette is. (Some day, incidentally, the influence of Hemingway on Pinter will be properly assessed.) 'The Killers' is a classic story in its open-endedness, culminating with Ole Andreson stretched on his bed, resigned to his eventual fate for some undisclosed offence.

Early Kipling is often anecdotal in the Maupassant manner, but whereas Maupassant felt constrained by the form and eventually did his best work in the novels *Bel-Ami* and *Une Vie*, Kipling made a virtue out of the limitation imposed on him by the form. By employing narrators, he was able to squeeze more into the story. *Plain Tales from the Hills* employs a catch-phrase that finally becomes irritating – 'But that is another story' – yet it serves as an index of Kipling's awareness of the constraints of his chosen medium. Late Kipling, however, circumvents the difficulty. M. Voiron, for example, in 'The Bull that Thought', narrates a story which takes place over a number of years, but because he is a character he is allowed to edit his material openly: 'And next year,' he says, 'through some chicane which I have not the leisure to unravel . . .' An author could not permit himself this transition which amounts to the phrase, 'to cut a long story short'. Kipling's narrators allow him, without breach of decorum, to ramble, to recap, to circle, to backtrack, to anticipate, as real people do, and therefore to deal with long periods of time over a short space. The narrators, too, permit Kipling to avoid explanation, where necessary, because the responsibility for the story appears to rest with them, the author's role being that of auditor. In this way, Kipling crams into the short story the substance of a full-length novel, while the privilege of occlusion is retained.

'Mrs Bathurst' is probably the most notorious example of these techniques at work, though ' "The Finest Story in the World" ' employs them too. The narrative in the latter is, as the Kipling-figure remarks, 'a maddening jumble'. Charlie Mears can remember not just one previous existence but two, which, in his mind, are inseparable. In fact, as the narrator finally realizes, each tale told separately would be banal: 'The adventures of a Viking had been written many times before; the history of a Greek galley-slave was no new thing.' The details are luminous because they are deprived of a coherent setting and context. They exist in the dark – inexplicable and end-stopped – hence their potency. 'The Dream of Duncan Parrenness' further illustrates the point: for most of its length, Kipling revisits the theme of self-haunting. (Despite his often-repeated determination never to repeat himself, he had already touched on this in 'At the End of the Passage': 'the first thing he saw standing in the verandah was the figure of himself'.) After

Parrenness has donated his trust in men and women, and his boy's soul and conscience, to the dream-presence of his older self, he is left with his reward – 'When the light came I made shift to behold his gift, and saw that it was a little piece of dry bread.' Perhaps this piece of dry bread alludes to Matthew 4:4 ('Man shall not live by bread alone, but by every word that proceedeth out of the mouth of God'), thus illustrating the nature of his transaction, the swap of morality for materialism. Perhaps it alludes to 'the bread of affliction'. Either is possible. Reading the story, however, the image is strangely satisfying in itself. It tells, and tells profoundly, without explaining itself. It is the man, this shrivelled piece of bread, and hardly needs the Bible to underpin it.

At the centre of 'Mrs Bathurst' is another famously baffling image, which once read is never forgotten: two tramps, one squatting, one standing, by the dead-end of a railway siding in South Africa.

> 'There'd been a bit of a thunderstorm in the teak, you see, and they were both stone dead and as black as charcoal. That's what they really were, you see – charcoal. They fell to bits when we tried to shift them. The man who was standin' up had the false teeth. I saw 'em shinin' against the black. Fell to bits he did too, like his mate squatting down an' watchin' him, both of 'em all wet in the rain. Both burned to charcoal, you see. And – that's what made me ask about marks just now – the false-toother was tattooed on the arms and chest – a crown and foul anchor with M.V. above.'

When everything has been said about this story, it is this image which continues to grip the heart and squeeze it. Like the piece of dried bread, it never relaxes its hold on the imagination. Is any explanation, then, possible? Kipling approaches this *coup de théâtre* by a very circuitous route, using several narrators, and yet each apparent digression contributes to the whole.

Most readers see 'Mrs Bathurst' as an obscure tale of elective affinities – the core of which is the passion of a middle-aged warrant officer called Vickery for Mrs Bathurst, a widowed New Zealand hotel keeper. What has passed between them is only guessed at by the narrators. But they agree that Mrs Bathurst is something special. She has 'It', hence Vickery's obsession which manifests itself suddenly and feverishly when, in Cape Town, he sees her for a few seconds on film. She is arriving at Paddington station in search of Vickery. Night after night Vickery watches her – then deserts. Another narrator, Hooper, supplies the grisly denouement above, at the point where the other two, Pyecroft and Pritchard, break off. Vickery's tattoo shows up white, like writing on a burned letter. There is some dispute as to whether the other body is that of Mrs Bathurst: Pritchard plainly thinks it is, but critics have differed, myself included.

Though the rambling narration has been denounced by both Kingsley Amis and Angus Wilson, the story is as precise as a Swiss watch. Everything fits, but the reader has to wind it up. The theory of elective affinity stems from the narrators. They fit Vickery's story to their own experience: sailors, they know, constantly desert for reasons of the heart. Moon has jumped ship in the South Seas for a woman, 'bein' a Mormonastic beggar'; Spit-Kid Jones married a 'cocoanut-woman'. Hooper agrees that some women can drive a man crazy if he doesn't save himself. Hence the theory. Kipling, however, is careful to show the observant reader that his narrators are unreliable, and to tuck away the truth of the matter. The credulity of Pyecroft and Pritchard is established in the framing story of Boy Niven who dragged them off on a wild goose chase through the woods of British Columbia. In addition, there is a persistent motif of unreliable machinery – trains derailed on straight lines, a gyroscope that goes on the blink, a brake-van chalked for repair, damaged rolling stock, sprung midship frames, ill-fitting false teeth, and so on. It is a broad hint that the machinery of this story is also unreliable.

Moreover, on ascertainable facts, the narrators are shown to be wrong. Hooper hears a clink of couplings, 'It's those dirty little Malay boys, you see.' It isn't. It's Pyecroft and Pritchard. Similarly, Pyecroft gets an expert to 'read' the captain's face – wrongly as it turns out. Further, Kipling makes Pyecroft employ a variety of foreign phrases, all italicized, adding an extra one to the magazine version – *moi aussi, verbatim, ex officio, status quo, résumé, peeris* and *casus belli*. Taken with other biblical props from Acts – the beer ('Others, mocking, said, These men are full of new wine') and the strong south-easter ('a sound from heaven like a rushing mighty wind') – these phrases add up to a parody of the gift of tongues.

In other words, Pyecroft speaks more than he knows, trusting to erroneous inspiration, as when he compares Vickery's false teeth to a 'Marconi ticker', hinting at strange communication with Mrs Bathurst. Hooper's tic of dialogue is to say 'You see', a total of sixteen times. The point is that his companions don't see at all.

The truth is concealed in the words of 'The Honeysuckle and the Bee', sung by some picnickers on the beach, words by A. H. Fitz, music by W. H. Penn. They tell us what Vickery only hints at in the phrase 'my *lawful* wife', namely that he has married Mrs Bathurst bigamously, in a Moon-like way. A 'lawful' wife implies an unlawful wife and the song confirms this suspicion:

> As they sat there side by side,
> He asked her to be his bride
> She answered 'Yes' and sealed it with a kiss.

Vickery's eventual fate, death by lightning, tells us what happened after the bigamy, for it is paralleled in the framing story of Boy Niven. 'Heavy thunder with continuous lightning' is, according to Pyecroft, the punishment for *desertion*. Vickery, then, is a double-deserter, from Mrs Bathurst and the navy. We don't know much about Mrs Bathurst, but we know enough to understand why Vickery is afraid, 'like an enteric at the last kick': first, 'she never scrupled to . . . set 'er foot on a scorpion'; secondly, as Pritchard's anecdote of the beer-bottles demonstrates, she never forgets. After five years, she remembers Pritchard's name and his 'particular' beer, unlike the servant girl who chucks him a bottle in mistake for someone else. The contrast is telling.

Vickery has committed a crime, bigamy, and that presumably is why the captain connives at his absence without leave – desertion being less of a disgrace than legal proceedings from the navy's point of view. The element of criminality also explains why Vickery watches the film so compulsively, yet with such dread: in the oldest of traditions, he is revisiting the scene of his crime. The film explains, too, that Vickery, unlike the others, has found Mrs Bathurst forgettable. He takes Pyecroft along for confirmation – so much for their romantic interpretation.

In 'Mrs Bathurst' nothing is wasted. Every digression contributes to the total meaning. It is like a closed economy, as parsimonious as a city under siege, despite its air of beery reminiscence. In 'The Wrong Thing', Kipling makes it clear that his art had no place for guesswork. Though he believed in his Daemon, as any writer must if he is not to force his talent, he was conscious and critical after the Inner Voice had played its part: 'Iron's sweet stuff,' says Hal, 'if you don't torture her, and hammered work is all pure, truthful line, with a reason and a support for every curve and bar of it.' Though one can scarcely imagine any child grasping this piece of aesthetic theory from *Rewards and Fairies*, it is a plain warning to adults that nothing can be skipped, that every detail is relevant – as it is in 'Mrs Bathurst'.

Does this affect the status of the charcoal figures? Ultimately, it does not. Are we to assume an accident? Or an act of God? Clearly, the fate of Vickery carries an element of poetic justice, but we cannot speculate beyond that point. The reader untangles the thread of the narrative only to discover that Kipling, at the crucial moment, has deliberately snapped it in order to preserve the shock at the heart of the tale. There is no insulating context, only raw voltage.

The same thing, though less strikingly, is true of 'Dayspring Mishandled', when Manallace draws on his black gloves at the crematorium. The gesture has a power and solemnity which are unaccountable. This story illuminates one difference between Kipling's early work and his late work. In *Something of Myself*, Kipling dilates briefly on his art: 'The shortening of them, first to my own fancy after rapturous rereadings, and next to the space available, taught me that a tale from which pieces have been raked out is like a fire that has been poked.' Kipling, rightly in my view, never deviated from this prescription. Yet there are those who have argued that, whereas in the early work excision creates intensity, in the later stories it merely creates obscurity. However, in the later work, the reader is often expected, as in 'Mrs Bathurst', to reinstate what Kipling has eliminated. Links are suppressed to involve the reader in the tale: close reading implicates the reader as he deciphers the encoded text. In Henry James's formula from *The Golden Bowl*, the writer forgoes 'the muffled majesty of authorship' – in order to compel us to 'live and breathe and rub shoulders and converse with the persons engaged in the struggle'. 'Dayspring Mishandled' is a case in point.

The plot is as neat in its way as the resolution of Tom's antecedents in *Tom Jones*. Alured Castorley has, in his youth, been a member of a literary syndicate which provided pulp fiction for the undiscriminating mass-market. Manallace, another member of the group, decides to ruin Castorley's carefully nurtured reputation as a Chaucer expert by getting him to authenticate a planted forgery of a previously unknown Chaucer fragment. While Castorley has risen in the world of letters, Manallace has made a reputation of a different kind in 'the jocundly-sentimental Wardour Street brand of adventure'. Manallace's income goes towards nursing 'Dal Benzaquen's mother through her final illness, 'when her husband ran away'. For about half the length of the tale, Kipling conceals the revenge plot so that, like the narrator, we believe that when 'Dal's mother dies, 'she seemed to have emptied out his life, and left him only fleeting interest in trifles'.

Part of our pleasure resides in the simple realization that the series of apparently pointless hobbies are, in fact, related to each other and have a profound purpose – that of revenge. Each step is lucid and mesmerizingly technical – Kipling's impersonation of the insider with special knowledge was never put to better use. Everything contributes – the experiments with ink, the medieval paste, the handwriting, the early Chaucerian tale – as if Kipling was demonstrating to his readership that, in his work, the diversion is always in fact central and germane. In this tale of revenge and literary hoax, where the avenger is finally compassionate, Kipling is careful not to explain two things – the motive for Manallace's subterfuge and the reason why he finally forbears. Castorley's careerism, his lack of generosity, his 'gifts of waking dislike' – these are all inadequate reasons for a scheme which is designed to kill its victim. The narrator is told the real motive, but we are not: 'He told it. "That's why," he said. "Am I justified?" He seemed to me entirely so.' Most readers assume that Castorley grossly insulted the mother of 'Dal Benzaquen, in conversation with Manallace during the war, because she had turned down his proposal of marriage: 'He went out before the end, and, it was said, proposed to 'Dal Benzaquen's mother who refused him.'

That parenthetical 'it was said' carries its own charge of doubt and, taken with the warnings against passive readership that are scattered through the story – like Manallace's reiterated 'if you save people thinking, you can do anything with 'em' – it should put us on our guard. The truth about Castorley and 'Dal's mother comes out under the influence of illness and Gleeag's liver tonics. (Kipling was always willing, perhaps too much so, to use drugs as a way of speeding up necessary disclosure, as in ' "Wireless" ' and 'A Madonna of the Trenches'.) The fuddled, dying but truthful Castorley begins by saying that 'there was an urgent matter to be set right, and now he had the Title and knew his own mind it would all end happily'. His rambling monologue concludes with his naming 'Dal's mother. The crucial words are *and knew his own mind*. Castorley is the person who *didn't* know his own mind. The phrase would be meaningless if Castorley, as 'it was said', had proposed and been refused. Clearly, he proposed and was accepted – only to desert her in order to better himself and get on in the world. Like Wilkett, in 'The Tender Achilles', he opts for career rather than caress. Manallace's motive, then, is that Castorley has rejected 'Dal's mother and perhaps boasted of it – a thing hard for Manallace to bear because he has 'adored' her.

Castorley is such a repellent character, so bereft of redeeming features, that this may seem implausible. We find it almost impossible to believe that 'Dal's mother actually loved him. Kipling, though, has thoughtfully provided an analogue – in Mrs Castorley, who, if equally ghastly, is having a passionate affair with the surgeon, Gleeag. It is obvious enough, yet Manallace doesn't realize for a long time: 'But she's so infernally plain, and I'm such a fool, it took me weeks to find out.' The heart has its reasons – reasons which transcend mere appearances and unworthy personalities. Castorley may be snobbish, selfish and bellied – but neither is Vickery such a catch, or the 'unappetizing, ash-coloured' Mrs Castorley.

Once we have grasped that Castorley has loved and left 'Dal's mother, the story falls into place. For instance, the scrap of Latin, which incorporates an anagram of Manallace's name, now has its full significance. The text is not simply a vehicle for Manallace's device to prove the fragment is a forgery. Translated, it reads, 'Behold this beloved Mother taking with her me, the accepted one.' We are never told 'Dal's mother's name. She is, as it were, 'this beloved Mother' and the words 'the accepted one' refer to Castorley's proposal. The Nodier poem, which provides the story with its epigraph, now makes fuller sense: 'Dal's mother is 'la fille des beaux jours', the old Neminaka days, whose memory is now poisoning Castorley's system like mandragora. The Chaucerian fragment, too, with its account of a girl 'praying against an undesired marriage', slips into place. 'Dal's mother is forced to marry someone else, by default. When she is enduring her fatal illness and is 'wholly paralysed', we are told that 'only her eyes could move, and those always looked for the husband who had left her'. Clearly, if this was her legal husband, the obvious candidate, Manallace would have been better employed in mounting a campaign of revenge against *him*. In fact, 'the husband who left her' must be Castorley. Kipling again resolves the doubt by another careful parallel. At Castorley's cremation, Mrs Castorley's eyes turn, like 'Dal's mother's eyes, to her real passion, her illicit lover, Gleeag.

Dowson's 'Non Sum Qualis Eram Bonae', glancingly alluded to by Manallace, also finds its true place in this structure. The poem is an account of sleeping with a prostitute, while actually being sick with love for someone else – Cynara, who comes as a vision in the grey dawn:

> But I was desolate and sick of an old passion,
> When I awoke and found the dawn was grey:
> I have been faithful to thee, Cynara! in my fashion.

Dowson's poem is yet another example of dayspring mishandled, like Nodier's poem. Kipling's text is so richly worked that one wonders finally whether it is totally fanciful to see the motif of the grey dawn punningly reiterated in Graydon's name.

Graydon's factory, which produces pulp literature for mass consumption, makes its contribution to the whole. Kipling seldom wastes a frame in any of his stories. Here he is warning us against literature which does not require the reader to think, as well as touching on the idea of forgery, fakery and substitution: 'So, precisely as the three guinea hand-bag is followed in three weeks by its thirteen and sevenpence ha'penny, indistinguishable sister, the reading public enjoyed perfect synthetic substitutes for Plot, Sentiment, and Emotion.' The single word, 'sister', alerts us to the parallel between literature and women: Castorley, instead of marrying the real thing, has chosen an ashen-faced substitute, who has never believed him 'since before we were married'. As a consequence, Castorley has to endure a concealed, corrosive passion. It is *this* that Manallace finally takes pity on. Like many another in Kipling's work, Castorley is compelled to eke out his emotional life on 'perfect synthetic substitutes' for sentiment and emotion.

One last detail of 'Dayspring Mishandled' remains to be accounted for – the twice-repeated phrase, 'for old sake's sake'.

This comes from a poem in Kingsley's *The Water Babies*, which describes a doll lost on a heath and rediscovered:

> I found my poor little doll, dears,
>   As I played in the heath one day:
> Folk say she is terribly changed, dears,
>   For her paint is all washed away,
> And her arm trodden off by the cows, dears,
>   And her hair not the least bit curled:
> Yet, for old sake's sake, she is still, dears,
>   The prettiest doll in the world.

The paralysis of 'Dal's mother and Castorley's sick-bed declaration of love are encapsulated and underlined by Kingsley's poem. The gloves so mysteriously donned by Manallace continue to hoard their meaning – as so often in Kipling's work.

For those to whom Kipling is merely a crude jingoist, the almost Joycean meticulousness of his art will come as a surprise. But his abiding concern with love, in all its desolate manifestations, will come as a revelation. Love in Kipling's oeuvre isn't often happy: in *Plain Tales* it is mainly adulterous or disappointing or competitive; in 'Without Benefit of Clergy', it is tragic, with Ameera and the child dead, the mother greedily acquisitive and Holden's home suddenly wrecked by the rains: 'he found that the rains had torn down the mud pillars of the gateway, and the heavy wooden gate that had guarded his life hung lazily from one hinge. There was grass three inches high in the courtyard; Pir Khan's lodge was empty, and the sodden thatch sagged between the beams.' What had once seemed secure and solid is wiped out virtually overnight, the house mirroring the frail relationship – a symbolic scene possible only in the tropics. Desolation, sacrifice and waste are the words that present themselves when one considers Kipling's treatment of love.

There are, of course, moments when sacrifice isn't entirely negative. Even 'The Wish House' has its positive side – grim and thankless though Grace Ashcroft's sacrifice is. She may herself be doubtful, for all her toughness, and seek reassurance from her friend Liz Fettley ('It *do* count, don't it – de pain?') but there is something movingly tenacious in her emotional commitment which Kipling captures in one sentence: 'The lips that still kept trace of their original moulding hardly more than breathed the words.' If Kipling had added the indefinite article – and written 'the lips that still kept *a* trace' – how much weaker this statement of willed beauty in the face of old age and imminent death would have been. If we compare 'The Wish House' to Chekhov's great story of old age, 'A Dreary Story', the power of Grace Ashcroft is evident. Chekhov's hero, Professor Nikolay Stepanovitch, is the incarnation of Yeats's summation of age – 'testy delirium and dull decrepitude'. The Professor's sense of mortality infects his entire life, empties him of profundity, interest and affection, even for his ward Katya whom he loves. 'Farewell, my treasure!' the story ends, but these are the hollow words of a man recalling the memory of emotion, not the thing itself. By comparison, Grace Ashcroft isn't such a desolate figure.

The sacrifice in 'Dymchurch Flit' is difficult and touching, too. The Pharisees ask for a boat to take them to France 'an' come back no more'. There is a boat but no one to sail it, and so they ask the widow to lend them her sons: 'Give 'em Leave an' Good-will to sail it for us, Mother – O Mother!' The conflict is then between her own delimited maternal feelings – 'One's dumb, an' t'other's blind . . . but all the dearer me for that' – and her mother's heart which goes out to the invisible Pharisees and *their* children: 'the voices justabout pierced through her; an' there was childern's voices too. She stood out all she could, but she couldn't rightly stand against *that*.' Finally, she consents, shaking 'like a aps-tree makin' up her mind'. She is rewarded for her charity by the return of her sons and by the promise that psychic gifts will run in her family, but Tom Shoesmith makes it clear that her sacrifice was not made for gain: 'No. She loaned her sons for a pure love-loan, bein' as she sensed the Trouble on the Marshes, an' was simple good-willing to ease it.'

Kipling's stories return ceaselessly to the nature of parental love, its ability to expend inexhaustible passion on apparently worthless objects. There is Wynn Fowler in 'Mary Postgate', 'an unlovely orphan of eleven', who repays Mary's devotion 'by calling her "Gatepost", "Postey", or "Packthread", by thumping her between her narrow shoulders, or by chasing her bleating, round the garden, her large mouth open, her large nose high in the air, at a stiff-necked shamble very like a camel's'. Kipling, artistically generous as ever, doesn't reserve strong feeling for the handsome. Nor are the recipients of this love perfect. In 'Friendly Brook', Mary, the adopted Barnardo girl, garners no praise from Jabez and Jesse; 'It don't sometimes look to me as if Mary has her natural right feelin's. She don't put on an apron o' Mondays 'thout being druv to it – in the kitchen *or* the henhouse. She's studyin' to be a school-teacher. She'll make a beauty! I never knowed her show any sort o' kindness to nobody . . .' For this plain, vinegary girl, whose 'Maker ain't done much for her outside nor yet in', her foster-father, Jim Wickenden, is prepared to commit murder – loosening a plank so that her real father is drowned on one of his visits to blackmail the foster-parents. Eliot, understandably in wartime, chose to read this story as a kind of pagan celebration of England, with the brook as a tutelary deity. It isn't. Jim Wickenden's relationship with the brook is made clear in the implicit pun with which Kipling ends the story. Wickenden is happy when the brook floods and takes a snatch of his hay because that represents hush-money: 'The Brook had changed her note again. It sounded as if though she were mumbling something soft.' His secret is safe with the brook.

In the same story, there is the Copley family and their 'Bernarder cripple-babe', whom they foster, but not for the financial inducement: 'It's handy,' says Jabez. 'But the child's more. "Dada" he says, an' "Mumma" he says, with his great rollin' head-piece all hurdled up in that iron collar. *He* won't live long – his backbone's rotten, like. But they Copley's do just about set store by him – five bob or no five bob.' For Kipling, this isn't an extreme case. It is a human constant he can effortlessly empathize with.

It is this knowledge of parental love, too, which produces some of Kipling's most savage stories. He knows it can be

476

murderous if threatened – as it is, most obviously, in 'Mary Postgate', where the wizened old spinster stands over a German airman with a revolver, luxuriating first in his death (from injuries sustained in a fall from his aircraft) and then in a hot bath. This act of barbarism, her refusal to fetch a 'Toctor', Mary knows, would not gain Wynn's approval were he alive. Nor does it, I think, elicit Kipling's approval – only his understanding. The same theme is examined in 'A Sahibs' War', where Kipling's attitude is less ambiguous. The narrator, Umr Singh, is a Sikh who is a kind of adopted father to a Sahib called Kurban: 'Young – of a reddish face – with blue eyes, and he lilted a little on his feet when he was pleased, and cracked his finger-joints.' How carefully Kipling implies, in the first three phrases, this young man's virtual anonymity, and how carefully he conveys the immense emotional investment of the narrator in the last two descriptive touches, singling out characteristics invisible except to the eye of love. In this story, the narrator attempts to revenge himself on a treacherous Boer family who have killed his 'son', Kurban Sahib.

They are not prepossessing: 'And old man with a white beard and a wart upon the left side of his neck; and a fat woman with the eyes of a swine and the jowl of a swine; and a tall young man deprived of understanding. His head was hairless, no larger than an orange, and the pits of his nostrils were eaten away by a disease. He laughed and slavered. . .' When the Sikh narrator plans his revenge, he intends to be exact, a child for a child: 'and the idiot lay on the floor with his head against her knee, and he counted his fingers and laughed, and she laughed again. So I knew they were mother and son . . .' He means to hang the son in front of the mother and Kipling accurately records her anguish: 'The woman hindered me not a little with her screechings and plungings.' Umr Singh, who has taken opium to sustain him, is deflected from his purpose by a vision of the dead Kurban Sahib who orders him to refrain, telling him that this is a Sahibs' War. Mary Postgate has no such assistance back to civilized values and the rule of law – only her tortured instinct, in its full atavism. Nevertheless, though the Boer family survive,

Kipling makes us know the force of parental grief. If it is the eye of love that isolates and cherishes that habit of cracking the fingers, it is the same eye, hideously inflamed, that registers the wart on the left side of the Boer's neck.

In his stories, Kipling often measures love by its opposite, and O *Beloved Kids*, his letters to his children, also shows how deep this habit of thought and expression went. His expressions of affection are rarely straightforward. Except for two occasions ('You see, I love you'), Kipling prefers the ironical mode: 'Mummy is better I think every day than she was (perhaps because two yelling pestiferous brats are away)'; 'she says as long as she hasn't you two horrid brats to look after she can stand most things'; 'I regret I have not kicked you enough'; 'if it had been you I should have chastised you with a cricket stump'. Examples of this knock-about stuff would be easy to multiply. Clearly, they conceal an almost embarrassing concern and tenderness, a passion more single-minded and obsessive than the sexual. Despite the tough front, Kipling is evidently infatuated and showers gifts on his son while the letters keep up a saving pretence of sternness. Squash courts are built, there are treats at Brown's Hotel followed by music halls, motor bikes are bought, gramophones, and finally a Singer car. There can be no question – Kipling was a sugar daddy.

With this, and the death of his beloved daughter, Josephine, in mind, we come to Kipling's most tender story, ' "They" ', which unfolds in a way that gives new meaning to that old cliché: its progress is as grave, delicate and measured as Mrs Bremmil, in 'Three and – An Extra', 'turning over the dead baby's frocks'. Kipling's treatment of the theme of bereavement is simple and reticent. There is none of the bravura prose with which 'The Gardener' ends, when Helen Turrell confronts the military cemetery: 'She climbed a few wooden-faced earthen steps and then met the entire crowded level of the thing in one held breath. She did not know that Hagenzeele Third counted twenty-one thousand dead already. All she saw was a merciless sea of black crosses, bearing little strips of stamped tin at all angles across their faces.' This difference granted, to the detriment of neither, ' "They" ' and 'The Gardener' are intimately connected. Behind each lies the death of one of Kipling's children, Josephine, and John who was lost in action during the First World War. Both, too, share the theme of reticence. Helen Turrell is prevented from expressing her grief by the threat of social exposure, the narrator of ' "They" ' by an emotional fastidiousness, which is clearly related to Kipling's own personality – as we see it in his ironic letters to his children and in the very title of his autobiography, *Something of Myself*. Kipling was shy about his emotions, shy indeed about using his own voice, preferring to speak through others or adopting the bluff clubman's tone of his caste and its grating air of worldliness: 'for he did me the honour to talk at me plentifully' and 'it is not always expedient to excite a growing youth's religious emotions'. ' "They" ', however, has none of this ponderous archness, except deliberately.

The narrator is, at first, in marked contrast to Miss Florence, who is blind and therefore openly sensitive as an exposed membrane: 'we blindies have only one skin, I think. Everything outside hits straight at our souls. It's different with you. You've such good defences . . .' The defences are apparent in the narrator's response to Miss Florence's question, 'You're fond of children?'; 'I gave her one or two reasons why I did not altogether hate them.' This is recognizably the Kipling who told his children he loved them by brandishing a cricket stump. And, of course, the narrator's shyness is more than matched by the elusive children, 'the shadows within the shadow'. The narrator's attitude to Miss Florence is one of straightforward pity, without a trace of condescension: like her, he accepts that he is more capable, less vulnerable. To the other parents who have suffered bereavement, he is less neutral, more superior: 'I saw the Doctor come out of the cottage followed by a draggle-tailed wench who clung to his arm,' he coldly notes, and we are reminded of Helen Turrell's refusal to meet the hysterical, 'mottled' Mrs Scarsworth on equal terms.

By the story's end, everything has been reversed. His grief is such that Miss Florence pities him: 'And, d'you remember, I called you lucky – once – at first. You who must never come here again.' The narrator is included in the democracy of grief, but when his heart is opened the pain is so great that the consolation provided by the children of the House Beautiful is, after all, no consolation but an unbearable torment. The unseen touch of *his* dead child is just not enough – and therefore too much. Finally, Kipling's attitude is there in the inverted commas which surround his title, ' "They" ': the children are wraiths, necessary to some, but they do not exist, and it is this which the narrator finds impossible to endure.

Kipling's poem, 'The Road to En-Dor', specifically warns against dabbling in the supernatural and in *Something of Myself* he is equally firm: 'I have seen too much evil and sorrow and wreck of good minds on the road to En-Dor to take one step along that perilous track.' Still, ' "They" ' is an exploration, even if Kipling does turn back: the tallies which feed Miss Florence's fire are an example of a more ancient form of communication; both the narrator and Miss Florence know about 'the Colours' and 'the Egg which it is given to very few of us to see'. Kipling doesn't explain what either is, though the Egg may be the Egg of the Universe, deposited by the First Cause from which Brahma came. It isn't important: the mere mention is enough to open up possibilities about the potential of the human mind – a theme Kipling considers in ' "Wireless" '.

There, a consumptive chemist, Mr Shaynor, is in love with a girl called Fanny Brand, 'a great, big, fat lump of a girl', who distantly resembles 'the seductive shape on a gold-framed toilet-water advertisement'. Shaynor, weakened by TB, takes a drink prepared by the narrator from random drugs and goes into a trance. Once under, he stares at the advertisement and writes snatches of 'The Eve of St Agnes' and the ode 'To a Nightingale', occasionally lapsing into the deadest prose. The poetry (Shaynor has never heard of Keats) is inspired by his surroundings – vulgar druggist's dross, a hare hanging up outside *the* (Kipling's use of the definite article is always superb) Italian warehouse next door and so on. The narrator, desperate for an explanation, tries analogies with radio waves and faulty receivers, since the story is framed by some early broadcasting experimentation. The frame, however, is completely ironic, though the jargon of Cashell, the enthusiast, comes so thickly that Kipling's deflating irony is easily missed in the welter of Hertzian waves and coherers. ' "That's all," he said, proudly, as though himself responsible for the wonder.' How much more wonderful, Kipling implies, is the transmutation of life's pitiful fragments into art – Spinoza, falling in love, the noise of the typewriter or the smell of cooking. Eliot's comment on his list might have been Kipling's: 'When a poet's mind is perfectly equipped for its work, it is constantly amalgamating disparate experience; the ordinary man's experience is chaotic, irregular, fragmentary.' Kipling prefers a description closer to Yeats's rag-and-bone shop of the heart: 'Followed without a break ten or fifteen lines of bald prose – the naked soul's confession of its physical yearning for its beloved – unclean as we count uncleanliness; unwholesome, but human exceedingly; the raw material . . . whence Keats wove the twenty-sixth, seventh and eighth stanzas of his poem.' Beside the miracle of the gifted human coherer, that rare occurrence, stand the pathetic transmissions achieved by science – 'Signals unintelligible'.

This fascinated respect for the miracle of the mind isn't logically opposed to a disbelief in the supernatural. But perhaps the more exact word for Kipling's position would be distrust. Clearly, he felt it dangerous to meddle, as we can see from 'The Disturber of Traffic', where the lighthouse-keeper, Dowse, is driven mad by his ceaseless contemplation of 'the wheel and the drift of Things'. The prefatory poem pleads, 'Lay not Thy toil before our eyes', and in the story itself Kipling touches on the same message, alluding to I Corinthians 13:12, as the narrator is lent 'a pair of black glass spectacles, without which no man can look at the Light unblinded'. As often in late Kipling, the narrator, Fenwick, is unreliable: he takes Dowse's account more or less at face value, though Challong, with his webbed hands and feet and the ability to survive being tipped into the sea from the Light, is patently a figment of Dowse's imagination. Challong is, we are told, an 'Orang-Laut' – that is, a man of the sea.

The epithet points us towards the old man of the sea, Proteus, the god renowned for constantly changing his shape. Dowse's madness takes the form of a fascination with shapes and patterns: when he is finally rescued, he is barely able to speak because 'his eye was held like by the coils of rope on the belaying pin, and he followed those ropes up and up with his eye till he was quite lost and comfortable among the rigging, which ran criss-cross, and slopeways, and up and down, and any way but straight along under his feet north and south.' Once Dowse is absorbed in the changing shapes of things his mental stability deserts him. The Protean world doesn't bear looking at, any more than the Light.

Kipling's attitude is similar to that of Stephen, the abbot in 'The Eye of Allah', who takes the decision to destroy the microscope – even though his mistress is dying of cancer. The possible benefits are outweighed by the immediate dangers – inquisition and execution ('You can hear the faggots crackle') and the longer-term threat to the Christian religion, whereby the war between Good and Evil would become merely an endless struggle between two morally neutral forces of creation and degeneration – without any hope of a final outcome. The short-term danger of 'more torture, more division' is clear enough, a transparent conclusion, but the route to it is subtle and any reading must account for the details of the story.

'The Eye of Allah' groups itself naturally with 'The Manner of Men', a story in which Kipling describes the progress of St Paul (described by one of the narrators, from his limited viewpoint, as 'a Jew philosopher') by sea from Myra to Rome, with a shipwreck at Malta en route. Like Browning's Karshish, who witnesses the raising of Lazarus by one he describes as 'a leech', Quabil and Sulinor are witnesses whose testimony is reliable as to fact, but perhaps unreliable as to interpretation. Sulinor is the more sympathetic to Paul, who has nursed him through dysentery and, more importantly, intuited Sulinor's life-long fear of the Beasts in the circus. As an ex-pirate of dubious status, Sulinor is justifiably leery and the Beasts are a grumbling presence through the story: even the *'hrmph-hrmph'* of the oars in a trireme reminds Sulinor 'of an elephant choosing his man in the Circus'. The story poses the question: who has saved the ship? From a Christian standpoint, Paul is clearly responsible – with God's help. From the seamen's position, it is finally their skill which brings off the safe beaching of the boat. Kipling, I believe, doesn't express a bias, unlike Browning, and the reader is left to adjudicate between the rival claims of miracle and pragmatic technique. Either way, Paul's fearless calm, whether justified or not, plays its part in the operation. If, at the story's outset, Kipling appears to incline towards Paul – since Quabil mistakes Paul much as he himself is mistaken for a landlubber when he is actually a master-mariner – the finale's emphasis is on technique, pure seamanship, as Sulinor and Baeticus indulge in a war game.

The theme of miracle versus the purely natural explanation of phenomena is central to 'The Eye of Allah', taking the form of medicine or metaphysics. Despite the monastic setting, sceptics are well represented. John of Burgos, the artist, is an unbeliever, although he is attacked to St Illod's: '"*Thy* soul?" the sub-cantor seemed doubtful.' Roger Bacon is a freethinker: '*Every* way we are barred – barred by the words of some man, dead a thousand years, which are held final.' Roger of Salerno also resents Church interference. The infirmarian, Thomas, won't be other than a lay-member of the community because he fears his heresy: 'I confess myself at a loss for the cause of the fever unless – as Varro saith in his *De Re Rustica* – certain small animals which the eye cannot follow enter the body by the nose and mouth, and set up grave diseases. On the other hand, this is not in Scripture.'

The story shows, however, that the 'certain small animals' *are* in Scripture, since they now form part of John of Burgos's illustration for the Gadarene swine. How does Kipling want us to interpret this? Are we to believe that scientific discovery is inherent in the gospel once it is *illuminated*? After all, in a glancing reference to Colossians 4:14, Stephen reminds John that Luke is a physician. Similarly, when Roger of Salerno sees John's picture of the devils leaving Mary Magdalene, he immediately recognizes what has been depicted – not a miracle but 'epilepsy – mouth, eyes, and forehead – even to the droop of her wrist there. Every sign of it! She will need restoratives, that woman, and, afterwards, sleep natural.' He pays the artist a physician's compliment: 'Sir, you should be of our calling.' This reconciliation of the theological and the physical is matched by another profound pun, however, to set against that of 'illumination': John's great Luke begins with the Magnificat and he has literally *magnified* the Lord, using the microscope, so that what, when unexplained, seemed miraculous, becomes part of the natural world. The Lord is no longer outside his creation: he *is* his creation, a position which is theologically untenable. Christ – if this line of argument is pursued to its conclusion – is nothing more, or less, than the gifted leech identified by Karshish. Stephen seems the only person to reach out towards this possibility – and he destroys the microscope, to save a system which, however imperfect, ensures a necessary order against chaos. The chaos he fears is not purely social. He fears, too, 'that man stands ever between two Infinities' and I think Kipling shared this fear.

The impersonal scale of things and the smallness of the individual made him flinch, as Kim's crisis and breakdown show: 'He tried to think of the lama – to wonder why he had stumbled into a brook – but the bigness of the world, seen between the forecourt gates, swept linked thought aside.' And at last the outcry of the threatened ego is heard: 'I am Kim. I am Kim. And what is Kim?' Mental breakdown interested Kipling. He himself was twice afflicted as a young man and his sister was troubled for most of her life. He treats the subject directly in 'The Janeites', where the shell-shocked Humberstall is restored to a sanity of sorts by Macklin, who persuades him to memorize the works of Jane Austen, by pretending that they will give him an entrée to a quasi-Masonic society of 'Janeites', with attendant perks. It is, of course, a gentle conspiracy of a different kind – to exercise and re-educate a mind which has been disturbed by trench warfare and experiences that are the more horrific for Humberstall's insouciant Cockney retelling: 'then I saw somethin' like a mushroom in the moonlight. It was the nice old gentleman's bald 'ead. I patted it. 'Im and 'is laddies 'ad copped it right enough.' *I patted it.* Kipling didn't flinch from much.

Eliot, Orwell, Edmund Wilson, Randall Jarrell, Borges, Kingsley Amis, Angus Wilson, and the most gifted Kipling critic of all, Miss J. M. S. Tompkins, have all spoken out for Kipling – without success. His work remains ignored by the literary intelligentsia, largely for political reasons. Yet his politics are more various than their reputation. It isn't difficult to find attitudes in his work which are unpleasant and one could compile a damning little anthology. There is the anti-Semitism of ' "Bread Upon the Waters" ', where McPhee remarks, 'Young Steiner – Steiner's son – the Jew, was at the bottom of it' and the prejudice is reinforced by McRimmon's 'there's more discernment in a dog than a Jew'. Sometimes it is possible to write off remarks like this as elements of characterization. For instance, the racial prejudice of Curtiss in *The Story of the Gadsbys*: 'Hang it all! Gaddy hasn't married beneath him. There's no tar-brush in the family, I suppose.' Kipling's 'Lispeth', 'Without Benefit of Clergy' or 'Beyond the Pale' show clearly enough that, though he saw the difficulties of mixed marriages, he was disinterested enough to register disapproval of the 'white' position: the clergyman in 'Lispeth' is exposed as a mendacious hypocrite. Similarly, Ortheris's prejudice is undermined by Learoyd's report of it: 'Orth'ris, as allus thinks he knaws more than other foaks, said she wasn't a real laady, but nobbut a Hewrasian. An don't gainsay as her culler was a bit doosky like. But she *was* a laady.'

All the same, there is, for example, Kipling's anti-Irish prejudice to consider. In *Something of Myself*, he asserts: 'the Irish had passed out of the market into "politics" which suited their instincts of secrecy, plunder, and anonymous denunciation'. There is, too, a callous Darwinism which is hard to accept, a sense that some life is acceptably cheap: 'the weakest of the old-type immigrants had been sifted and salted by the long sailing-voyage of those days,' he writes, deploring the imperfection of later immigrants to America who were preserved by the shorter steam voyage. And in 'Without Benefit of Clergy', he is cool about the function of cholera in this Malthusian aside: 'it was a red and heavy audit, for the land was very sick and needed a little breathing space ere the torrent of cheap life should flood it anew. The children of immature fathers and undeveloped mothers made no resistance.' Perhaps Kipling intends his tone to be stoical. *Tant pis*, it comes across as simply callous.

But if there is no difficulty in mounting a case against Kipling, it is also worth pointing out that his opinions are by no means as stereotypical as biased accountancy can make them. In *Something of Myself*, he also deplores the extermination of the American Indian: 'I have never got over the wonder of a people who, having extirpated the aboriginals of their continent more completely than any modern race had ever done, honestly believed that they were a godly little New England community, setting examples to brutal mankind. This wonder I used to explain to Theodore Roosevelt, who made the glass cases of Indian relics shake with his rebuttals.' The Boers, too, are seen clearly and prophetically by Kipling: 'we put them in a position to uphold and expand their primitive lust for racial domination'. He blames the white man for the importation of disease into Africa, ruining a 'vast sun-baked land [that] was antiseptic and sterile'. And for an establishment figure, Kipling is capable of savaging the highest, as in this plea for regulated prostitution as a way of controlling venereal disease: 'visits to Lock Hospitals made me desire, as earnestly as I do today, that I might have six hundred priests – Bishops of the Establishment for choice – to handle precisely as the soldiers of my youth were handled'. This isn't the predictable voice Kipling's detractors would have us expect, and if it doesn't excuse other lapses into illiberalism, it certainly complicates our picture.

'The soldiers of my youth' is a significant phrase. We know that Kipling didn't mean 'the officers of my youth'. For preference, Kipling always took the part of the inarticulate, the anonymous, the helpless – and it is typical that his version of Browning's 'The Bishop Orders His Tomb' should be 'The Mary Gloster', a poor relation but full of passion and coarse pathos.

And written in the demotic. It was a mode that Kipling consciously gave himself over to, as we can see from the poem which follows 'The Manner of Men', spoken by the St Paul whom Quabil mistrusts because 'he had the woman's trick of taking the tone and colour of whoever he talked to':

> I am made all things to all men –
> Hebrew, Roman, and Greek –
> In each one's tongue I speak . . .

There is something of himself in these verses, and in the plea with which the poem ends: 'Restore me my self again!'

Browning expresses a similar pang in 'One Word More':

> Love, you saw me gather men and women,
> Live or dead or fashioned by my fancy,
> Enter each and all, and use their service,
> Speak from every mouth – the speech, a poem.
> Hardly shall I tell my joys and sorrows,
> Hopes and fears, belief and disbelieving:
> I am mine and yours – the rest be all men's,
> Karshish, Cleon, Norbert and the fifty.
> Let me speak this once in my true person . . .

Whatever the regrets, the achievement, in both cases, is bound up with the artistic choice 'to have gathered from the air a live tradition'. Pound's words apply to every writer engaged in the endless rediscovery of the oral and the liberation of literature from the tyranny of the classical, the received, which was once itself 'language really used by men', in Wordsworth's famous phrase. Isaac Bashevis Singer adapts the Yiddish folk tradition, with its generous allowance of formulaic phrases, old-fashioned omniscience and biblical directness. Whitman revels in his 'barbaric yawp' and the escape from European habits. Twain's fiction introduces the drawl into American prose: 'You don't know me, without you have read a book by the name of *The Adventures of Tom Sawyer*, but that ain't no matter.' Almost exactly a hundred years later, Saul Bellow, after a false and frigid beginning, has fought the literary until he can confidently begin 'Zetland: By a Character Witness' with the words, 'Yes, I knew the guy.' We should see Kipling in this company of essentially oral writers who insist on talking in the library – and then remember how many more voices he can command. Kipling deliberately chose to work with 'unpromising' material, just as his allegorical artist, the bull Apis, chooses ordinary Chisto, rather than Villamarti – the result, for both, is immortality.

I have quoted freely in this essay, frequently from work which I haven't selected for inclusion, in the hope that readers will be encouraged to explore Kipling further. *Kim* in particular should be read and I had to fight the temptation to extract from it. Let me conclude, then, with one last quotation from that work. 'The sullen coolies, glad of the check, halted and slid down their loads.' It seems an ordinary sentence, doesn't it? But how different it would have been, how much lighter their load, if Kipling had written 'set down their loads', instead of 'slid down their loads'.

# Kipling's Poetry

At the outset of his long literary career Rudyard Kipling was apparently content to recognize the distinction between verse and poetry, and, if we are to judge from his letter to Caroline Taylor of 9 December 1889, equally content to accept that his own place was below the salt: 'I am not a poet and never shall be – but only a writer who varies fiction with verse.'

Almost a year later, in September 1890, Oscar Wilde recorded a similarly modest assessment of *Plain Tales from the Hills*, turning his phrase like a bayonet. If Kipling's title could boast of its artlessness, the unvarnished simplicity of its artistic means, Wilde was not inclined to disagree: 'one feels as if one were seated under a palm tree reading life by superb flashes of vulgarity'. (Interestingly, Wilde's use of the final *mot injuste* is foreshadowed in *Departmental Ditties*, where Sleary 'Bade farewell to Minnie Boffkin in one last, long, lingering fit', rather than the 'kiss' one might justifiably expect.) This atmosphere of placid congruence – that Kipling's place was with hoi polloi – is misleading. What Wilde ruefully perceives as a limitation is precisely what Kipling knew to be his originality – the discovery for literature of the underdog. This is a bent which determines the arc of Kipling's career from early tales of Anglo-Indians to the later poem 'A Charm':

> Take of English earth as much
> As either hand may rightly clutch.
> In the taking of it breathe
> Prayer for all who lie beneath.

Not the great, nor well-bespoke,
But the mere uncounted folk
Of whose life and death is none
Report or lamentation.

When T. S. Eliot, in the course of an essay of fine advocacy, identifies, as a weakness, Kipling's lack of 'inner compulsion', the absence of a Figure in the Carpet, he overlooks Kipling's uncommon fascination with the common man and the common woman – his helpless under-doggedness.

The atmosphere of congruence between Wilde and Kipling is also misleading because, a year earlier, Kipling had already struck against 'long-haired things / In velvet collar-rolls', preferring to side with the less fashionable military types in India who 'hog their bristles short'. Kipling's acceptance of the distinction between verse and poetry, between high and low art, was not simply benign, but also a wry, bitter, bristling recognition of the way the battle-lines were drawn. That note of resignation, the calm declaration ('I am not a poet and never shall be') could quickly alter to a timbre of puckish aggression, as it does in 'The Conundrum of the Workshops' (1890), where the tower of Babel is an early casualty in the history of criticism:

They builded a tower to shiver the sky and wrench the
stars apart,
Till the Devil grunted behind the bricks: 'It's striking, but
is it Art?'

The poem itself is striking and memorable, but is it poetry? Or is it merely verse? For myself, I find the Old Testament cadence of 'builded' finely judged and the two verbs 'shiver' and 'wrench' beautifully economical in the way they adumbrate, first, the height and the breadth of the tower, and, second, the scale of the driving ambition – the desire to 'wrench the stars apart', a desire whose scope is curtailed by the unbiblical bathos of 'grunted' and 'bricks'. This is a particular instance where, as it were, the pigment of the language can be described by the critic

with a modicum of the vividness that Kipling brings to the scar
of Matun in 'The Truce of the Bear': 'Flesh like slag in the
furnace, knobbed and withered and grey'. In each example,
Kipling's language is patently not inert, but, like the harp of
True Thomas, birls and brattles in Kipling's hands.

We think of Kipling as a special, borderline case, but he is
not. Arnold memorably damned Pope and Dryden as 'classics
of our prose' in his essay 'The Study of Poetry', a critical
manoeuvre Eliot then used against Whitman in his essay on
Pound: 'Whitman was a great prose writer. It [his originality] is
spurious in so far as Whitman wrote in a way that asserted that
his great prose was a new form of verse.' As one who has fallen
short of poetry, then, Kipling is in the best possible company. It
is apposite that Pope should be a fellow defendant, since the
advertisement to 'An Epistle to Dr Arbuthnot' provided Kipling
with the title of his autobiography: 'Being divided between the
Necessity to say something of *Myself*, and my own laziness to
undertake so awkward a Task . . .'

To substantiate his case against Pope and Dryden, Arnold
quoted, maliciously:

> To Hounslow Heath I point, and Banstead Down;
> Thence comes your mutton, and these chicks my own.

Of course, counter examples could be cited against this damning
quotation from the 'Second Satire of the Second Book of Horace
Paraphrased'. One might list more obviously poetic lines of Pope
like 'Die of a Rose in aromatic Pain', but better are lines that
merely, yet perfectly, enact the unremittingly alert language we
call poetry: the exact comedy of bowls 'Obliquely waddling to
the mark in view'; the just comparison of learned commentary
to the silkworm and vice versa ('So spins the silkworm small its
slender store, / And labours, 'till it clouds itself all o'er'); the
finely calculated reversed foot in the middle of the line 'Keen,
hollow winds howl thro' the bleak recess'; the incriminating
guinea vividly 'gingling' down the tell-tale stairs; the punishment
for erring sylphs:

> Or Alom-*Stypticks* with contracting Power
> Shrink his thin Essence like a rivell'd Flower.

What a couplet. Elsewhere in Pope, the words 'power' and 'flower' are contracted to 'flow'r' and 'pow'r', which is what the metre requires here. Yet the words are written out in full, so that they exist, perfectly, precariously, between expansion and the threatened contraction. Notice, too, that Pope chooses not the obvious adjective 'shrivelled', but 'rivell'd', which calls to mind the expected word 'shrivelled', then gives it to us short of two letters – shrunken and contracted to 'rivell'd'. A further punishment for sylphs re-imagines drinking chocolate, and its preparation, with a paradoxical and poetic combination of microscopic intentness and boldly inverted perspective:

> Or as *Ixion* fix'd, the Wretch shall feel
> The giddy Motion of the whirling Mill,
> In Fumes of burning Chocolate shall glow,
> And tremble at the Sea that froaths below!

By now, even the accident of orthography, 'froaths', makes its illusory contribution to the poetry – seeming more frothy by virtue of its extra vowel, silent though it is.

Examples, however, do not answer the general point behind Arnold's particular example. To do that, one must establish what verse actually is. Once establish *that* with certainty and we can see if Kipling holds to the norm and does indeed write verse rather than poetry. By verse, however, I do not mean light verse. Though we seldom trouble to distinguish between them, verse and light verse are easily differentiated. In light verse, the interest, the meaning, resides, paradoxically and primarily, in the intricacies of the form: the content is merely the pretext to activate the elaborate metrical mechanics, just as the steel ball-bearing in a pin-table is only of interest in so far as it gets the pyrotechnics going. Verse, on the other hand, is a transparent medium which is important only as a vehicle for the meaning it carries – and which, therefore, is distinguished from prose only by the use of rhyme. Unsurprisingly, examples of pure verse are hard to find. Garrison Keillor's 'Mrs Sullivan', however, is the perfect instance, *das Ding an sich*: its message is wryly feminist and its medium, when Keillor reads it on radio, is the purest prose anecdote because the enjambement ensures that the unobtrusive rhymes are utterly inaudible.

'Function follows form,'
Said Louis Sullivan one warm
Evening in Chicago drinking beer.
His wife said, 'Dear,
I'm sure that what you meant
Is that form should represent
Function. So it's function that should be followed.'
Sullivan swallowed
And looked dimly far away
And said, 'Okay,
Form follows function, then.'

He said it again,
A three-word spark
Of modern arch-
Itectural brilliance
That would dazzle millions.
'Think I should write it down?'
He asked with a frown.
'Oh yes,' she said, 'and here's a pencil.'
He did and soon was influential.

The mystery here – why is this prose anecdote set out as verse? – is solved as soon as one realizes the problem facing Garrison Keillor. His material is too short to be a prose anecdote and it would be ruined by padding or elaboration. However, it is too subtle to be a straightforward joke taking up two lines. So it is awarded the poetic treatment – capital letters and rhymes. In fact, it would make a respectable prose poem, did we not have the mistaken conviction that the prose poem should have a heightened quality of 'froathy' language. In reality, there is no reason why a prose poem should be anything other than a piece of prose which is too short, too short to be even a very short short-story – what the Germans call *eine kleine Prosa*. Eliot understood this perfectly in his prose poem 'Hysteria'. The prose poem, however, is not a remedy one might expect Garrison Keillor to discover. The solution he finds is ingenious enough.

Even if we accept the Keillor as a singularly pure example of verse – and therefore as a standard which Kipling's poetry manifestly surpasses – we are still obliged to confront the issue of versification. Surely, as we try to distinguish between poetry and verse, a further difficulty arises when, unlike the Keillor verse, the lines are differentiated from prose not only by rhyme but also by versification?

> To Hounslow Heath I point, and Banstead Down;
> Thence comes your mutton, and these chicks my own.

Is this merely versified prose? Further, why does versification seem to imply the versifier, an epithet with unmistakably derogatory connotations, while the poet somehow escapes the mechanical universe of metrics into the more plastic and subtle dimension of rhythm? Of course, the two terms are supposedly neutral and interchangeable, because versification (the principles of metrical practice) and rhythm both depend on the repetition of stress.

Nevertheless, our prejudice is that metre is less subtle in its repetition than rhythm, however strained and inaccurate this looks when seen against the long tradition of English poetry. Modernism in poetry did not go metric in this country. In Russia, things were different, despite the best efforts of Mayakovsky. The metres of Russian poetry, from Pushkin to Pasternak, demonstrate enormous subtlety. The Russian poet can deploy metres which, in English, arrive in the ear tainted with comedy, whereas in Russian their associations are majestic.

There *is* an element of pure prejudice in our unthinking, negative response to complex metre. At the same time, the

494

Russian example isn't a clinching counter instance because it is on the English milieu that Kipling is dependent. English culture is no longer receptive to metrical virtuosity. Readers can no longer identify or name even the easier reaches of prosody. In fact, translations from the Russian which attempt to preserve the original metrical complexities only succeed in investing the host language with laughable syncopations. Given this negative predisposition, Kipling's detractors might adapt a phrase of his own and use it against him to evoke the unseemly air of vigorous, even raucous, improvisation in his verse. The phrase comes from 'Naaman's Song': 'In tones like rusty razor-blades to tunes like smitten tin'. While one can acknowledge the drift of the charge easily enough, one could not concede either its accuracy or justice without first citing passages, like the biblical cadences of 'Gertrude's Prayer', which, finally, make the charge implausible.

Even a professed admirer like T. S. Eliot enters the caveat that Kipling is musically deficient: 'what fundamentally differentiates his "verse" from "poetry" is the subordination of musical interest'. In an earlier and less well-known review in *The Athenaeum* of 9 May 1919, Eliot's view of Kipling was more decidedly negative but the limitations in Kipling's poetry were substantially the same: Kipling, the young Eliot found, had 'ideas' but no 'point of view', no 'world', and the music of his poetry was music only 'as the words of orator or preacher are music', persuading 'not by reason, but by emphatic sound'. The older Eliot has the same reservations, but is less dismissive. Nevertheless, though he hedges the judgement with modifications, the charge, that Kipling's verse is musically deficient, remains on the charge-sheet, damningly. Kipling, we are given to understand, writes terrific tunes but misses out on melody; we like his songs, but where are his Lieder?

Obviously, one can point, as Eliot could, to Kipling's free verse in 'Song of the Galley-Slaves' and 'The Runners', but these are exceptions which simply prove the rule. Which is that, for every poem like 'The Runes on Weland's Sword', with its curt, two-stress line, there are hundreds of poems whose metre is as subtle as a barn-dance, as predictable as the fiddler at a ceilidh. One thinks, for instance, of 'The Ballad of the *Bolivar*':

> Leaking like a lobster pot, steering like a dray –
> Out we took the *Bolivar*, out across the Bay!

Yet consider these lines, from earlier in the same poem:

> We put out from Sunderland loaded down with rails;
> We put back to Sunderland 'cause our cargo shifted . . .

The line 'Leaking like a lobster pot, steering like a dray' is actually made up of a trochaic tetrameter catalectic, followed by a trochaic trimeter catalectic. Which only means that the stresses fall as follows:

> Leaking like a lobster pot, steering like a dray –
> / v / v / v /,  / v / v /

The tetrameter has four stresses, while the trimeter has three. The pattern here is repeated in the earlier line: 'We put out from Sunderland loaded down with rails'. But the effect is completely different since the pattern hasn't yet established itself in the ear. Thus the absence of a caesura – a pause in the line to divide the tetrameter catalectic from the trimeter catalectic – means that there is a double stress at 'Sunder*land load*ed' which enacts rhythmically what the line depicts, which is a loading down, a weightiness at the centre.

And the following line is another tiny miracle of rhythmic subtlety: 'We put back to Sunderland 'cause our cargo shifted.' Again, deprived of the caesura, the ear cannot decipher and demarcate the two halves of the line, so that the whole line is poised ambiguously between the (as yet unresolved) metre and the natural rhythm of speech. On the one hand, 'We' wouldn't naturally take a stress, whereas 'put' would. On the other hand, the metrical imperatives reverse this natural pattern of stress: 'We' is stressed and 'put' recedes. The line, then, is decidedly shifty about its rhythmic status and the instability is added to by Kipling's use of a full trimeter and the 'extra' syllable (making thirteen in all) – so that the cargo's shift is embodied in the line itself.

These are not crude effects 'like smitten tin', nor are they isolated effects in Kipling. We do not discover them because, like Eliot, we do not expect to discover them. Instead we listen impatiently for the blunter satisfactions of the chorus, eradicating subtleties along the way by assimilating them to the main template. Yet the subtleties are everywhere. To take an example readily to hand, 'smitten tin' contains its own tinny, off-key echo, exactly inexact – not *tin-tin*, but *ten-tin*.

I can't think of a poet in the language who attracts more prejudice than Kipling. Orwell, an avowed admirer, is perfectly prepared to rewrite the poetry so that the dialect is standardized. But dialect is Kipling's greatest contribution to modern literature – prose and poetry – and he is the most accomplished practitioner since Burns. Without his example, Eliot's great avant-garde coup, the cockney pub conversation in 'A Game of Chess', would have been inconceivable. The bonus of dialect is easy to illustrate: which is the more lascivious, the standard English 'lascivious', or McAndrew's Scots version, 'those soft, lasceevious stars'? To the non-dialect speaker, at least, the Scots variant is infinitely more seductive than its less wheedling standard English version. Orwell would probably concur about Kipling's use of Scots – for some reason, the Scots dialect is exempt from the snobbery which attaches to other dialects. The real problem for Orwell is the cockney dialect of Kipling's soldiers, which he finds intrinsically comic – though he attributes his own 'underlying air of patronage' to Kipling. In the short stories, Mulvaney's Irish is a similarly insoluble problem for many readers. It is, the argument runs, a caricature with no foundation in phonetic reality. It is stage Irish. In fact, just as Scots would make a distinction between the urban Glaswegian accent and the more refined delivery of Edinburgh's Morningside, Irish-English likewise contains multitudes – the harsh accent of Protestant Belfast, the soft erosions of Catholic Killi-

ney. In Mulvaney's speech, Kipling offers us only one of many
alternatives – the broadest of dialects, true – but one which,
however unrepresentative, has its counterpart in rural reality.
The inability to pronounce 'th – ', which means that 'thousands'
comes out as 't'ousands', while not universal, is easily observable. ('Inability', though, is the wrong word, because it suggests
deficiency where in truth there is only difference.) I do not
believe that Kipling intended, in Orwell's words, 'to make fun
of a working-man's accent'. I think it more likely that Orwell,
an old Etonian and a writer who, in *Down and Out in Paris
and London*, worries that his accent will instantly discover him
as a gentleman, is transferring his own attitudes to Kipling.

After all, Orwell is not a reliable reader of Kipling's poetry:
faced with the dove-tailed ironies of 'The Winners', its 'water-
tight, fire-proof, angle-iron, sunk-hinge, time-lock, steel-faced
Lie', Orwell is taken in: 'Sooner or later you will have occasion
to feel that he travels fastest who travels alone, and there is the
thought, ready made and, as it were, waiting for you.' Orwell has
missed the warning signals sent out by Kipling to dissociate
himself from his ostensible ruthless moral: '*Down to Gehenna*,
or up to the Throne, / He travels the fastest who travels alone';
'Win by his aid and the aid disown – / 'He travels the fastest who
travels alone'. Kipling knows that the recommendation of ingrati-
tude as a moral precept is repugnant. Orwell is more concerned
with the poem's alleged proverbial memorability. For him, it is a
moral mnemonic – good bad poetry whose survival is its justification. It is a tag. As praise, this is decidedly back-handed – and I
should like to remove the curse by quoting the end of D. J.
Enright's British Council leaflet on T. S. Eliot at the time of his
centenary in 1988. 'Many of his lines, felt "as immediately as the
odour of a rose", have entered the language in the form of catch-
phrases or adages.' Enright goes on to quote, lavishly, without
any sense that there is some impropriety in the gift of memorability. Of course, Eliot's intellectual bona fides is impeccable. It will
be some time, however, before the taint attached to wide popularity leaves Kipling, as, at last, it has left Dickens – another
writer of genius belittled for decades by our cultural custodians.

For them, Kipling's very virtuosity is suspect. The sestina is the artiest of poetic forms, almost Fabergé in its insistence on surface over substance. Successful sestinas, though, invert the given limitations of the form, subduing the obtrusive repetition until it is invisible. Elizabeth Bishop's 'A Miracle for Breakfast' is one perfect example. The other is Kipling's 'Sestina of the Tramp-Royal'. The strict, cramped, formal demands are belied by the unbuttoned dialect and its illusion of relaxation and roominess. The tone rambles and spreads itself and Kipling solves the technical problem of the sestina by making its repetitiveness part of his speaker's character. He does this boldly and immediately in the first stanza, by adding an *extra* repetition at the beginning of the third line:

> Speakin' in general, I 'ave tried 'em all –
> The 'appy roads that take you o'er the world.
> Speakin' in general, I 'ave found them good . . .

Throughout, too, Kipling's way with the iambic pentameter is as varied as any comparable passage in Tennyson, partly because of caesurae, partly because the emphases of the speaking voice run over the metre's metronome. 'Sestina of the Tramp-Royal' isn't a great poem – even though it manages to modulate from the button-holing style of explanation to the poetic bravura of 'An', out at sea, be'eld the dock-lights die, / An' met my mate – the wind that tramps the world!' – but it is a very good sestina.

And what it illustrates is the strength of not being poetic. Kipling's use of dialect is usually associated with the music hall – that is to say, a popular art form – whereas perhaps it would be more helpful and truer to classify it with modernism, with Stravinsky's use of jazz and Russian folk melodies, with Picasso's restless appropriation of African sculpture and everyday materials like the daily paper. Unquestionably, Kipling, though popular, was as prepared as Stravinsky or Picasso to flout conventional standards of beauty. Kipling's aesthetic position is the argument from authenticity:

> *Ah! What avails the classic bent*
> *And what the cultured word,*
> *Against the undoctored incident*
> *That actually occurred?*

(Note the extra 'undoctored' syllable in line 3.) This italicized quasi-manifesto from 'The Benefactors' attracts examples to itself from Kipling's entire oeuvre, where the 'beauty' of each example is the beauty of accuracy rather than the beauty of eloquence. For instance, the political background of the Marconi scandal is now almost irretrievably lost, so that 'Gehazi', once a topical poem, now survives as an unforgettable evocation of leprosy:

> The boils that shine and burrow,
> The sores that slough and bleed –

Four verbs that one can hardly bear to dwell on – so vivid that one almost flinches.

In this category, one can include the olfactory shock of 'the mud boils foul and blue'; the sticky candour of ' "Snarleyow" ' where a gun-carriage wheel is said to be 'juicy' after it has gone over a body; and the unpleasantly palpable details which Kipling relishes in 'Mandalay': the 'Beefy face an' grubby 'and' of housemaids in a London of 'gritty pavin'-stones', far from the 'sludgy, squdgy creek' back East. Kipling's poetry has a strong stomach and it hardly ever looks away. There is very little in the way of whiffling sensibility. Rather there is a determination to include the unaesthetic: 'breech-blocks jammed with mud'; 'the lid of the flesh-pot chattered high'; 'the ten-times fingering weed'; 'the club-footed vines'. Rather than the baby seal with its soap-bubble eye, seal culling means gloves 'stiff with frozen blood'. Barren, featureless, and therefore indescribable landscapes are not a problem for Kipling, because he doesn't feel the constraint of literary decorum and takes his similes where and as he finds them: 'Old Aden, like a barrick-stove / That no one's lit for years an' years.' He casts a cold eye on death, too – on 'the wide-eyed corpse', on 'Blanket-hidden bodies, flagless, followed by the flies', on ''Is carcase past rebellion, but 'is eyes inquirin' why'.

It would be easy to continue quoting in this heterogeneous way. Sounds and the sea, however, provide two conveniently unified anthologies of excellence. Perfectly captured sounds include: 'And the lisp of the split banana-frond / That talked us to sleep when we were small'; 'To hear the traffic slurring / Once more through London mud'; 'the sob of the questing lead!'; the 'snick' of a breech-bolt; 'the thresh of deep-sea rain'; 'the first dry rattle of new-drawn steel' at the battle of Edgehill.

The sea is an equally generous provider, bringing us 'wind-plaited sand-dunes' and 'rain-squalls' that 'lash and veer'. Kipling's beach is as real as Joyce's Sandymount Strand:

> In the heel of the wind-bit pier,
> Where the twisted weed was piled.

'Piled' somehow evokes very precisely the illusion of immense and slightly inept labour that is suggested by the accumulation of seaweed on a shore – as if it had been put there, deliberately, untidily, rather than accidentally. Kipling is good on the sea *solus* ('the drunken rollers comb') and in conjunction with ships: 'The shudder, the stumble, the swerve, as the star-stabbing bowsprit emerges'; 'the shouting of the back-stay in a gale'.

When it comes to the sinking of ships, Kipling surrenders everything to the task of seeing the object as in itself it really is: the most famous example occurs in 'The *Mary Gloster*':

> Down by the head an' sinkin', her fires are drawn and
> cold,
> And the water's splashin' hollow on the skin of the empty
> hold –
> Churning an' choking and chuckling, quiet and scummy
> and dark –

In ' "The Trade" ', Kipling catches the aftermath: 'only whiffs of paraffin / Or creamy rings that fizz and fade'. 'The Destroyers' again consults the entrails of catastrophe: 'Till, streaked with ash and sleeked with oil, / The lukewarm whirlpools close!' Here, 'lukewarm' adds immeasurably to the reality of the scene. As an adjective, it is calculatedly unpoetic compared to the more obviously rhetorical lines which follow:

> A shadow down the sickened wave
> Long since her slayer fled.

Here we are recognizably in the presence of poetry, whereas with 'lukewarm' poetry was not a consideration.

In 'The King' (1894), Kipling shows himself fully aware of his aesthetic position – which is completely counter to Arnold, who felt Victorian England to be intractably unpoetic. Arnold's supposition was indubitably correct in his own case, as a glance at 'East London' and 'West London' will show. Kipling's allegiance is rather with Baudelaire and Eliot, poets determined to write in the present, with its gamps, galoshes, gaslights, spats, stove-pipe hats and area gates. Kipling's King is the spirit of Romance – a figure generally considered to be incompatible with, say, the railway season ticket. Kipling's King brings up the 9.15 train, in the driver's cab, the 'unconsidered miracle'.

Kipling is a modernist rather than the dated Edwardian of conventional criticism. Looked at thus, his poetry can surprise us with its affinities. Eliot, for instance, is indebted to 'The Long Trail' for the metre of 'Skimbleshanks' – the greatest modernist significantly taking the serious metric of Kipling and transposing it downwards to the frankly lighter mode. But more importantly Eliot is Kipling's debtor in 'The Hollow Men' and in the third of his 'Preludes':

> You dozed, and watched the night revealing
> The thousand sordid images
> Of which your soul was constituted;
> They flickered against the ceiling.

Kipling's 'Gentleman-Rankers' not only foreshadows Eliot's use of the nursery rhyme in 'The Hollow Men' ('We're poor little lambs who've lost our way, / Baa! Baa! Baa!') but also contributes:

> Every secret, self-revealing on the aching whitewashed
> ceiling.

When one reads 'Gertrude's Prayer', one looks back to Chaucer and to Ecclesiastes, but also ahead to Ezra Pound's *The Pisan Cantos* in their closing pages. The subject of both poems is irremediable error, for which a language drenched in contrition and self-denial is appropriate – so each poet chooses an impersonal, ritual dialect, a diction of hallowed simplicity, worn smooth with centuries of use, which yet avoids the taint of archaism, of mere quaint pageantry:

> The ant's a centaur in his dragon world.
> Pull down thy vanity, it is not man
> Made courage, or made order, or made grace,
>     Pull down thy vanity, I say pull down.
> Learn of the green world what can be thy place
> In scaled invention or true artistry,
> Pull down thy vanity,
>               Paquin pull down!

Pound's rhyme is more intermittent than Kipling's, but both men are masters of the refrain whose measured simplicity eventually amounts to what one can only call a scourged eloquence. 'Dayspring mishandled cometh not againe!'

Reading Kipling's poetry now is to realize how far ahead of his time his writing was. 'The Return' returns to a constant theme of Kipling's – the soldier's discontent in civvy street – and looks ahead to the laconic specificity of Auden. In 'Memorial for the City', Auden brings a scene alive with a single bizarre image: 'The soldiers fire, the mayor bursts into tears.' 'The

Return' anticipates Auden's economical documentation of the war-zone:

> Towns without people, ten times took,
>     An' ten times left an' burned at last;
> An' starvin' dogs that come to look
>     For owners when a column passed . . .

Whose concentration camp is more vivid? Auden's or Kipling's? 'Barbed wire enclosed an arbitrary spot / Where bored officials lounged (one cracked a joke) / And sentries sweated for the day was hot . . .' I think Kipling's is less mannered and contrived: 'Be'ind the pegged barbed-wire strands. / Beneath the tall electric light . . .' There are two words in the Kipling which expose Auden's effortful authenticity. They are 'pegged' and 'tall'.

I do not wish to overstate Kipling's modernism. It would be slightly fanciful, for instance, to insist on the *poésie pure* of 'McAndrew's Hymn' – the pure sound of catalogued technicalities like crosshead-gibs, the coupler-flange, the connecting-rod, the spindle-guide – since the poem is by way of being Kipling's earliest manifesto and fraught, therefore, with meaning. As a poem, it belongs with those others that declare the figure in Kipling's carpet – 'The Glory of the Garden', 'The Survival' and 'Alnaschar and the Oxen'. McAndrew is Kipling's lifelong subject. He is one of the Sons of Martha. He is an underdog – essential, but ignored by 'the passengers, wi' gloves an' canes'. In 'The Glory of the Garden', the lawns are not everything: 'the Glory of the Garden lies in more than meets the eye':

> For where the old thick laurels grow, along the thin red
>                                                     wall,
> You find the tool- and potting-sheds which are the heart
>                                                     of all;
> The cold-frames and the hot-houses, the dungpits and the
>                                                     tanks,
> The rollers, carts and drainpipes, with the barrows and
>                                                     the planks.

This is the metrical source, as it happens, for 'Growltiger's Last Stand'. How was it, then, that T. S. Eliot overlooked this vital connecting-rod? Eliot's selection of Kipling was made in 1941 and, in a sense, represents an aspect of the poet's war-work. France had capitulated, the evacuation at Dunkirk had taken place, and Germany had begun what looked like a successful invasion of Russia. All this finds its reflection in Eliot's selection, which draws heavily and understandably on Kipling's patriotic verse. As a result, Eliot's selection, though an enduring land-mark, has some extraordinary omissions: the ballad 'The Gift of the Sea', the chilling and pitiless masterpiece 'A Death-Bed', 'My Boy Jack', 'A Nativity', the powerfully nostalgic 'Lichtenberg', whose refrain ('Riding in, in the rain') contains its own swallow of emotion, and 'Bridge-Guard in the Karroo'. This last poem, written in 1901, is one of Kipling's most characteristic master-pieces. Its territory is familiarly foreign. It deals with soldiers. Its narrative is easy to follow. It has none of the chilly parallelism of 'A Death-Bed', where the course of the First World War and the progress of a cancer patient towards certain death are juxtaposed with cold relish. The stamp of Kipling's authority is everywhere in 'Bridge-Guard in the Karroo' – from the beauty of the sunset ('Opal and ash-of-roses, / Cinnamon, umber, and dun') to the quiet desolation of the homesick guard:

> We slip through the broken panel
>     Of fence by the ganger's shed;
> We drop to the waterless channel
>     And the lean track overhead;
>
> We stumble on refuse of rations,
>     The beef and the biscuit-tins . . .

Kipling is our laureate of litter, our bard of homesickness, capable of capturing the very details of despair: 'the click of the restless girders / As steel contracts in the cold – '; 'A morsel of dry earth falling / From the flanks of the scarred ravine'. The 'hosts of heaven' themselves are seen 'Framed through the iron arches – /Banded and barred by the ties' – and remind one, yet again, of Pound:

> a sinistra la Torre
>        seen through a pair of breeches.

Perhaps it is appropriate to conclude with the coupling of two politically unpopular poets – with their beleaguered sympathies and their discriminating ears. However, the sceptic will respond, with some justice, that it is easy to justify 'Bridge-Guard in the Karroo' but where is the poetry in the famous, unexcludable 'If – '?

The case for 'If – ' has never been made. Neither has the case against it. For admirers and detractors alike, I imagine, the verdict seems self-evident. Those who dislike Kipling on principle would frame their objections as follows: 'If – ' is nothing more than the complacent aggregation of impossible precepts and as far from poetry as the average school song.

I agree that 'If – ' is a test case. Personally, I feel the poem's power, but is that power the power of verse or the power of poetry? The advice is by and large sound, and line 8 ('And yet don't look too good, nor talk too wise') takes off the curse of complacency. What the sensitive reader responds to is not the particularities of advice but the impossibly stretched rhetorical structure. 'If – ' is a single sentence, endlessly burdened by the weight of hypotheticals. The conclusion – 'you'll be a Man, my son!' – depends on more qualifications than it seems possible for one sentence to bear. The poem, then, mimics the moral difficulty posed by Kipling – and yet the successful negotiation of the impossibly cumbered sentence to its end demonstrates, in miniature, the possibility of achieving something genuinely difficult. As single-sentence poems go, it is one of the longest, and it possesses all the poetry of the lovingly deferred finale of Dvořák's Cello Concerto. The form tells as much as the substance – and is, indisputably, poetry of a high order.

# Hopkins in His Letters

Gerard Manley Hopkins used to wait outside Miss Burdett Coutts's house at Highgate in the hope of seeing the Queen. He had no luck, but once, in Oxford, managed to glimpse a princess: 'I put myself in her way as she went to the station and got a good passing look, and, as I was alone at the particular spot, I think a bow.' We readers of writers' letters are not so very different from Hopkins, or from those *Sun* readers who yearn to be intimate with royalty – with its glamour and its gaffes. In both cases, the concept of incarnation has been adapted for everyday use. We prize letters for their *actualité*, for their entrée into the actual presence of genius. The letter, we hope, is the spirit. Allowing for tact and heated overstatement, we assume, reasonably enough, that letters are non-fiction and can, therefore, minister to a deep human instinct – the desire to see celebrity in the flesh. Rather than remain contented, as we ought, with the artistic personality as manifested in the work, we yearn to know the ordinary side of the extraordinary. Though it is the work which lends importance to the life, many of us prefer the authentic, imperfect, untouched-up reality. We want to see for ourselves, without the artist's interference, focus and selection. Just as, in this case, one would prefer Hopkins's complete letters to this selection.

When I agreed to review Hopkins's letters, I naturally assumed that, at last, the unsatisfactory publishing history of

*Gerard Manley Hopkins: Selected Letters*, edited by Catherine Phillips, Oxford University Press.

Hopkins's correspondence was going to be solved. Instead of individual volumes – to Robert Bridges, to Canon R. W. Dixon, and miscellaneous correspondents including Alexander Baillie and Coventry Patmore – I imagined an indispensable, annotated and chronologically arranged complete edition. Instead, Oxford University Press has published a £30 volume which is full of gaps – unsewn, the book gapes at every 32-page signature. Catherine Phillips prints the rest of the letter which begins this review, not the besotted royalism – presumably to make room, elsewhere, for this little gem of almost intolerable interest and immediacy: 'Dear Bridges, Your letter has been forwarded. I am most happy to come any day in the first week of September which you like to name. We go home to Hampstead tomorrow. I hope you are better than when you wrote. Believe me affectionately yours, Gerard M. Hopkins.' Rather than this 'mere Lloyd's Shipping Intelligence', might not place have been found for one of Hopkins's metaphorical frisks? 'No, Philip Rathbone never wrote. The teapot of inclination has been tilted several times till the spout of intention very nearly teemed out the liquor of execution (I am speaking of myself now, not of Mr Rathbone, and must point out the extraordinary merit of the figure I am employing: I shall work it up), but till now it has not filled the cup and saucer of communication.' Or even the facetious parody of Francis Bacon, which ends: 'Bay our negst beetigg be berry add birthful, but dow I have a cold. Your affegtiodate friedd, GERARD EB HOPKIDS.' Further, having no replies here means that one cannot assess how much Hopkins's friends valued his detailed and forthright criticisms of their work. He can resemble a non-smoker crushing out a cigarette thoroughly enough to rule out its being lit up again. And yet, we have Coventry Patmore's word for it: 'My dear Sir – Your careful and subtle fault-finding is the greatest praise my poetry has ever received.'

For all that, what remains is instinct with Hopkins's great gifts, even in something as unremarkable as 'a grunting harmonium'. Hopkins's critical penetration is threefold – he has a genius for theoretical formulation, seen here at its best in the famous letter to Baillie about Parnassian, which was written almost unbelievably at the age of twenty, when Hopkins was a second-year undergraduate. Secondly, he is a first-class close reader, as Patmore bears witness, though this aspect is under-represented in this selection. Thirdly, Hopkins has a unique talent for metaphorical encapsulation that brings a Dickensian quality to literary criticism. Browning is caricatured as having, like Charles Kingsley and the Broad Church school, 'the air and spirit of a man bouncing up from the table with his mouth full of bread and cheese and saying that he meant to stand no blasted nonsense'. Arnold's poems, he says, 'have all the ingredients of poetry without quite being it – no ease or something or other – like plum pudding at the English ambassador's'. Has anyone ever hit off better that moment in Arnold when conscious classicism and restraint decline into social stiffness and verbal etiquette? Hopkins is tough, too, on the worst of Tennyson – a 'downright haberdasher', who should have called *The Idylls of the King* by the franker title *Charades from the Middle Ages*. When our 'pleasing modern author', as the unpublished Hopkins refers to himself, is in this irreverent, bloodletting mood, we forget his unsleeping earnestness, as he does, too. Wordsworth's sonnets, though beautiful, have 'an odious goodness and neckcloth about them which half throttles their beauty'. The repetitive Aeschylus 'goes at it again and again like a canary trying to learn the Bluebells of Scotland'. High spirits. All the same, Hopkins was earnest and deeply unhappy in his job as fellow in Classics and Professor of Greek and Latin Literature at University College, Dublin. The Aeschylus fling is followed by: 'To bed, to bed: my eyes are almost bleeding'.

As early as 1885, it is clear that Hopkins is clinically depressed: 'I think that my fits of sadness, though they do not affect my judgement, resemble madness.' A month earlier, Hopkins narrowed his mental affliction to 'anxiety' and saw no grounds for thinking he should ever 'get over it'. Holidays, rare enough anyway, soon lost their efficacy as cures. When he meets the poet Katharine Tynan, he reports that she took him at first for twenty, ignorant of his 'heart and vitals, all shaggy with the whitest hair'. Faced with another gruelling heap of examination scripts to be marked, he fancies 'the fallen leaves of my poor life between all the leaves'. But how unhappy *was* Hopkins? *Really?*

To answer the question, consider his eyes. In March 1887, 'the irises of the present writer's eyes are small and dull, of a greenish brown; hazel I suppose; slightly darker at the outer rims'. By September 1888, despite an afternoon off in the Phoenix Park, his eyes are 'very, very sore'. Hopkins complains frequently about his eyes until, in October 1888, he gets a pair of glasses – and reports his oculist's verdict that 'my sight is very good and my eyes perfectly healthy'. So what was the problem with the eyes? Was it actually a problem with the mind's eye? I think so. What depressed Hopkins more than anything was the strain of marking, hence this horrible story which he passes on to Bridges, before complaining that his eyes are 'very, very sore': 'This reminds me of a shocking thing that has just happened to a young man well known to some of our community. He put his eyes out. He was a medical student and probably understood how to proceed, which was nevertheless barbarously done with a stick and some wire. The eyes were found among nettles in a field.'

That last unbearable sentence is surely a plea for help as much as it is objective narrative. The facts we have no reason to think untrue. Yet those eyes among the nettles, only lines away from his own stinging eyes, are also an involuntary poetic emblem, a 'found' emblem, of his predicament and that of his suffering 'sleek and seeing ball'. During his fatal illness, it is scarcely surprising that he should console his mother with his escape from the drudgery of his job – to which the discomfort of dying didn't compare.

# Dr Johnson's Last Letters

'The testicle continues well,' writes Dr Johnson to his intimate friend the Revd Dr Taylor in December 1783. One of my unrealized projects, when I worked as a publisher, was the *Faber Book of Ageing*. It was to have included Michelangelo's equation of elderly respiration with a torpid, autumnal fly in a leather sack; Yeats's 'Slow decay of blood, / Testy delirium / Or dull decrepitude'; Wallace Stevens's unforgivingly vivid 'We hang like warty squashes, streaked and rayed'; Betjeman's 'My head is bald, my breath is bad'; and Forster's documentary dismay recorded in his journal for 2 January 1925: 'famous, wealthy, miserable, physically ugly . . . stomach increases, but not yet visible under waistcoat. The anus is clotted with hairs, and there is a great loss of sexual powers . . .' Undoubtedly, Dr Johnson's testicle would have found a prominent place in such an anthology.

At first, surgeons thought it was a hydrocele. On examination, however, they pronounced it a sarcocele and pierced it experimentally. 'The experiment was made about a month ago, since which time the tumour has encreased both in surface and in weight, and by the tension of the skin is extremely tender, and impatient of pressure or friction. Its weight is such as to give great pain, when it is not suspended, and its bulk such as the common dress does but ill conceal, nor is there any appearance that its growth will stop. It is so hot, that I am afraid it is

*The Letters of Samuel Johnson 1782–1784*, edited by Bruce Redford, Clarendon Press.

in a state of perpetual inflammation.' The chirurgeon's knife was poised to remove the tumour when, abruptly, the experimental incision reopened and the fluids began to evacuate. The predicted danger of gangrene disappeared and the testicle ceased to mirror the craze for ballooning which raged in the world outside the sick-room.

A difficulty with my projected anthology was that potential editors seemed sceptical about the tonic and stoical and humorous values which I imagined would inhere in the collection. To a man almost they found the concept depressing – except for Anthony Burgess, who could envisage, as well as decrepitude, a kind of wry passion. In the end, though, even he decided that ageing wasn't something it was possible to focus on: it was too close for that. The idea languished when he dropped out of the jogging.

Johnson, though he was terrified of dying, brings to the business of affliction the objectivity of arithmetic. Writing to Mrs Thrale's daughter, Hester, Johnson manifestly prizes clarity above almost every other virtue: 'you will find yourself to think with so much clearness and certainty that the pleasure of arithmetick will attract you almost as much as the use'. It is this arithmetical objectivity which Johnson brings to that troublesome testicle: 'I now no longer feel its weight; and the skin of the scrotum which glistened with tension is now lax and corrugated.' *Glistened.*

More than physical unwieldiness and decay, Johnson feared mental debility. This volume of impeccably edited letters begins with Johnson's doctor, Dr Laurence, suffering a stroke which left him half paralysed. To the daughter Johnson writes: 'if we could have again but his mind and tongue, or his mind and his right hand, we would not much lament the rest'. Accordingly, the high point of these letters, if that doesn't sound too paradoxical, is Johnson's own stroke – which he describes in two letters that rival Orwell's famous assertion (in *Homage to Catalonia*) that being wounded is a very interesting experience, well worth retailing.

The stroke deprives him of speech. 'As it is too early to send [his letter] I will try to recollect what I can that can be suspected to have brought on this dreadful distress.' A minute account of his medicines and complaints follows. Two days later, he writes to Mrs Thrale, disclosing that his immediate worry was for his mental faculties: 'I was alarmed and prayed God, that however he might afflict my body he would spare my understanding. This prayer, that I might try the integrity of my faculties I made in Latin verse. The lines were not very good, but I knew them not to be very good, I made them easily, and concluded myself to be unimpaired in my faculties.' The letter continues in the same calmly curious vein: 'I had no pain, and so little dejection in this dreadful state that I wondered at my own apathy.' He takes wine to restore his speech. It is unsuccessful. He retires again to bed – 'and, strange as it may seem, I think, slept'. Later, he notices that, writing, his hand tends to make the wrong letters.

There is something candidly heroic as well as tedious in Johnson's meticulous and repetitive catalogue of his ailments, as correspondent succeeds correspondent. The last two years of his life are an epic of blisterings, bloodletting, costiveness (castor oil and klyster pipes), dropsy (diuretics included vinegar of squills, turpentine and Spanish Fly), toothache, opium-taking, asthma, insomnia and flatulence. From this ordeal Johnson emerges with dignity and real moral distinction – a man capable of facing fear itself fearlessly, with open eyes.

# Aristotle

Yesterday my wife drove my father to the Spiritualist chapel in Oxford's Summertown. They passed Aristotle Lane. 'Aristotle,' said my father. 'Wasn't he a Greek millionaire?'

Since my wife was driving, she didn't catch the expression on his face and therefore asked me afterwards whether he was cracking a joke. The tone of his voice gave nothing away. Either explanation – humour or ignorance – is possible. My father isn't an educated man. On the other hand, as a patronizing Oxford undergraduate, I once offered to play him a bit of *La Traviata*, my latest (belated) cultural discovery. He could smell improvement and snobbery in the air and gave a bravura performance of pained reluctance. But I wouldn't let him off. On went the record. As Montserrat Caballé soared and sank, my father sang along. 'I know this. My mother used to sing me this.' His mother had been a music hall artiste and had once given a Command Performance for Edward VII.

*History: The Home Movie*, my epic, grew out of this sort of thing. It is partly about the Pasternaks, my wife's famous relations, and partly about my own much more ordinary family. Except that, as the story above shows, I don't think my own family is ordinary. In fact, I'm not sure that *any* family is ordinary. Ask an audience at a poetry reading, as I once did, to raise a hand if they know someone who has been to prison – and about 75 per cent put their hands up. Maybe my father was making a sly deadpan joke about Aristotle. Maybe he's read the *Nichomachean Ethics*. Or maybe he's the equivalent of the Glaswegian in *History: The Home Movie* who talks about the great violinist, Hughie McEwan. (Better known to the rest of the world as Yehudi Menuhin.)

I've written about my father before – a 25-page memoir called 'A Silver Plate' in *Rich* (1984). So he isn't the central figure in *History: The Home Movie*. But he is crucial to its inception – crucial because he illustrates, in his life and his person, precisely and intimately, that life is a series of surprises. Look at him now, aged eighty-three, in his plastic Panama hat, his polyester lightweight linen jacket, as he gropes and groans his way downstairs, and you wouldn't think that this frail, uncertain individual was once a professional boxer. But then you might register the broken nose or the huge hands, hands which are still full of strength. On the fiftieth anniversary of D-Day, this simple paradox has been brought vividly home to me. Bifocalled, Brylcreemed veterans, their lower lips trembling between words, tell us how, as they waded ashore, the waves slapped their faces under their helmets.

The cover illustration for *History: The Home Movie* is a photograph of a steam train and four carriages crossing a sea. Waves break, close enough to splash up to the tender. There are seagulls, five of them. It looks like photomontage. But it isn't. It's a photograph of the Hindenburg dam and the train is real. I bought it in Berlin in 1983 or 1984. I was eating a Kaiser-schnitzel in a pub called the Restaurant Jahrmarkt off Savigny-platz. First someone tried to flog me a single rose. Next I tried to wave away a postcard seller, but my wife wanted to look through the fifty or so antique postcards on offer. About half-way through, she flipped a card across the table. 'For the cover of your epic.' It was the train in the sea. And it wasn't cheap. But I needed it.

As far as I remember, I hadn't, at that point, actually written anything. I had done a lot of dreaming and planning, however, and it is clear from the Jahrmarkt anecdote that I had my idea. My wife and I both recognized the appropriateness, the justice of the image. By then, too, I had the title. And I had several episodes pressing to be written. Of course, some of these had been pressing for most of my life – my father, drenched in sweat, asleep, lit by the street light through thin curtains, delivering a tirade, utterly fluent in a foreign tongue we have never been able to identify. This episode was so pressing that it found its way into the short prose memoir and, when it came to a poetic reprise in *History: The Home Movie*, I found that I had 'used' it.

There were plenty of other untold stories. My wife's aunt and uncle were trying to cross the border into Austria from Germany. They were both Jews. He was the head of the Deutsches Vereinsbank in Munich. They were travelling in the chauffeur-driven company car. At the border-control, they were stopped because the photograph in her passport didn't match her face. It had been taken in Russia during the famine, when she was nineteen, but she was so starved her picture looked about fifty – considerably older than she was even fifteen years on. A member of the Gestapo suddenly appeared at the car window. The officer glanced from photograph to face to photograph and said: 'It *is* Frau Pasternak. You can let her through.' He had been a taxi-driver and, before German anti-Semitism became rampant, had driven my wife's uncle fairly frequently. The uncle was, the Gestapo man remembered, 'a generous tipper'. These days, taxis were too risky and the uncle preferred the company car. The Gestapo man wanted a lift into Austria. In the car, the uncle fell asleep. His wife remembered to the end of her life how he nodded off on to the officer's shoulder.

On the jacket of the American edition of *History: The Home Movie* is an ordinary coffee cup resting on a matching white saucer. In the swirl of coffee you can see three soldiers going over the top, one in a gas mask, one who has been shot in the throat. You get the picture: Aristotle *was* a Greek millionaire. The other, ordinary Aristotle spoke with a lisp, wore rings and was a schoolmaster. You get the picture: one of his pupils was Alexander the Great. Maybe I made up the bit about the lisp.